EURYTHMY FORMS
FOR
TONE EURYTHMY

EURYTHMY FORMS FOR TONE EURYTHMY

VOLUME IX

RUDOLF STEINER

Reproductions of the original pages

With an Introduction to the English by Dorothea Mier

German Edition Introduced and Edited by Eva Fröbose

Translated by Marsha Post

2009
SteinerBooks

Published by SteinerBooks
402 Union Street No. 58
Hudson, New York 12534
www.steinerbooks.org

The drawings are reproduced from the original drawings by Rudolf Steiner. The forms were drawn from the viewpoint of the audience on various kinds of paper with pencil, indelible pencil, or ink and are given at nearly their original size (93%).

This edition is translated by Marsha Post from the German Bibliographic No. K 24, *Eurythmieformen: Eurythmieformen fur die Ton-eurythmie, Band IX*, published by Rudolf Steiner Verlag, Dornach, Switzerland, 1994.

CONTENTS

FORMS ALPHABETICALLY BY COMPOSER

(If not otherwise indicated, the compositions are for the piano.)

BWV = List of Bach's Works
HWV = List of Händel's Works
KV = List of Mozart's Works

Armand, Atirta Zsadányi (see Kossowits, Jósef)

INTRODUCTION TO THE ENGLISH EDITION

DOROTHEA MIER

At last the book of tone eurythmy forms is now available to the English-speaking world. Though the forms themselves have been in print since the end of the 1980s, the collected notes and indications of Rudolf Steiner therein have now been translated.

Among all the gifts that Rudolf Steiner showered on humanity are the many riches he poured into the development of eurythmy. One of these jewels is this collection of forms for tone eurythmy. As with all things of value, the more you live with them, the more they reveal of themselves. Each form is unique, no two are alike. It is my personal experience that just when you think you have discovered a principle, the next refutes it. I have also often found that when puzzling how to bring a form and music together, something in the form makes me aware of an element in the music that I had not considered. These forms are not just a convenience, saving one the trouble of making a form oneself, but are in themselves a new and challenging element. The form is like a bridge into another world of experience and expression, a path to the archetype of the music.

I believe, in all instances, individual eurythmists asked Rudolf Steiner for a form for a specific piece of music. One can feel gratitude toward these first eurythmists for their initiative, which generated this treasure. It is interesting to see their preferences; some chose dramatic pieces, others lyrical, etc. In speech eurythmy it was more often Marie Steiner who made the request, and then the form was given to a eurythmist.

There are various people I would like to acknowledge and thank, first and foremost Eva Froböse, who brought out *Die Entstehung und Entwicklung der Eurythmie* (CW 277a) in 1965, recently translated into English by Alan Stott and published as *Eurythmy: Its Birth and Development*, 2002. This book contains the first lessons in eurythmy and, as the title suggests, its further development until the major courses in 1924 [also published as books: *Eurythmy as Visible Singing* (CW 278) and *Eurythmy as Visible Speech* (CW 279)]. Eva Froböse then undertook the second mammoth task of collecting all the forms and indications together, an especially hard task for the tone eurythmy forms which, in many cases, had been in private possession. Now all the forms, for both speech and tone eurythmy, are available in nine volumes. This tone eurythmy volume is the first to have the text translated into English. We hope the volumes for English poems, Rudolf Steiner's verses, and the *Calendar of the Soul* will follow. Thanks to Marsha Post, translator; Mary Giddens; production, Gene Gollogly of SteinerBooks, publisher; and last but not least, warmest thanks to Gabriele Knecht whose generosity has made this edition possible.

INTRODUCTION TO THE GERMAN EDITION

EVA FROBÖSE

Within Rudolf Steiner's complete works there came out over the years [in German], in addition to the two eurythmy courses, *Eurythmy as Visible Speech* (CW 279) and *Eurythmy as Visible Singing* (CW 278), also *Eurythmy: Its Birth and Development* (CW 277a). The last of these contains both of the courses from 1912 and 1915, the so-called Dionysian course and the Apollonian course. The volume titled *Eurythmie, die Offenbarung der sprechende Seele* [Eurythmy, the revelation of the speaking soul] includes introductions for the eurythmy performances from 1915–1924. [Rudolf Steiner's] notes and, where available, the programs were added. In addition, *Entwürfe zu den Eurythmiefiguren* [Sketches for the eurythmy figures] and *Eurythmieformen zu den Wochensprüchen des Anthroposophischen Seelenkalendars* [Eurythmy forms for the verses of the Calendar of the Soul] were published.

In connection with Rudolf Steiner's forms for the *Calendar of the Soul* (in CW 40), now all the other existing [eurythmy] forms for his poetry and verses, as well as all the forms for texts by other authors, are given in several volumes. These are lyric, epic, and drama works by authors in the German, English, French, and Russian languages. Also [in the volumes published] are the tone eurythmy forms for classical and romantic compositions.

The necessity for these publications came about because the original drawings were being copied [by hand] and passed on to others, resulting in many distortions. In addition, the paper on which the originals were drawn is turning yellow, and the drawings themselves are fading. In light of this and the fact that the eurythmy forms have gradually been spread worldwide, it is time to round off the eurythmy publications with a set of Rudolf Steiner's standard eurythmy forms. An important note for this first publication of the eurythmy forms: to execute these forms eurythmically, a training in eurythmy is required. In no way are these eurythmy forms to be compared with any kind of choreography.

For decades this artistic spiritual property was protected, because certain verses and forms were reserved only for the Eurythmy Group of the Goetheanum. On the other hand, a schooling had to be taken on for these difficult-to-manage forms within the eurythmy training. In the 1960s an overview of the complete form-work first appeared. However, sixty years after Rudolf Steiner's death this extraordinary, artistic work, which proceeded out of eurythmy and was meant for the work of eurythmy, may be made public with full justification.

*

The texts for the eurythmy forms, along with the indications for lighting and costumes given by Rudolf Steiner, are printed separately [in German] in four volumes.

MUSIC IN COMPARISON TO THE OTHER ARTS

Lecture in Cologne, December 3, 1906

RUDOLF STEINER

For those who have thought about it, music has always been something like a riddle in connection with the aesthetic point of view. On the one hand, music is most understandable for the soul, for the immediate sensing of the human heart and mind (Gemüt); on the other hand, it is difficult for those who want to understand its effect. If we want to compare music with the other arts, we must say that, actually, all other arts have a model or example in the physical world. When, for instance, a sculptor fashions a statue of Apollo or Zeus, he works from the ideal of the human world. It is the same in painting. Indeed, today one wants to let only a direct impression of reality be valid. Poetry, too, strives to create a reproduction of the reality. Whoever wanted to apply this theory to music would hardly be able to come to any kind of result. One must ask: Where does the artistically-formed tone come from? To what in the world is it related?

Schopenhauer, a luminary of the nineteenth century, brought clear and fitting concepts in relation to art. He gave music a special place among the arts and held art as such to have a quite special value in human lives. Basically, he had as the leading motif of his philosophy the sentence: "Life is unpleasant, and I seek to make it bearable by contemplating it." According to his presentation, a blind, unconscious will reigns in the whole world. This will builds the stone, and then, out of the stone, the plant, and so on, because it is never satisfied. Thus, in everything there lives the yearning toward something higher.

Human beings feel this themselves, but there are great differences. Those primitive souls who live in a dull consciousness feel the lack of satisfaction of the will much less than individuals who can sense much more clearly the pain of existence. Schopenhauer said that there is a second element that the human being knows besides the will; that is the mental image or idea. It is like a Fata Morgana, like a mist-structure or a rippling of the waves in which the form of the will, of the blind, dark impulse, is reflected. In the human being the will rises up to this phantom creation. When through this human beings see the will, they become even more unsatisfied. However, there are means through which they can be released from the blind urge of the will. One of these remedies is art. Through art human beings are able to remove themselves from and set themselves above the lack of satisfaction of the will.

When human beings create a work of art, they work out of the imagination or mental image. Whereas other mental images are merely pictures, it is different with art. For instance, the Zeus by Phidias did not come about by reproducing the image of a real person. The artist combined many impressions; all the positive elements were kept in memory, and the weaknesses were omitted. Out of many human beings he created an archetype, which does not exist anywhere in nature, but which is divided among many individual human beings. Schopenhauer said that the true artist presents the archetypes and not the mental images that people otherwise have; not reproductions, but archetypes. By entering, as it were, into the depths of creative nature, human beings redeem or release themselves.

Thus it is with all of the arts, except music. The other arts must go through the imagination or mental image, therefore giving pictures or images of the will. Tone, however, is the direct expression of the will itself, without the involvement of the imagination. When human beings are artistically active with tone, they are listening with their ear on the heart of nature itself. They perceive the will of nature and reproduce it in the sequence of tones. Thus—Schopenhauer says—human beings are in a trusting relationship to the things themselves; they penetrate to the innermost being of things. Because human beings feel themselves near this being or essence in music, they feel deep satisfaction in it. Thus, out of an instinctive knowledge, Schopenhauer assigned to music the role of representing the nature or being of the cosmos directly. He had a kind of instinctive inkling of the real facts. Why music can speak to everyone, and why music works on the human being from earliest childhood, will become clear in the realm of existence where music has its true models.

When musicians compose, they cannot imitate anything. They have to draw the motifs for the music out of their soul. Where they get them will come to light when we point to the worlds that are not sense-perceptible. We must look at how the higher worlds are actually made up. Human beings are in the position to open up in their soul higher capacities that otherwise slumber there. Just as a man born blind might have an operation that would enable him to see the physical world, so too can inner organs open up for human beings that enable them to know the higher, spiritual worlds.

When human beings develop such capacities, which otherwise slumber in them, when they begin to develop their soul through meditation, concentration, and so on, they climb upward step-by-step. The first thing they experience is a special transformation or re-organization of their dream world. When human beings are able to shut out the memories of the outer sense world and other experiences, and when they still, however, have a content in their soul, their dream world begins to acquire a great regularity. When they awaken, it is then as if they raised themselves out of a flowing cosmic ocean. They know that they have now experienced something new; it is as if they have come out of an ocean of light and color that they have never known in the physical world. Their dream experiences become ever clearer. They remember that, in this world of light and color, the things and beings there were different from other objects [of the physical world], because one could pass through them; the objects gave no resistance. They learned to know a number of beings whose essence, whose bodies, were the colors. These are beings who reveal and embody themselves in the colors. Gradually, people expand their consciousness and extend it over this world and remember, upon awaking, that they took an active part in this world. The next step is that they take this world with them into the day-waking world. Then human beings gradually learn to see what we call the human astral body. They experience a world that is much more real than the ordinary, physical world. The physical world is a kind of condensation crystallized out of the astral world. In this manner human beings have two stages of consciousness: the everyday, waking consciousness and the dream consciousness.

Human beings reach a still higher stage when they are able to transform the completely unconscious state into a conscious state. The *chelas*, or pupils of spiritual science, learn to attain continuity of consciousness for that part of the night that is normally dreamless and completely unconscious. They learn to be conscious in a world of which they would otherwise know nothing. This is not a light-and-color world, but one that shows itself at first to be a world of tone. In this state of consciousness human beings attain the capacity to hear spiritually; they learn to perceive combinations of tones and tone varieties that cannot be heard by the physical ear. This world is called devachan.

Now we should not think that when we hear the spiritual, intoning world rising up, it does not also contain the world of light and color. Also, the tone world is permeated by light and color, but these belong to the astral world. However, the element belonging to devachan itself is the flowing ocean of tones. Human beings can also bring this intoning element out of this world of the continuity of consciousness and can, because of this, hear it in the physical world. A tone lies at the foundation of everything in the physical world. Every face represents specific devachanic tones. All objects have at the foundation of their being a spiritual tone, and each human being is such a spiritual tone in his or her deepest being. For this reason Paracelsus said: "The realms of nature are the letters and the human being is the word that is composed of these letters."

Every time we go to sleep, become unconscious, the astral body leaves the physical body. Then we are unconscious, but living in the spiritual world. The spiritual sounds or tones make an impression on our soul. Every morning we awaken out of a world of the music of the spheres. We enter into the physical world from a realm of harmonious, melodious sound. If it is true that human beings experience devachan between two incarnations, so we may also say that the soul lives luxuriously during the night in flowing tone as the element out of which it is actually woven. This is really the soul's home.

Creative musicians transpose into physical sounds the rhythm, harmonies, and melodies that have imprinted themselves into their astral body during the night. That is the mysterious relation between music that resounds here in the physical world and hearing spiritual music in the night.

When a light shines upon a person, a shadow of the person is formed. That shadow is not the real human being. Thus is the music that is created in the physical world a shadow, a real shadow of the much higher music of devachan. The archetype or model of music is in devachan. The physical music is only a reflection of the spiritual reality.

After we have become clear about this, we want to try to grasp what effect music has on the human being. Esoteric examination shows that the human being is made up of a physical body, etheric body, astral body, and the "I." The etheric body is an etheric archetype of the physical body. A still finer body, which is related to the etheric body and tends toward the astral body, is the sentient body. In these three levels of the bodily nature we see the soul. The soul is connected first with the sentient body. The sentient soul is as if incorporated in the sentient body; it is within the sentient body. Like a sword and its scabbard form a whole, so too, the sentient body and sentient soul form a whole. In addition, we have the mind or intellectual soul and a still higher member of our being, the consciousness soul. The consciousness soul is connected with the spirit self or manas. When we are asleep, the sentient body lies in bed with the physical body and the etheric body; the higher members—thus also the sentient soul—are in the world of devachan. In physical space, we feel all other beings as outside of us. In devachan we do not feel ourselves outside of other beings; rather, they permeate us, and we are within them. For this reason, in all esoteric schools the spheres of devachan and the astral realm have been called the world of permeability.

While human beings live and weave in the world of flowing tones, they themselves are saturated with these tones. When they return from this devachanic world, their own consciousness soul, intellectual soul, and sentient soul are permeated with the vibrations of the devachanic world; they have them within themselves. With these vibrations they penetrate the physical world. When human beings have taken in the vibrations, these vibrations are such that human beings can work back upon the sentient body and etheric body from out of the sentient soul. Because they brought the vibrations with them out of devachan, they can transfer them to the etheric body. Then their own etheric body vibrates along with these vibrations. Actually, the essence of the etheric body and of the sentient body is based on the same element: on spiritual tone and spiritual vibrations. The etheric body is lower than the astral body, but the activity performed by the etheric body is higher than that of the astral body. The development of the human being consists of the "I" transforming the bodies: first the astral body into manas; then the etheric body into buddhi; and then the physical body into atman. Because the astral body is the finest, the least amount of force is necessary to work into it. The force needed to work into the etheric body has to come from devachan. The force necessary for the transformation of the physical body must come from upper devachan. One can work on the astral body with forces from the astral world itself, but one can work on the etheric body only with forces from devachan. And one can work on the physical body only with forces from upper devachan.

During the night human beings receive from the world of flooding tones the force to carry the tones over to the sentient body and etheric body. When they create or perceive musically, it is because they already have these sounds or tones in the sentient body. Though human beings, upon awakening in the morning, are not aware of having taken tones into themselves in the night, they feel, however, that when they listen to music these impressions of the spiritual world are within themselves. The clairvoyant can see, when hearing music, how the tones flow, take hold of the firmer substance of the etheric body, and let the etheric body vibrate along with them. From this, human beings have the feeling of well-being. This feeling of well-being comes about because they feel themselves as conquerors over the etheric body through their astral body. This is strongest when people manage to overcome what is already in the etheric body. The etheric body is always intoning in the astral body. When one hears music, the impression is in the astral body first. Then one sends the tones consciously into the etheric body and overcomes the tones that are already in the etheric body. That is the feeling of well-being one has in listening to music and in creating music. With certain musical sounds something goes out of the astral body and into the etheric body. The etheric body has now received new tones. A kind of struggle arises between the sentient body and the etheric body. If these tones are so strong that they overcome the etheric body's own tones, then joyful music in a major key comes about. When the music is in a major key, one can see that the sentient body is the conqueror over the etheric body. With music in a minor key, the etheric body is the conqueror over the sentient body. The etheric body resists the vibrations of the sentient body.

When human beings live in the musical element, they are living in a reflection of their own spiritual home. In the shadow-picture or reflection of the spiritual, the soul finds the highest elevation, the most intimate connection to the primal element of the human being. It is for this reason that music works so deeply even on the simplest soul. Even the simplest soul feels in music an echo of what it experienced in devachan. The soul feels itself at home. Every time the human being hears music, he or she feels: yes, I am from a different world!

Out of this intuitive knowledge Schopenhauer ascribed to music the central place among the arts, and said that in music the human being perceives the heartbeat of the will of the world.

In music, human beings feel the echoes of what lives and weaves in the inner depths of things; echoes of what is so akin to them. Because feelings are the most inward element of the soul and related to the spiritual world, and because the soul has its element in tone, in which it actually moves, the soul lives in a world where the bodily mediators of the feelings are no longer present but where the feelings still live. The archetype of music is in the spiritual, while the archetypes of the rest of the arts lie in the physical world itself. When human beings hear music, they have a feeling of well-being because the tones coincide with what they have experienced in their spiritual home.

The Inner Nature of Music and the Experience of Tone (CW 283)

ABOUT THE EURYTHMY FORMS

Eva Froböse

With eurythmy Rudolf Steiner created a new movement art built on speech, on the word, on the sound—and *not* a dance-art. This new art unites the human being with the cosmos: the vowels with the planets and the consonants with the zodiac.

During the second, so-called "Apollonian," course of 1915 Rudolf Steiner wrote, for presentation through eurythmy, his cosmic poetry: "The Dance of the Planets" and "The Twelve Moods." At this time there appeared the first indications for tone eurythmy. (See *Eurythmy: Its Birth and Development*, CW 277a, p.71.)

The first standard form for speech eurythmy, "Chor der Urtriebe" (1-12) [The chorus of the primal drives], by Fercher von Steinwand, was performed in November 1918. The verses for December from the *Calendar of the Soul* (in CW 40) followed. At the end of 1919 the following came from Goethe's works: "Howards Ehrengedächtnis" [Howard's memorial]; the cloud verses titled "Stratus," "Cumulus," "Cirrus," and "Nimbus;" "Hymn to Nature;" and "The Metamorphosis of the Plants." In 1920 came verses and the fairy tales from Rudolf Steiner's Mystery Dramas.

At the end of 1920 the first tone eurythmy pieces were performed: "Pastorale," "Hirtenmusik" [Pastorale, shepherd's music] from the *Weihnachtsoratorium* [Christmas oratorio] by Johann Sebastian Bach. This came about through the initiative of the piano teacher, Hendrika Hollenbach. Several months later, in September 1921, followed a form for "Trauermarsch" [Funeral march] by F. Mendelssohn-Bartholdy and, at the request of a young eurythmist, a form for "Schmetterling" [Butterfly] by Edvard Grieg. (See the essay by Hendrika Hollenbach, "The First Beginnings of Tone Eurythmy," page 187.)

From 1922 on an abundance of music pieces enriched the eurythmy programs. Rudolf Steiner created forms for serious as well as the humorous pieces, and for classical and romantic pieces, often with quite interesting instructions for shaping them eurythmically.

In contrast to the speech eurythmy forms, Rudolf Steiner drew the forms for the musical pieces during rehearsals. Thus, the eurythmists became witnesses to the creation. It must have been a wonder to experience how, while he was listening to the music being played for him, the forms arose: harmonious in spatial arrangement in waves, loops, points, and zigzags. Great mobility was exacted of the eurythmists.

An extraordinarily difficult form is the one for the "Prelude, D-flat major" by F. Chopin. Rudolf Steiner drew it right after the eurythmist involved had executed her own form-composition for it. This process is reported quite vividly on pages 180-181.

Rudolf Steiner listened a number of times to duets, trios, or compositions, such as for the septet by Ludwig van Beethoven, in order to draw forms for them.

From his sick-bed Rudolf Steiner also created, besides for speech eurythmy, forms for tone eurythmy, but now, as one could not play music for him, he worked from the notes on the music sheets! Not every musical piece that was brought to him received a form; however, he often gave indications for lighting or costumes. (See "Beleuchtung und Kostumangaben zur Toneurythmie" [Instructions concerning lighting and costumes for tone eurythmy], publication from the Archive of the Rudolf Steiner Estate, Dornach, Switzerland 1975.)

The compositions were performed—and thus the forms were also given—with no repetitions. They were shortened here and there. Over one hundred tone compositions with forms had already been performed when Rudolf Steiner gave the tone eurythmy course: *Eurythmy as Visible Singing* (CW 278). Other courses were to follow, such as the speech eurythmy course: *Eurythmy as Visible Speech* (CW 279).

Rudolf Steiner ended on February 27 with the words: "If I had given fourteen lectures instead of the eight given, I would be concerned that it would not be properly assimilated. Thus, let us remain with what we have now received first as an impulse, as a stimulus."

The following is Rudolf Steiner's report on the tone eurythmy course in the "Nachrichtenblatt" [News page] from *Das Goetheanum* of March 1924:

> There was an inner necessity in the Section for Speech and Musical Arts, whose leader is Frau Marie Steiner, to hold a course on tone eurythmy. In a few sentences here the statement of intention and position shall be given. The art of eurythmy has thus far developed speech eurythmy to a certain degree. We ourselves are our strictest critics and know that everything that has been accomplished already is only a beginning. What has been started must be developed further.
>
> We were not as far along with tone eurythmy (visible singing) as with speech eurythmy (visible word). If the beginnings that we have thus far made are to progress on the right path, then precisely now a further development must take place in the stage in which tone eurythmy has been practiced. That is to happen through this course. At the same time, however, the nature of music itself must be pointed out. For in eurythmy, music becomes visible; and we must have a feeling for where music has its true source in human nature if we want to make its fundamental essence visible.
>
> In tone eurythmy what lives in the un-seeable-audible element in music becomes visible. There is precisely the greatest danger present to become un-musical. I hope to have brought, in the lectures of this course, the proof that then, when music streams over into movement, the need arises to push all of the un-musical elements out of the music and let only "pure music" carry over into the realm of the visible. Whoever is of the opinion that the musical element ceases when the audible is carried over into the visible movement and form will have concerns about tone eurythmy as a whole. However, such a view is not artistic in its deepest nature. For those who experience art within themselves must be filled with joy at

every expansion of the artistic sources and forms. That is just how it is that music, like every true art, springs forth from the innermost being of the human being. And this inner being reveals its life in the most manifold ways; and only that which lies in the human organism as possibilities of movement are brought out into speech and tone eurythmy. It is the being of the human being that is made manifest. The human form is only understandable as "frozen" movement, and only the human being's movement reveals the meaning of his or her form. One may say: whoever disputes the justification of tone and speech eurythmy objects to the emerging of the whole, full human being. Now, materialism refuses to let the spirit manifest in human knowledge. And most likely a similar attitude stands behind the rejection of eurythmy as an art among the other arts and as a justified art in connection with them.

It is hoped that the eurythmists have received some ideas and impulses through this course, and that through this, a contribution has been made to the further development of our art of eurythmy.

The original pages of the tone eurythmy forms—in contrast to those for speech eurythmy—are nearly all dated and bear the name of the eurythmist who received the form. One recognizes the handwriting of Marie Steiner, Rudolf Steiner, and of Hendrika Hollenbach, or the eurythmist in question. It was not Rudolf Steiner who initiated the giving of forms for the pieces of music. It was always at the request of the eurythmists, who wanted to do musical eurythmy. Hendrika Hollenbach, for instance, asked for forms for music she had chosen (see page 187).

Ilona Bögel (Schubert) wanted to perform "Schmetterling" [Butterfly] by E. Grieg, which she had just practiced on the piano. H. Hollenbach describes quite precisely how Rudolf Steiner listened to the music and then brought the form the next day.

Then Ilona rehearsed her "Schmetterling" and left the music lying behind. Later Flossy von Sonklar came into the hall, saw the Grieg music, and also chose from this book a piece of music for which she also received a form (page 6). This was the beginning of the solo forms.

Gradually, eurythmists began to develop forms for some music, which they then would show Rudolf Steiner. That was the moment [when they showed him their work] when he could then take hold and begin to sketch. We have a wonderful example of this with the "Regentropfen Prelude" [Raindrop prelude] (pages 24 and 180).

Thus, we have with tone eurythmy the possibility to follow along step-by-step the course of development of the eurythmy forms.

Never did Rudolf Steiner choose the music for the tone eurythmy. Nor did Marie Steiner choose the music, but she wove it quite wonderfully into the eurythmy programs. As if self-evident, the chronological order of the forms fit together. Much historical information could be added. One exception is the so-called "musical form" (page XXVIII) that Rudolf Steiner gave to Jan Stuten.

Musical Fundamental Form

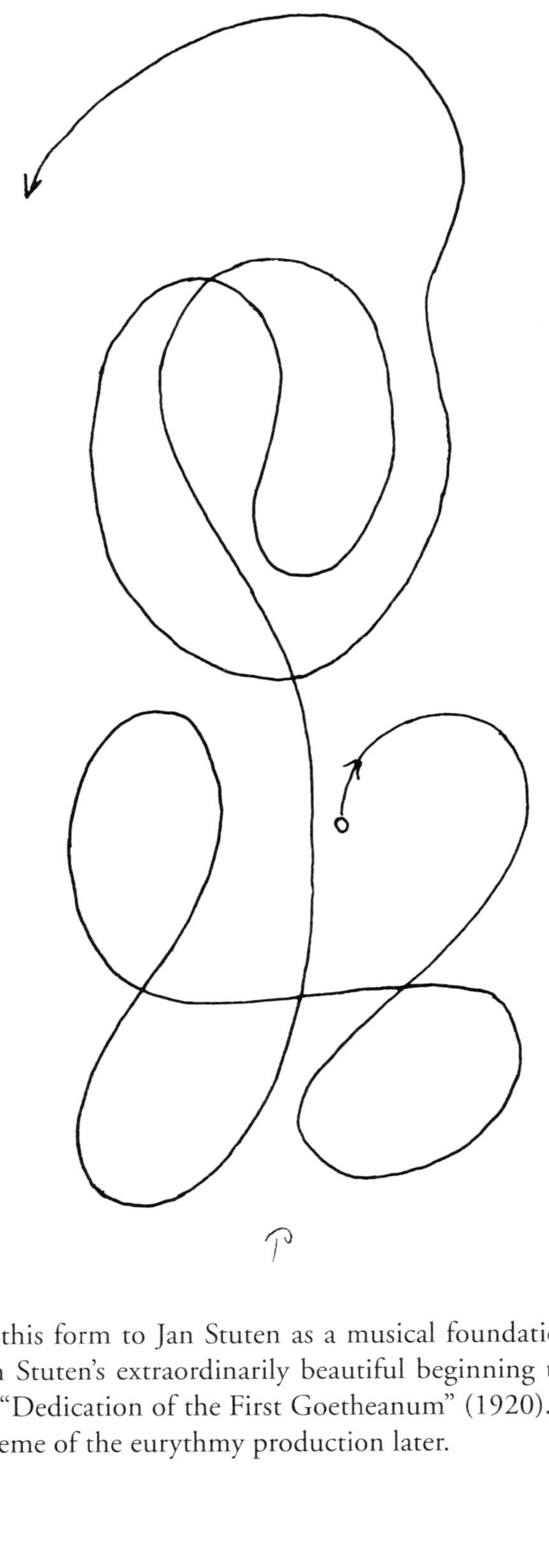

Rudolf Steiner gave this form to Jan Stuten as a musical foundational, or fundamental form. It inspired Jan Stuten's extraordinarily beautiful beginning theme of the prelude to the music for the "Dedication of the First Goetheanum" (1920). It was also made the basis of the initial theme of the eurythmy production later.

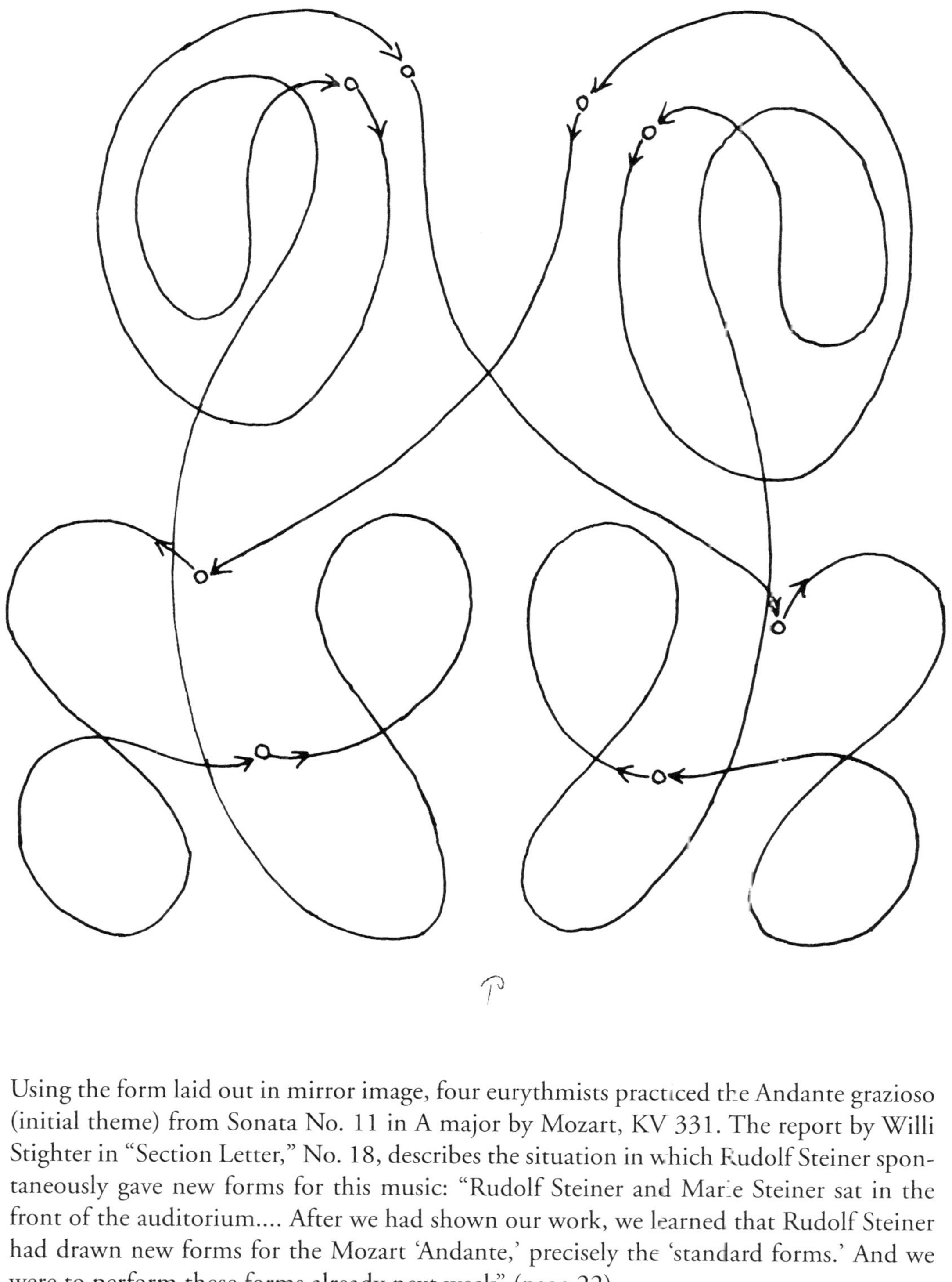

Using the form laid out in mirror image, four eurythmists practiced the Andante grazioso (initial theme) from Sonata No. 11 in A major by Mozart, KV 331. The report by Willi Stighter in "Section Letter," No. 18, describes the situation in which Rudolf Steiner spontaneously gave new forms for this music: "Rudolf Steiner and Marie Steiner sat in the front of the auditorium.... After we had shown our work, we learned that Rudolf Steiner had drawn new forms for the Mozart 'Andante,' precisely the 'standard forms.' And we were to perform these forms already next week" (page 22).

RUDOLF STEINER'S STANDARD FORMS FOR TONE EURYTHMY
with Details for Their Arrangement

A Chronological Overview

Editor's Note: The number given in parentheses indicates the number of the form as listed in the Forms Alphabetically by Composer list. This will aid the reader in quickly finding additional information about the music pieces for the forms.

The sequence corresponds to the dates on the pages or the time of their appearance in the programs. Some eurythmy indications that were given first during practice or that were added later by Rudolf Steiner are included with the individual pieces. The situation in which these instructions arose will always remain important; above all, the fact that they were connected with a specific eurythmist in each case. See in addition, the Additional Instructions and Details on pages 177 ff.

1920

The first eurythmy form came about as a result of a question by Hendrika Hollenbach, in December, for

Sinfonia Pastorale, G major, from the Weihnachts-Oratorium [Christmas oratorio], part II (from F on), arranged for harmonium, piano, cello, and violin, by J. S. Bach (23)............1

The forms were arranged as follows on the two-tiered platform on the stage: below, in front of the platform, are three forms for cello among which the form for the violin moves; on the top tier is one eurythmist for the harmonium part; and on the lower tier, for the piano part, are two eurythmists who can do all the forms.

1921

In August—again because of a question from Hendrika Hollenbach—came a form for

Andante maestoso, "Trauermarsch" [Funeral march] from Lieder ohne Worte, Op. 62/3 [Songs without words], by F. Mendelssohn-Bartholdy (99)............2

The minor tones were to be practiced on this music. (See pages 179-180 in the Appendix concerning the indications for each of the measures.)

At the same time Ilona Bögel asked for a form for

"Schmetterling" [Butterfly] from Lyrische Stücke Heft III, [Lyrical pieces, book III], Op. 43/1, by E. Grieg (76)............3

It was performed on August 26. Rudolf Steiner listened to both music pieces in the evening at the Goetheanum and brought the forms for both of the pieces the next morning. For

"Butterfly" he drew two forms, of which he thought the bottom one was the better one. (The form is repeated.)

After the "Butterfly" came a form in September for music from

"Poetische Tonbilder" [Poetic tone-picture], Op. 3/2, by E. Grieg (74) 4

The performance of this piece took place first on November 13.

In the meantime, Rudolf Steiner drew a form for

"Kinderreigen" [Dances for children], by M. Schuurman (132) 5

1922

In 1922 the eurythmists again selected a composition by Edvard Grieg and performed it on February 24:

"Eroticon" (Name given by Marie Steiner: Lebenzauber [Life-magic]) from Lyrische Stücke [Lyrical pieces], Op. 43/5, by E. Grieg (79) 6

In the course of practicing the form, the eurythmists noticed that the form for the repeating initial motif was missing [and evidently asked about it]. Rudolf Steiner's answer: "When the first theme repeats itself, the first form can always be inserted."

The following humorous musical piece was included in the same performance:

"Nachtwächter" [Night watchmen], by Jan Stuten (138) 7

The notes for this composition were destroyed in the burning of the first Goetheanum. (See the costume sketch on page 170.)

The rehearsals of the five-part

Fuge No. 22 [Fugue], B minor, by J. S. Bach (12) 8/9

in April helped tone eurythmy to progress somewhat. The performance took place on May 6.

Two simple forms followed in the same month. They were for the spiritual songs:

"Bist du bei mir" [When you are with me], by A. Z. Armand (3) 10

The form can be arranged in different ways: forward, back, forward (1/2 fine) or forward and back three times; and

"Kein Hälmlein wächst auf Erden" [No blade of grass grows on earth], by Leonhard Emil Bach (24) 11

for two eurythmists: one does speech eurythmy; the second does the tone eurythmy. It was performed on May 6.

The performance on May 6 also included a duet for violin and piano:

Menuett, Allegretto, G major, by Ludwig van Beethoven (38) 12

This brought a new element through the charming instruction for the piano part: in every rest for the second measure in the bass, the foot position should be "sympathy." (See page 180.)

In the same month the forms for solos for two piano pieces were completed. The first was on May 4:

"Erinnerung" [Remembrance], by Anton Bruckner (49) 13

It was performed on June 9 in Vienna during the congress of June 1-12.
The second was on June 29:

"Sœur Monique," Rondeau pour Piano [Rondeau for piano], from Pièces de clavecin III [Pieces for piano], by F. Couperin (63) 14

(See page 180 for the division of the form.)

In July a new form was worked on for a group:

"Elfentanz," [Dance of the elves], Op. 12/4, from Lyrische Stücke [Lyrical pieces], by E. Grieg (75) 15

For this, the indication for the position of the head: head to the right; eyes to the left. The piece was performed in Dornach on July 30. At the same time, in speech eurythmy, the eurythmists worked on poetry about the elemental world. Various head positions, finger positions, and movement details were given.

In August the form came about for

Gavotte II (Musette), G major, from English Suite No. 3, G minor, by J. S. Bach (6) 16

During his lecture cycle in Oxford from August 16-29, during which four performances were held, Rudolf Steiner found the time to create four tone eurythmy forms:

Menuett (Aria), D minor, by A. Armand (2) 17

with the indications: with the major key the head position should be to the left and somewhat on the shoulder; with the minor key the head should be to the right and somewhat on the shoulder.

"Einsamer Wanderer" [Lonely wanderer], Op. 43/2, by E. Grieg (77) 18

"Humoristische Rondo" [Humorous rondo], by M. Schuurman (131) 19/20

Gigue, by G.P. Telemann (three-parts, or voices) (145) 21

The eurythmists ascribed this piece to J. S. Bach in error. (Bach had merely written it down for his son Friedmann on a page in his notebook.) The piece was played from the Bärenreiter edition and was performed first in April 1924.
Both solos were performed on September 17 and 24. Also included was the piece mentioned at the beginning:

Andante Grazioso, from Piano Sonata No. 11, A major, by W. A. Mozart, KV 331 (102) 22

(The form was done twice.), as well as the first movement of

Allegro, first movement from the Klaviersonate [Piano sonata] No. 12, F major, by W. A. Mozart, KV 332 (103) 23

On September 7 Rudolf Steiner gave the form for

Prelude No. 15, Op. 28/15 ("Regentropfen") [Raindrop], by F. Chopin (58) 24

after E. Wilke had performed her own work on it. Some excerpts from her letters communicate the atmosphere of an intensive time of work on the tone eurythmy. Under her form she wrote: "Joyous look upward with inner participation. Do not feel tormented." – Most likely a comment from Rudolf Steiner. (See pages 180-181.)
Drawings of various parts of the form on pages 172-175, according to Elly Wilke.

Besides this very difficult, hard-to-manage form there arose two further forms for compositions by F. Chopin. On September 17:

Nocturne in E-flat major, Op. 9/2 (See pages 181-182) (52) 25/26

Étude, F minor, from Trois nouvelles Études (as a duet) (61) 27

performed on October 11. Presumably, at this time Rudolf Steiner sketched the form for

Étude, F minor, (Allegro, molto agitato), Op. 10/9 (54) 28/29

which was performed on September 11, 1923.

In addition he gave a stylized form (also in costume with a hat) for

"Danse de la Fée Dragée" [Dance of the sugarplum fairy] from Casse Noisette [Nutcracker suite], by P. Tschaikowsky (146) 30

which was performed on September 24, and for

Allegro, from Klaviersonate [Piano sonata], E-flat major, Op. 7/4, by L. van Beethoven (27) 31/32

with a special instruction: "Alternating, look at the right thumb, the left thumb, the right big toe, the left big toe."

On November 7 in The Hague, while on a lecture tour on which the eurythmy group accompanied him, Rudolf Steiner drew the form for

"Caprice," G minor, from Improvisionen [Improvisations,] by M. Reger (112) 33

Soon thereafter in Dornach he drew the form for

"Träumerei" [Dreaming], D major, from Träume am Kamin [Dreams at the fireplace], by M. Reger (113) 34

and on November 30 a form for

Saraband, B major, for violin and piano, by G. F. Händel (81) 35

In December there followed forms for compositions by R. Schumann:

"Eintritt" [Entrance], from Waldszenen [Woodland scenes] (Form for children) (129) 36

and several forms for

"Papillons" [Butterflies], Nos. 1, 2, 9, and 12 (119, 120, 121, 122) ....37, 38, 39, & 40-42

The dates for these could not be ascertained.

At Christmas two forms were given:

Andante cantabile, for violin and piano, by G. Tartini (144) 43/44

Bourrée I & II, C major, from Suite No. 3 for violoncello, by J. S. Bach (5) 45/46

(Arranged for violin and piano) It was performed as a cello solo.

Before the tragic, fateful night of New Year's Eve 1922/23, the eurythmy program included the Allegro from "Klaviersonate No. 4" by L. van Beethoven; "Caprice" and "Träumerei" by M. Reger; and "Trauermarsch" by F. Mendelssohn. It also included the poem, "Zum neuen Jahr," [For the new year] by Vladimir Soloviev.

1923

In January and February the music, for which forms had been given the year before, was performed. Further new forms and indications for compositions by L. van Beethoven were developed quickly. In February the following pieces were performed.

February 11:

Scherzo Allegro, A major, from Klaviersonate [Piano sonata], Op. 2/2, by L. van Beethoven (25) 47

with the instructions, in the motives with sixteenths, to open the eyes and let the head go with it.

February 18:

Adagio cantabile, from Klaviersonate [Piano sonata], C Minor, Op. 13, (Pathétique), by L. van Beethoven (29) 48

Rondo Allegro, from the same sonata (30) 49

The instruction was given: "This form is to be done several times in different places and in different sizes." Both forms were given on January 20. For the third movement of the sonata *Pathétique* only the lighting exists.

On February 11 and 19, came two forms for each of the following:

Mazurka, B major, Op. 7/1, by F. Chopin (50) 50

"Vöglein" [Little bird] from Lyrische Stücke, Heft III [Lyrical pieces, book III], Op. 43/4, by E. Grieg (78) 51

Étude, A-flat major, Op. 25/1, by F. Chopin (55) 52

"Vorfrühling" [Early spring], by L. van der Pals (110) 53

Minore, from Klaviersonate [Piano sonata], Op. 7/4, by L. van Beethoven (28) 54

The form is to be done twice: the first time is up to the double bar; the second time is to be a repetition of the first and then proceed further to the end. Execute it as if dreaming, without any dramatic effect. (Ilona Schubert) and

Slavischer Tanz [Slavic dance], Op. 46/2, by A. Dvorak (to measure #85) (67) 55

performed on March 6, and

Menuett [Minuet], from Klaviersonate [Piano sonata], G major, Op. 78, by F. Schubert, (116) 56/57
performed on March 6 (I = the form once; II and III = the form three times).

In the spring of 1923 Rudolf Steiner stayed in Stuttgart several times. On February 27 and 28, as well as on March 6 and 7, eurythmy performances took place, and Rudolf Steiner gave an address before each of them. The Dornach eurythmists, who were in Stuttgart just at that time, were able to attend both lectures, which were held for Waldorf school teachers and musicians on March 6 and 8, in *The Inner Nature of Music and the Experience of Tone*. In the lecture on March 8, he gave first the spatial forms for the intervals and stressed that these are all contained in his "standard forms." In addition, Rudolf Steiner spoke, in the same lecture, about the "spiritual origin of the [musical] instrument." (See pages 178-179.)

It is to be assumed that he visited the Eurythmeum before March 8, as was his custom on his trips to Stuttgart. (The leadership and management of this conservatory was incumbent upon Marie Steiner.)

During one of these visits Hedwig Köhler, who taught tone eurythmy, did a performance with her students of an arrangement of the orchestral movement from Symphony No. 8 by A. Bruckner. After this performance Rudolf Steiner drew the spatial arrangement for a "eurythmic orchestral" piece, with quite differentiated forms for the string instruments, the reed instruments, and the brass. (An original is not available.) The lemniscate is the basis for the string instruments; the form of the instrument is the basis for the woodwinds. The percussion instruments stand on a raised platform in the center. (See pages 178-179.)

Rudolf Steiner was in Dornach again from March 11–23. During this time the question came to him anew concerning forms for children; specifically for "Andante con moto" from the "Klaviertrio" [Piano trio], Op. 100 by Franz Schubert, and for the "Arie" by D. Gabrielli, an arrangement for violin and bassoon. The similarity with the instrument is reflected clearly in the shape of this form.

The following forms came about on March 17:

Andante con moto, from Klaviertrio [Piano trio], Op. 100, by F. Schubert (117) 58-60
Unfortunately, Hendrika Hollenbach could find only an arrangement for piano and two violins. The piano should have both treble and bass. The "Andante con moto" was played several times while Rudolf Steiner drew.

Arie, an arrangement for violin and bassoon, by D. Gabrielli (70) 61
For the rests at the beginning and within the piece, Rudolf Steiner instructed the young girl who was to do these to do a particular movement: to move out of a closed O at shoulder-height over into an A with the forearms and on, with a flowing movement, to a small U with the forearms moving upward. The palms of the hands should

be turned inward. The upper arms always remain at shoulder-height. Then this same movement is to be done again in the same way in reverse. (Margarethe Eckinger, 1908-1993)

On April 4 came eight new forms:

Intermezzo, B minor/F sharp major, Op. 10/3, by Johannes Brahms (42) 62
Intermezzo, A-flat major, Op. 76/3, by J. Brahms (43) 63
Intermezzo, E minor, Op. 116/5, by J. Brahms (45) 64
Intermezzo, A major, Op. 118/2, by J. Brahms (46) 65
Davidsbündler Tänze [Davidsbündler dances], Op. 6/2, by R. Schumann (123) 66
Davidsbündler Tänze [Davidsbündler dances], Op. 6/11, by R. Schumann (124) 67
Schmetterling [Butterfly], Op. 33/6, by W. Niemann (109) 68
Berceuse Slave, Op. 11, for violoncello and piano, by F. Neruda (108) 69

On May 31 Rudolf Steiner gave a wonderful violin-form for R. Schumanns last composition:

Thema, [Theme], E-flat major, Op. 10/9, by R. Schumann (130) 70
Air, from the Orchestral Suite, D major, by J.S. Bach, arranged for violin and piano (17) 71

The sketch for page 71 72
and from Septet, Op. 20 by L. van Beethoven:

Tema con Variazioni [Theme and Variations] I and II, by L. van Beethoven (Form for adults) (40) 73-76
Menuett (Trio), by L. van Beethoven (Form for children) (39) 77

If one compares these forms for the wind and string instruments, as Rudolf Steiner created them, with the form for the bassoon in the "Arie" by D. Gabrielli, one will always see a characterization of the different instruments.

The St. John's-tide performance on June 24 presented the form given on June 12, described as the "St. John's Mood":

Nocturne, B minor, Op. 9/1, by F. Chopin (51) 78-79

and also both of the "Davidsbündler Tänze" [Davidsbündler dances], Op. 6/2 & 11, were deemed appropriate for St. John's-tide.

On June 26 the forms were done for:

Thema und Variationen [Theme and variations], from the Violinsonate [Violin sonata], G major, by W. A. Mozart, KV 379 (106) 80

With the instruction: occasionally in some places make a gentle, delicate circular motion with the hands and move the fingers too, like a smile. (Enrica Mohr-Senft)
In addition, the form was given for:

Präludium [Prelude] No. 8, E-flat minor, by J. S. Bach, BWV 853 (9) 81

From August 8 – September 4, nine performances by the eurythmy group took place during the conferences in Ilkley, Penmaenmawr, and London.

While Rudolf Steiner was in Vienna for his lecture cycle "Anthroposophie und der menschliche Gemüt" [Anthroposophy and the human soul] (in CW 223), he gave the solo form on October 1 for

and on October 5 the program in Gmunden included, as on October 11 in Salzburg, the performance by the same eurythmist of

Allegro spiritoso, fourth movement from Sonata for Violoncello, by J. E. Galliard (72) 115

first performed on January 3, 1924 (Archive No. 1372, presumably a preliminary to No. 1373) 116

1924

At the beginning of the new year, the forms that had been given in December were performed, as well as

Finale (Allegro), from the Piano Sonata, D major, by J. Haydn, HV 16:37 (91) 117

On January 4, Rudolf Steiner drew forms on two sheets of paper for

Largo, from Sonata for Violin and Oboe, Op. 2,/8, B Major, by G. F. Händel, HWV 393 (89) 118-119

This music had already been performed by students on December 23.

In February 11, 12, and 13, the following forms were given:

Prelude, B major, Op. 28/11, by F. Chopin (57) (See pages 182-183.) 120

Ballade [Ballad], A-flat major, 0p. 47/3 (To measure #51), by F. Chopin (60) 121

"Schmetterlinge" [Butterflies], by Jan Stuten (137) 122

"Reigen seliger Geister" [Dance of the blessed spirits], out of Orpheus und Eurdyke, by C.W. Gluck (73) 123

Intermezzo, B major, Op. 76/4, by J. Brahms (44) 124

Intermezzo, E-flat minor, Op. 118/6, by J. Brahms (48) 125

Romanze [Romance], G minor, from Faschingsschwank aus Wien [Carnival prank from Vienna], by R. Schumann (127) 126

The tone eurythmy course [Eurythmy as visible song (CW 278)] took place from February 19-27. See page 191 for an excerpt from the first lecture.

In February, in addition to others, the following piece was performed:

Präludium [Prelude] No. 22, B minor, by J. S. Bach, BWV 867 (11) 127

In March two forms were sketched for music by G. Tartini:

Larghetto affettuoso, first movement from Teufelsrillersonata [Devil's trill sonata], G minor, Op. 1/4 (140) 128

with directions for the hand position: thumbs, index fingers, and middle fingers should be extended outward; the fourth and fifth fingers are to be folded against the palms.

Presto ma non troppo (con fuoco), second movement from the second Violin Sonata, G minor, Op. 1/10 (142) 129

Come out with a pointing gesture "d" in walking. Gaze wide open. At the beginning to the A and also later with the stressed beats: step firmly with the heel of the right foot, then first come up to the front tip of the foot. Appeasing, soothing gestures. (Do the form two times.) Both pieces above were performed on May 16.

On April 20 the following was performed:

Menuett nach dem Lied [Minuet based on the song]: "Ehrlichkeit währt am längsten" [Honesty lasts the longest], for flute and piano, by W. Rosenberg (114) 130

(Brother of Baroness von Walleen). Rudolf Steiner created the form for this song at the request of Baroness von Walleen. The well-known hand position for wind instruments was given by Rudolf Steiner for this composition. (See page 177.) The composition came into an internal eurythmy program on April 20 and 22. In this closed performance the Foundation Stone mantram was done with eurythmy for the first time.

Additional forms arise on April 5 for:

"Mozart," Menuett [Minuet], E-flat major, by F. Bendel (41) 131

Andante for violoncello, by W. Lewerenz (94) 132

Presumably also

Scherzo, by W. Lewerenz (95) 133

Saraband, from Suite No. 11, D minor, (4-voices), by G. F. Händel, HWV 437 (80) 134

On April 28:

Präludium [Prelude] No. 12, F minor, by J. S. Bach, BWV 857 (10) 135

Molto Allegro, from the Piano Sonata, C minor, by W. A. Mozart, KV 457 (104) 136

Without the middle part, the first part is to be done in the minor range.

Andante, from the Piano Sonata, G major, by W. A. Mozart, KV 283 (101) 137

The form is to be executed through the whole piece one time, without repeating. (Originally measures 27-38 were omitted.)

Gigue, A major, by G. P. Telemann (145) 21

This was performed in April (presumably in 1922 in Oxford and ascribed to Bach in error).

On May 4:

Allegro Maggiore, from the Violin Sonata, G major, by W. A. Mozart, KV 301 (105) 138

On May 5:

Grave, from the Orchestra Suite, D major, arranged for violin and piano, by J. S. Bach, BWV 1068 (16) 139

The eurythmy group was present, at the express wish of Rudolf Steiner, during the Agriculture Conference from June 7-17 in Koberwitz. A eurythmy performance took place on June 9 in Lobe Theater.

From June 24-July 12, the Speech Eurythmy Course (CW 279) was held. Within this time period the following forms were created:

On June 27:

On July 10, either during a rehearsal or after the performance, Rudolf Steiner drew the forms for the following pieces:

Rudolf Steiner wrote on the form for the "Allegretto" Scherzo. He said, "You must do it this way," and made a kind of fourth, whereby he pressed his fingers together completely and made a teasing gesture. His eyes and countenance radiated a tremendous cheerfulness in that moment. (R. Kux, *Erinnerungen* [Remembrances].)

On July 10 two music pieces were performed:

And on July 11 three new forms were given for the following:

After the end of the speech eurythmy course, Rudolf Steiner traveled through Stuttgart and on to Arnheim, where the Anthroposophical Pedagogical Conference took place and where he held several lectures, also public lectures, from July 17-24.

From August 11-22, the eurythmy group accompanied Rudolf Steiner to Torquay to the second International Summer Course, and then immediately afterwards to London, until August 30. Rudolf Steiner traveled through Stuttgart on his way back to Dornach.

From September 5-28, Rudolf Steiner held seventy-one lectures.

Michaelmas 1924 brought a turning point for the Anthroposophical Movement because of Rudolf Steiner's illness. It was also a turning point for the eurythmy work. He could no longer come to rehearsals but had to lie in bed in his studio in the "Schreinerei" [carpentry workshop]. However, the connection with the eurythmists remained intact. Rudolf Steiner drew further forms for poetry and music. They brought sheet music to him, and he drew forms for the tone eurythmy without having the music played for him or ever having heard the music before. He created the forms from seeing the notes on the sheets themselves.

On November 19 he created forms for the following compositions:

Andante con moto, from the String Quartet, D minor, "Der Tod und Das Mädchen" [Death and the young girl] by F. Schubert (See page 171.) (118) 154

On November 21, the forms for:

Prelude, E-flat major, Op. 28/19, by F. Chopin (59) 155
"Gombei ga tane maku," Japanese folksong, by R. Dittrich (65) 156
"Konju Raku," Chinese dance melody, by R. Dittrich (66) 157
Prelude, Op. 11/14, by A. Scriabine (133) 158
Allegro, from the Violin Sonata, G minor, "Teufelstrillersonate" [Devil's trill sonata] (so-called First Allegro), by G. Tartini (141) 159
Allegro commodo, from the Violin Sonata, G minor, (so-called Second Allegro), Op. 1/10, by G. Tartini (143) 160
Allegro, from the Violin Sonata No. 7, A major, by F. M. Veracini (147) 161

On December 31 the following were performed:

Adagio, from Sonata No. 1 for Violin solo, G minor, by J. S. Bach, BWV 1001 (19) (Form top of page) 162
Gigue, from Suite No. 5 for violoncello solo, C minor, by J. S. Bach, BWV 1011 (21) (Form bottom of page) 162
Largo, second movement from Concerto grosso No. 2, B major, by G. F. Händel, HWV 313 (on December 28), arranged for violoncello and piano by A. Lindner (90) 163

1925

In January and February Rudolf Steiner sent, besides speech eurythmy forms, yet further forms for compositions by L. van Beethoven:

Andante con variazioni, from the Ninth Violin Sonata, A major, Op. 47 (36) 164
Adagio espressivo, from the Tenth Violin Sonata, G major, Op. 96, (Performed on February 8) (37) 165

Since 1921, not only tone eurythmy has developed further. Parallel with it, speech eurythmy expanded to include English, French, and Russian poetry.

Afterword

On page XXVI it was pointed out that the eurythmy musical pieces were always performed without repetitions. The forms were given in accordance with this. The double bar is dropped, and sometimes there are also abridgements. A few exceptions confirm the rule, such as, for instance, the Minuet in G major by Ludwig van Beethoven (page 12). This is executed eurythmically in the classical minuet style with all of its repetitions; they are also included in the form. Another example is the Minore from the Sonata in E-flat major, Op. 7/4 (page 54) in which the form is repeated. This Minore should be performed with the Allegro (page 31).

Because of all of this, questions arise for the musicians. Understanding will come about when one puts oneself into the situation of fashioning a program. A program must, in itself, be a work of art. It needs a certain balance. The texts must be, and remain to be, the main emphasis. The musical pieces should introduce, connect, and bring resolution, and should not, through their length, have a tiring effect. If a eurythmist selected a piece of music that was too long and put it into a program, it was shortened, abridged. Besides, tone eurythmy was just in its first beginnings.

It should also be mentioned—and that can be seen in their sequence—that a certain number of the forms were given for "children"; this means, given for the pupils in the School for Continuing Education at the Goetheanum. These pupils were also included in the program. Later these pieces were then taken over by the stage-eurythmists.

Eva Froböse

Eurythmy Forms for Tone Eurythmy

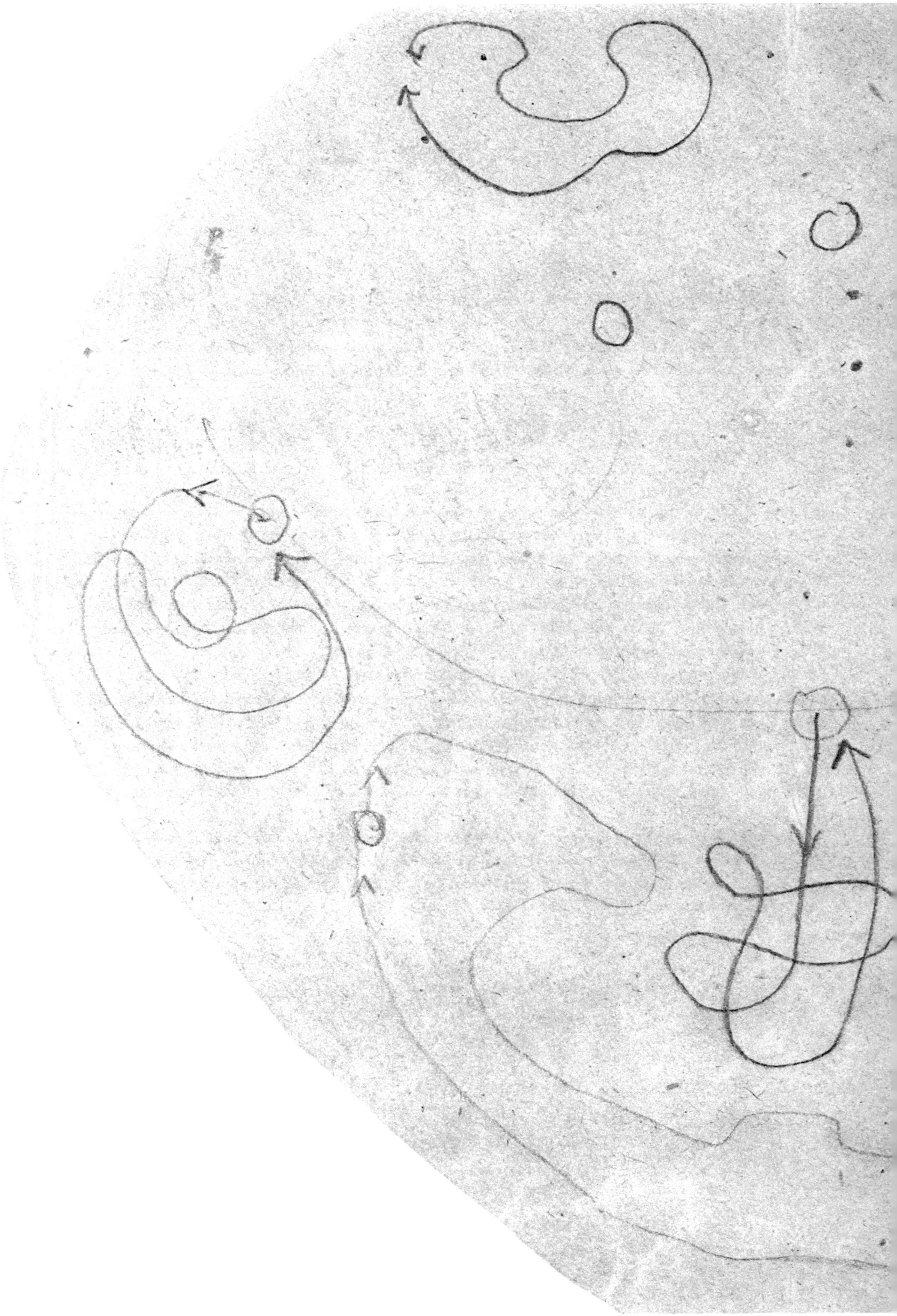

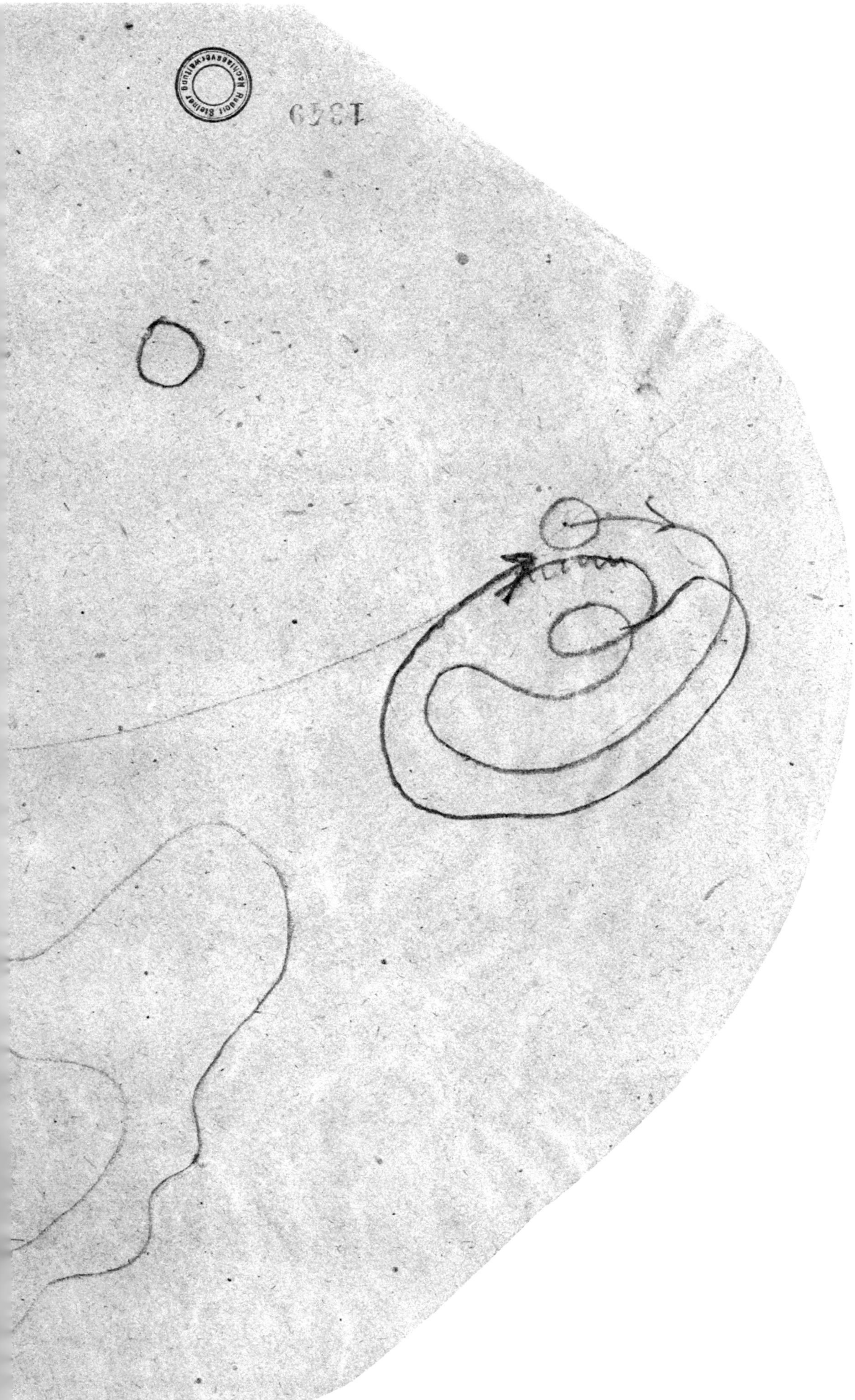

J. S. Bach – Sinfonia Pastorale, G major, from Weihnachts-Oratorium [Christmas oratorio] 1

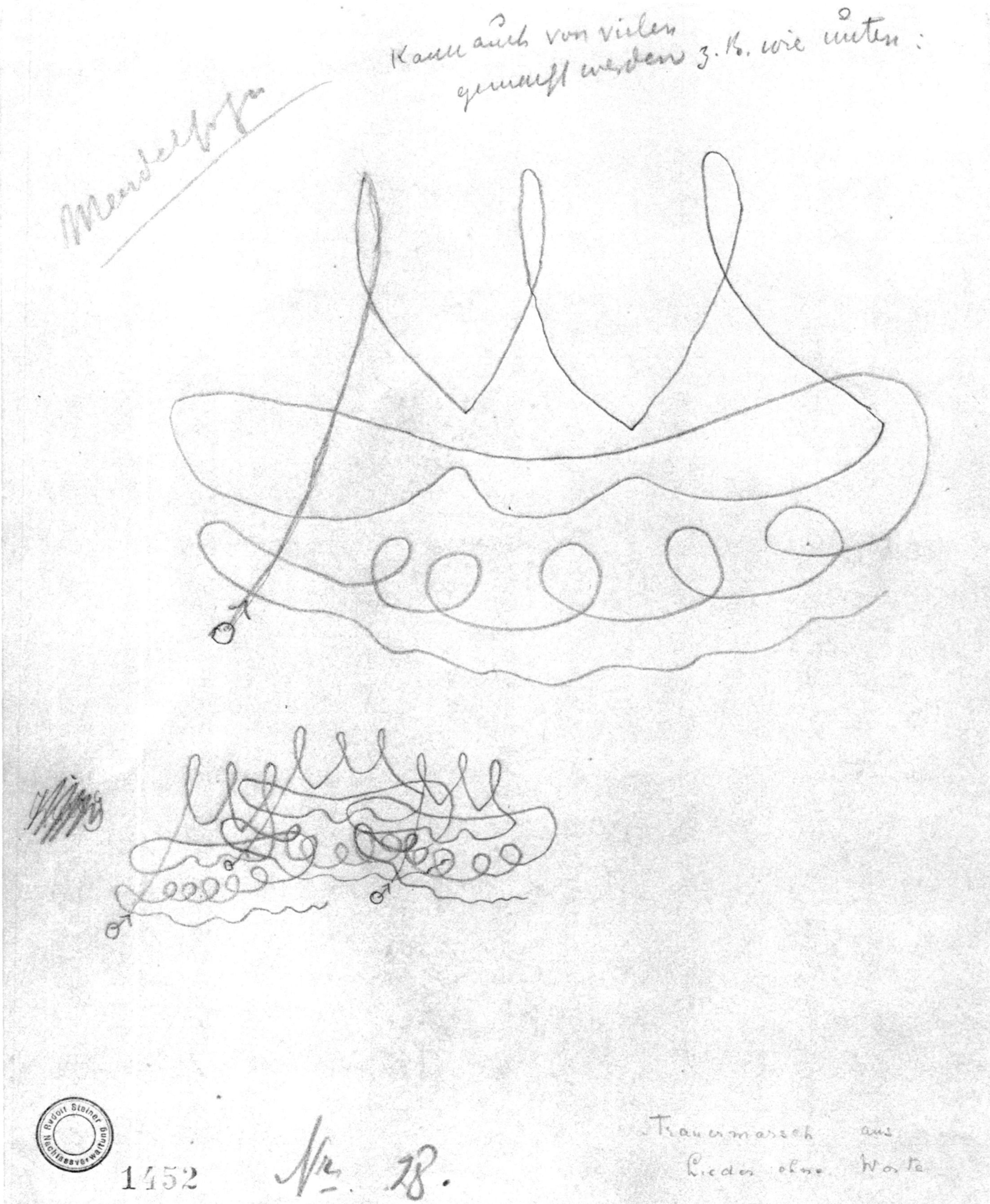

F. Mendelssohn-Bartholdy – Andante maestoso, "Trauermarsch" [Funeral march] from *Lieder ohne Worte* [Songs without words]

E. Grieg – "Schmetterling," [Butterfly] from *Lyrical Pieces*, Book III, Op. 43/1

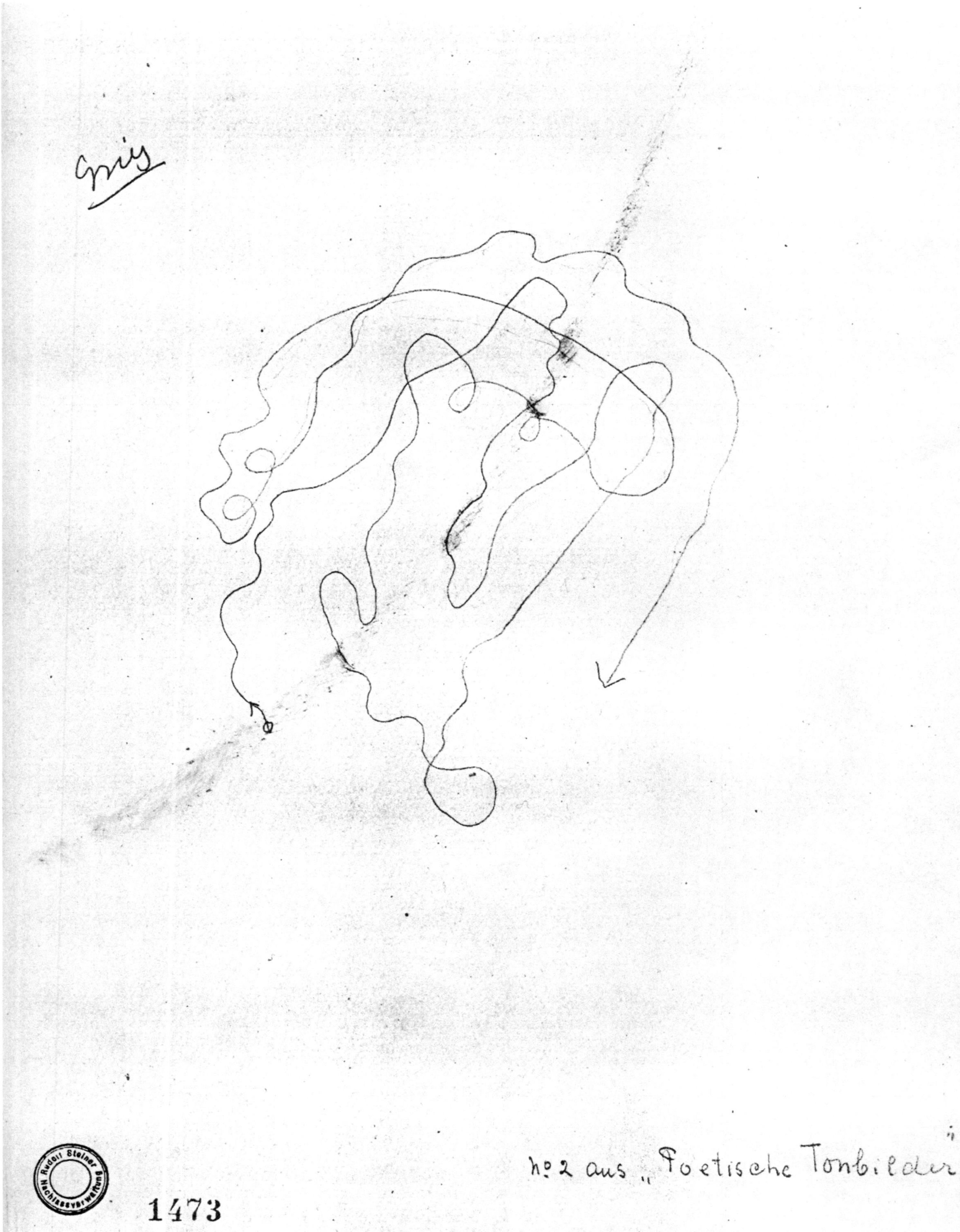

E. Grieg – from "Poetic Tone-picture," Op. 3/2

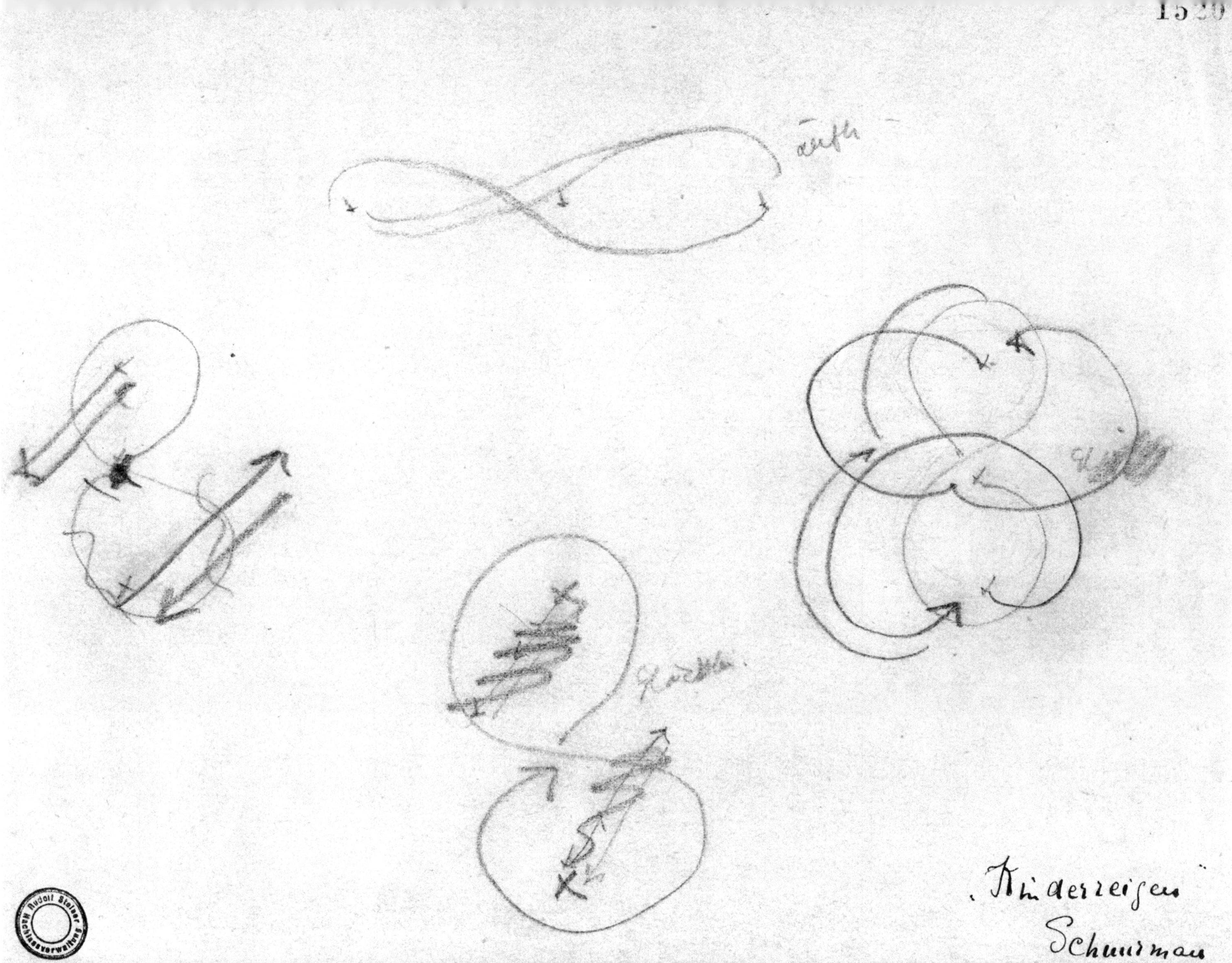

M. Schuurman – "Kinderreigen," [Dances for children], A major

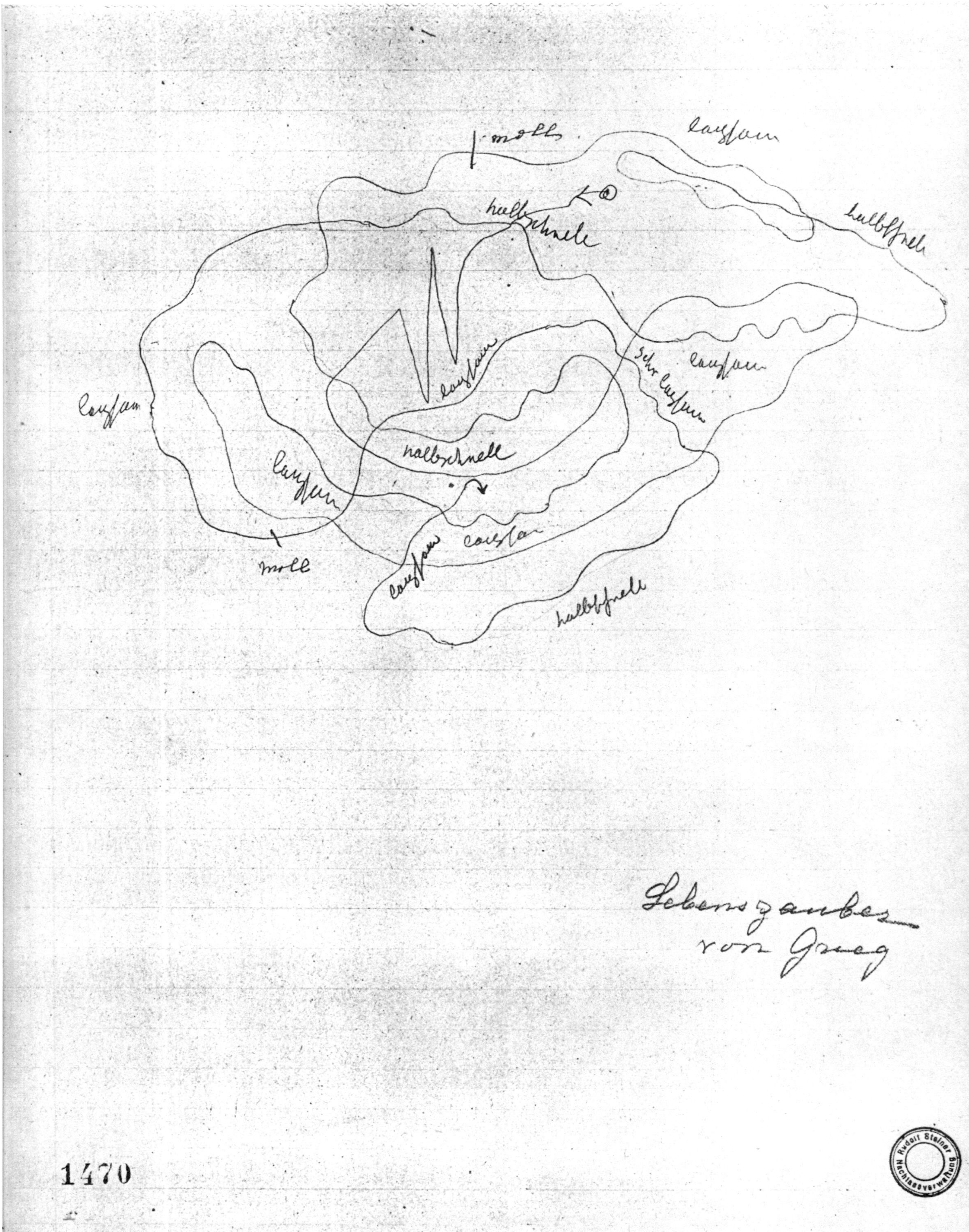

E. Grieg – "Eroticon" (Lebenzauber) [Life magic, (or also love poem)], from *Lyrical Pieces*, book III, Op. 43/5

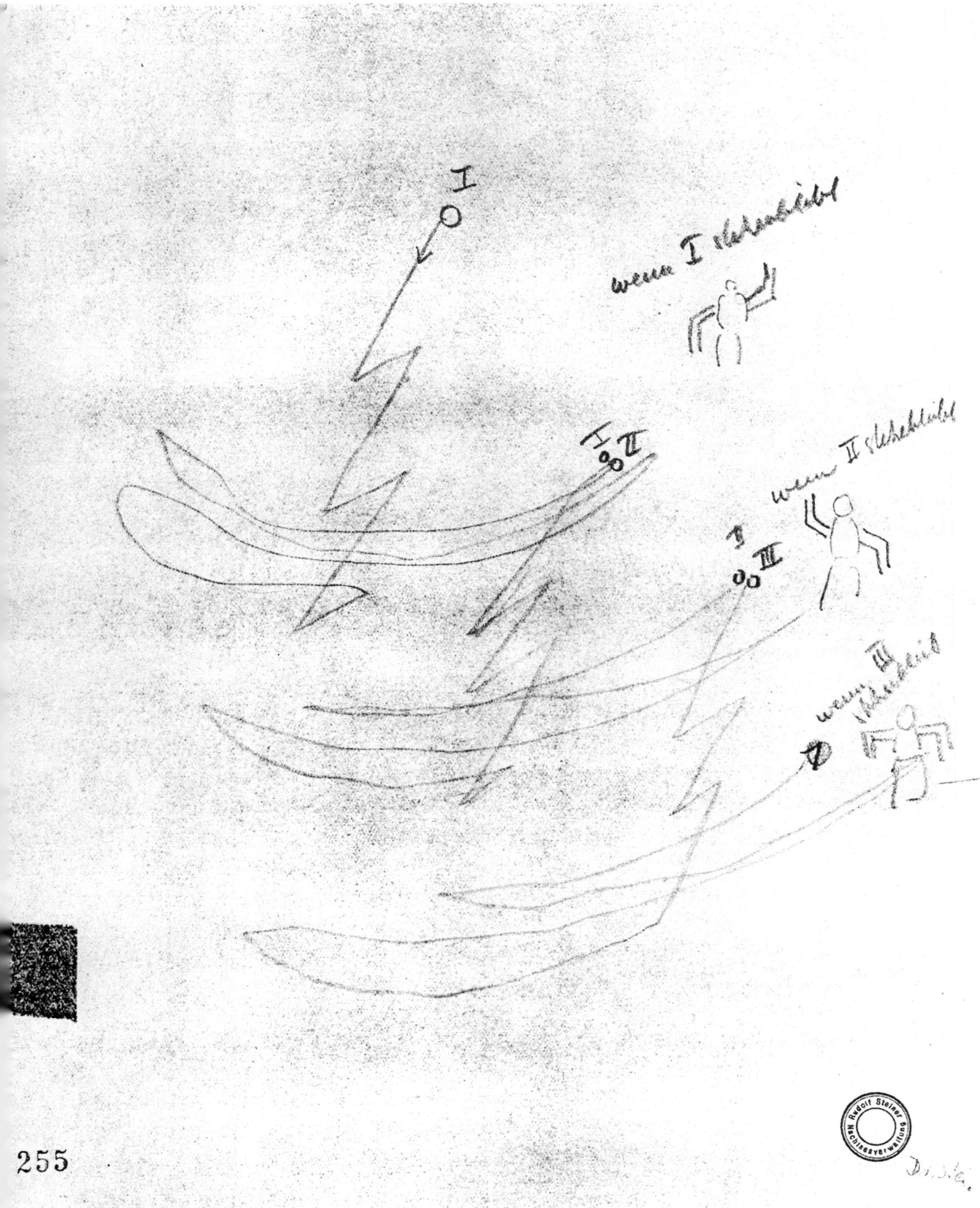

J. Stuten – "Nachtwächter" [Nightwatchmen] (music destroyed in the burning of the first Goetheanum)

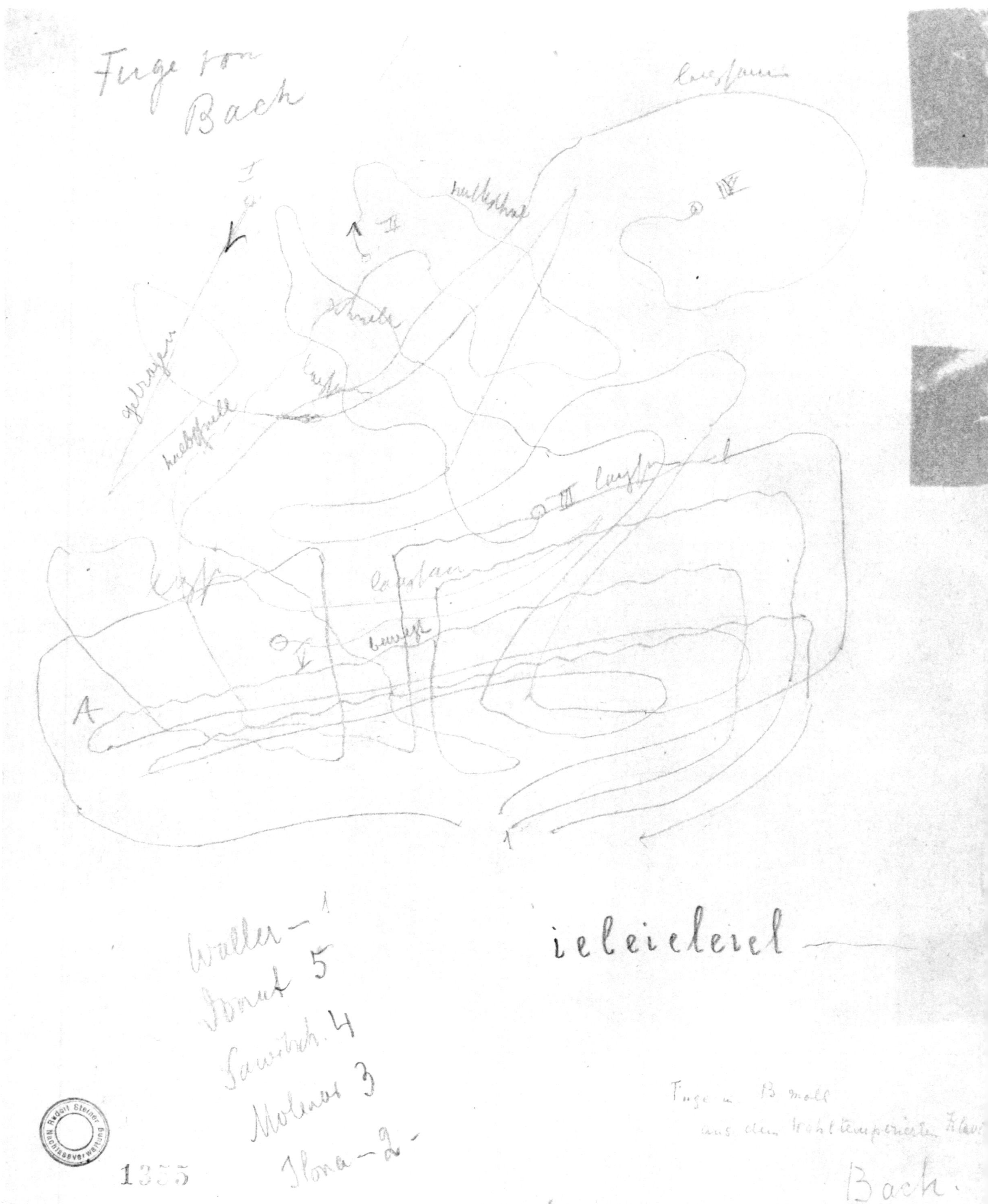

 J. S. Bach – Fugue No. 22, B minor, from *The Well-Tempered Clavier I*, (Form only for the first 25 measures) (page 1)

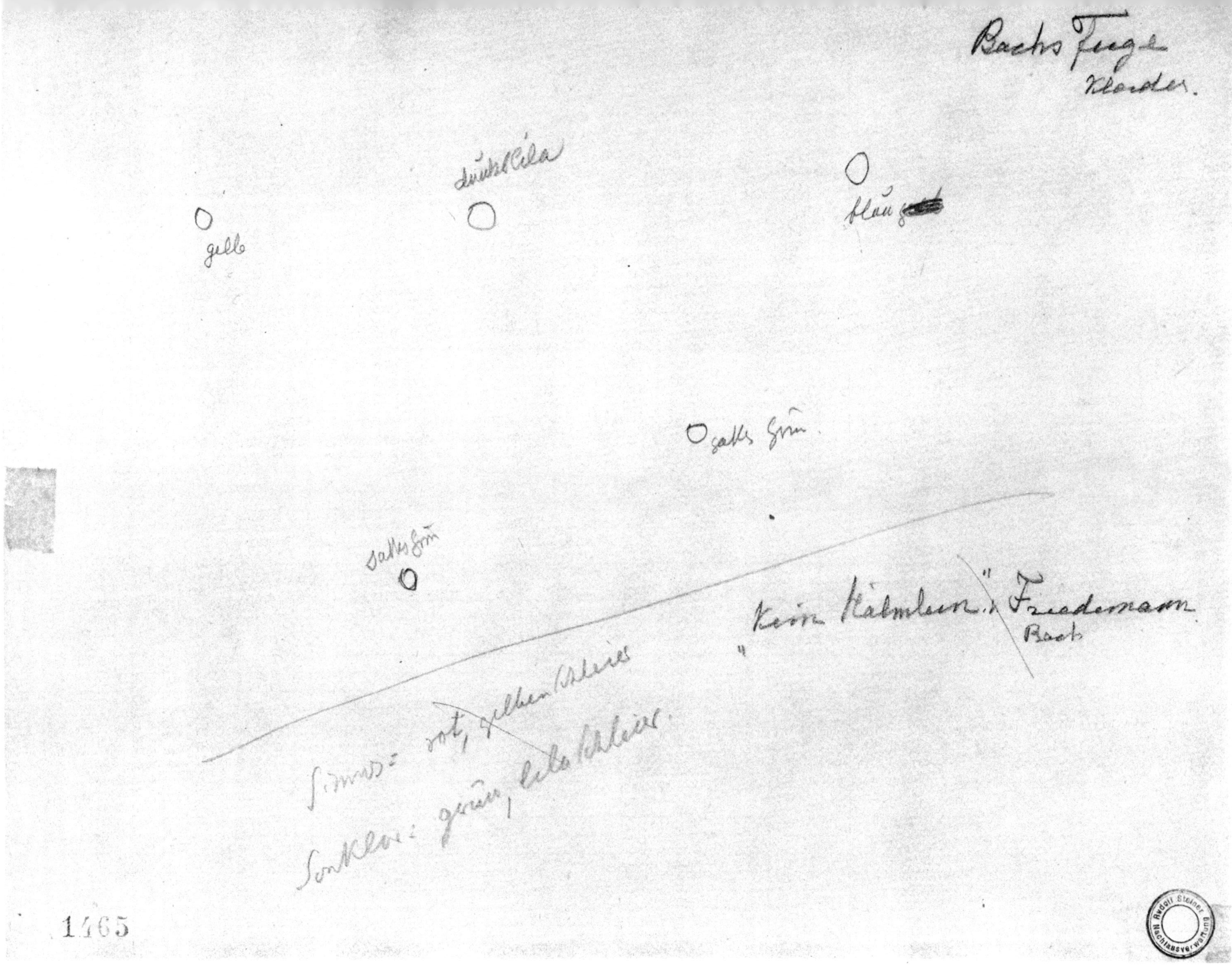

J. S. Bach – Fugue No. 22, B minor, from *The Well-Tempered Clavier I*, (Form only for the first 25 measures) (page 2)

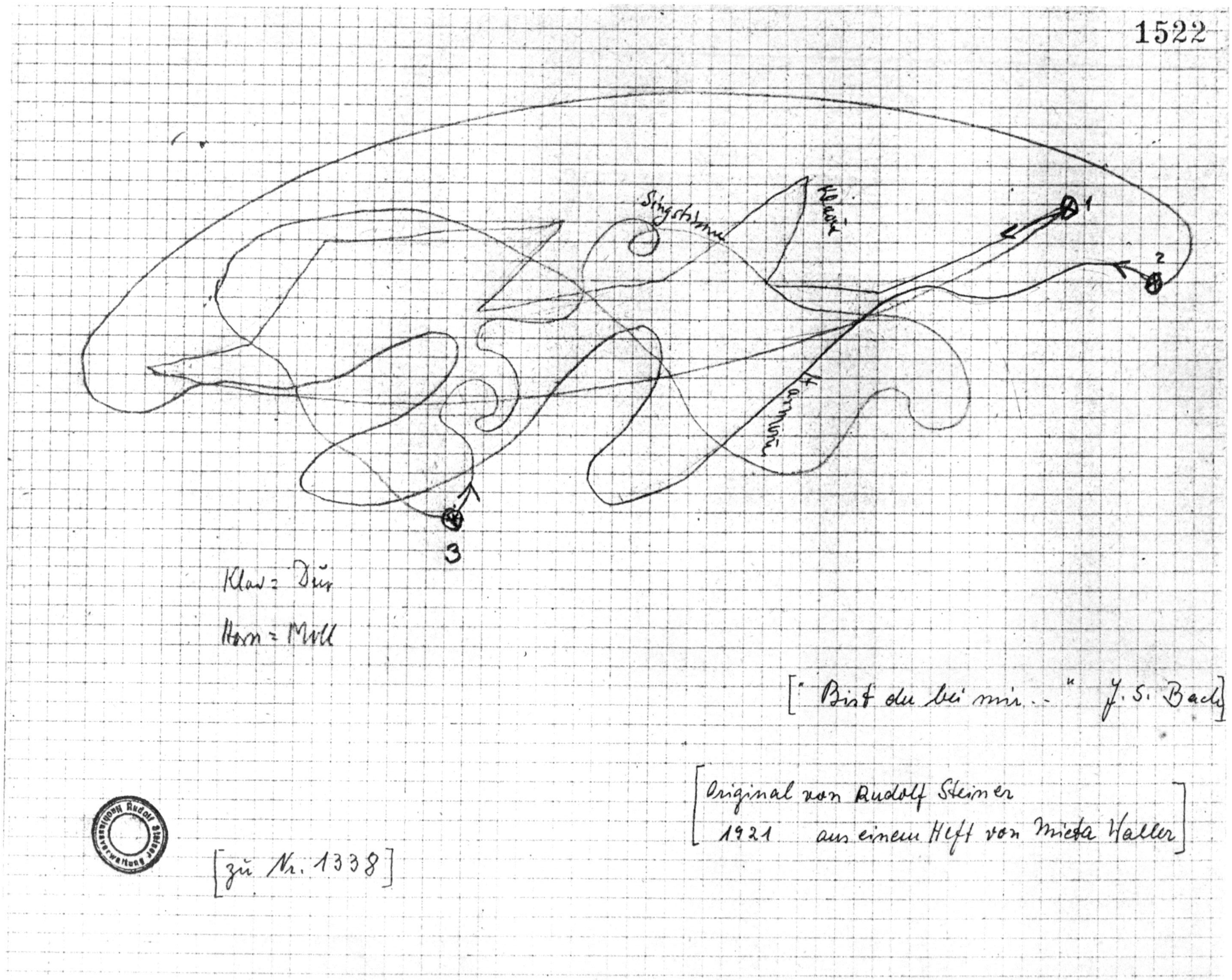

Notebook for Anna Magdalena Bach – "Bist du bei mir," [When you are with me] Aria, E-flat major

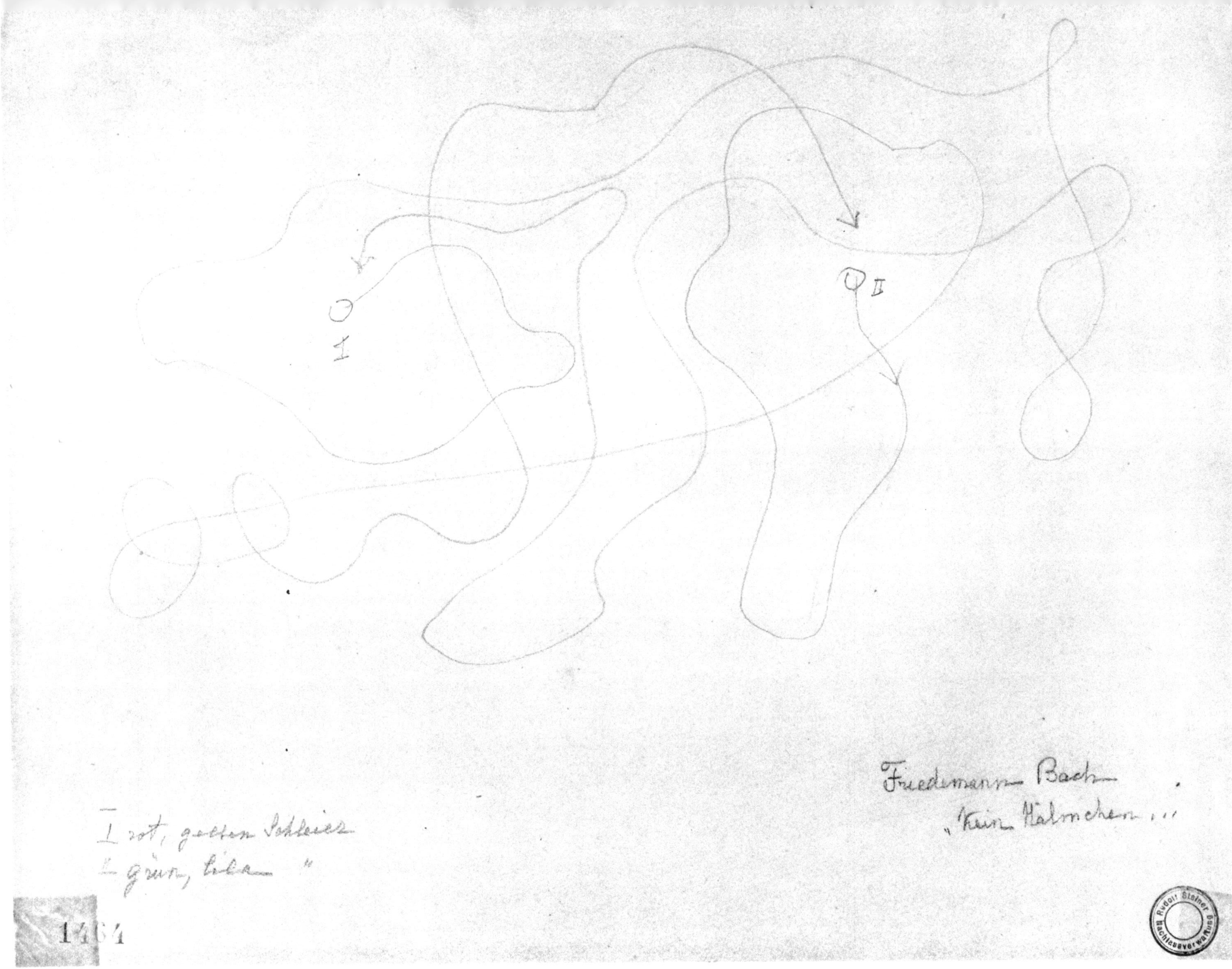

L. E. Bach – “Kein Hälmlein wächst auf Erden,” [No blade of grass grows on earth], Song, E-flat major (violin and piano)

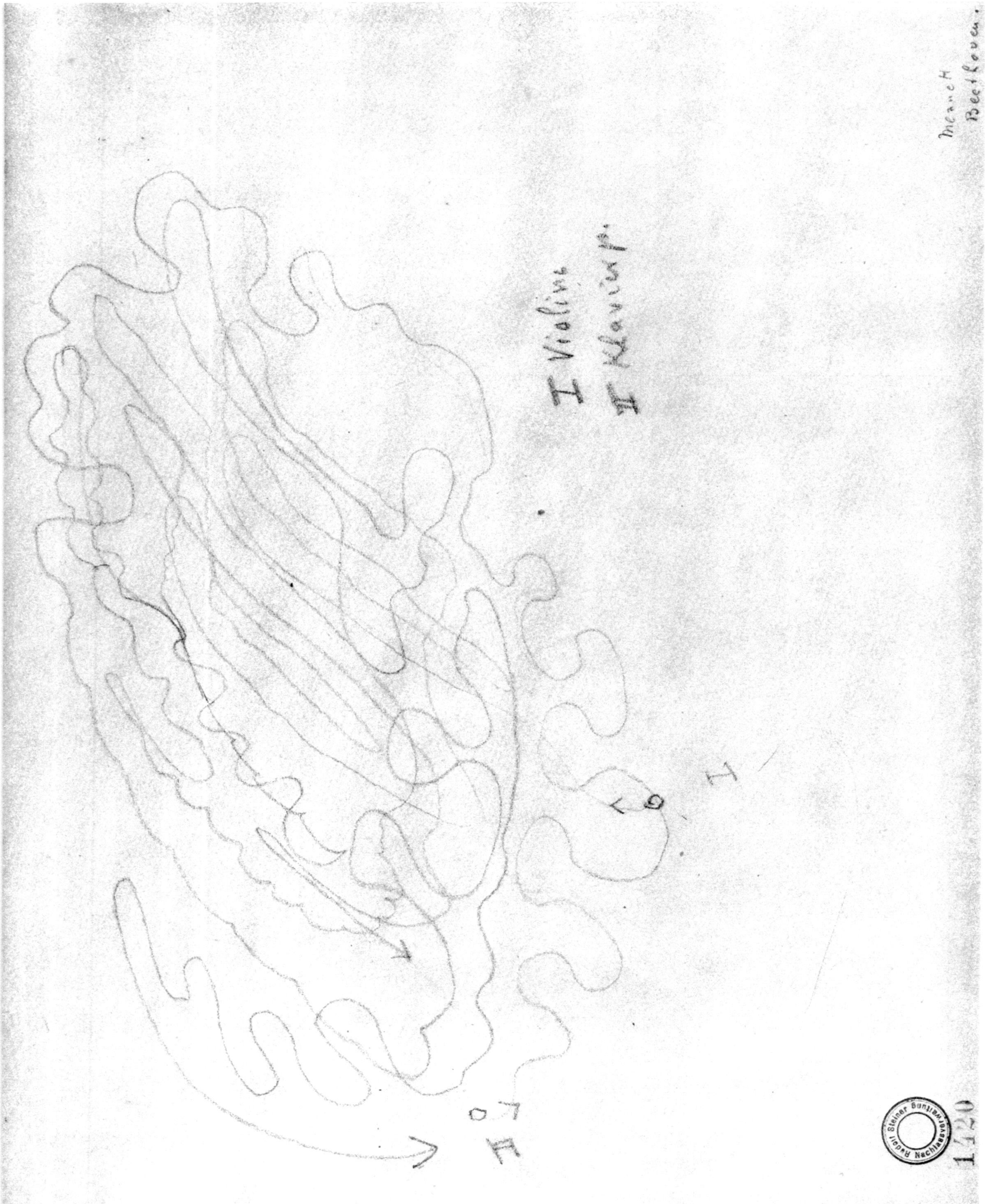

L. van Beethoven – Menuett, Allegretto, G major, No. 2

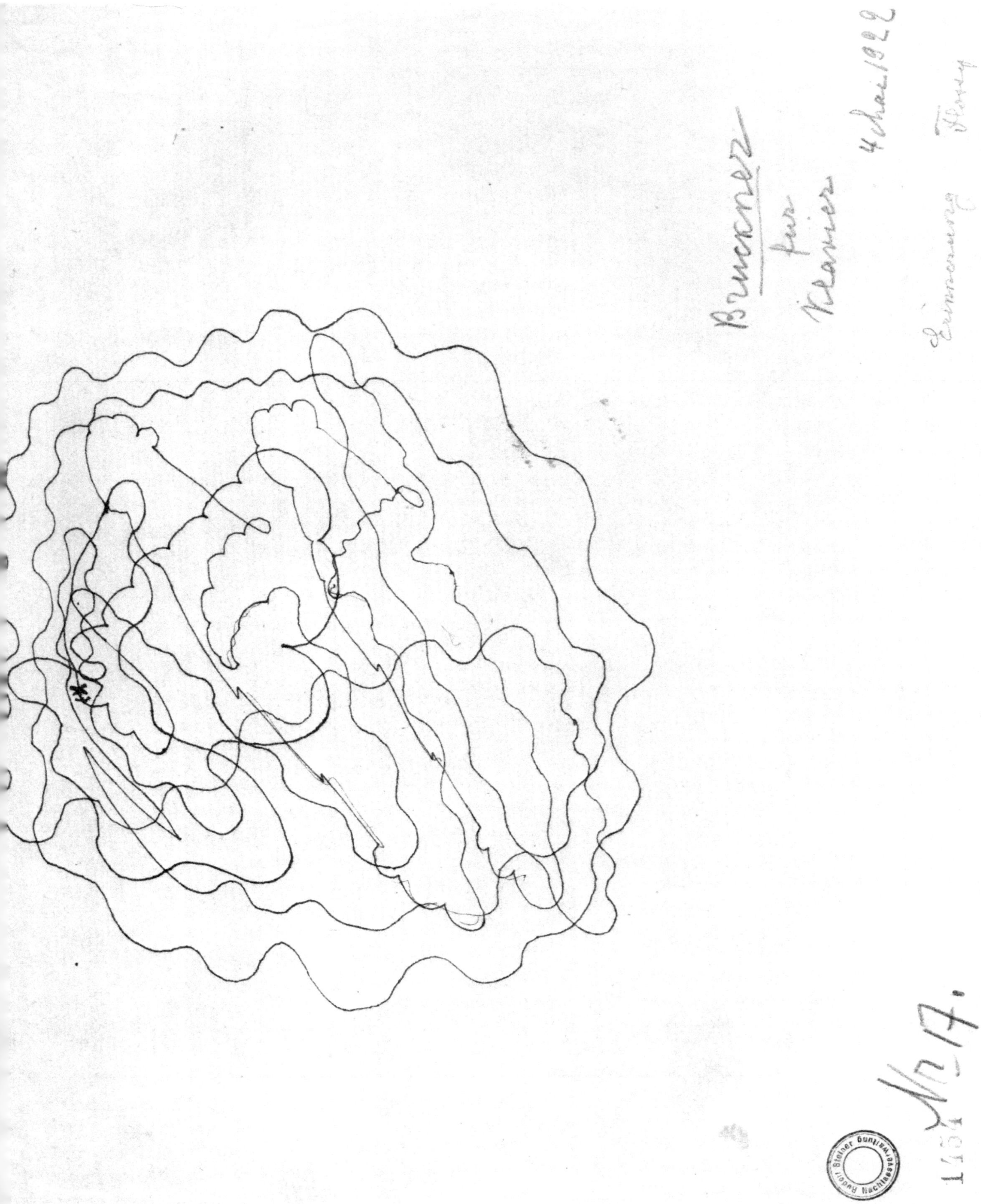

A. Bruckner – "Erinnerung" [Remembrance], slow, inward, A-flat major

14 F. Couperin – "Sœur Monique," [Sister Monica], Rondeau for piano in F major

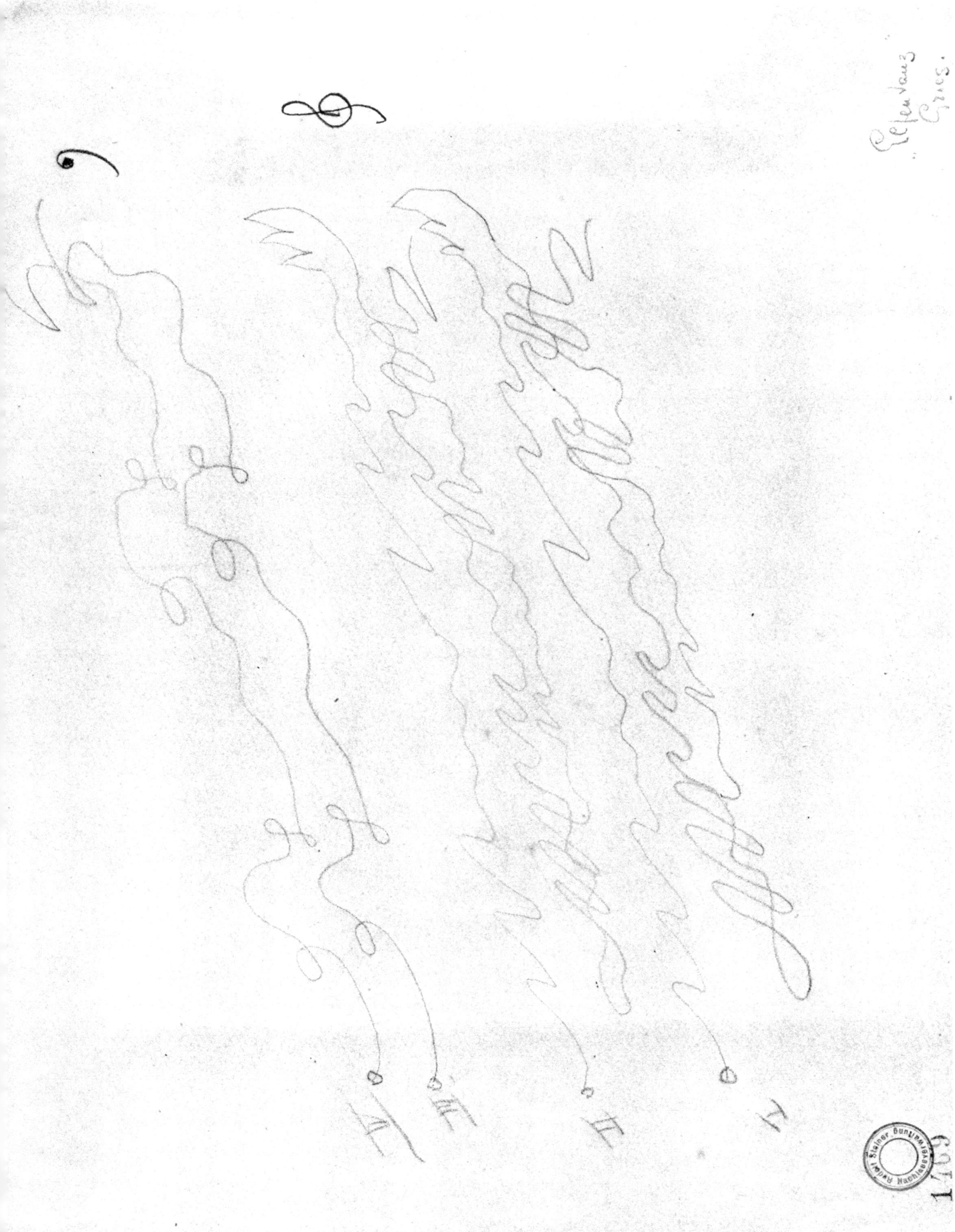

E. Grieg – "Dance of the elves" from *Lyrical Pieces*, book I, Op. 12/4

J. S. Bach – Gavotte II (Musette), G major, from English Suite, No. 3, G minor

Notebook for Anna Magdalena Bach – Minuet (Aria), D minor

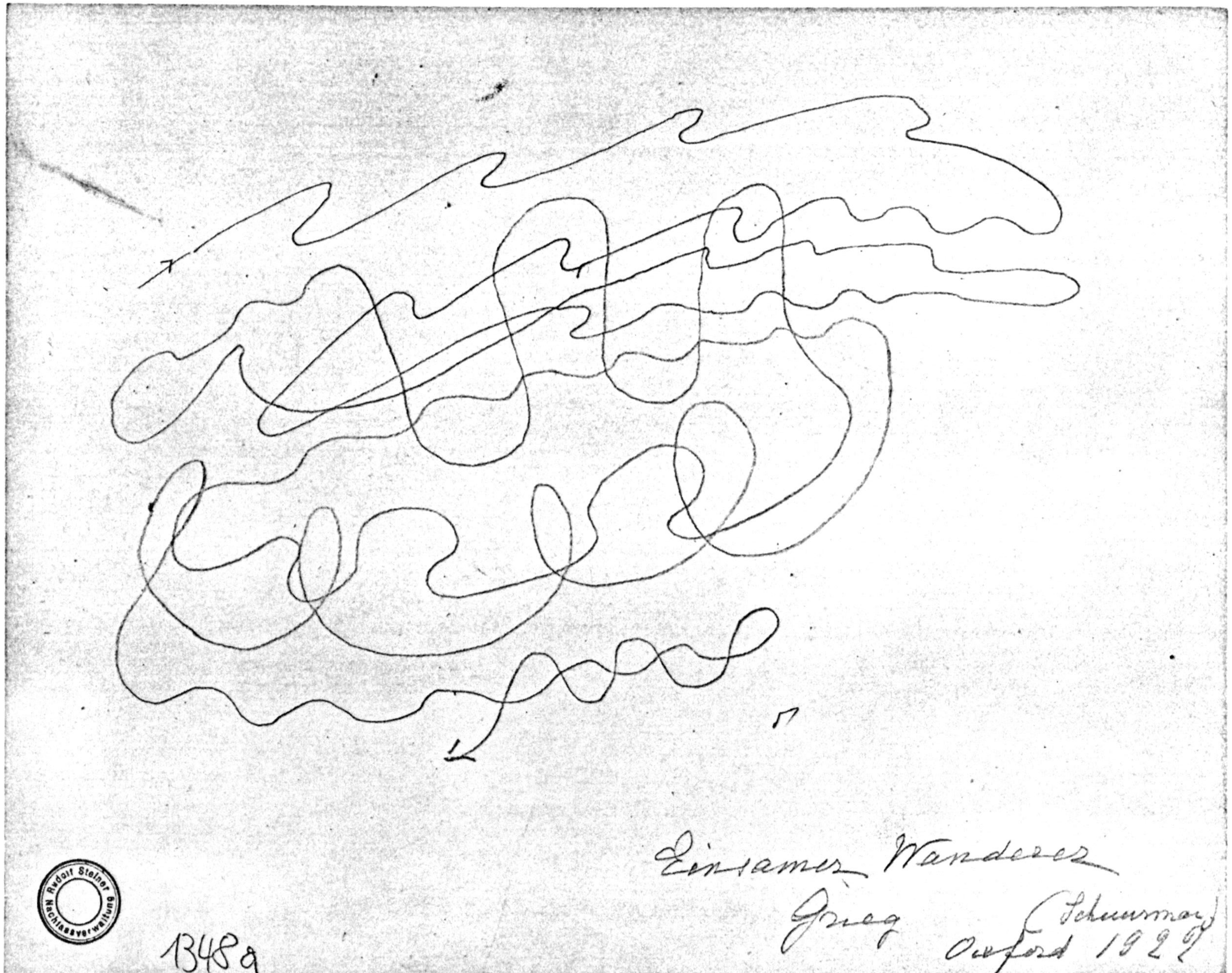

E. Grieg – "Lonely wanderer" from *Lyrical Pieces*, book III, Op. 43/2

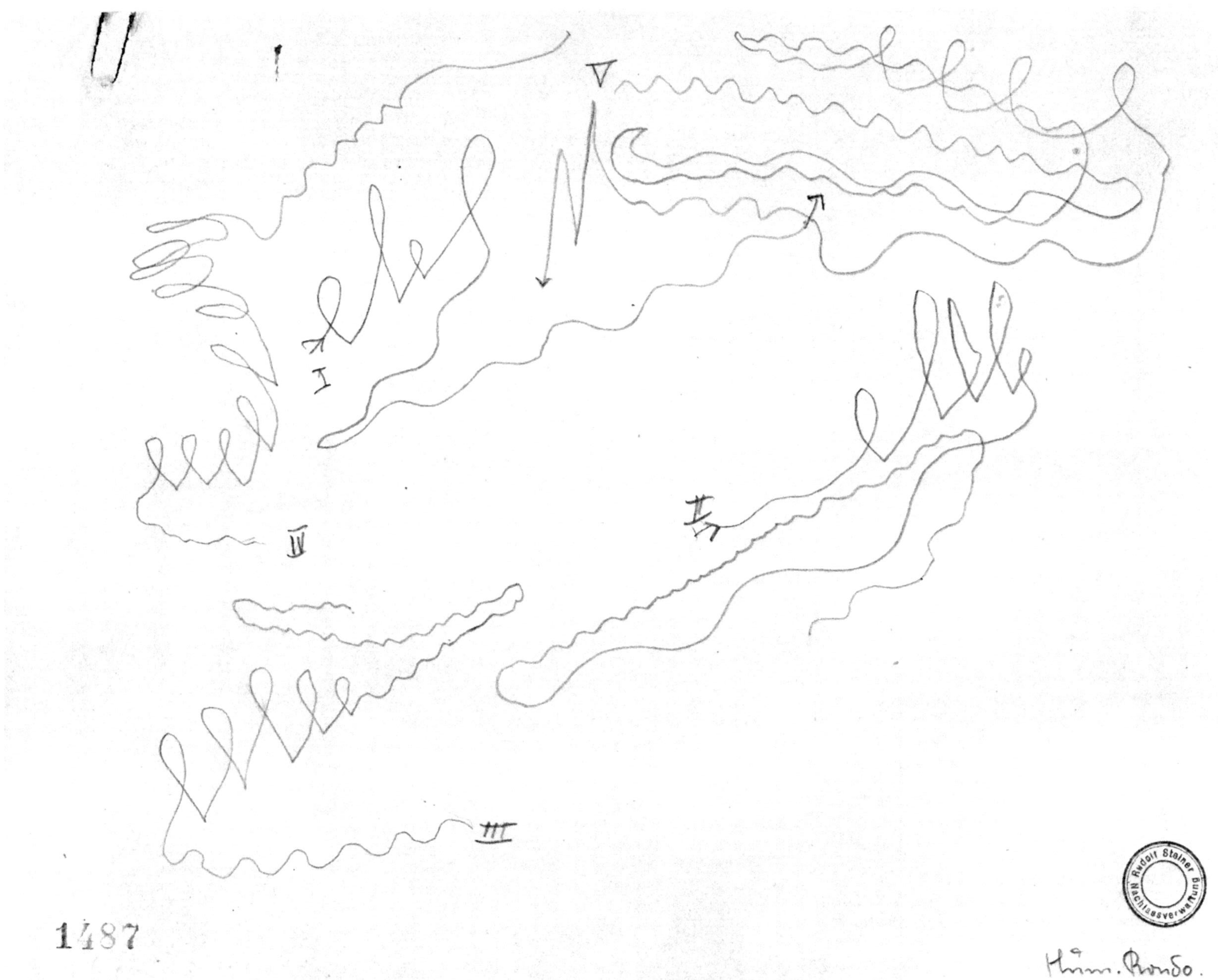

M. Schuurman – "Humoristisches Rondo" [Humorous rondo], (page 1)

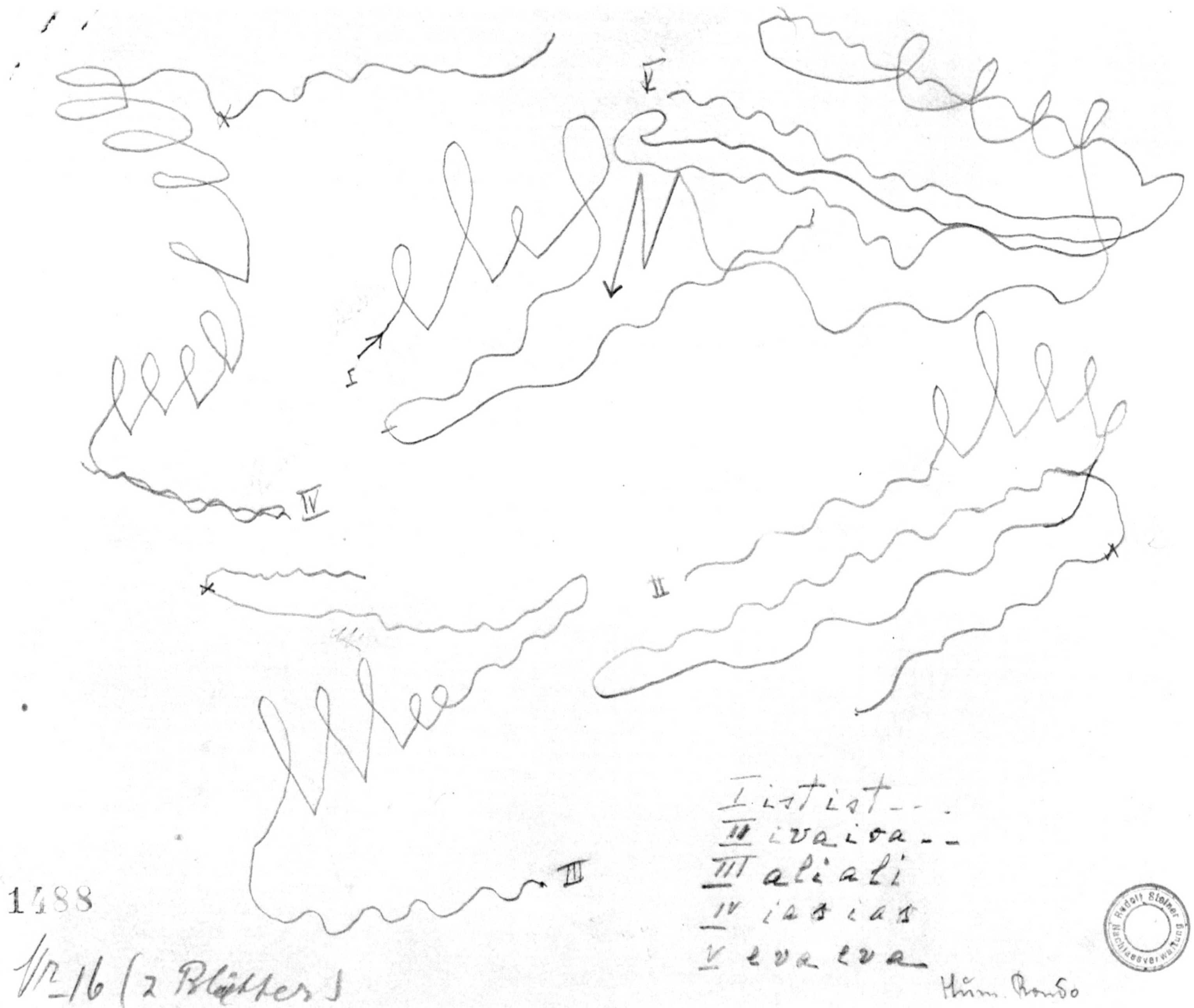

M. Schuurman – "Humoristisches Rondo" [Humorous rondo], (page 2)

G. P. Telemann – Gigue, from Suite A major

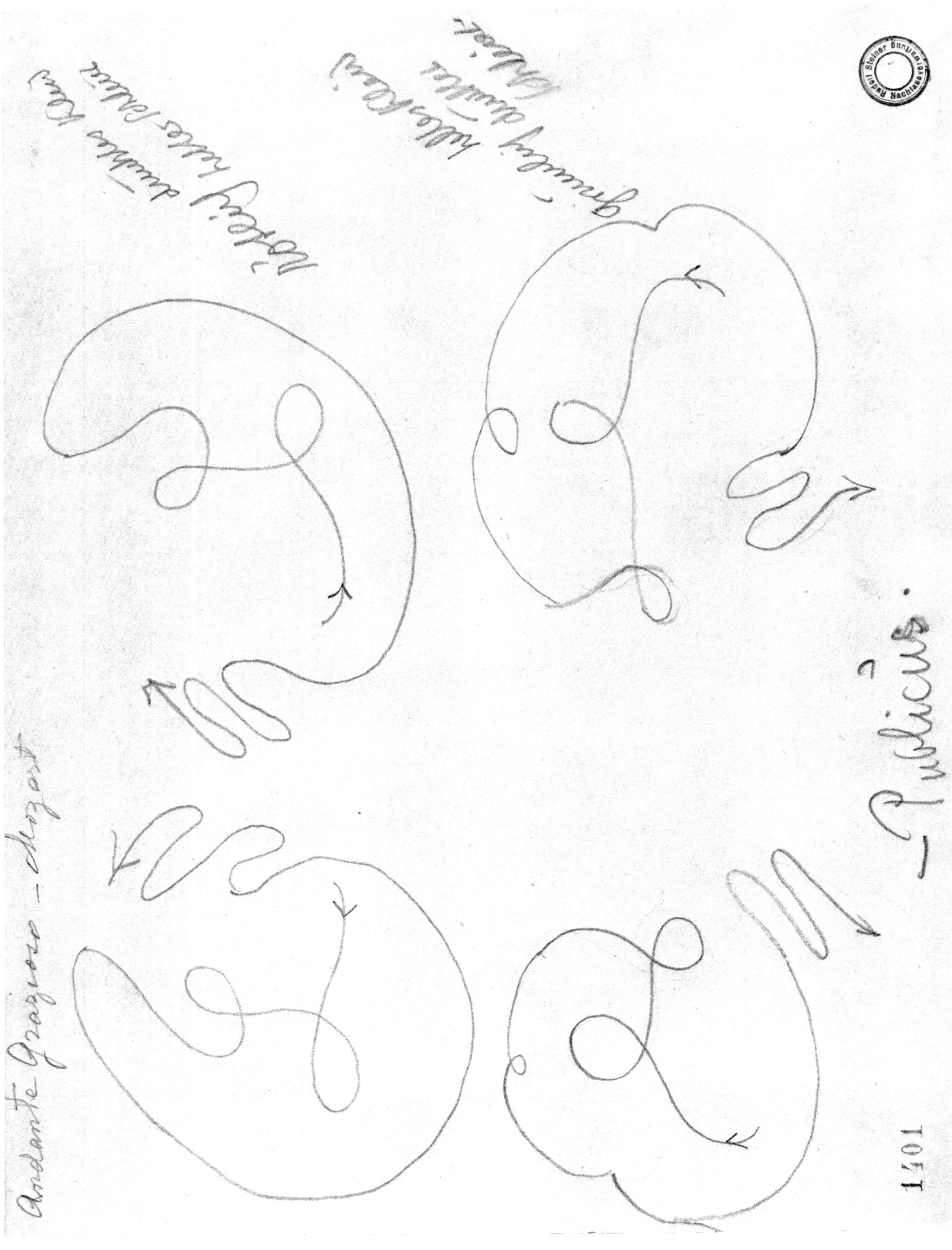

W. A. Mozart – Andante grazioso, the first movement from Sonata No. 11, A major

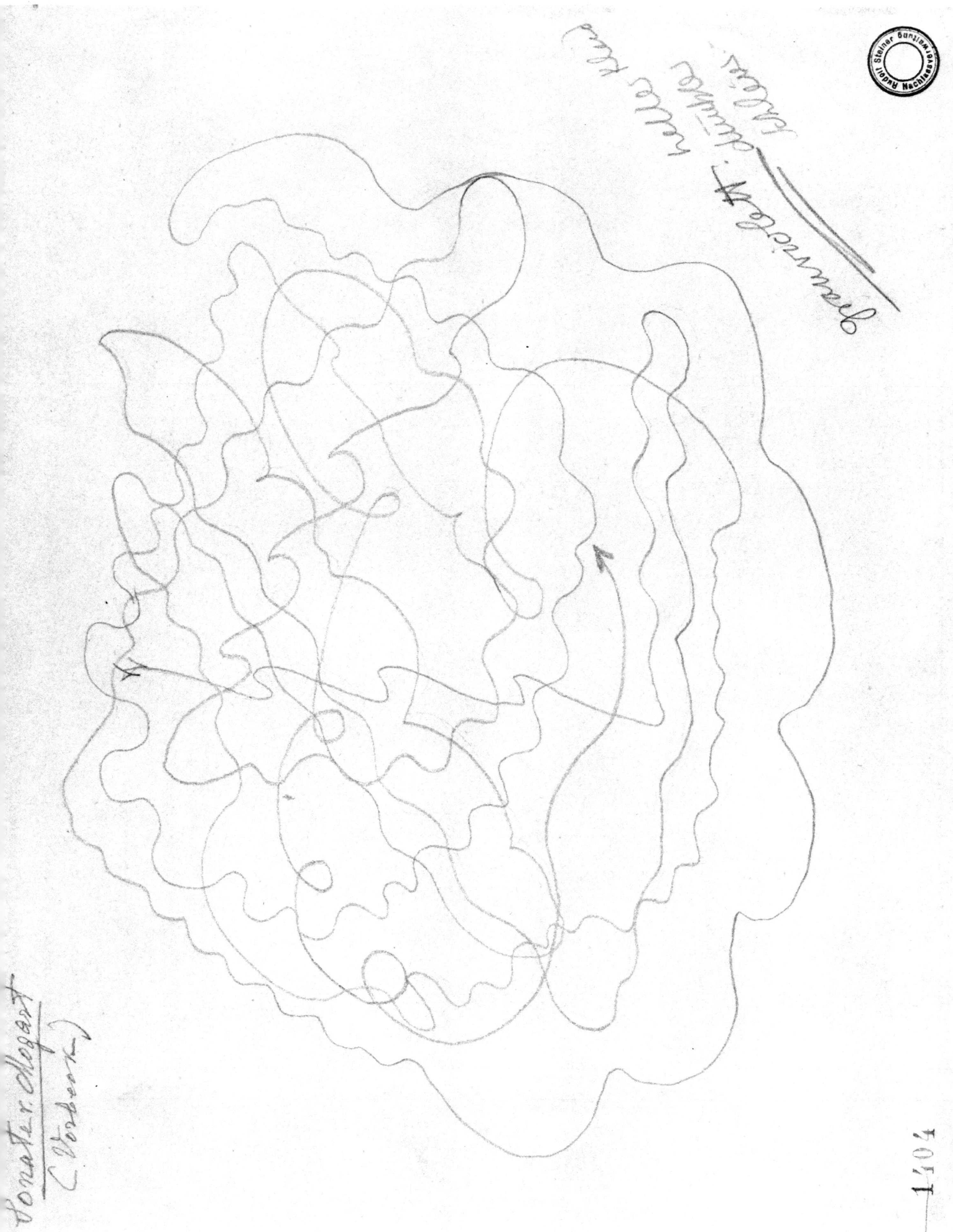

W. A. Mozart – Allegro, first movement from Sonata No. 12, F major

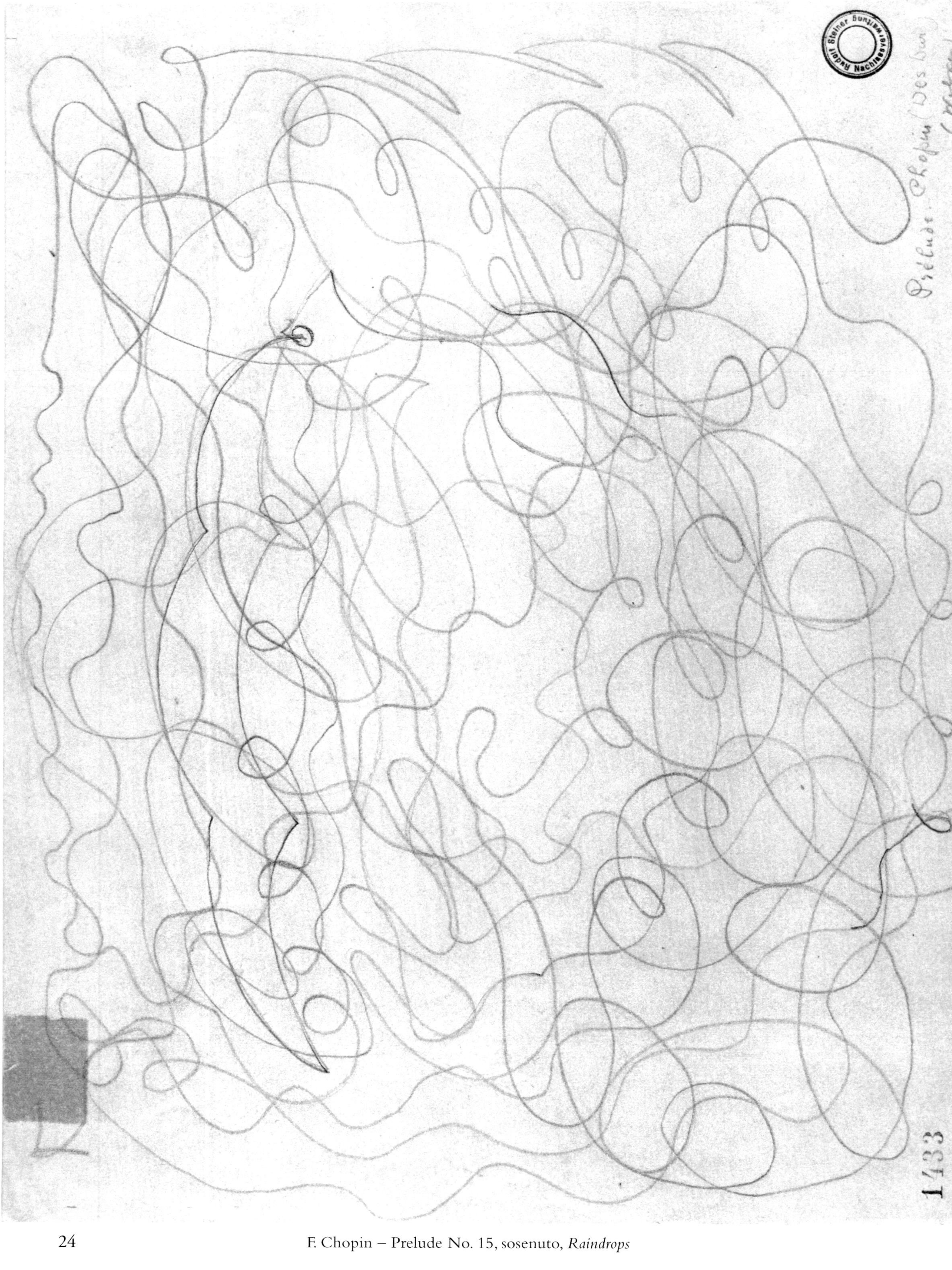

F. Chopin – Prelude No. 15, sosenuto, *Raindrops*

F. Chopin – Nocturne No. 2, Andante, E-flat major, Op. 9/2 (page 1)

F. Chopin – Nocturne No. 2, Andante, E-flat major, Op. 9/2 (page 2)

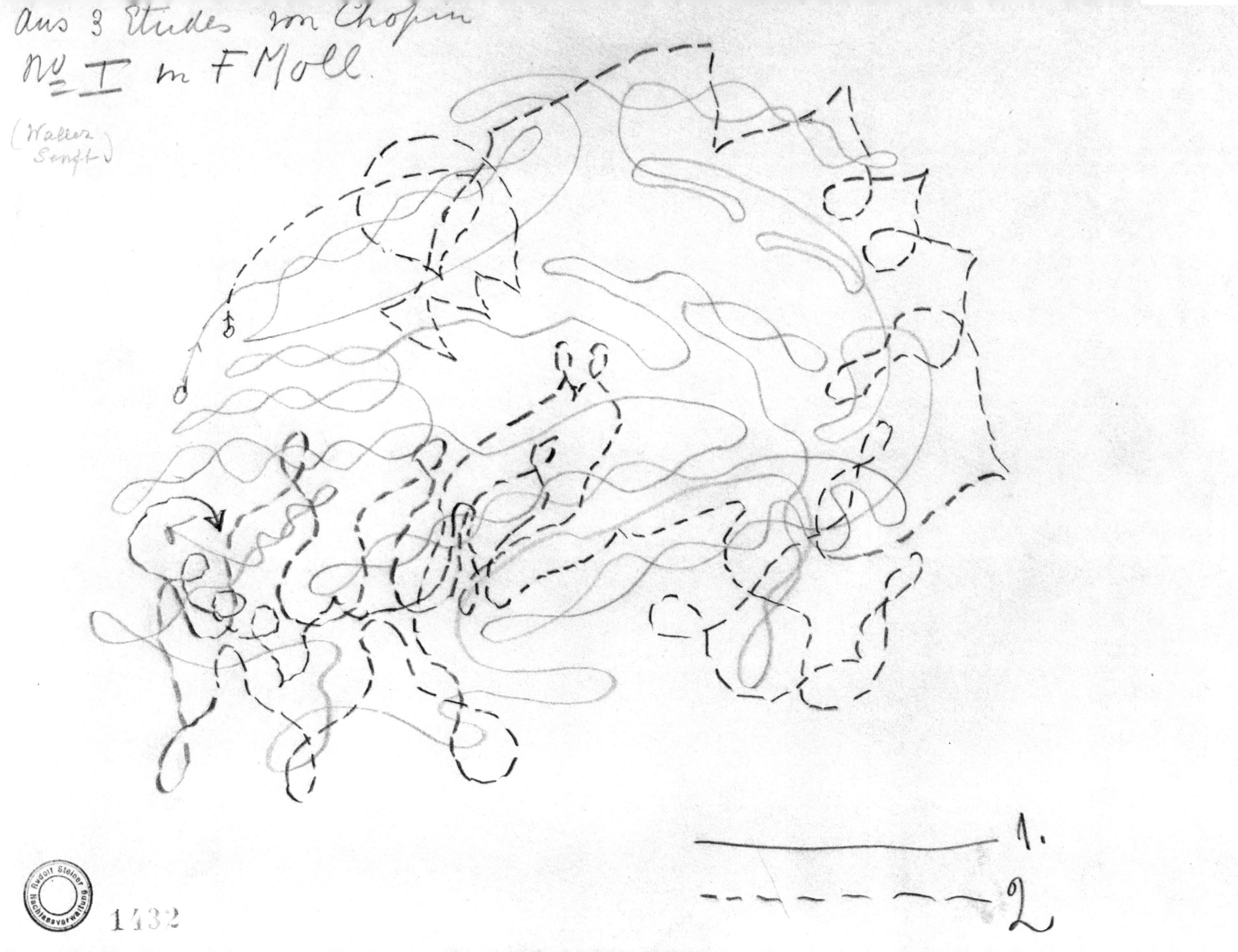

F. Chopin – Étude No. 25, Andantino, F minor, No. 1 from *Trois nouvelles Études* [Three new studies], Op. 1 (posthumous)

F. Chopin – Étude No. 9, Allegro, molto agitato, F minor, Op. 10/9 (page 1)

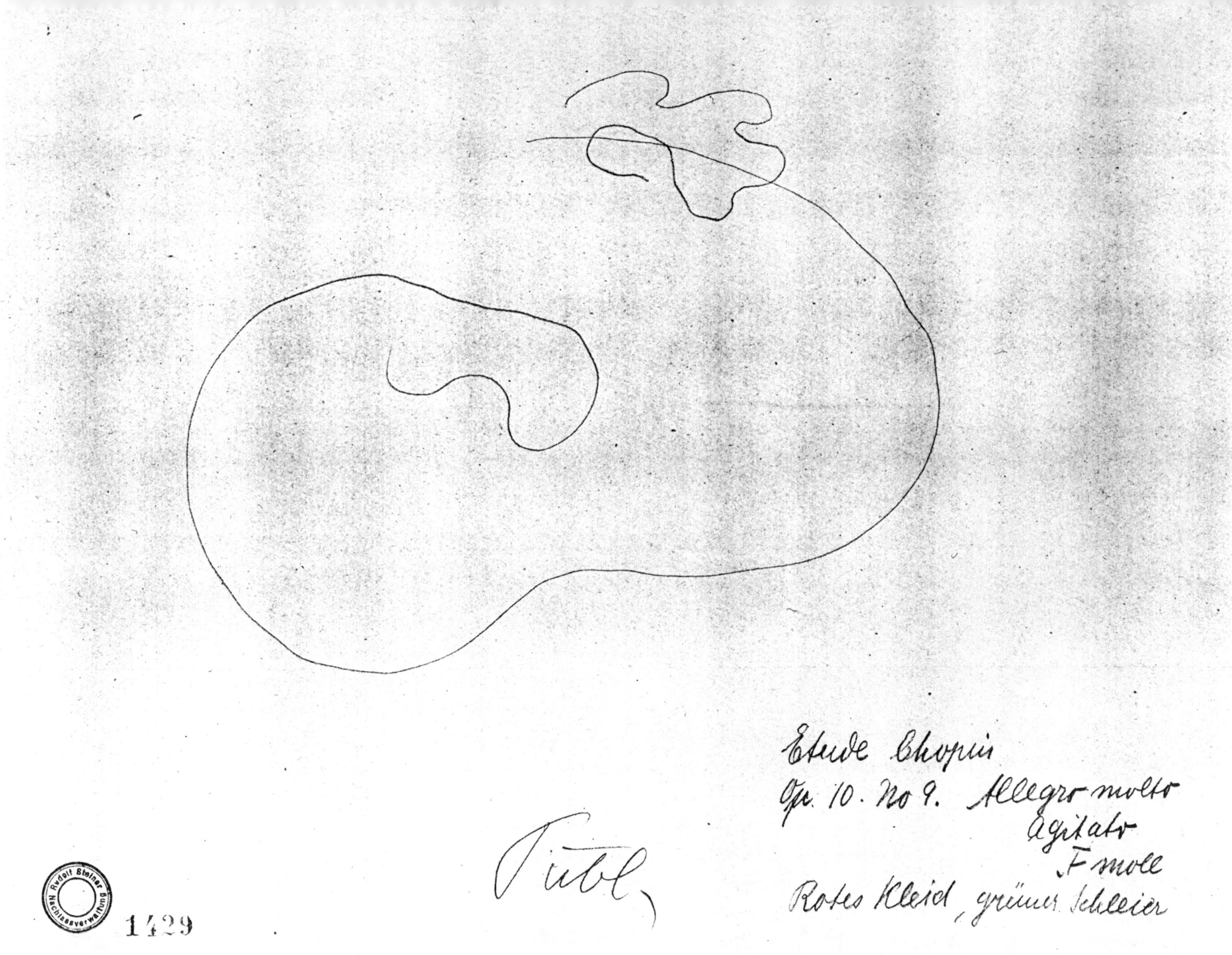

F. Chopin – Étude No. 9, Allegro, molto agitato, F minor, Op. 10/9 (page 2)

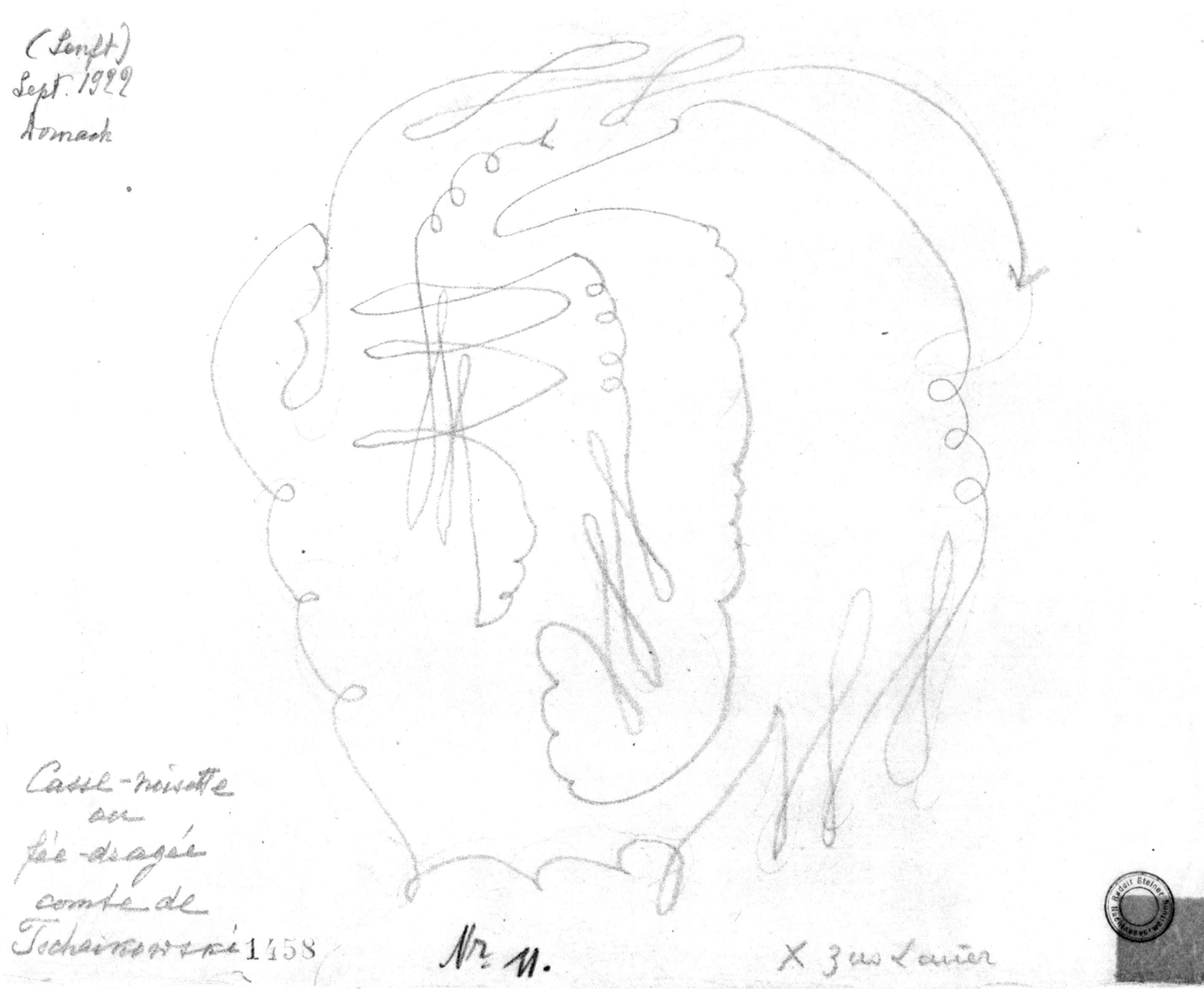

P. Tschaikowsky – “Dance of the Sugar Plum Fairy” from the *Nutcracker Suite*, for piano, Op. 71b

L. van Beethoven – Allegro, third movement from Sonata No. 4, E-flat major, Op. 7 (page 1)

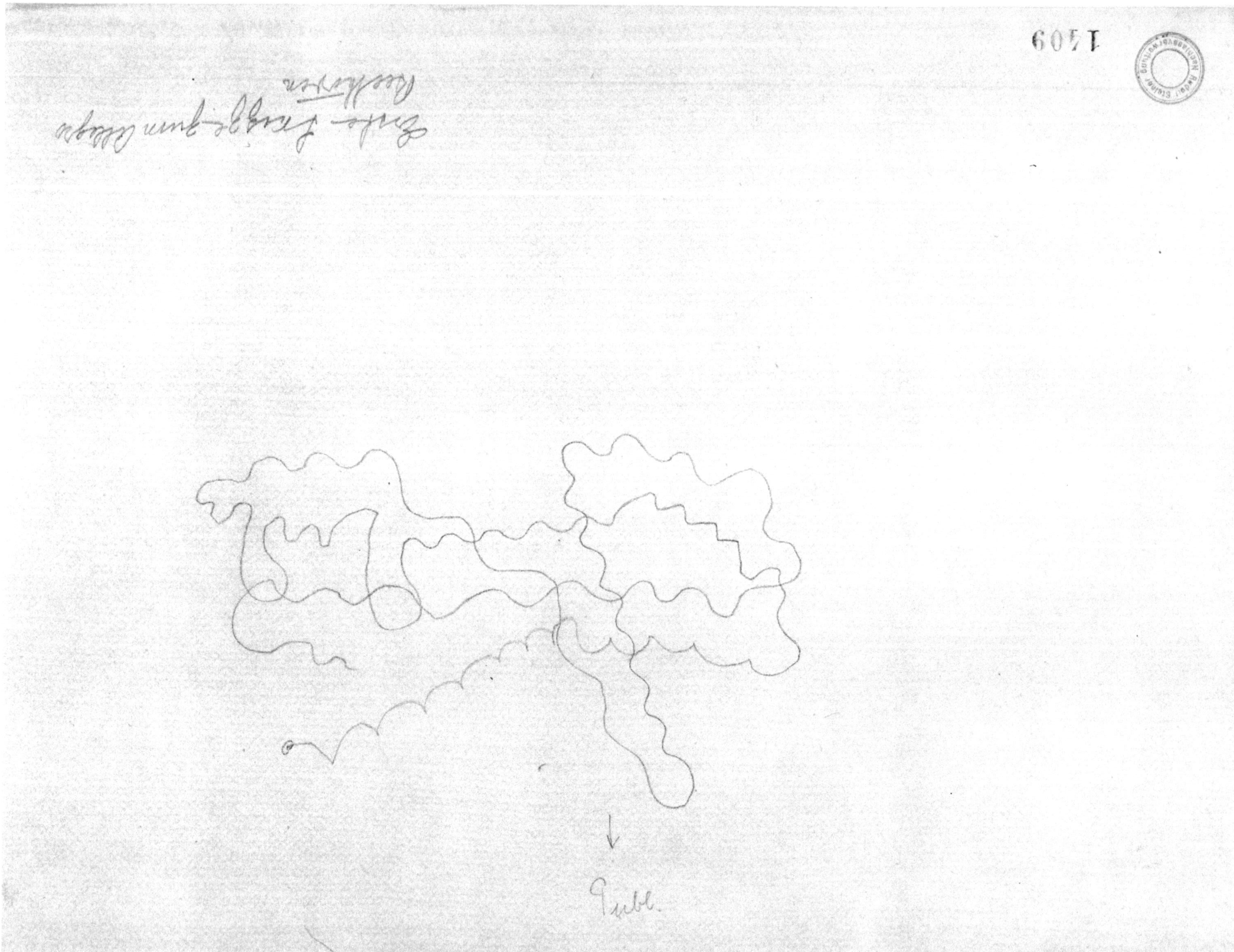

L. van Beethoven – Allegro, third movement from Sonata No. 4, E-flat major, Op. 7 (page 2)

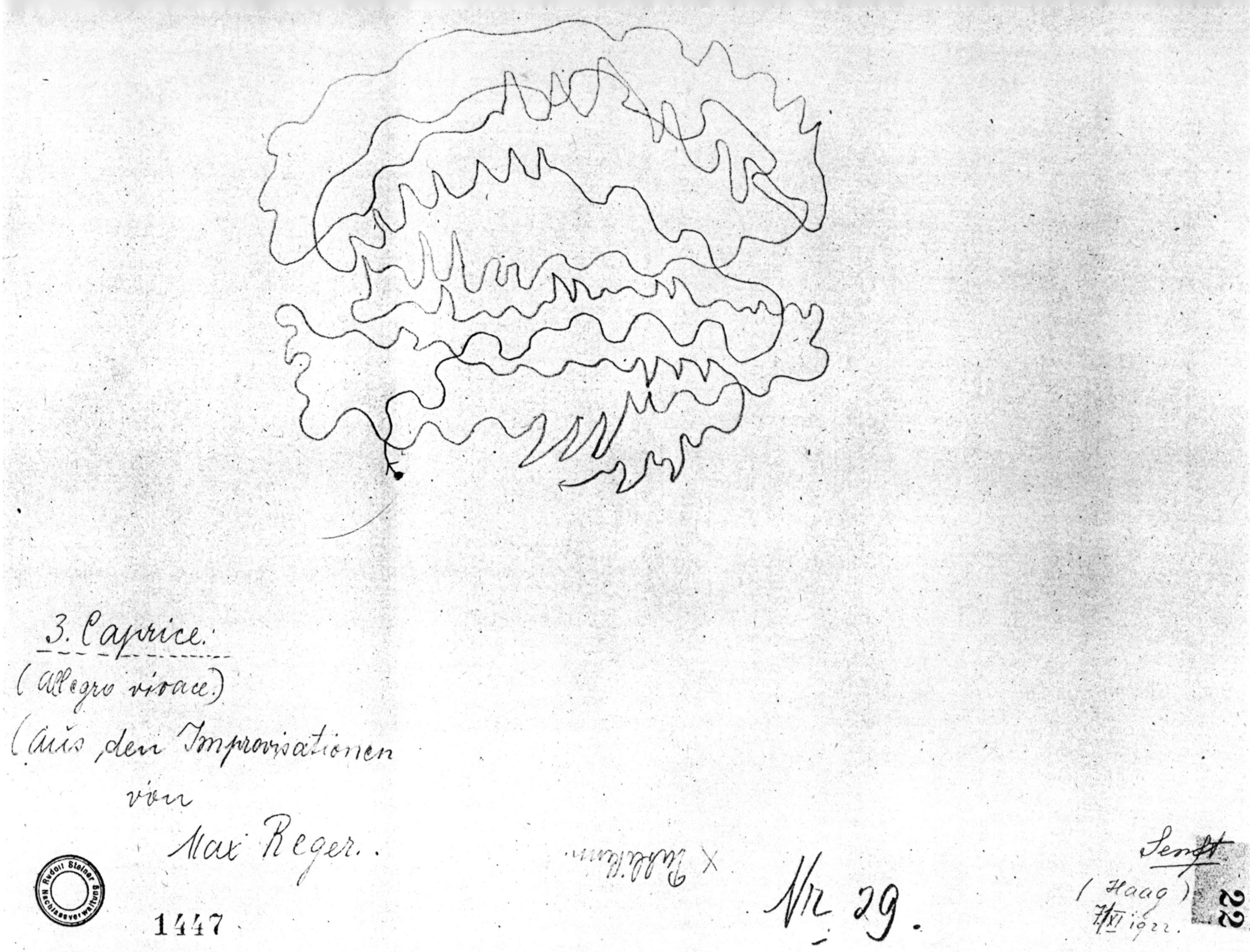

M. Reger – "Caprice," Allegro vivace from *Improvisationen*, [Improvisations], Op. 18/3

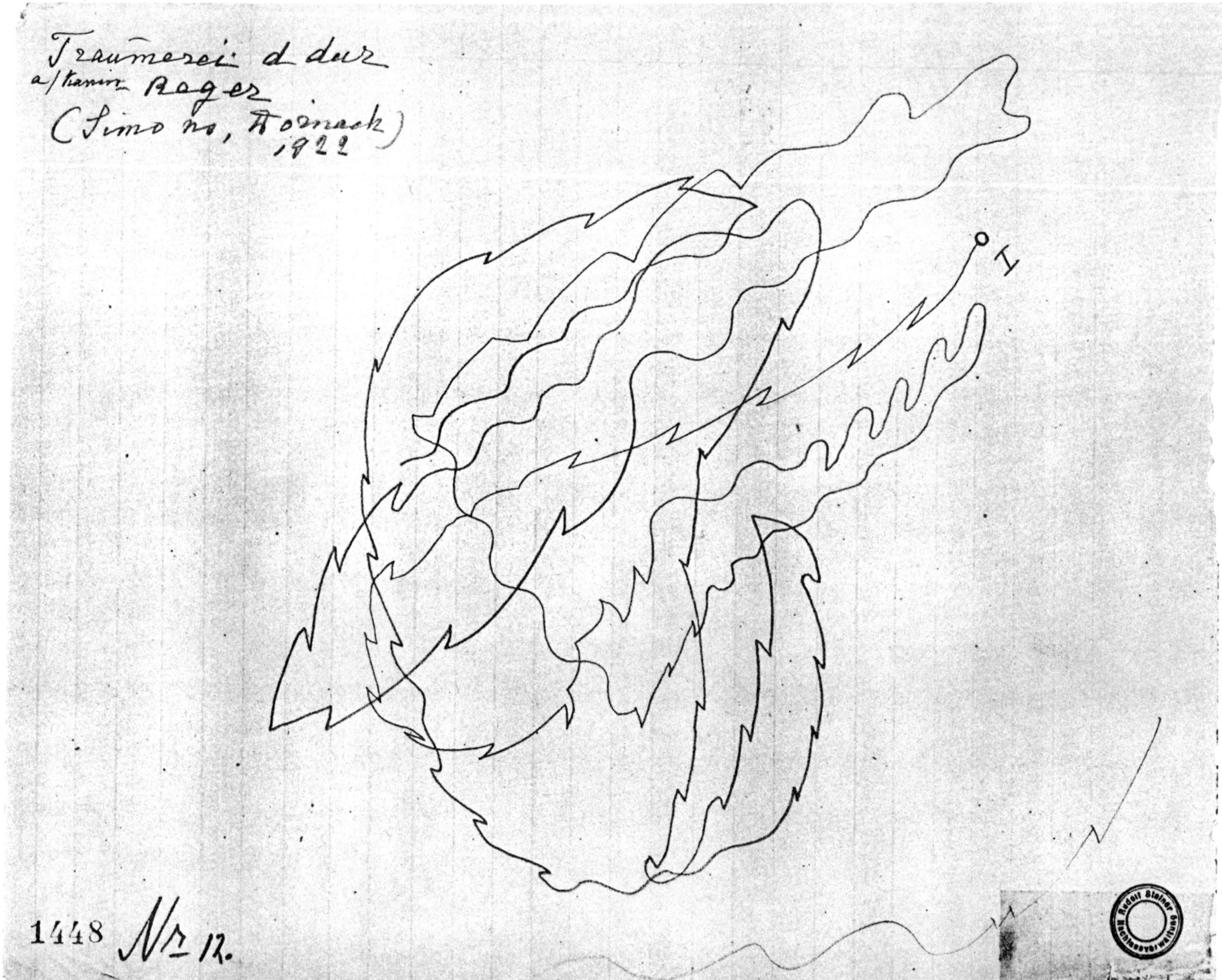

M. Reger – "Träumerei," [Dreaming], Molto sostenuto, D major from *Träume am Kamin* [Dreams at the fireplace], Op. 143/7

G. F. Händel – Saraband, B major for violin and piano

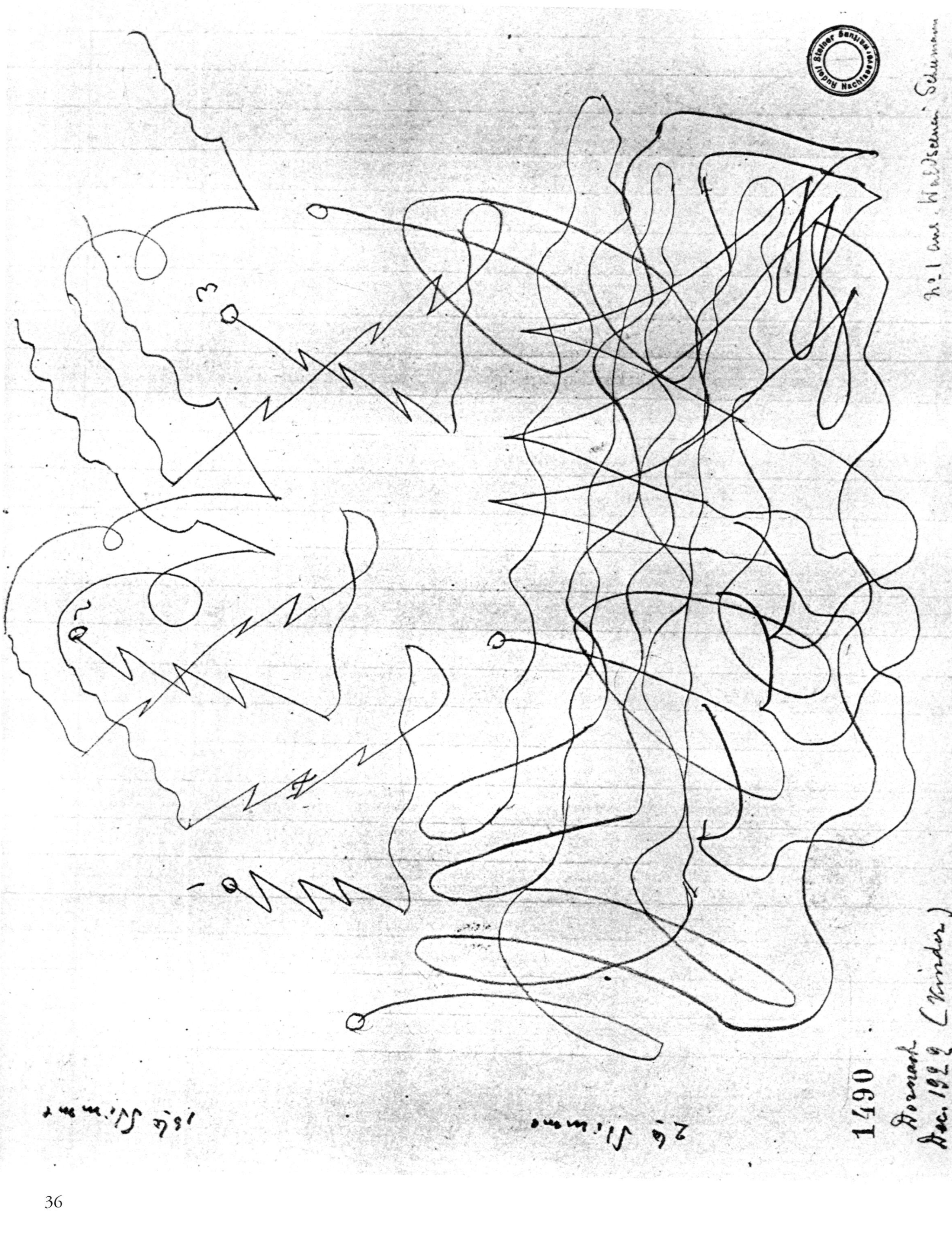

R. Schumann – "Eintritt" [Entrance] from *Waldszenen* [Woodland scenes], No. 1, Op. 82/1 (Form for children)

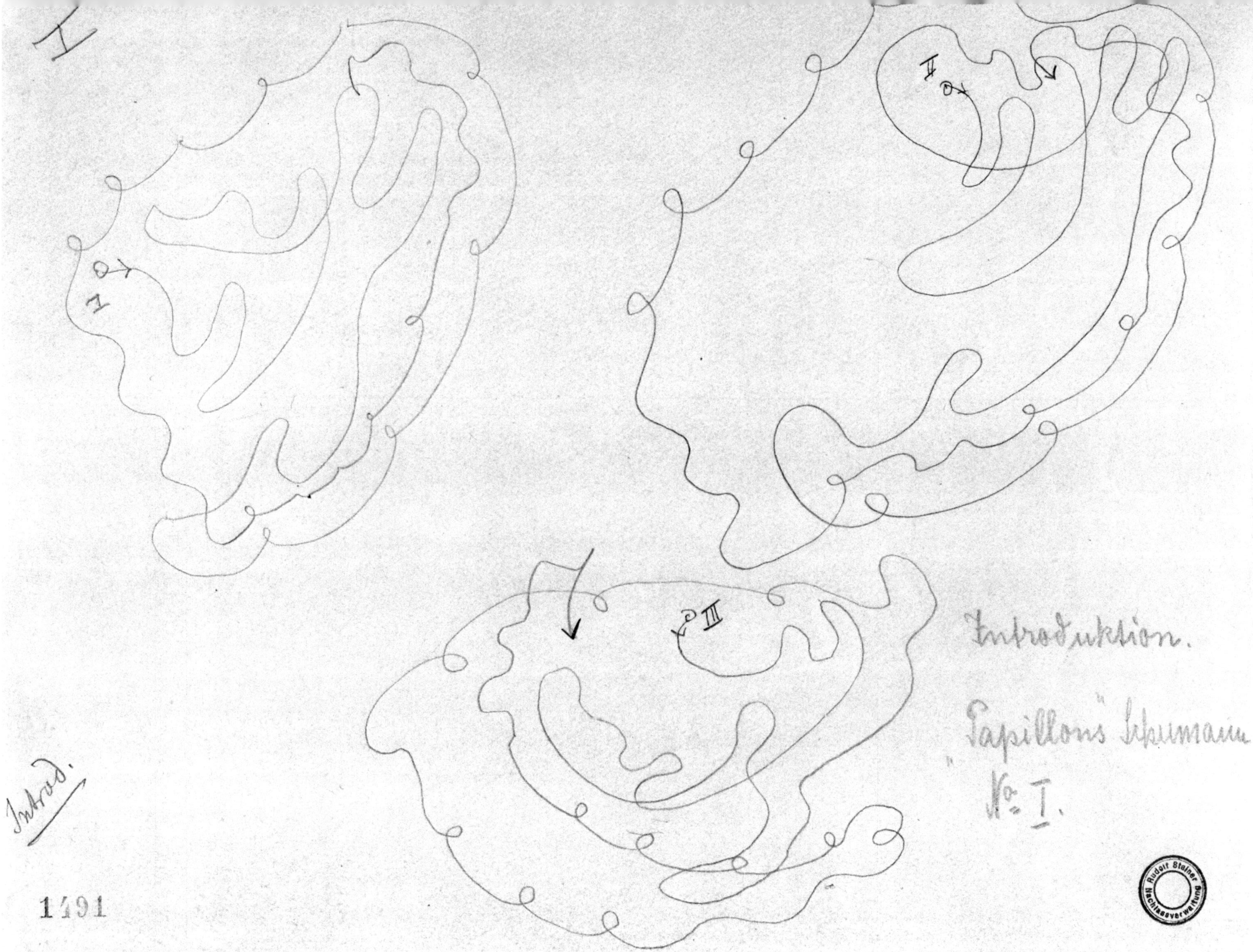

R. Schumann – "Papillons" [Butterflies], Introduction and No. 1, Moderato, D major, Op. 2/1

R. Schumann – "Papillons" [Butterflies], No. 2, Prestissimo, E-flat major/A-flat major, Op. 2/2

R. Schumann – "Papillons" [Butterflies], No. 9, Prestissimo, B minor, Op. 2/9

R. Schumann – "Papillons" [Butterflies], No. 12, Finale, D major, Op. 2/12 (page 1)

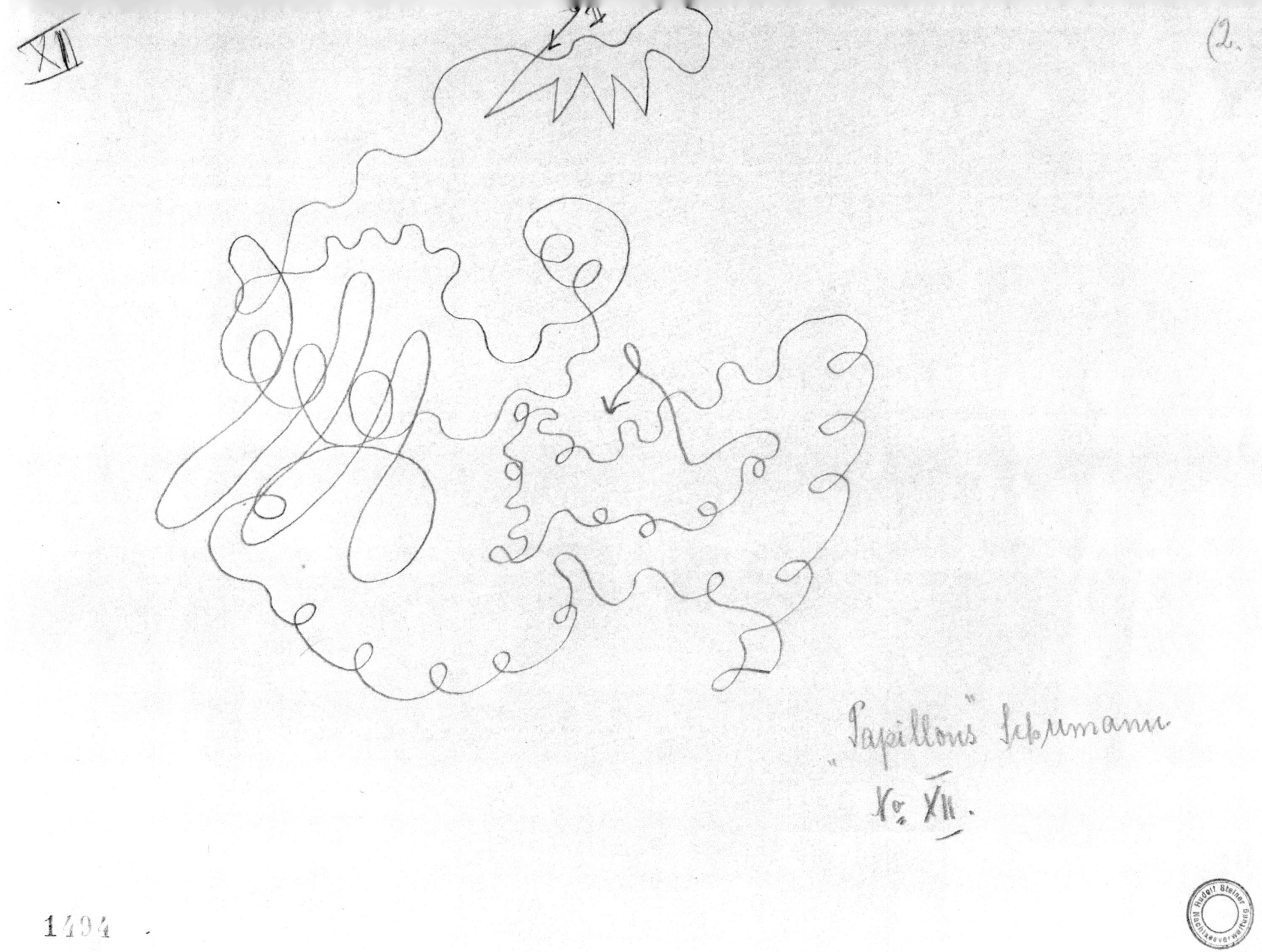

R. Schumann – "Papillons" [Butterflies], No. 12, Finale, D major, Op. 2/12 (page 2)

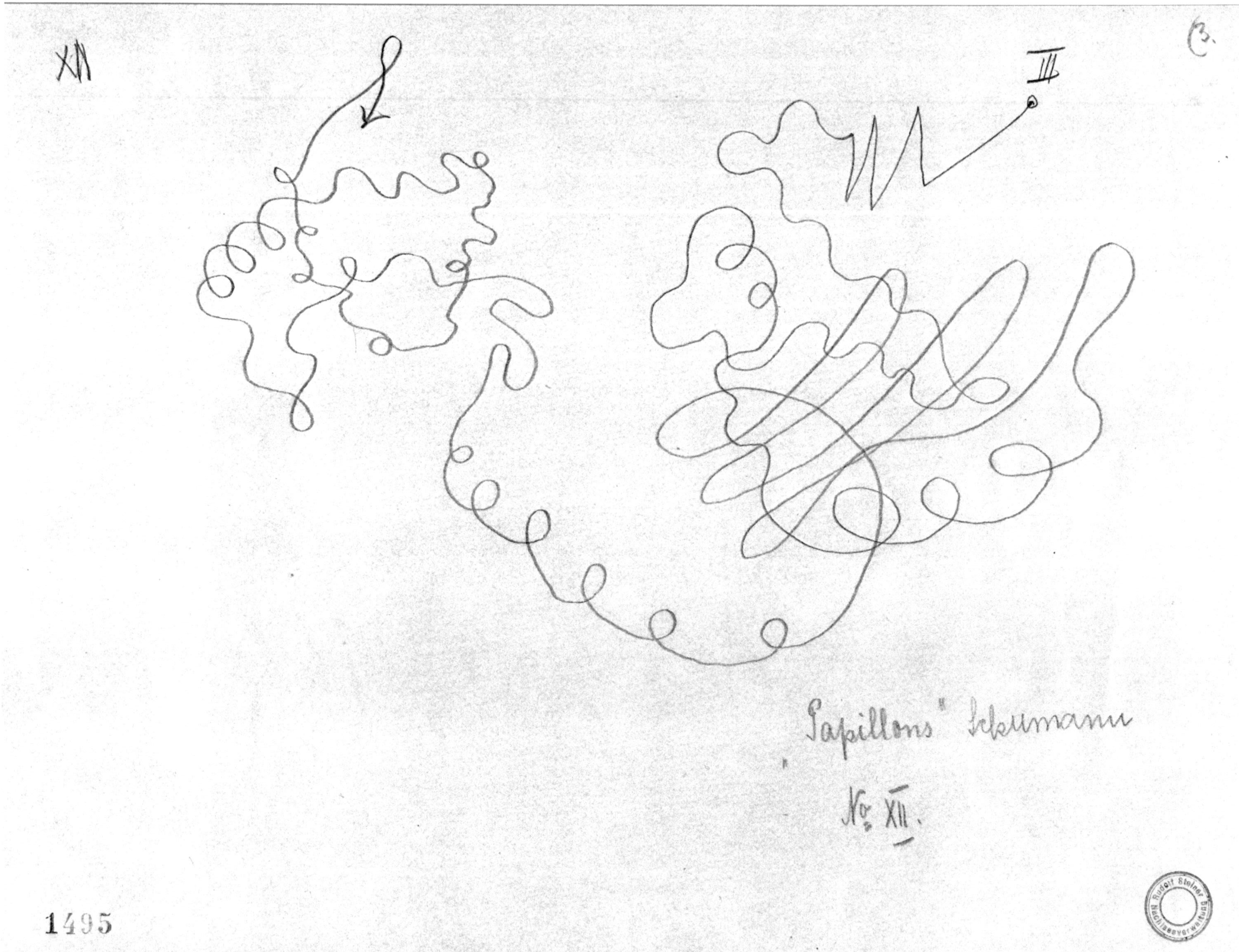

R. Schumann – "Papillons" [Butterflies], No. 12, Finale, D major, Op. 2/12 (page 3)

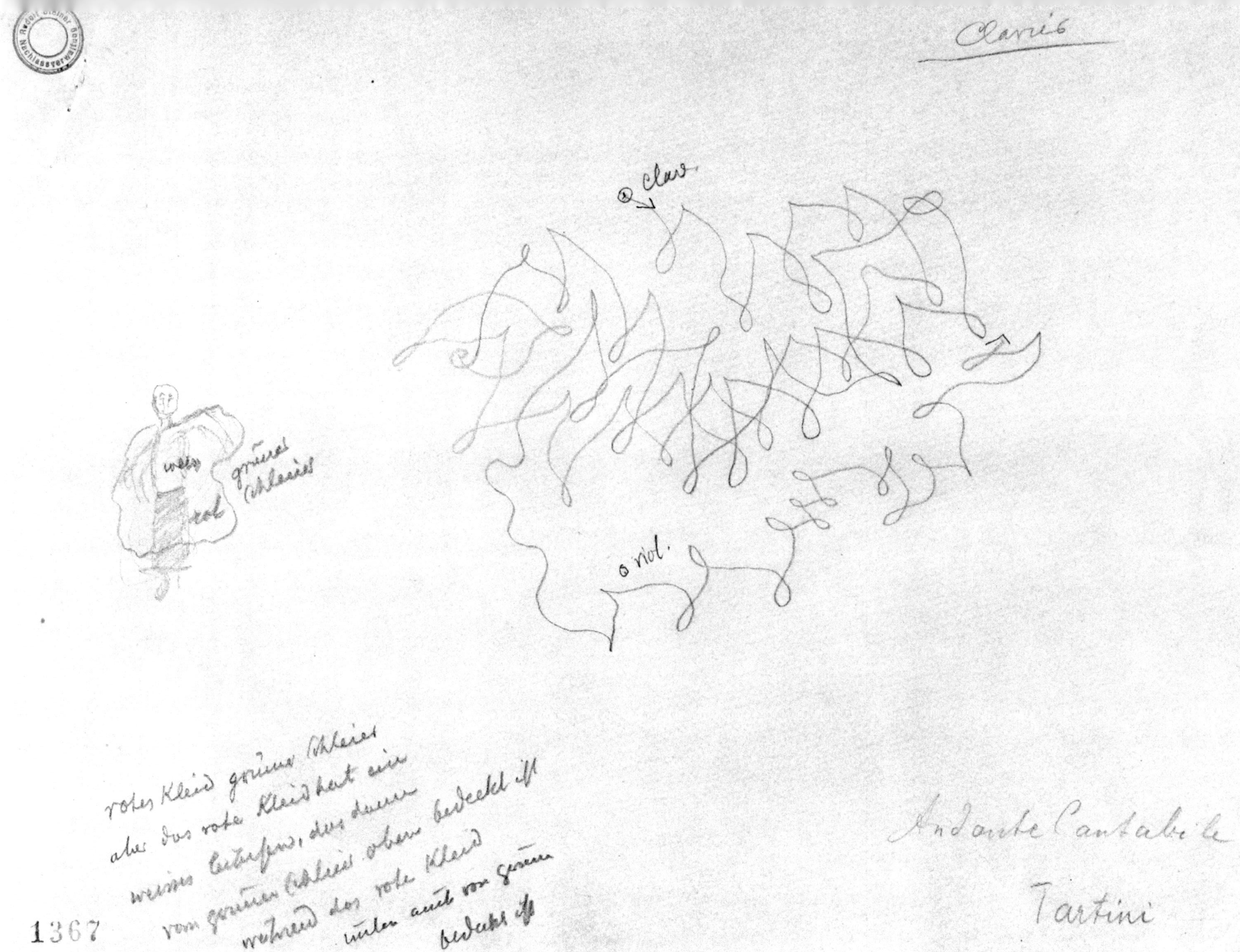

G. Tartini – Andante cantabile, first movement from Sonata in G major, Op. 2/12 (page 1)

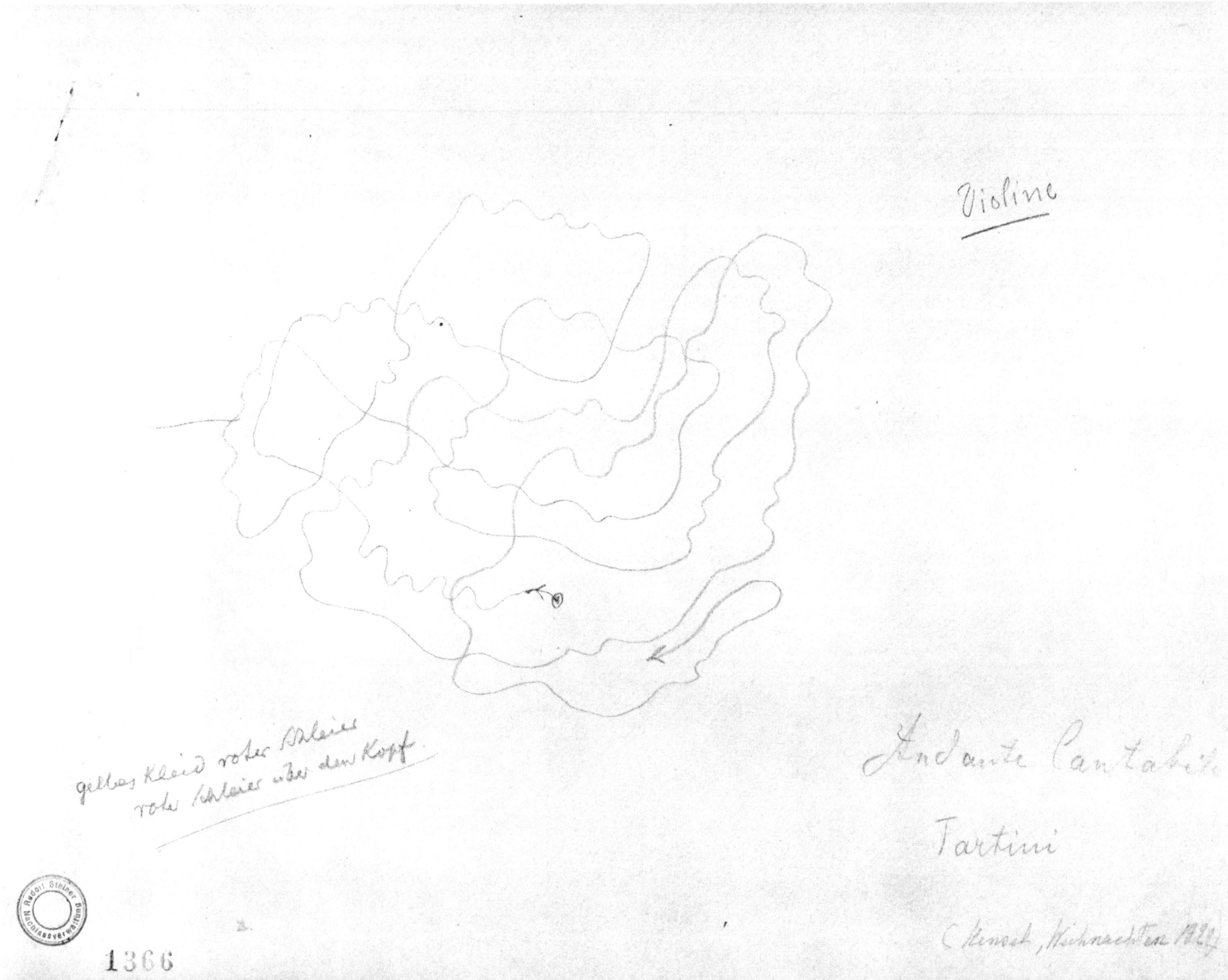

G. Tartini – Andante cantabile, first movement from Sonata in G major, Op. 2/12 (page 2)

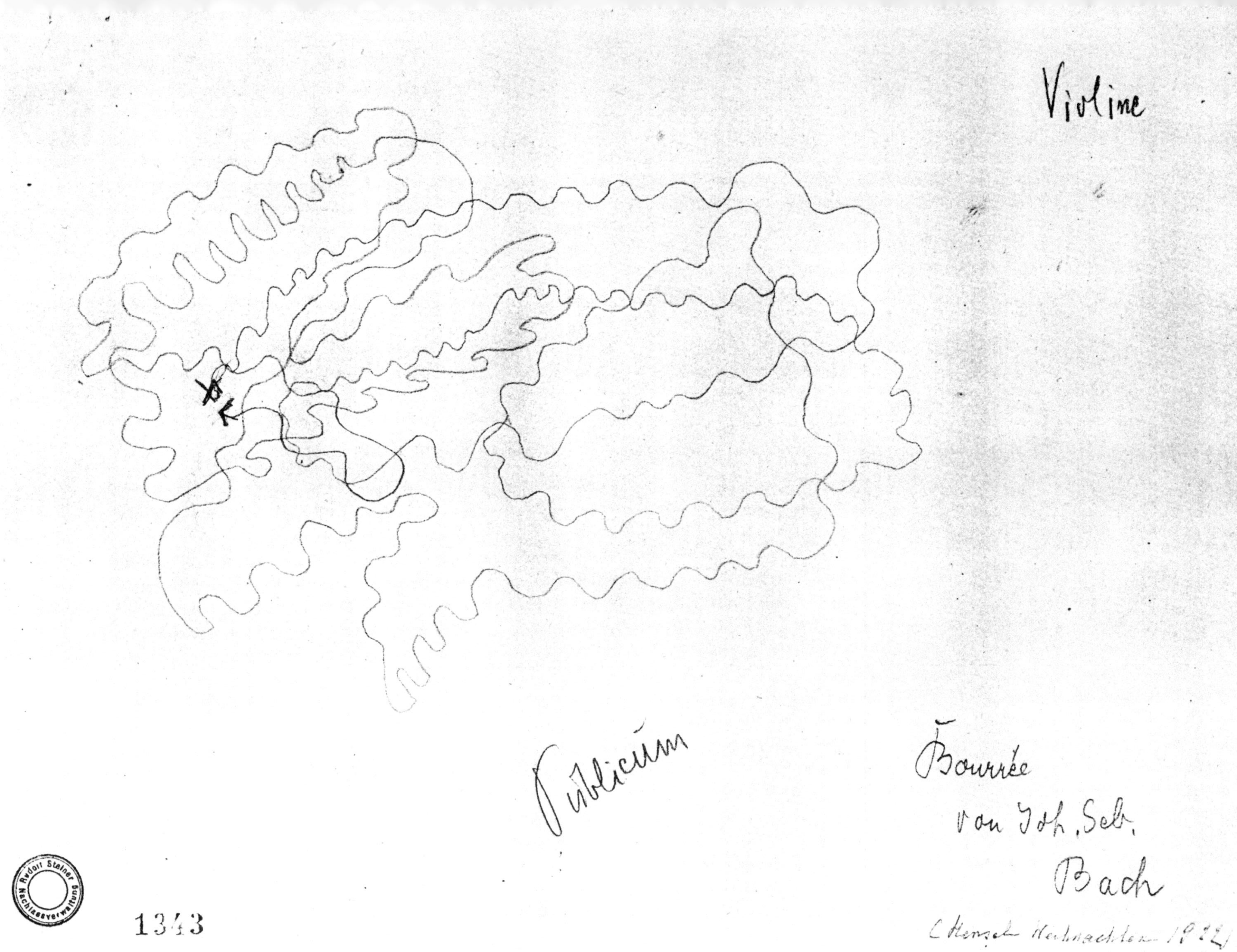

J. S. Bach – Bourrée I & II, from Suite No. 3 for violoncello solo, C major (page 1)

J. S. Bach – Bourrée I & II, from Suite No. 3 for violoncello solo, C major (page 2)

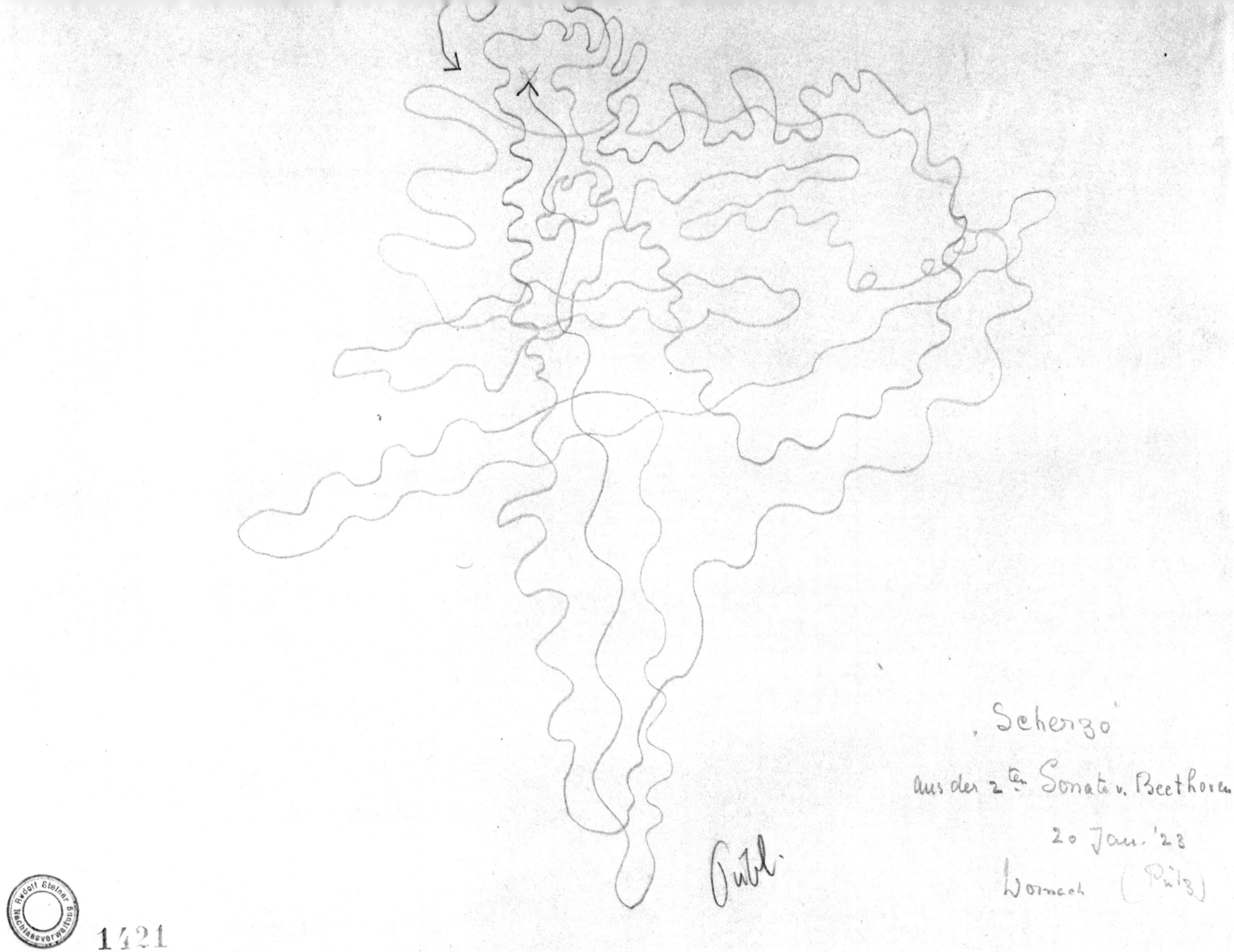

L. van Beethoven – Scherzo allegro, third movement from Sonata No. 2, A major

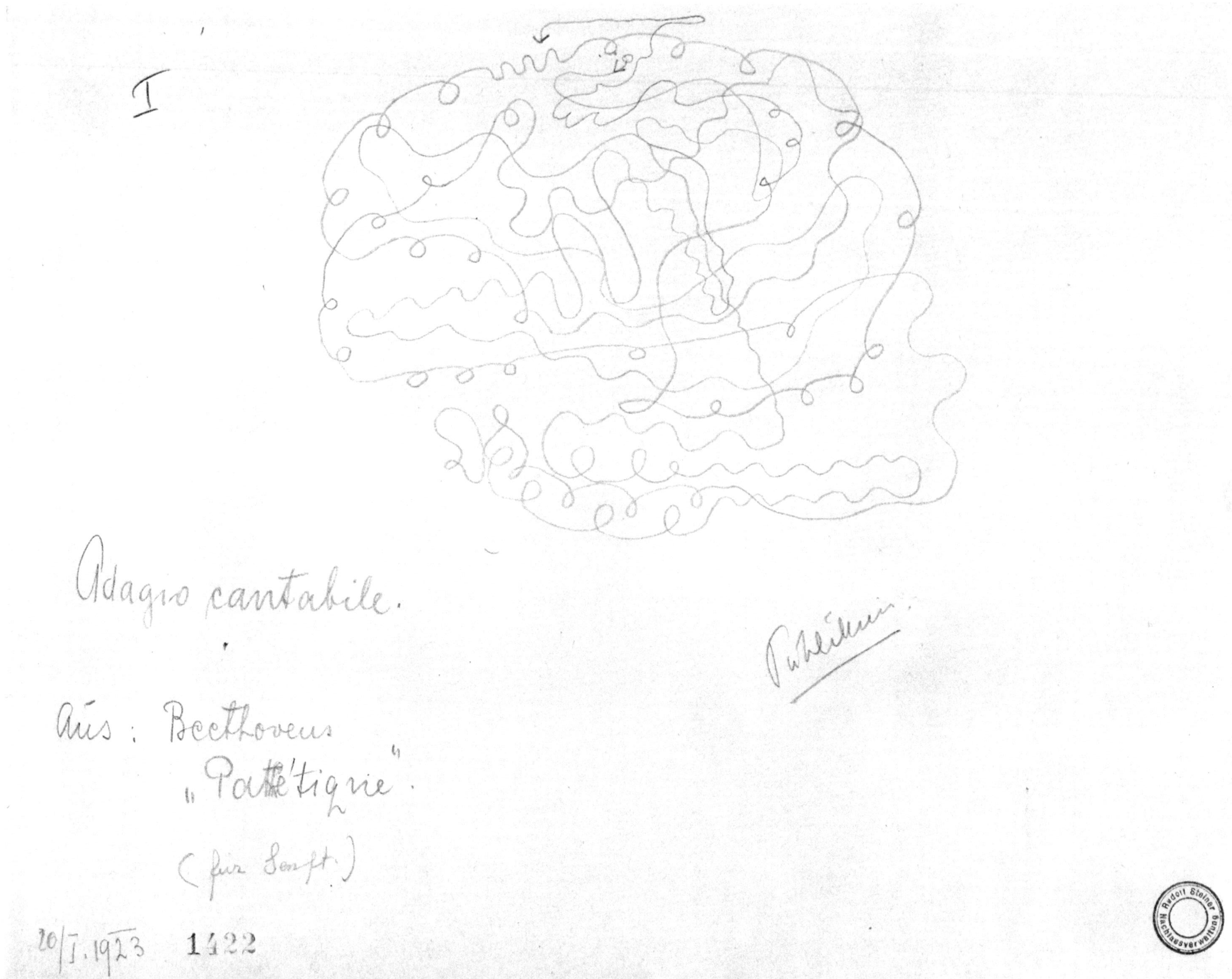

L. van Beethoven – Adagio cantabile, A-flat major, second movement from Sonata No. 8 (*Pathétique*), C minor, Op. 13

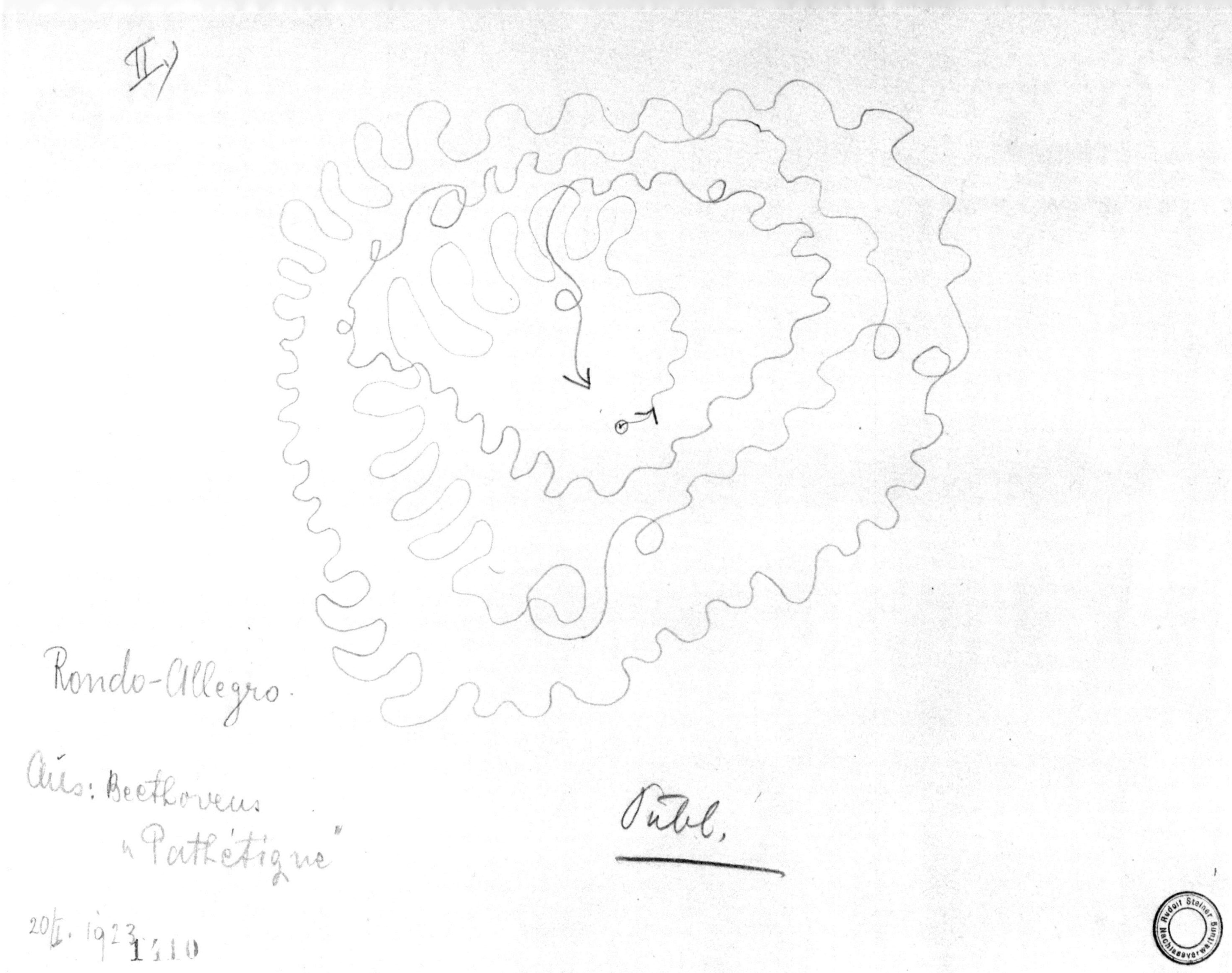

L. van Beethoven – Rondo Allegro, third movement from Sonata No. 8 (*Pathétique*), C minor, first part of the Finale, Op. 13

F. Chopin – Mazurka No. 5, Vivace, B major, Op. 7/1

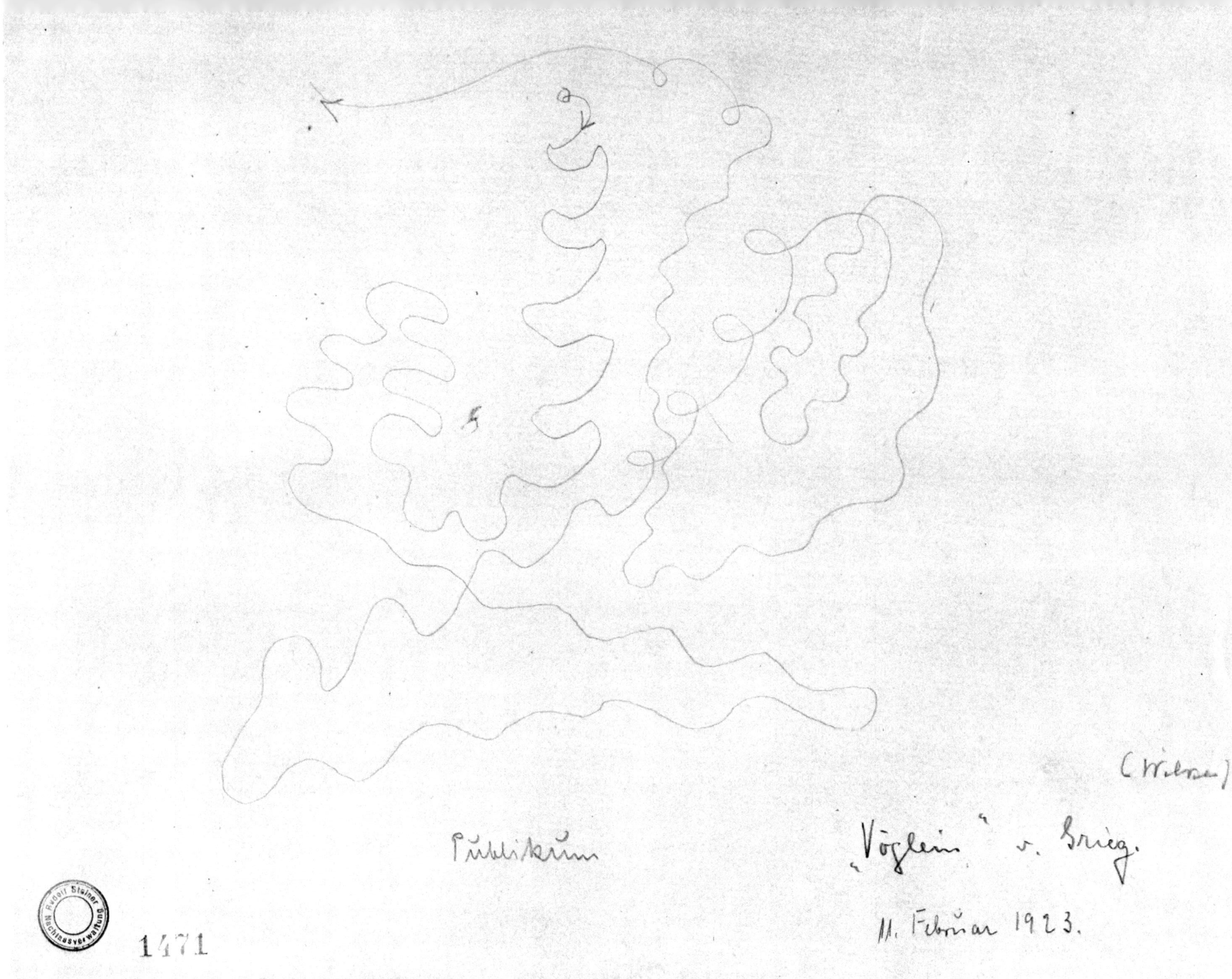

E. Grieg – "Little bird" from *Lyrical Pieces*, book III, Op. 43/4

F. Chopin – Étude No. 13, Allegro sostenuto, A-flat major, Op. 25/1

L. van der Pals – "Early spring" (slow)

L. van Beethoven – Minore, third movement from Sonata No. 4, E-flat major, Op. 7

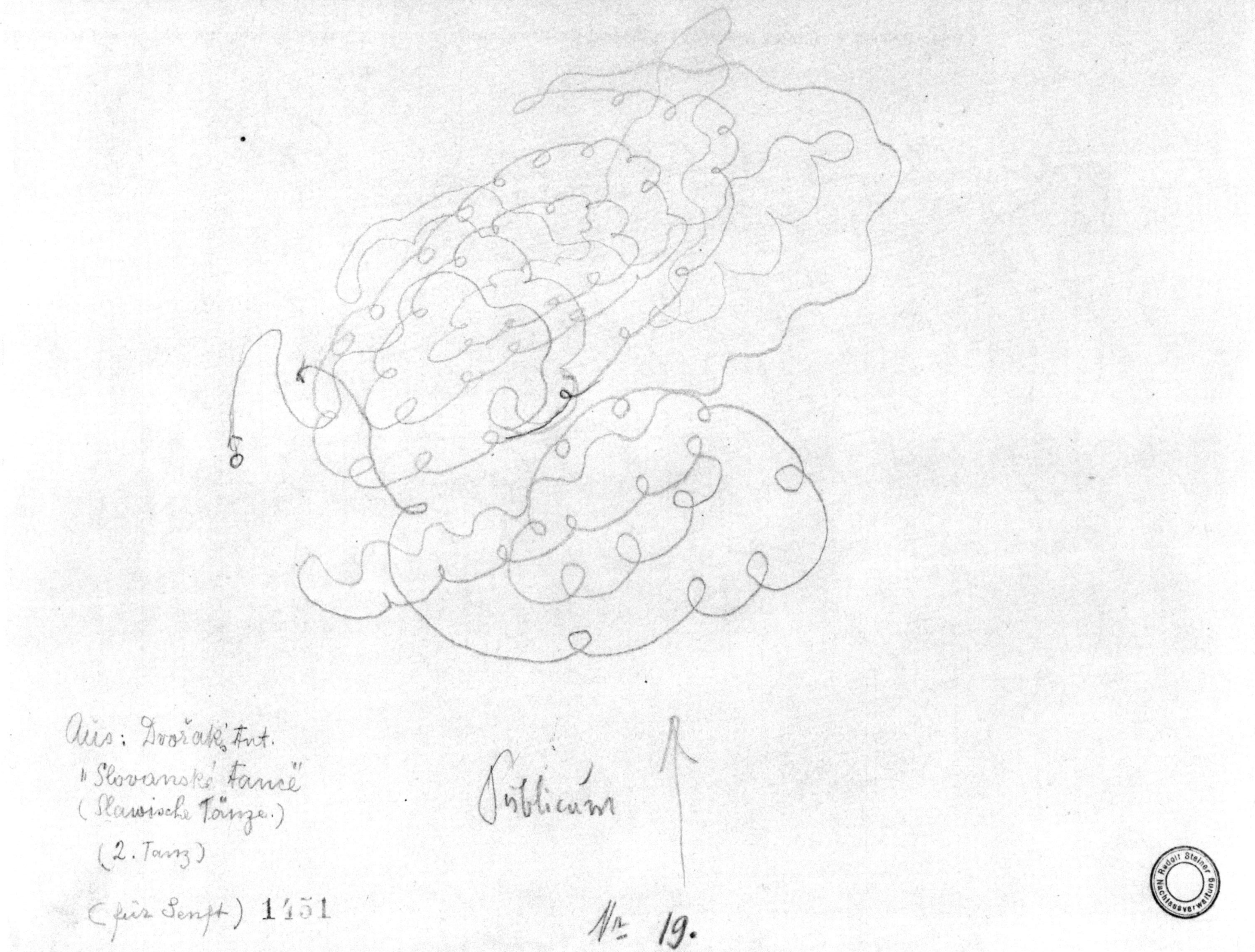

A. Dvorak – "Slavic Dance," Allegretto grazioso, E minor, No. 2

F. Schubert – Menuett, Allegro moderato, from the Sonata (*Fantasia*)[Fantasy], G major (page 1)

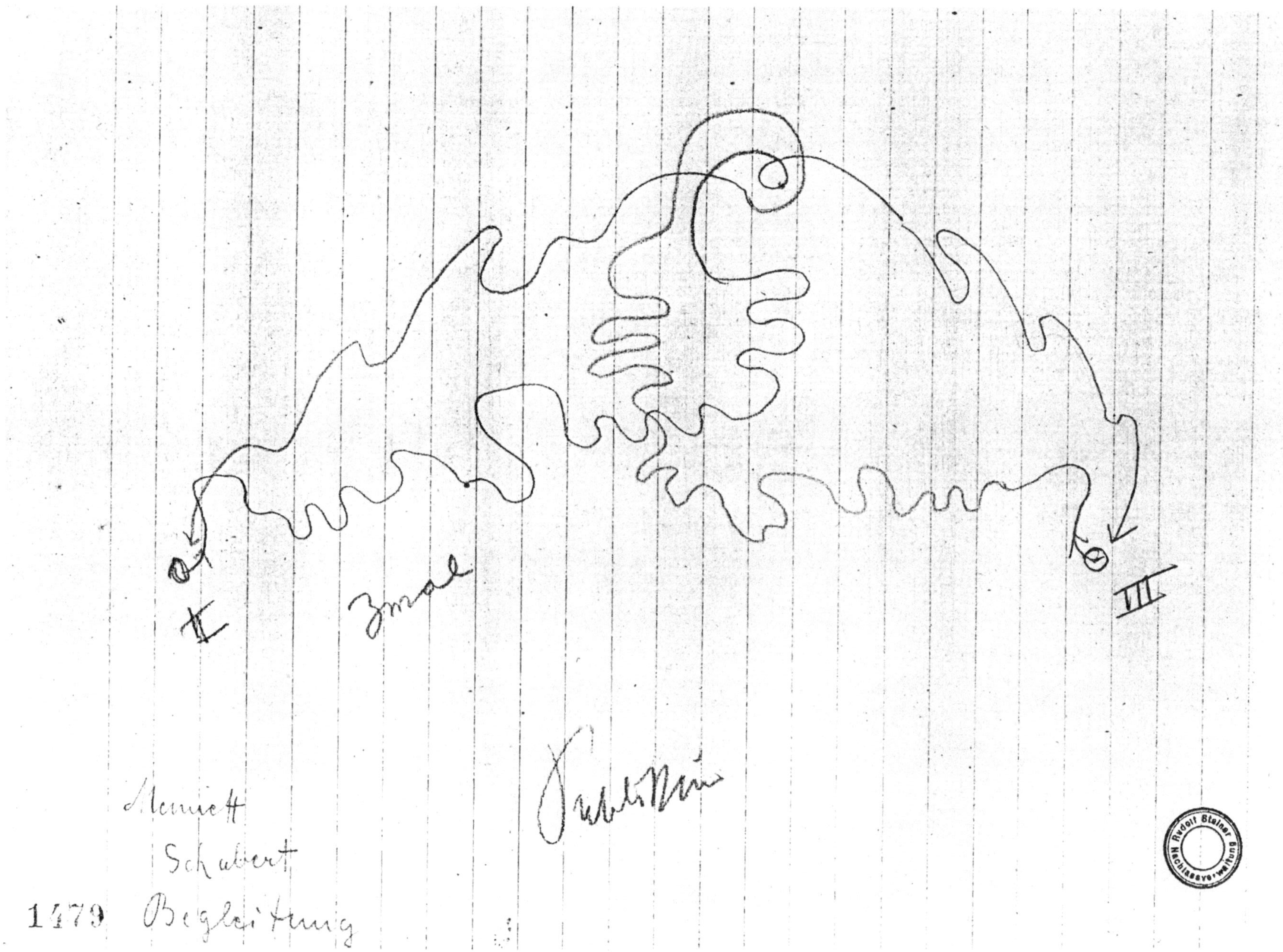

F. Schubert – Menuett, Allegro moderato, from the Sonata (*Fantasia*)[Fantasy],G major (page 2)

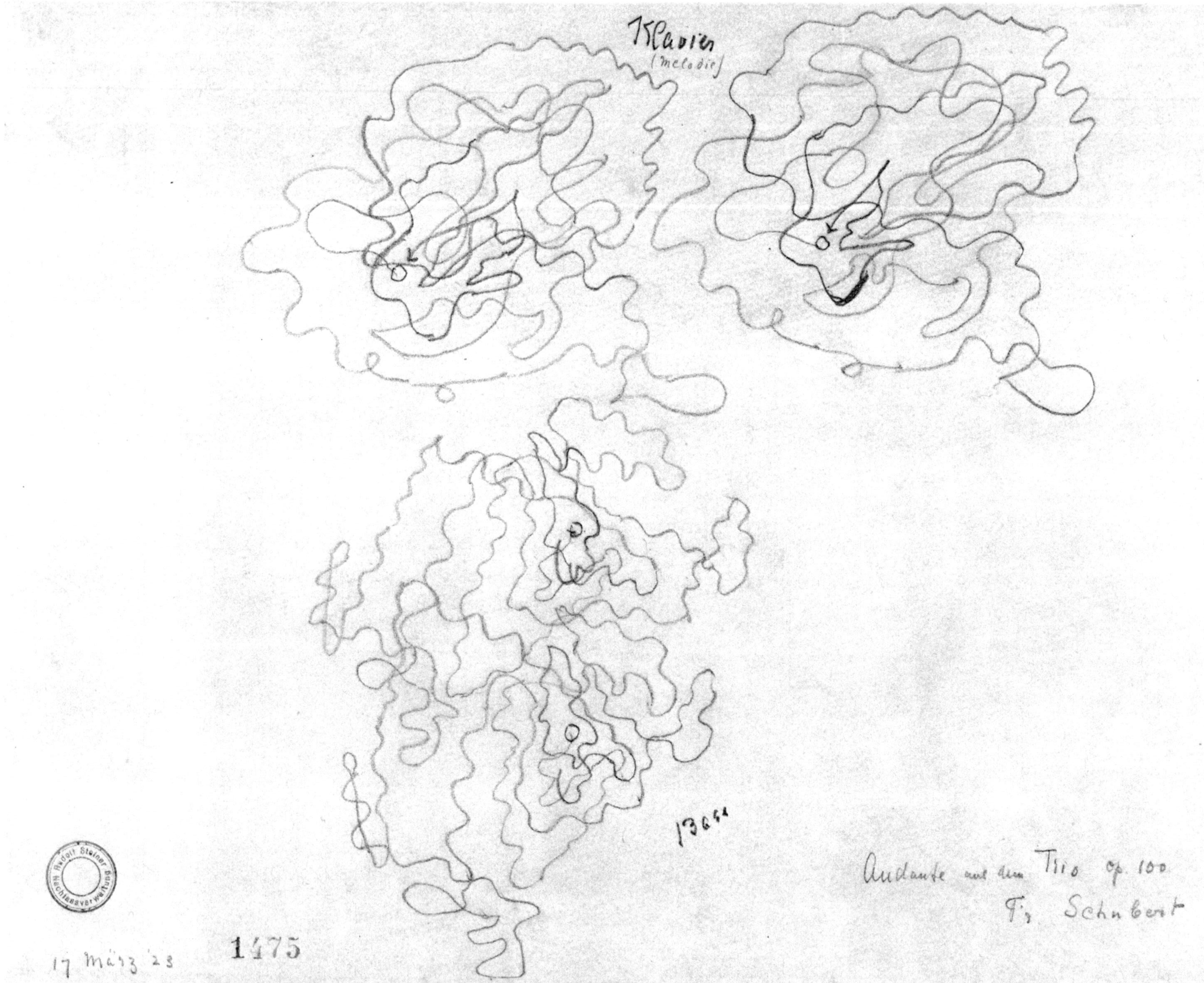

F. Schubert – Andante con moto, second movement from the *Klavier-Trio*, E-flat major, No. 2 (page 1)

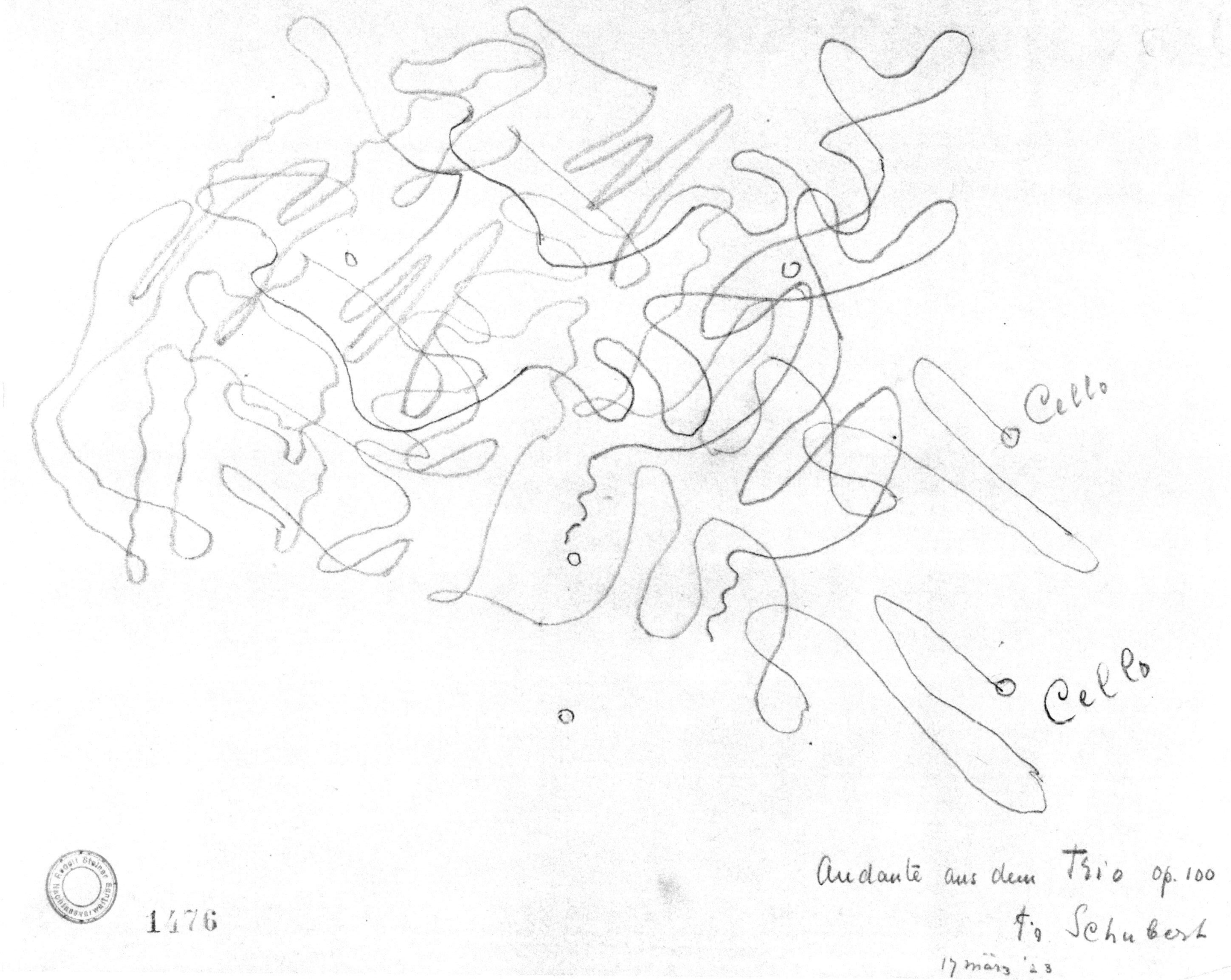

F. Schubert – Andante con moto, second movement from the *Klavier-Trio*, E-flat major, No. 2 (page 2)

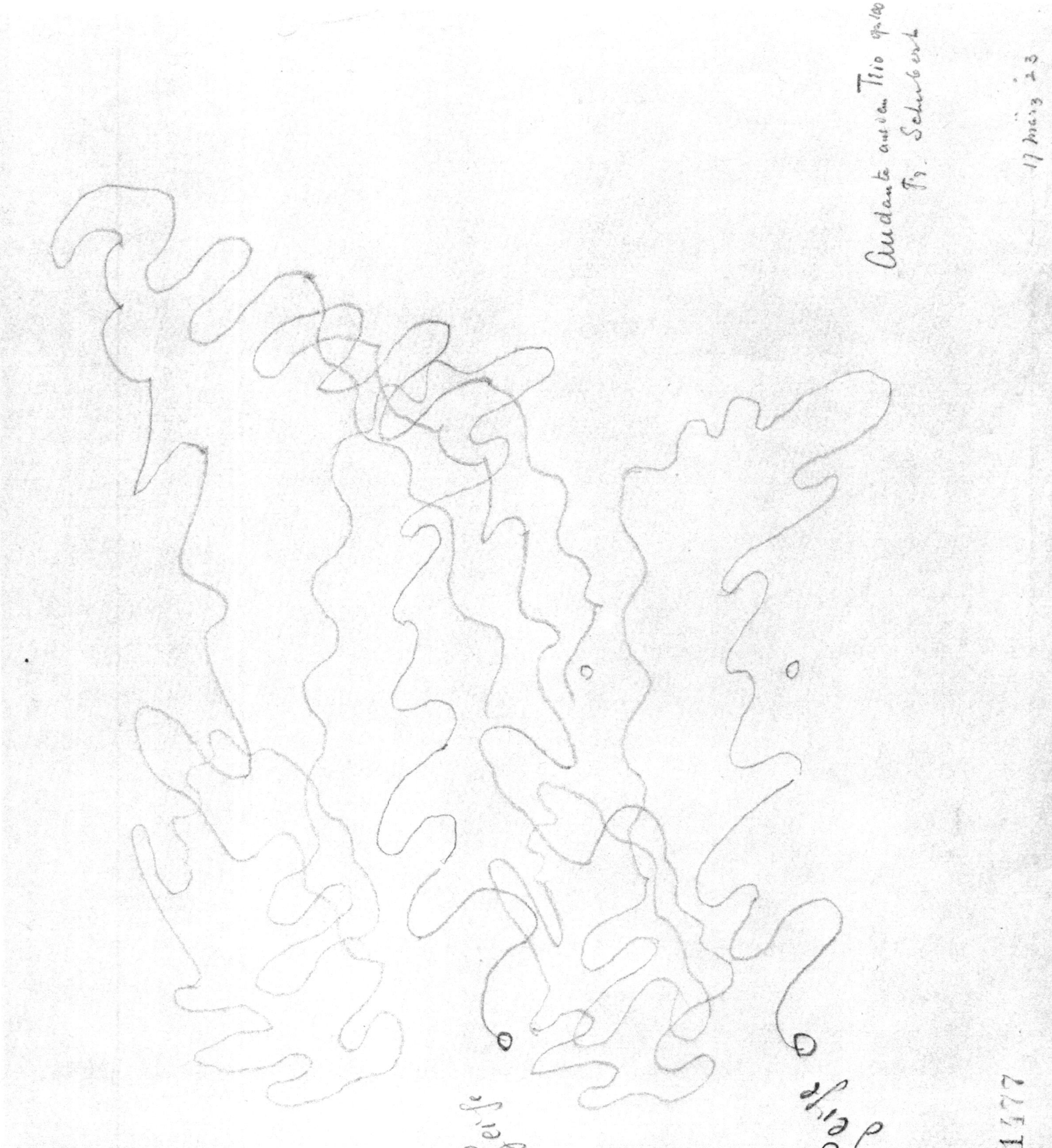

F. Schubert – Andante con moto, second movement from the *Klavier-Trio*, E-flat major, No. 2 (page 3)

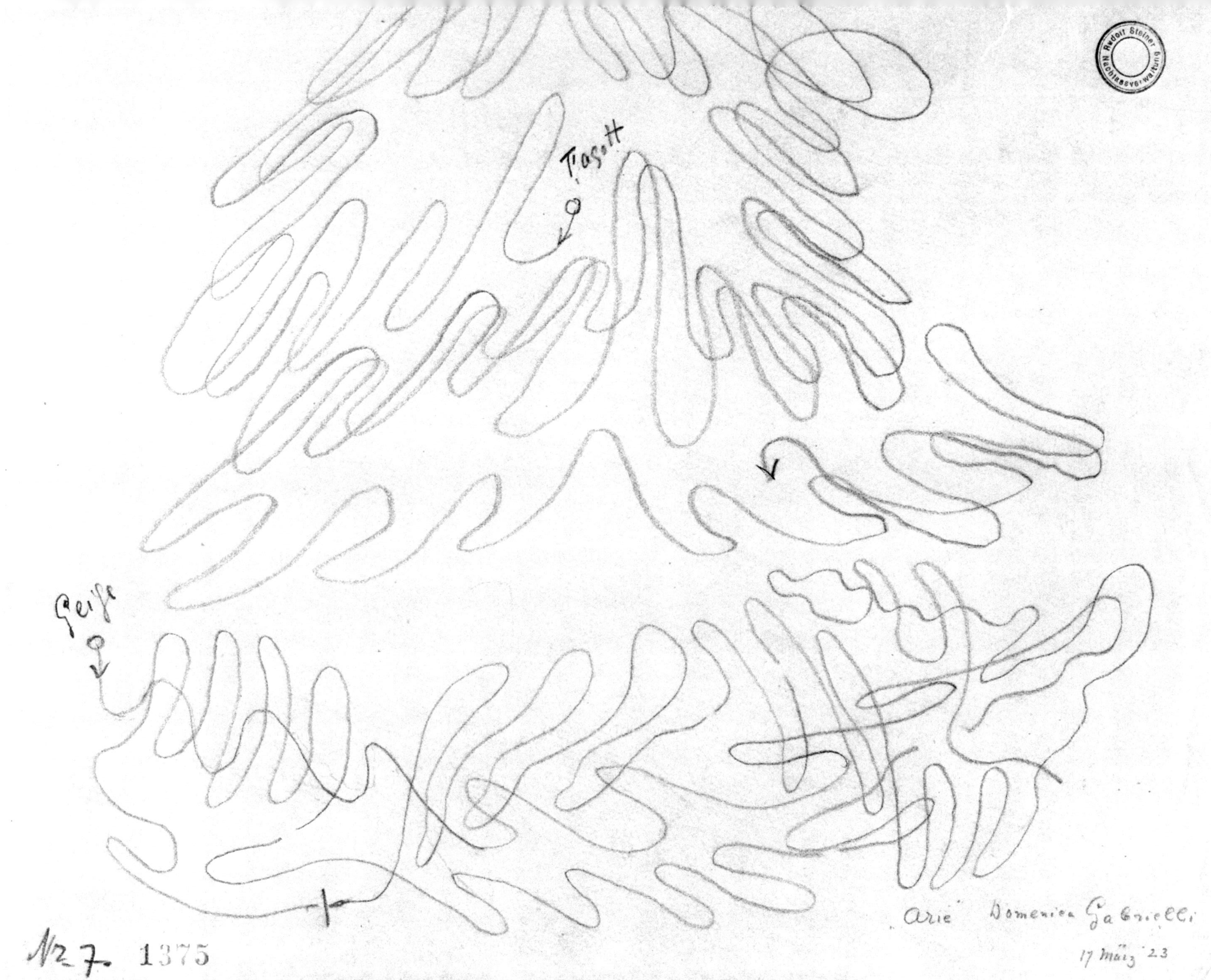

D. Gabrielli – Arie, "Bellezza Tiranna," Largo, G major, from the opera *Clearco in Negroponte*

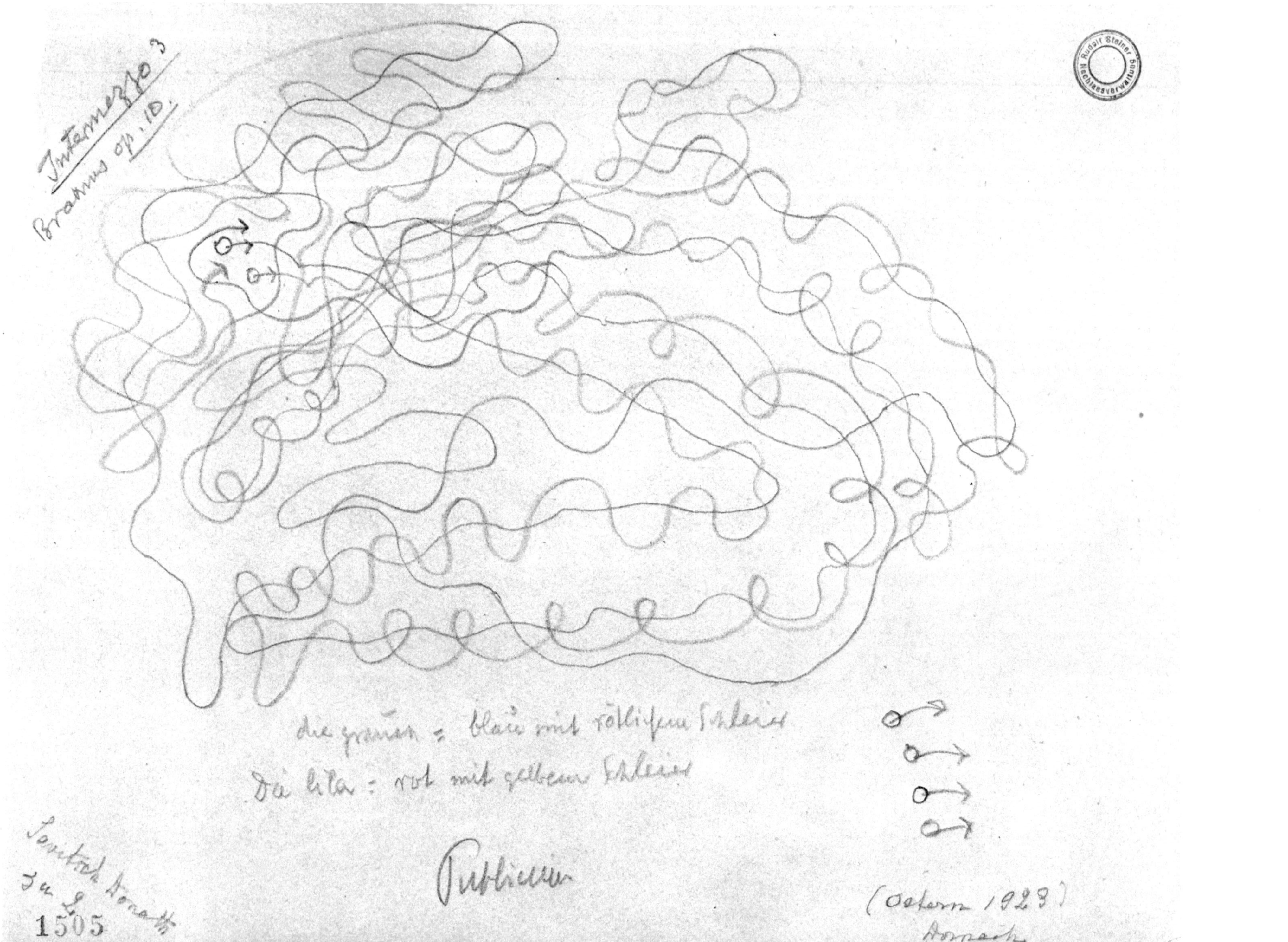

J. Brahms – Intermezzo, Allegro, B minor, No. 3 from *Ballads*, Op. 10/3

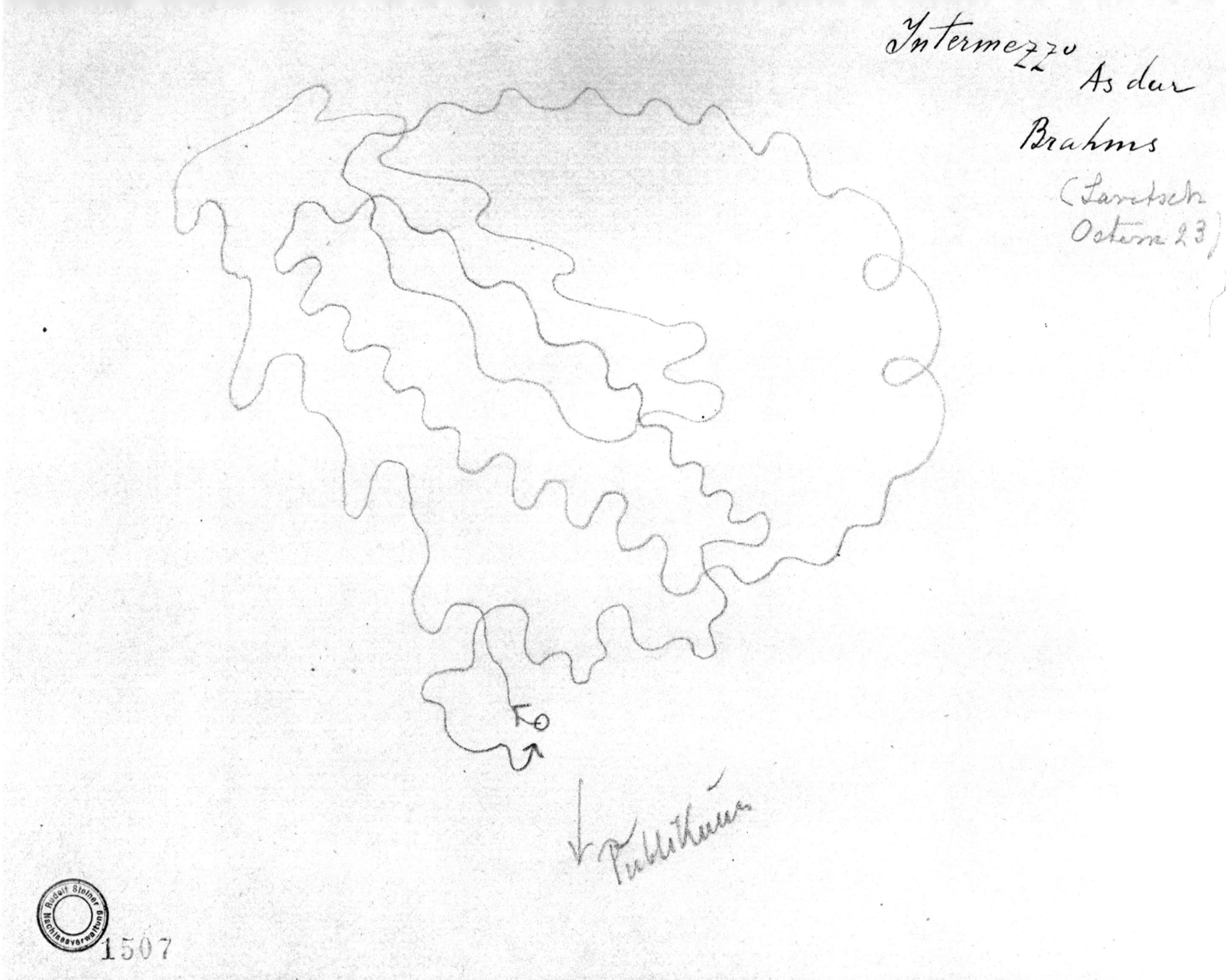

J. Brahms – Intermezzo, Grazioso, A-flat major, No. 3 from *Acht Klavierstücke* [Eight piano pieces], Op. 76/3

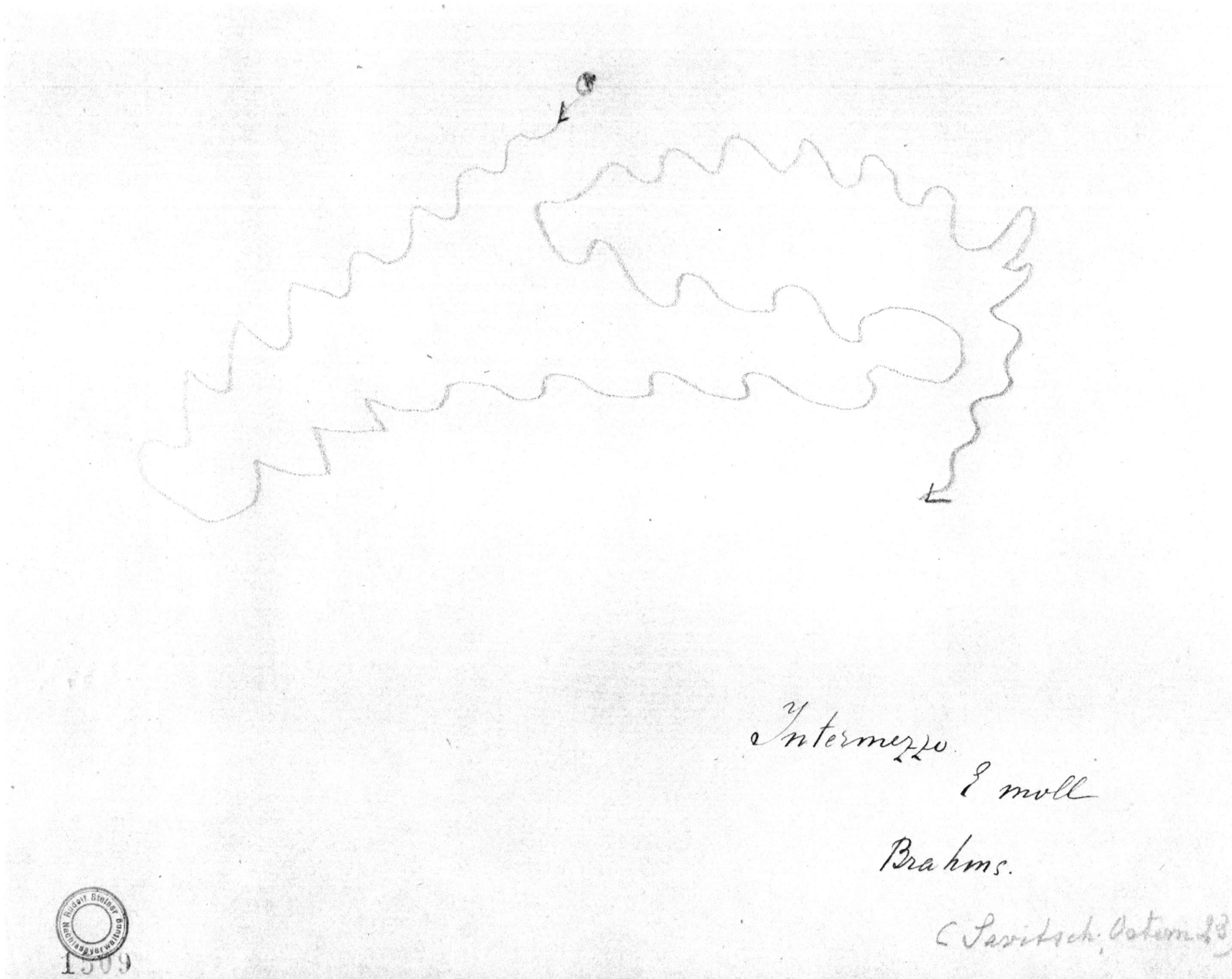

J. Brahms – Intermezzo, Andante con grazia ed intimissimo sentimento, E minor, No. 5 from *Fantasien*, Op. 116/5

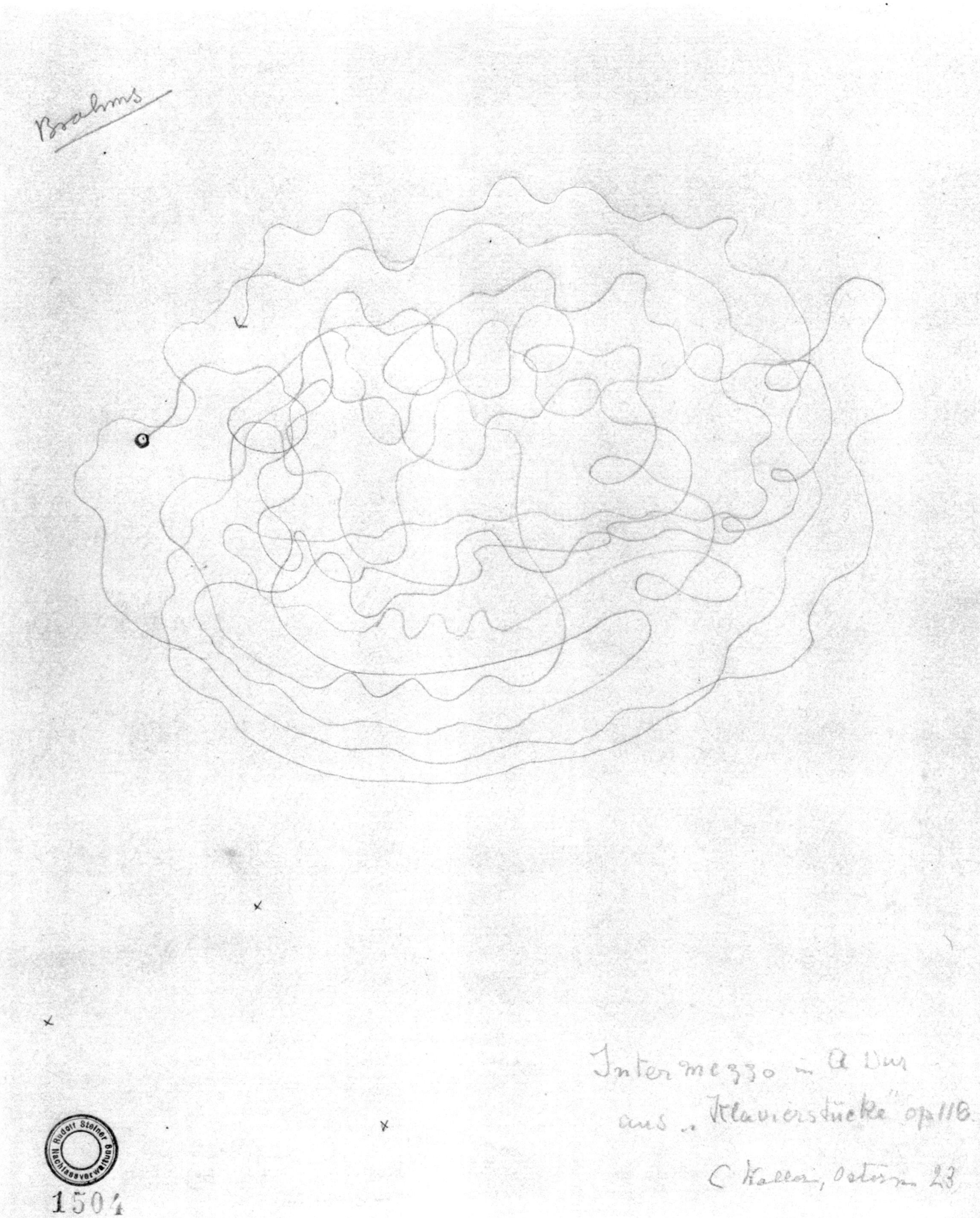

J. Brahms – Intermezzo, Andante teneramente, A major, No. 2 from *Sechs Klavierstücke* [Six piano pieces]

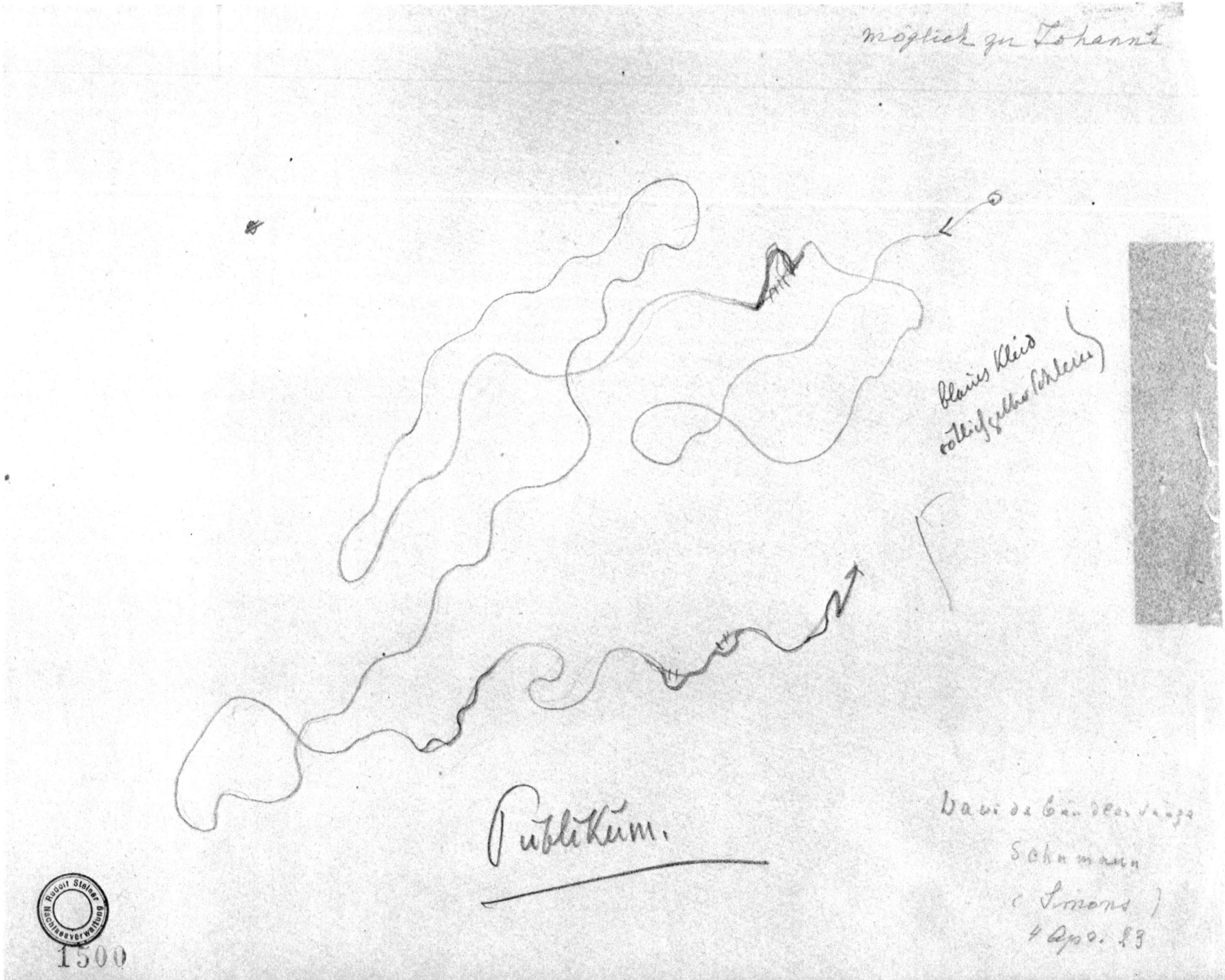

R. Schumann – “Davidsbündler Tänze” [Davidsbündler dances], No. 2, B minor, Op. 6/2 (Inward)

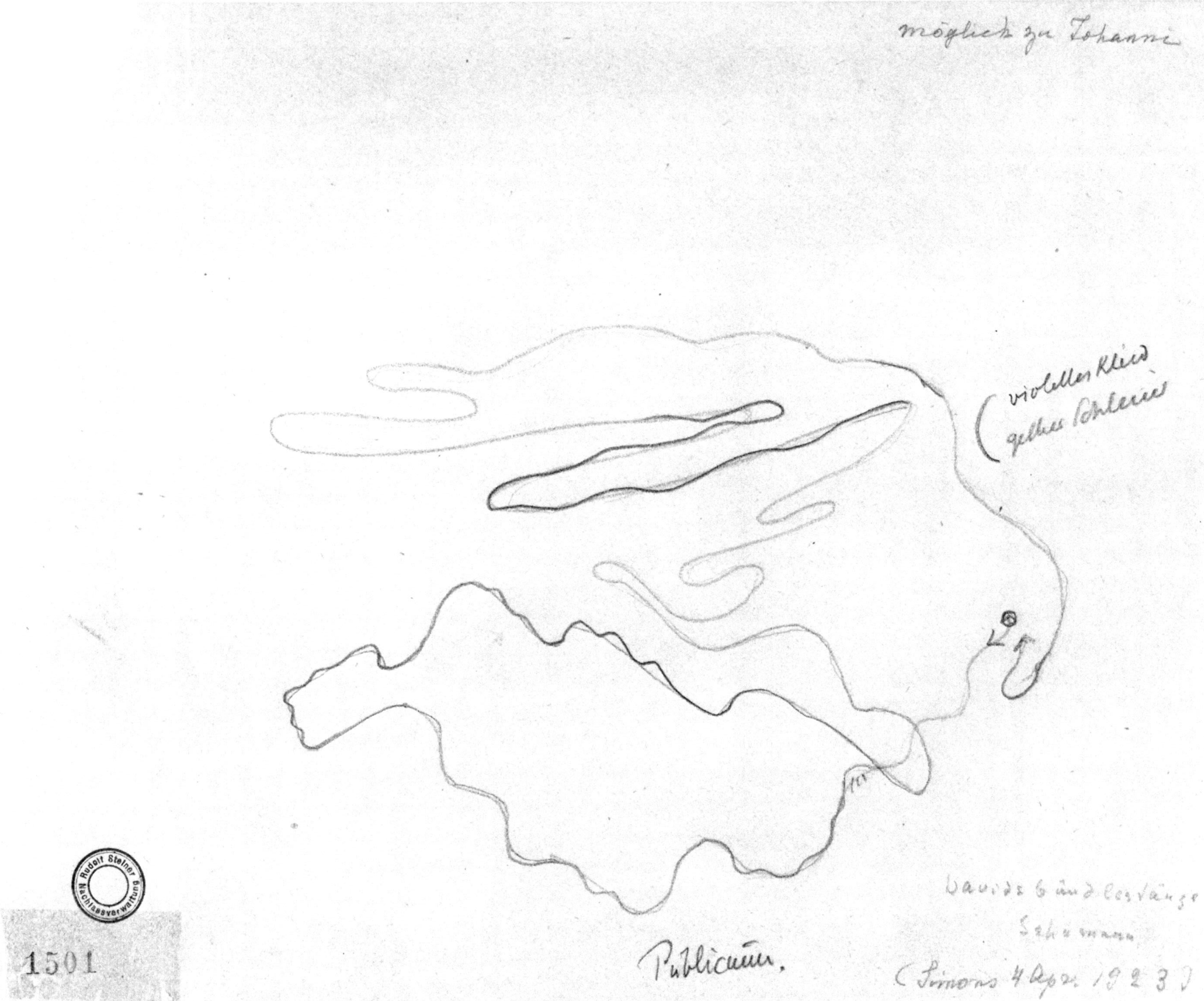

"Davidsbündler Tänze" [Davidsbündler dances], No. 11, D major, Op. 6/11 (simple)

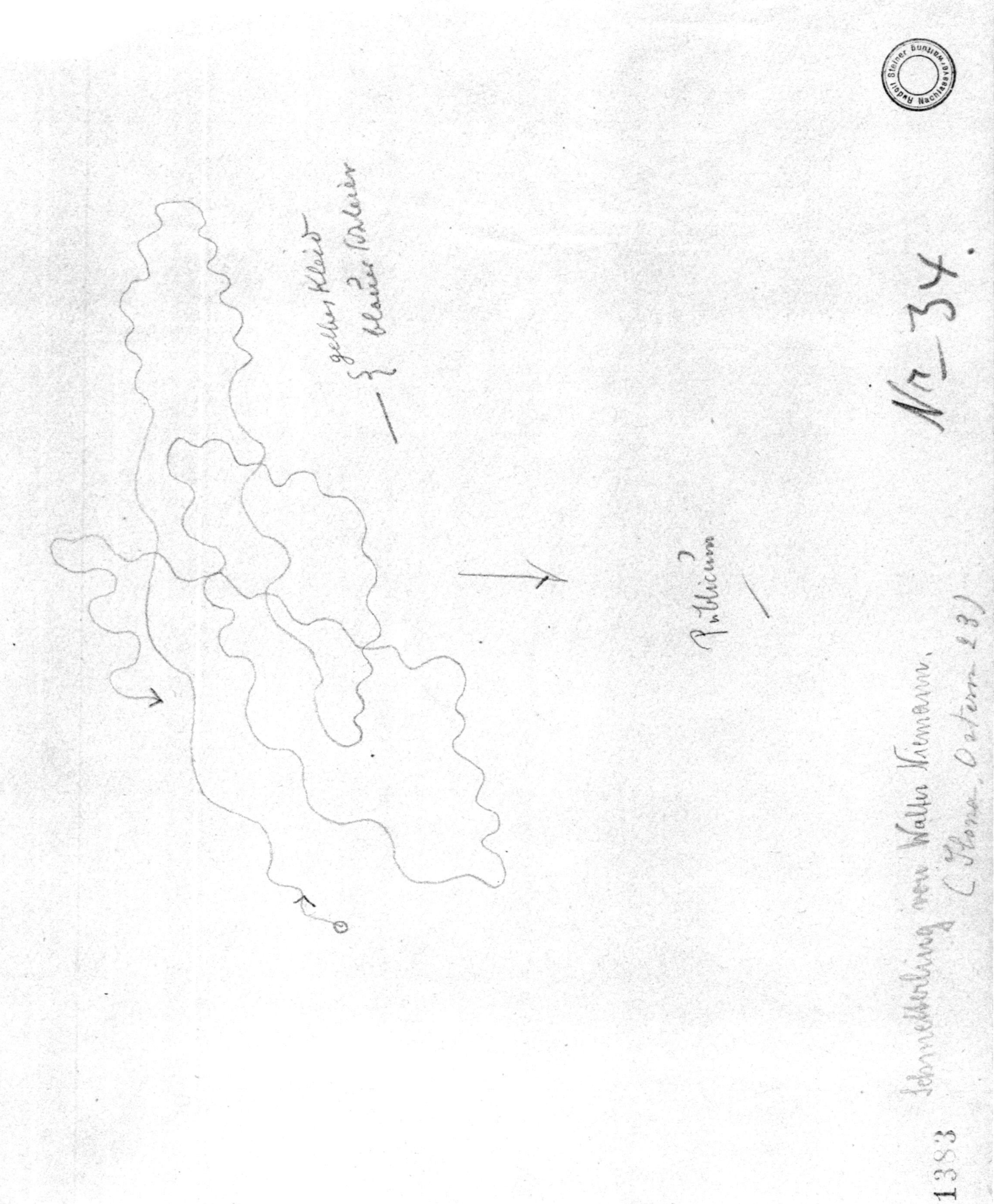

W. Niemann – "Schmetterling" [Butterfly] from *Romantische Miniaturen* [Romantic miniatures], Op. 33/6

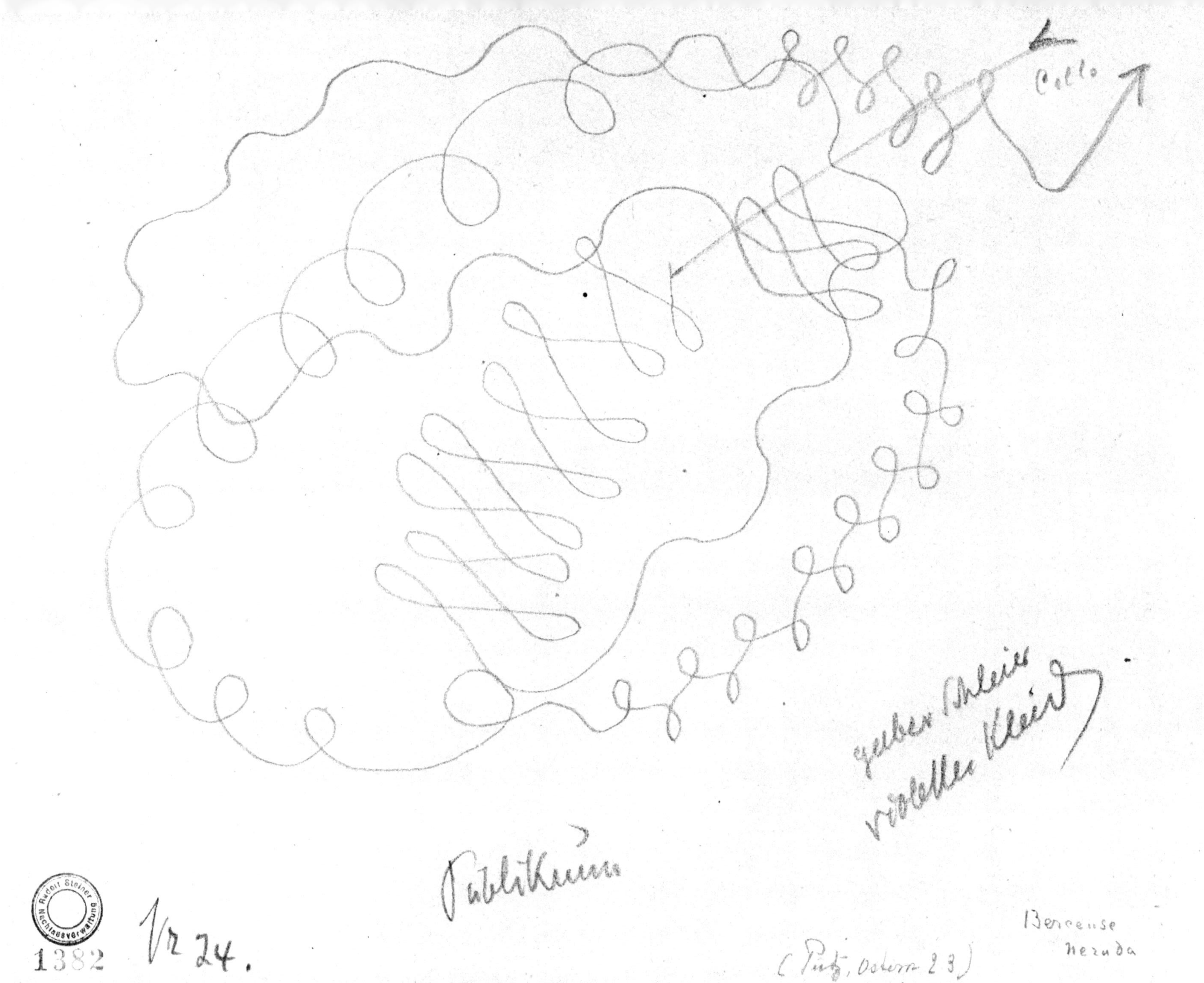

F. X. Neruda – "Berceuse Slave," Andantino, for violoncello and piano, Op. 11

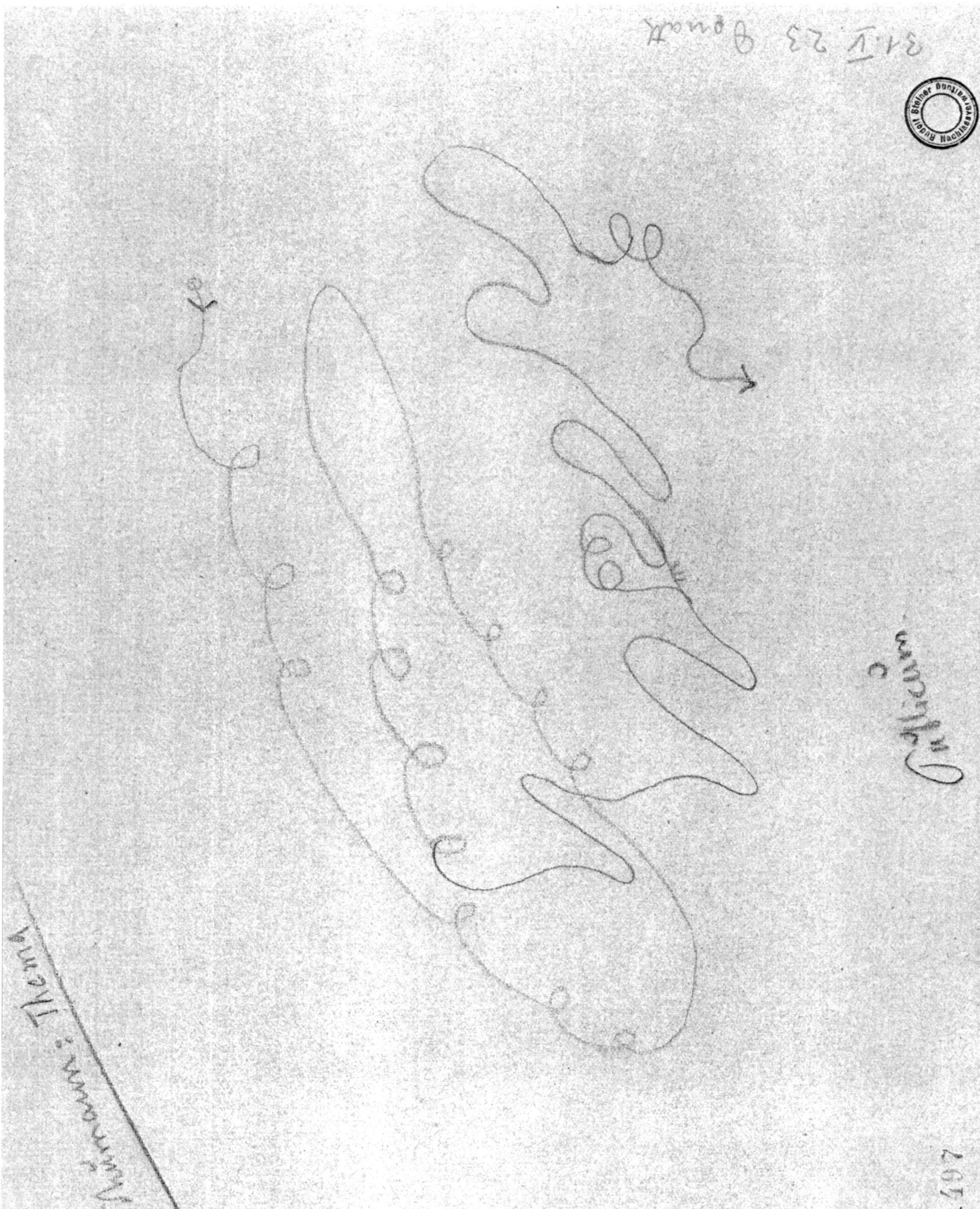

R. Schumann – Theme in E-Flat major, (Schumann's last composition) (quiet and inward)

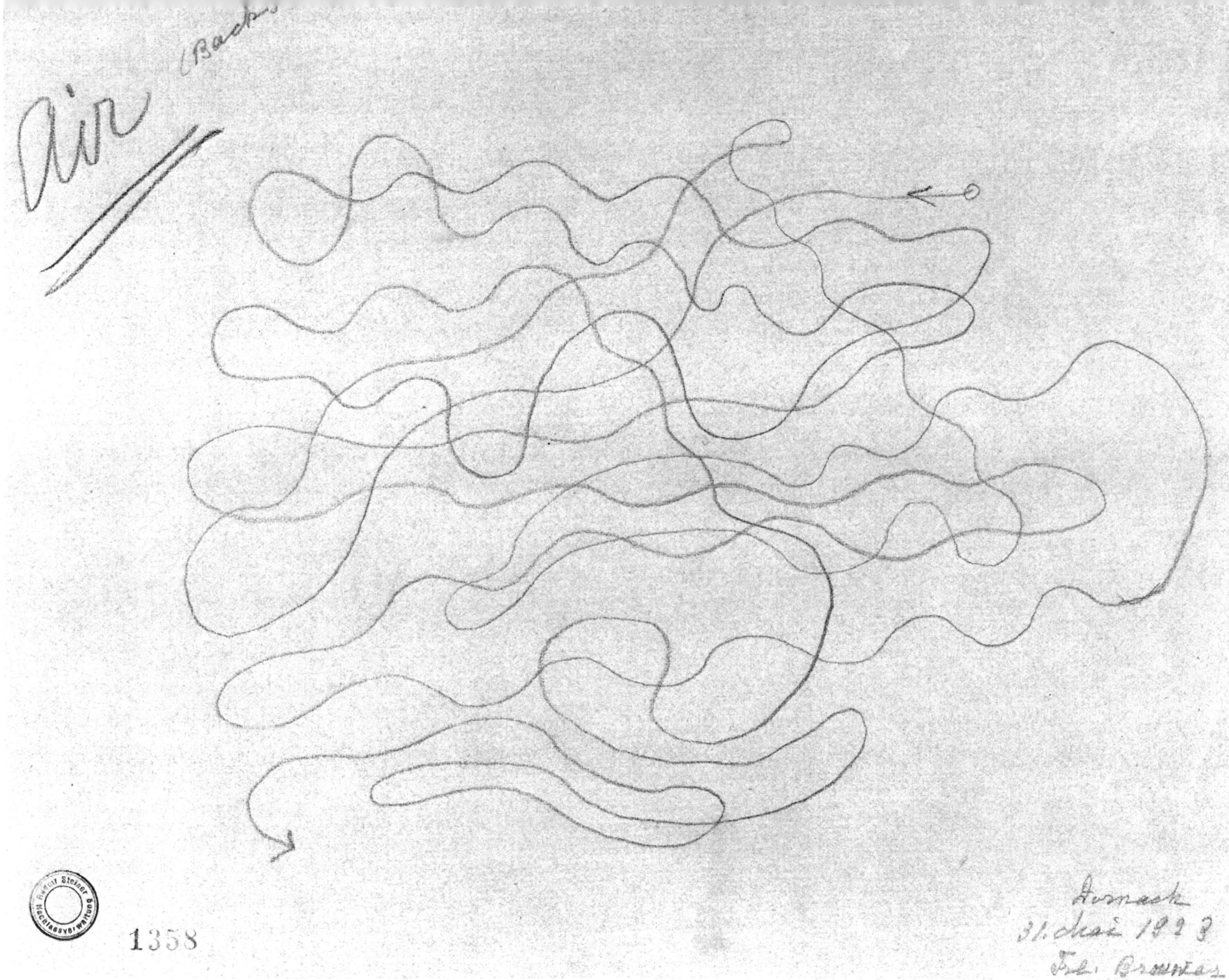

J. S. Bach – "Air," from the Orchestral Suite, D major, arranged for violin and piano (page 1)

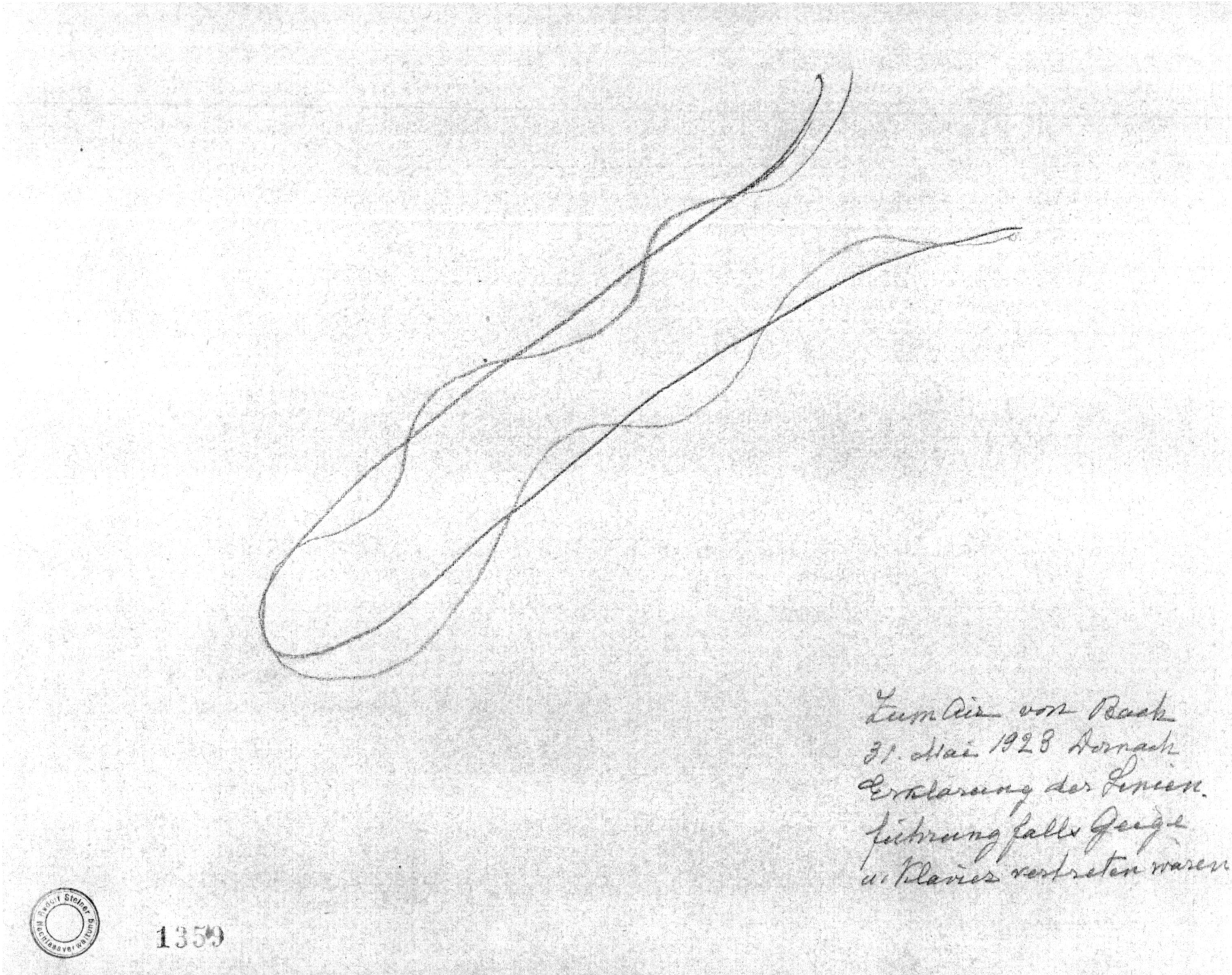

J. S. Bach – "Air," from the Orchestral Suite, D major, arranged for violin and piano (page 1)

L. van Beethoven – Tema con Variazioni (I & II) [Theme and variations], Andante, B major, fourth movement from the septet in E-flat major, Op. 20 (page 1)

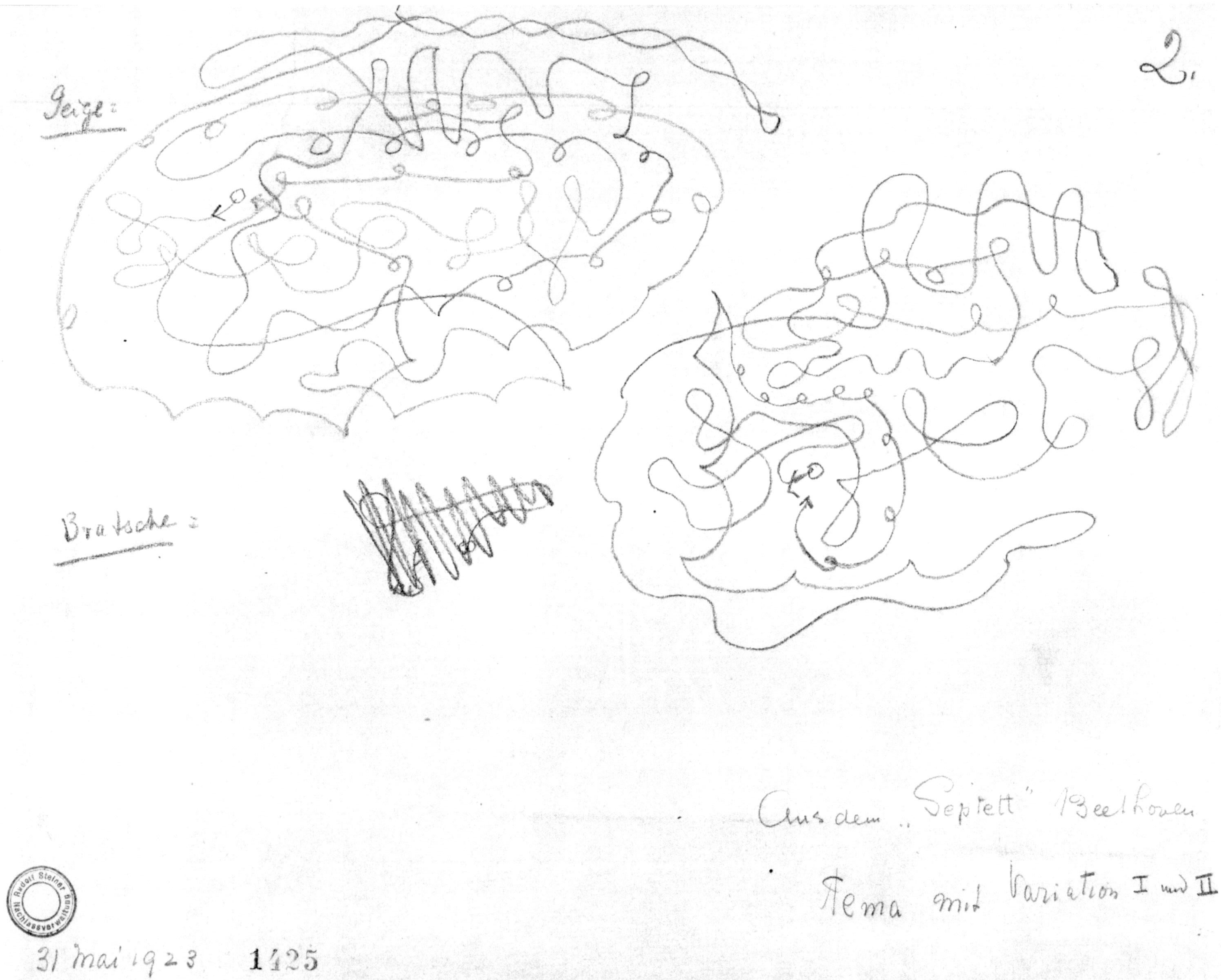

L. van Beethoven – Tema con Variazioni (I & II) [Theme and variations], Andante, B major, fourth movement from the septet in E-flat major, Op. 20 (page 2)

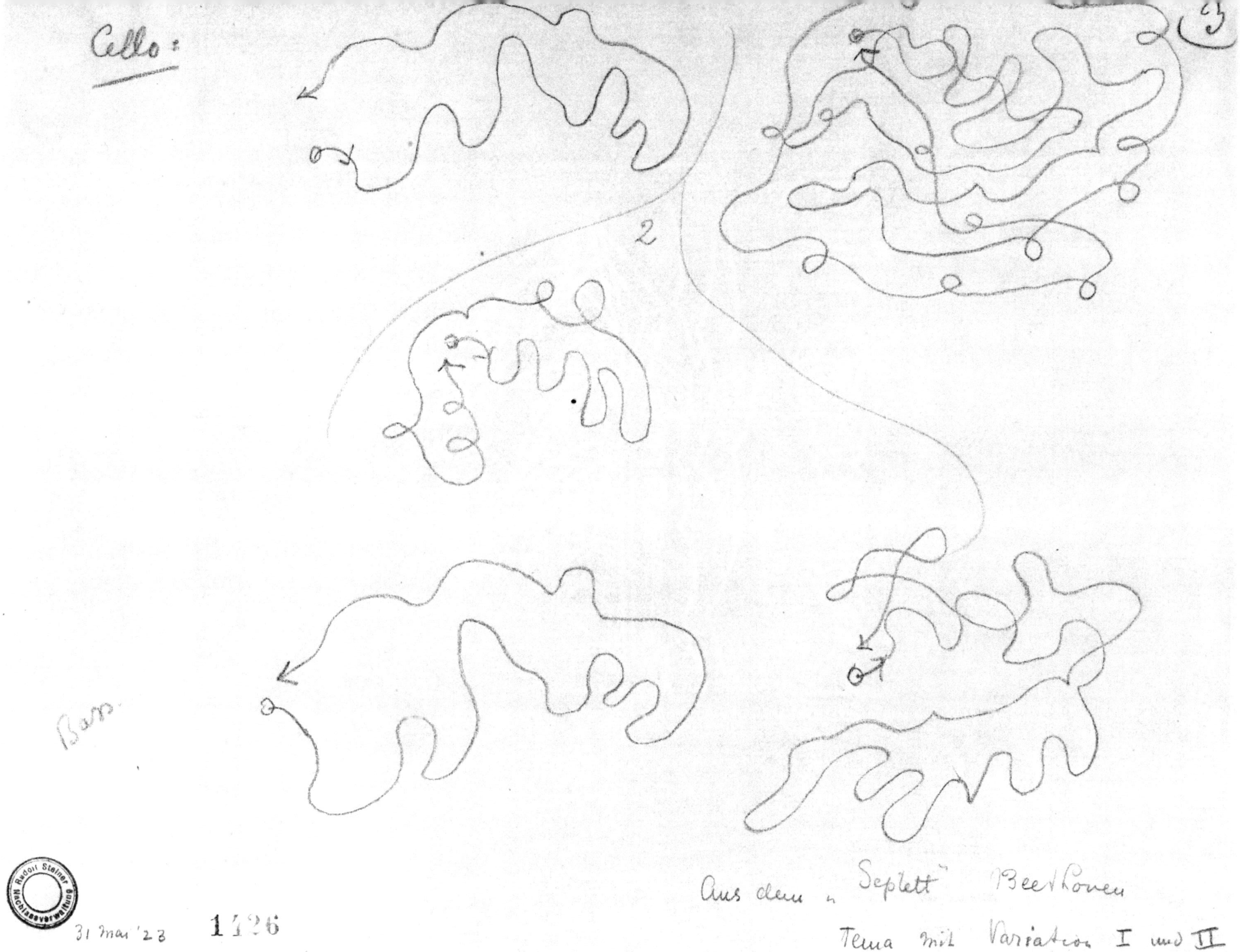

L. van Beethoven – Tema con Variazioni (I & II) [Theme and variations], Andante, B major, fourth movement from the septet in E-flat major, Op. 20 (page 3)

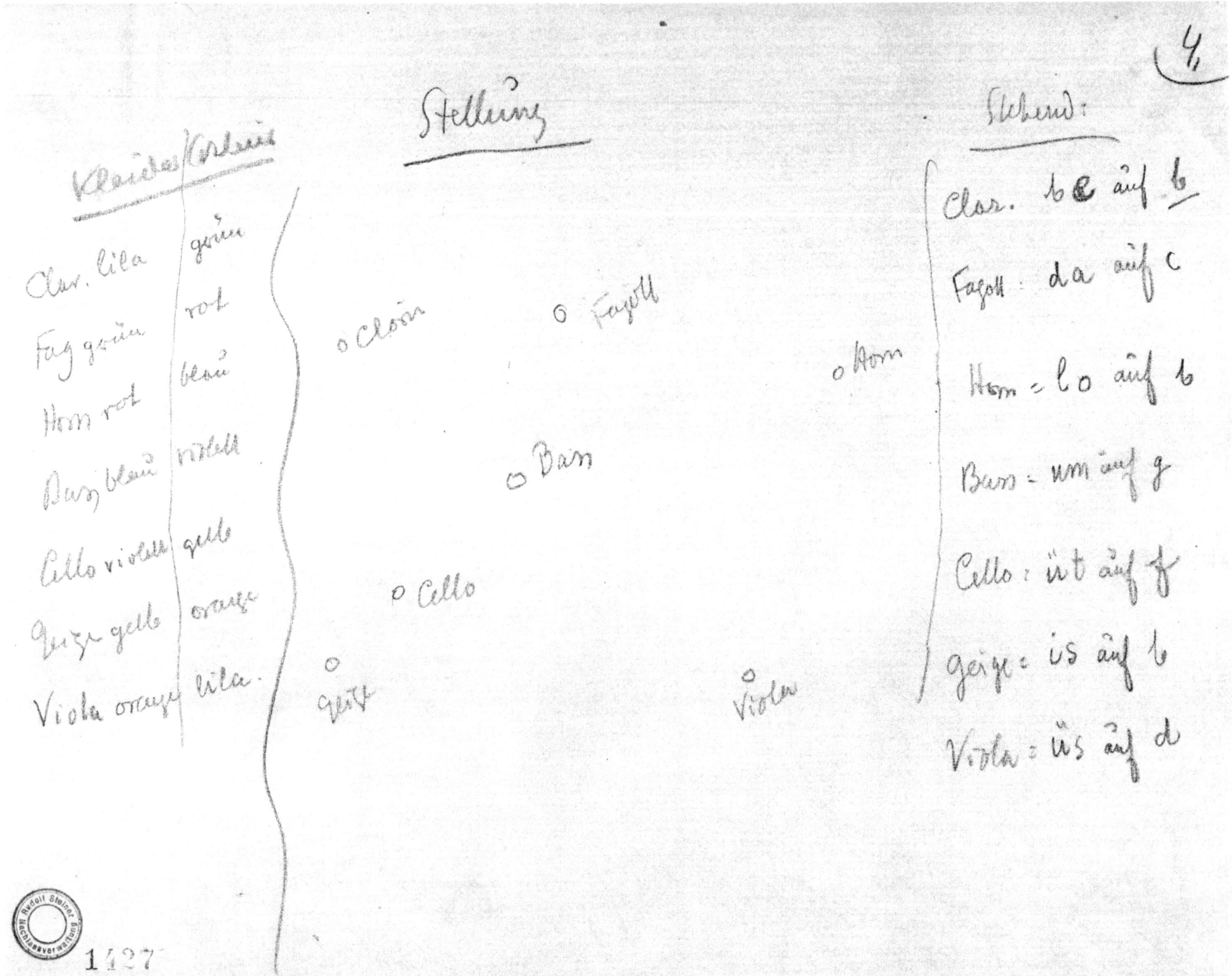

L. van Beethoven – Tema con Variazioni (I & II) [Theme and variations], Andante, B major, fourth movement from the septet in E-flat major, Op. 20 (page 4)

L. van Beethoven – Menuett (Tempo di menuetto), third movement from the septet in E-flat, major, Op. 20 (for children)

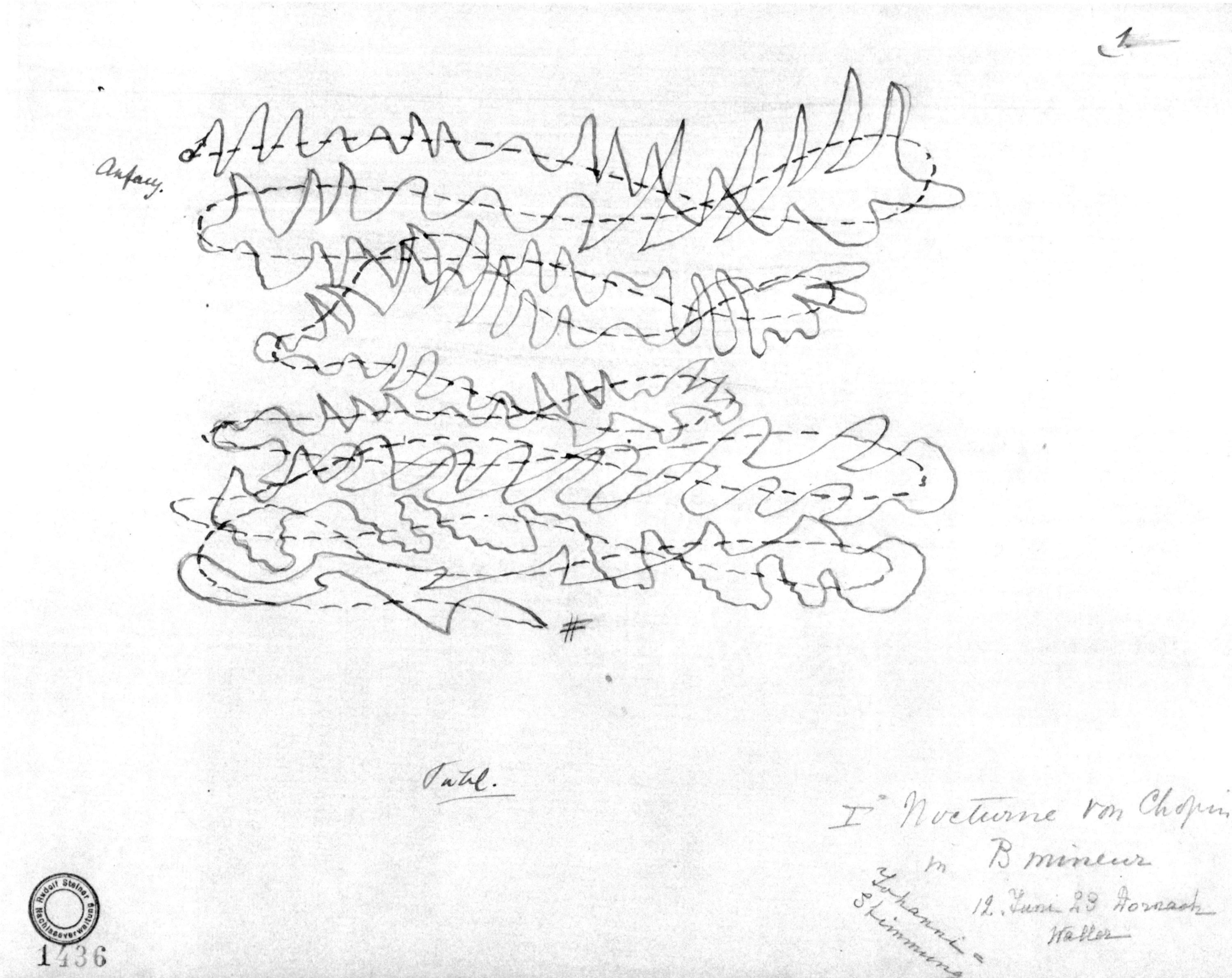

F. Chopin – Nocturne No. 1, Larghetto, B minor (Measures 27-34 omitted), Op. 9/1 (page 1)

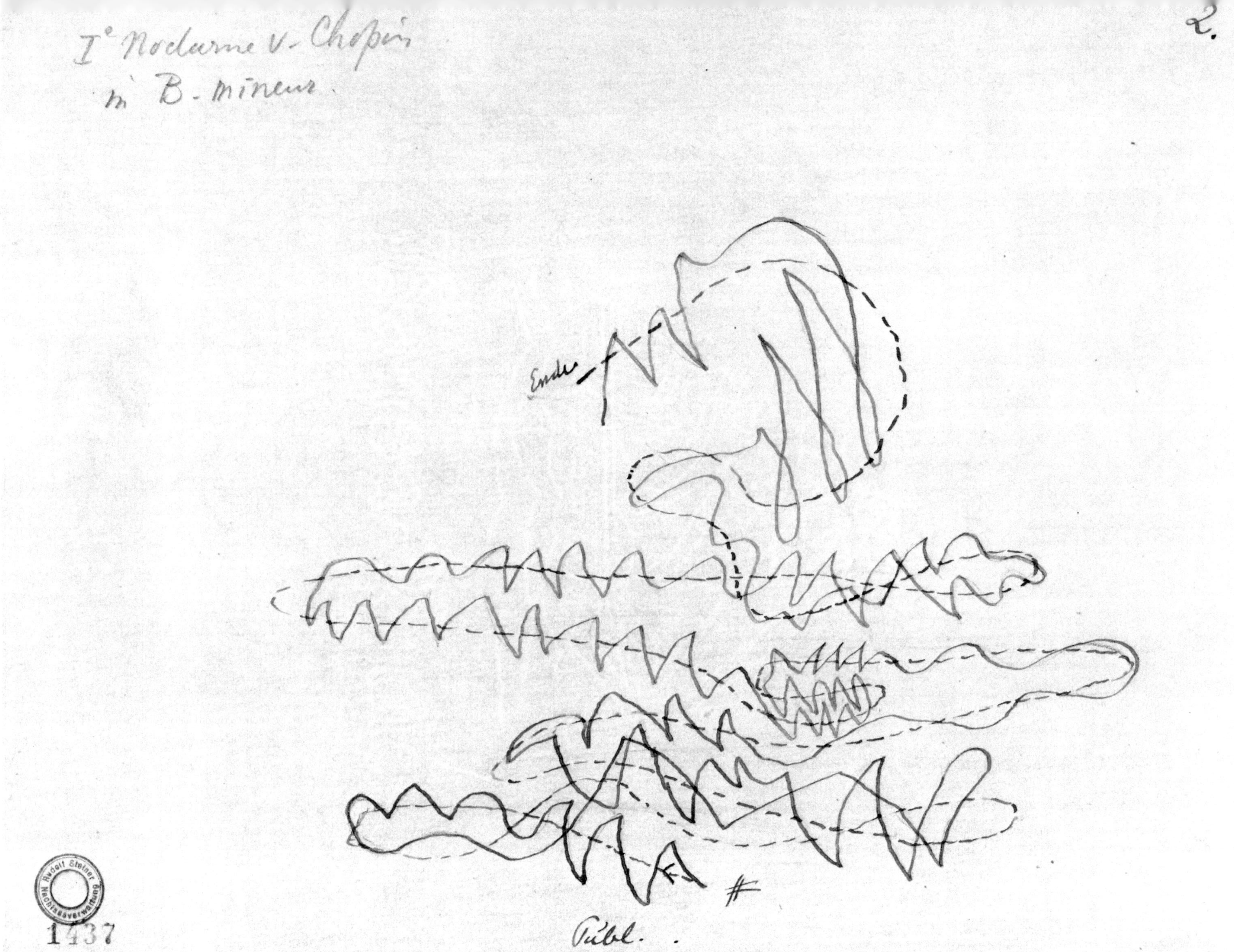

F. Chopin – Nocturne No. 1, Larghetto, B minor (Measures 27-34 omitted), Op. 9/1 (page 2)

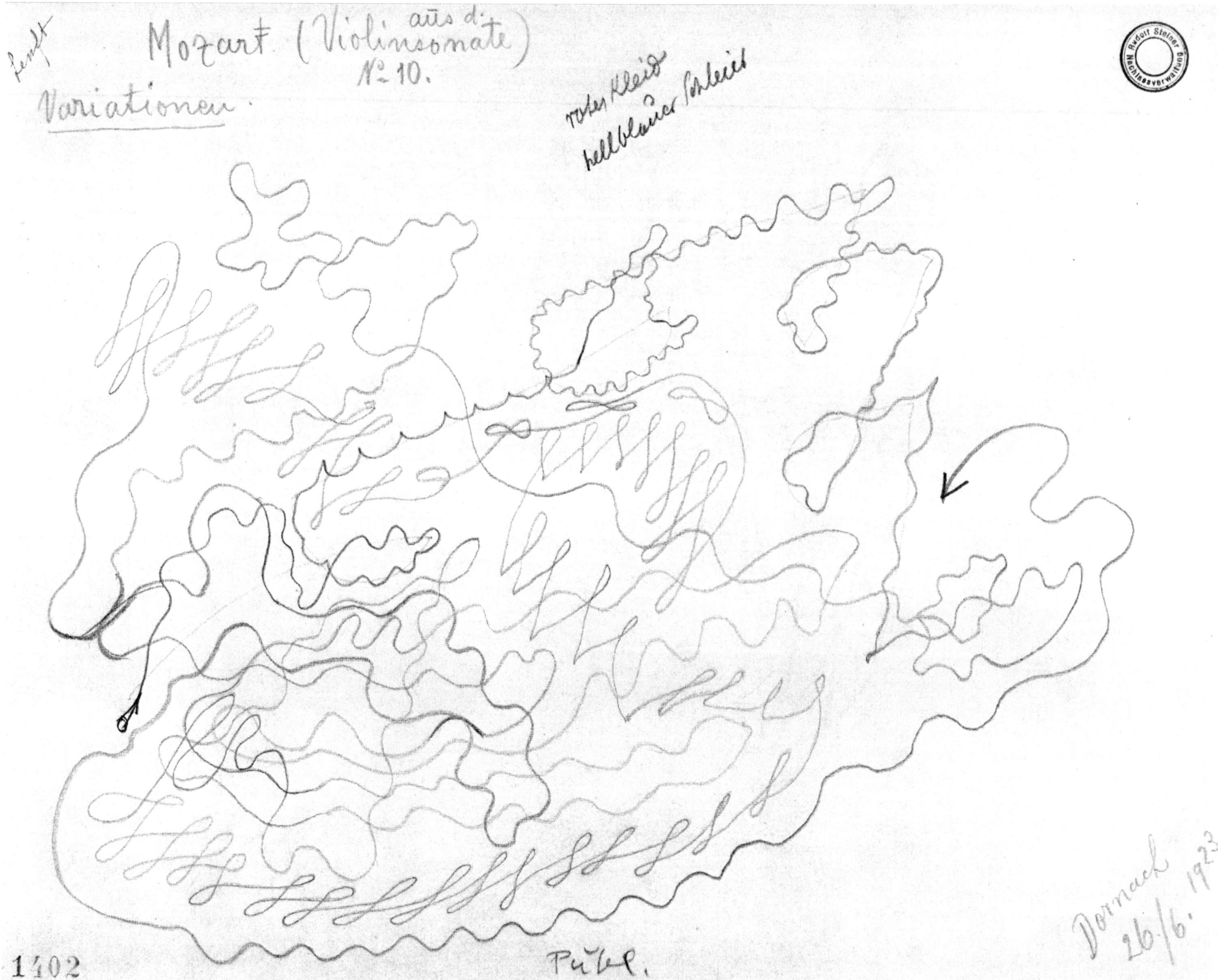

W. A. Mozart – Thema und Variationen [Theme and variations], Adantino cantabile, third movement from the Violin sonata, G major (without piano variation), KV 379

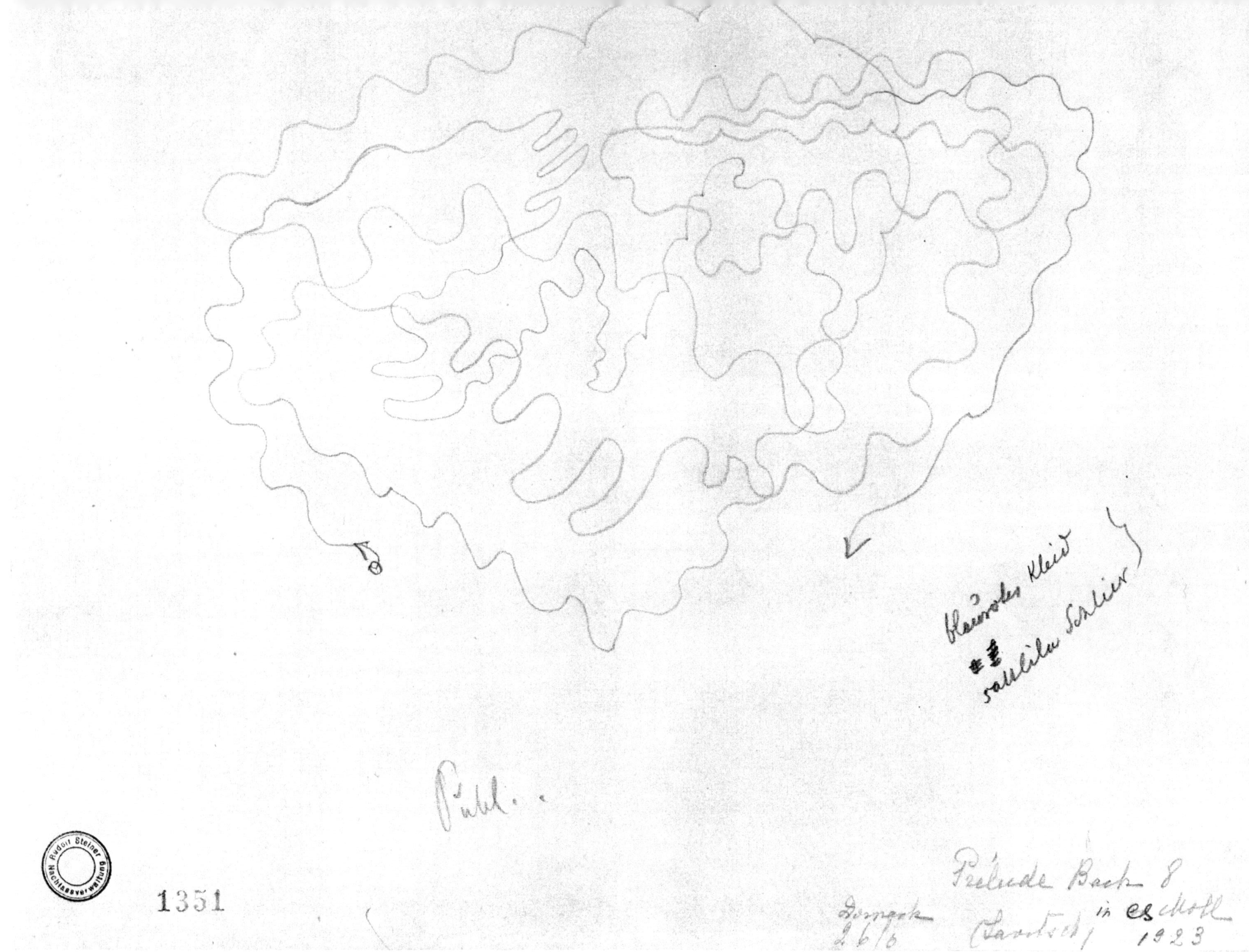

J. S. Bach – Prelude No. 8, E-flat minor, from the *Well-Tempered Clavier I*

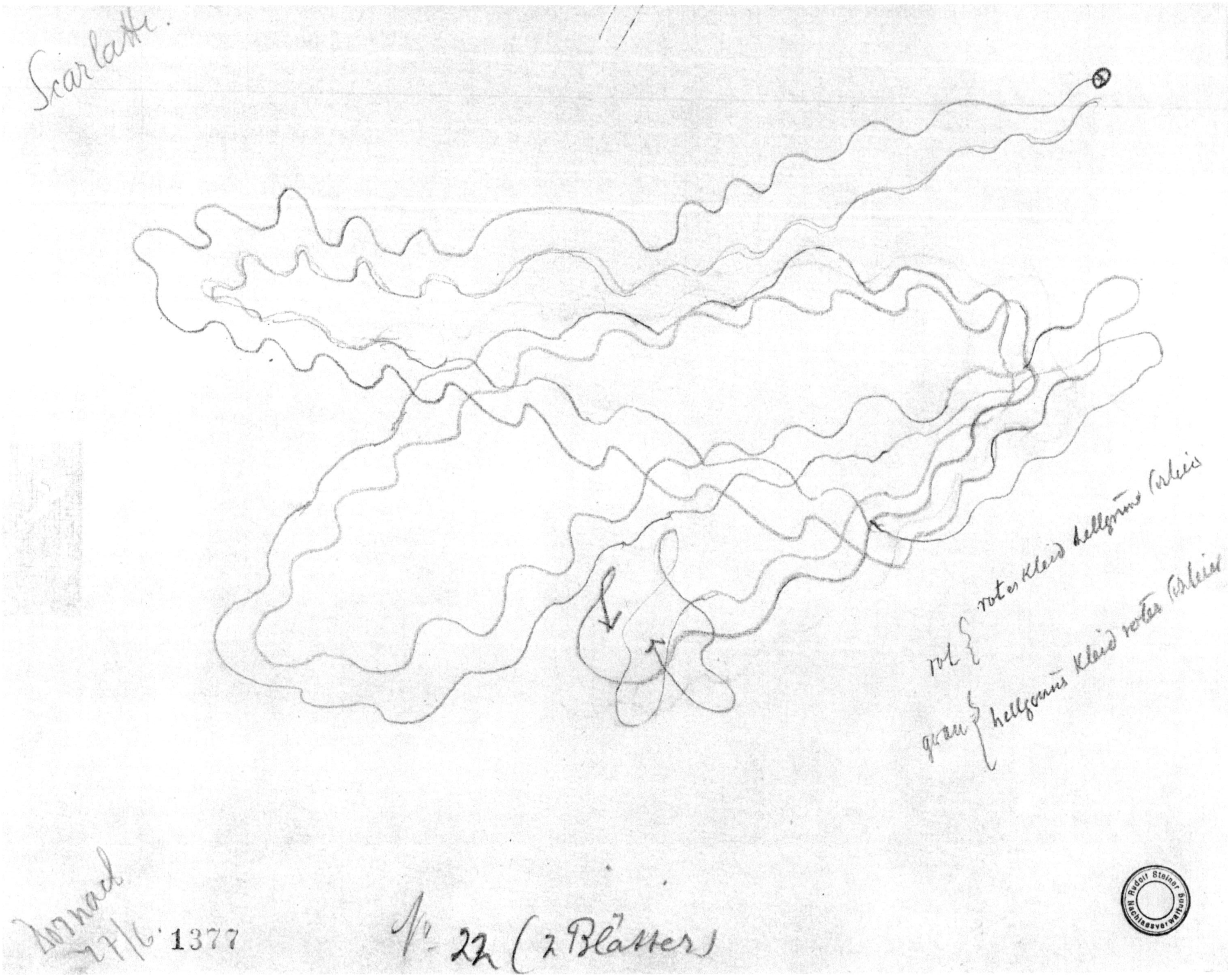

D. Scarlatti – Pastorale, from Sonata No. 5, D minor, arranged in E minor by Karl Tansig

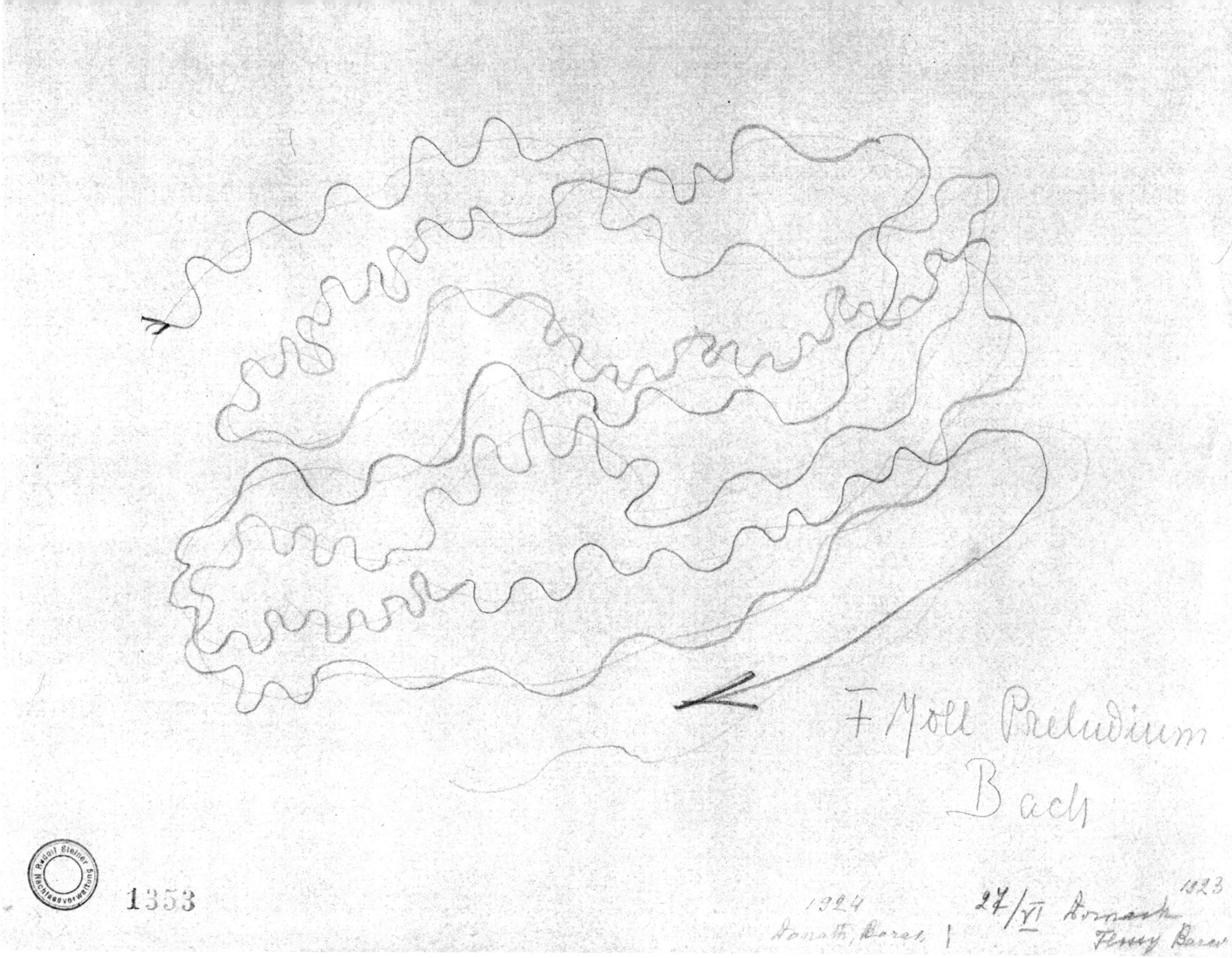

J. S. Bach – Prelude No. 12, F minor, from the *Well-Tempered Clavier II*

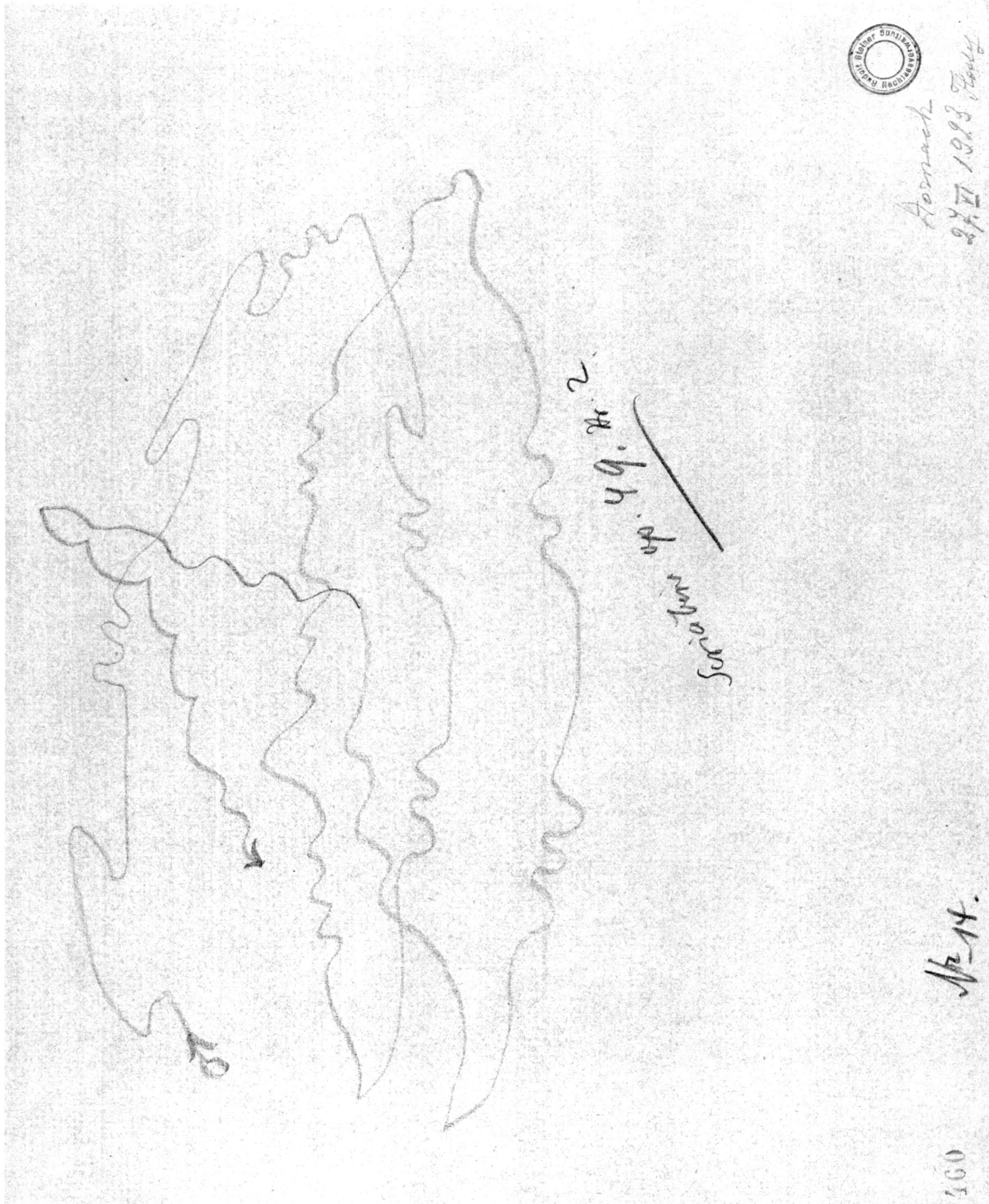

A. Scriabine – Prelude, Bruscamente, F major, Op. 49/2

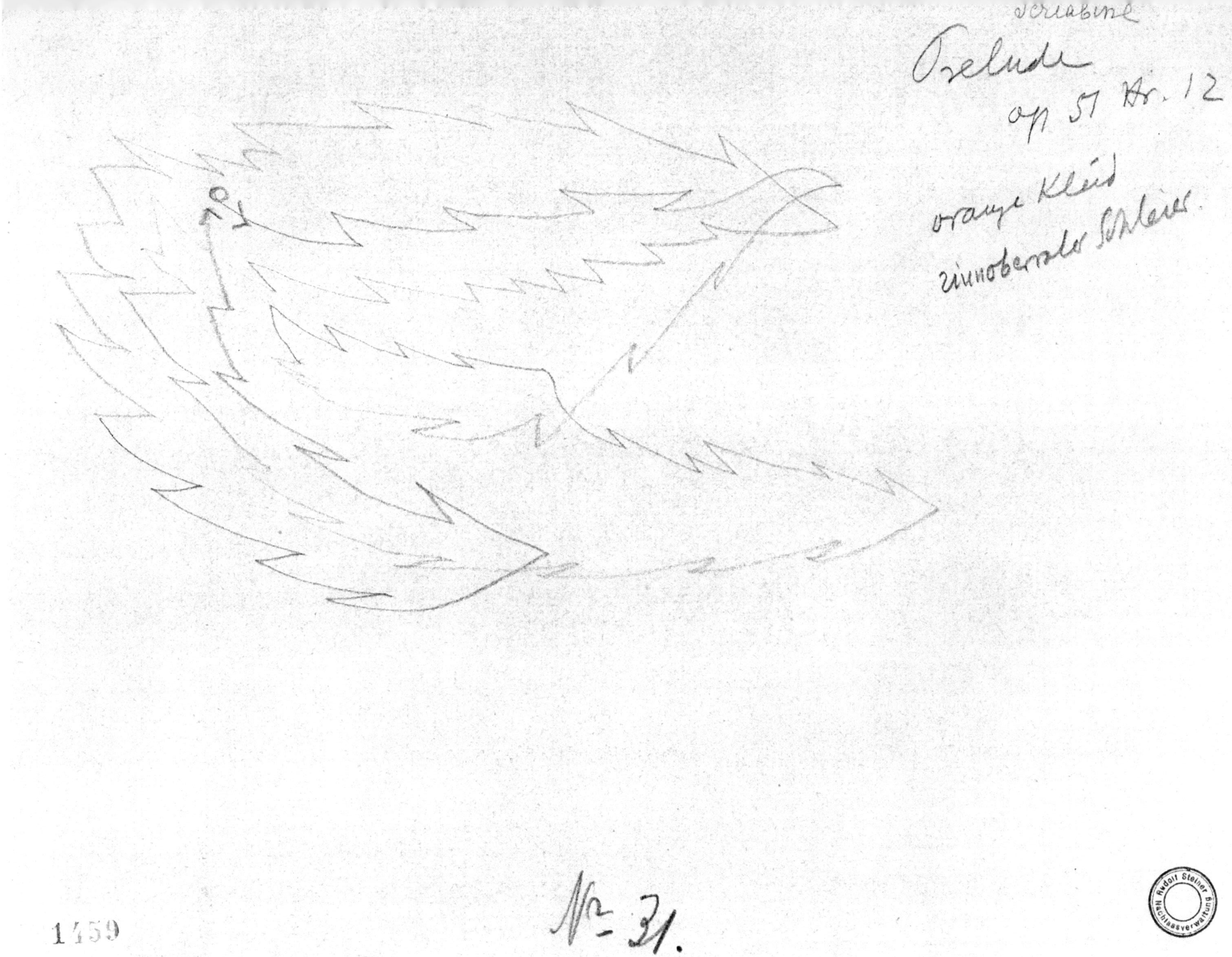

A. Scriabine – Prelude, Lugubre, A minor, Op. 51/2

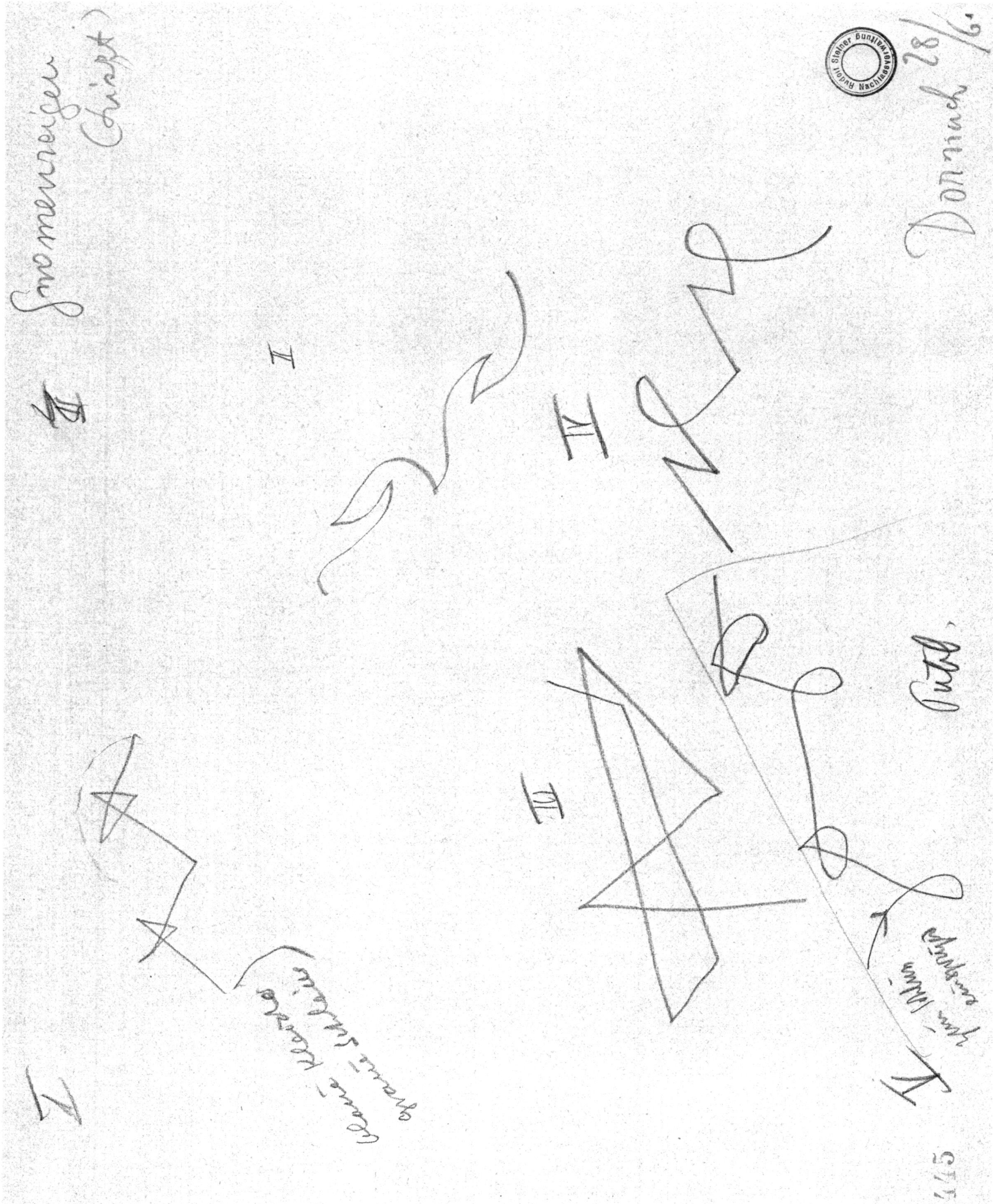

F. Liszt – "Gnomenreigen," [Dance of the gnomes], Presto scherzando, Konzertetüde No. 2 [Concert studies]

J. Brahms – Romanze, Andante, Allegretto grazioso, F major, No. 5 from *Sechs Klavierstücke* [Six piano pieces], Op. 11/5

G. F. Händel – Larghetto, third movement from the Sonata D Major (page 1, preliminary)

G. F. Händel – Larghetto, third movement from the Sonata D Major (page 2, preliminary)

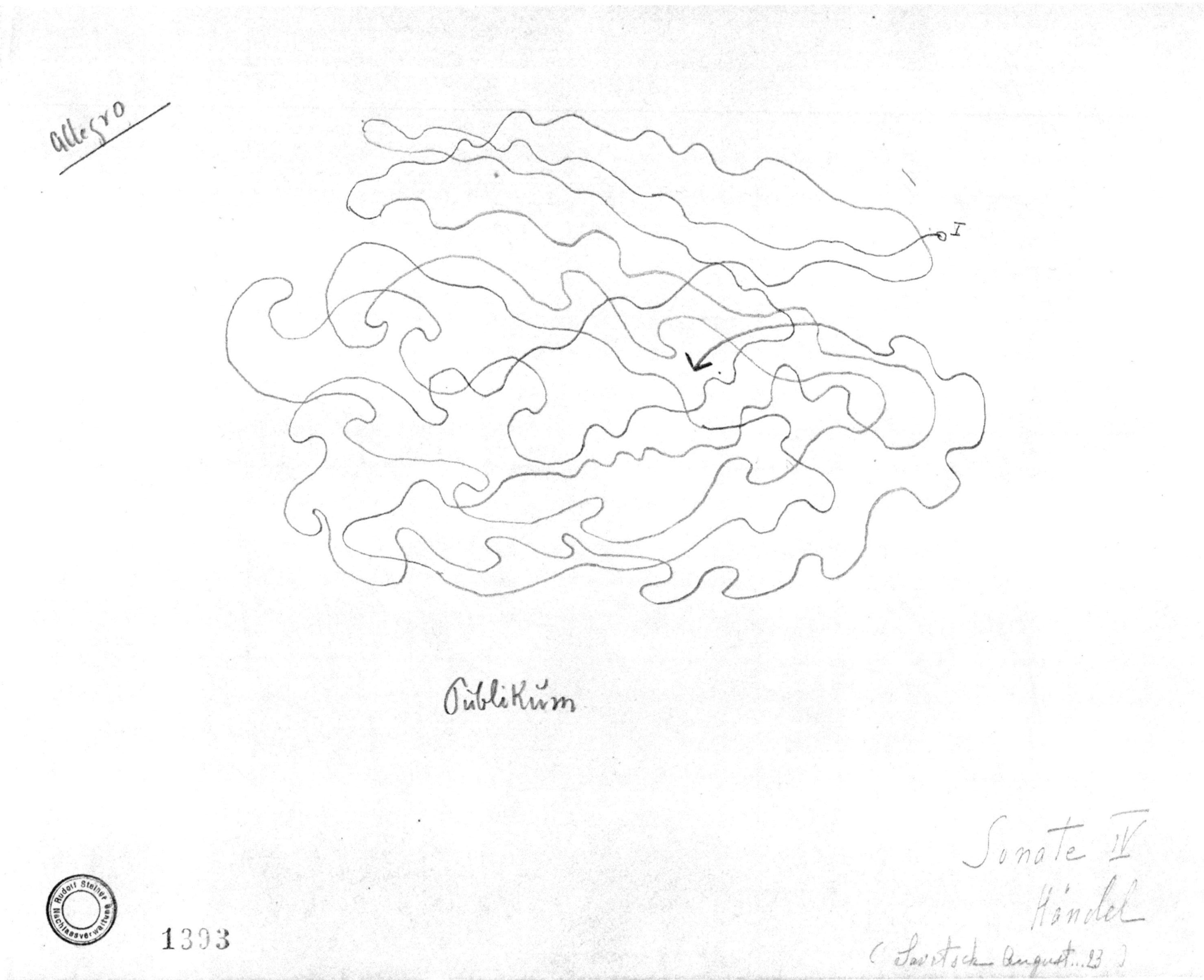

G. F. Händel – Allegro, fourth movement from the Sonata D Major

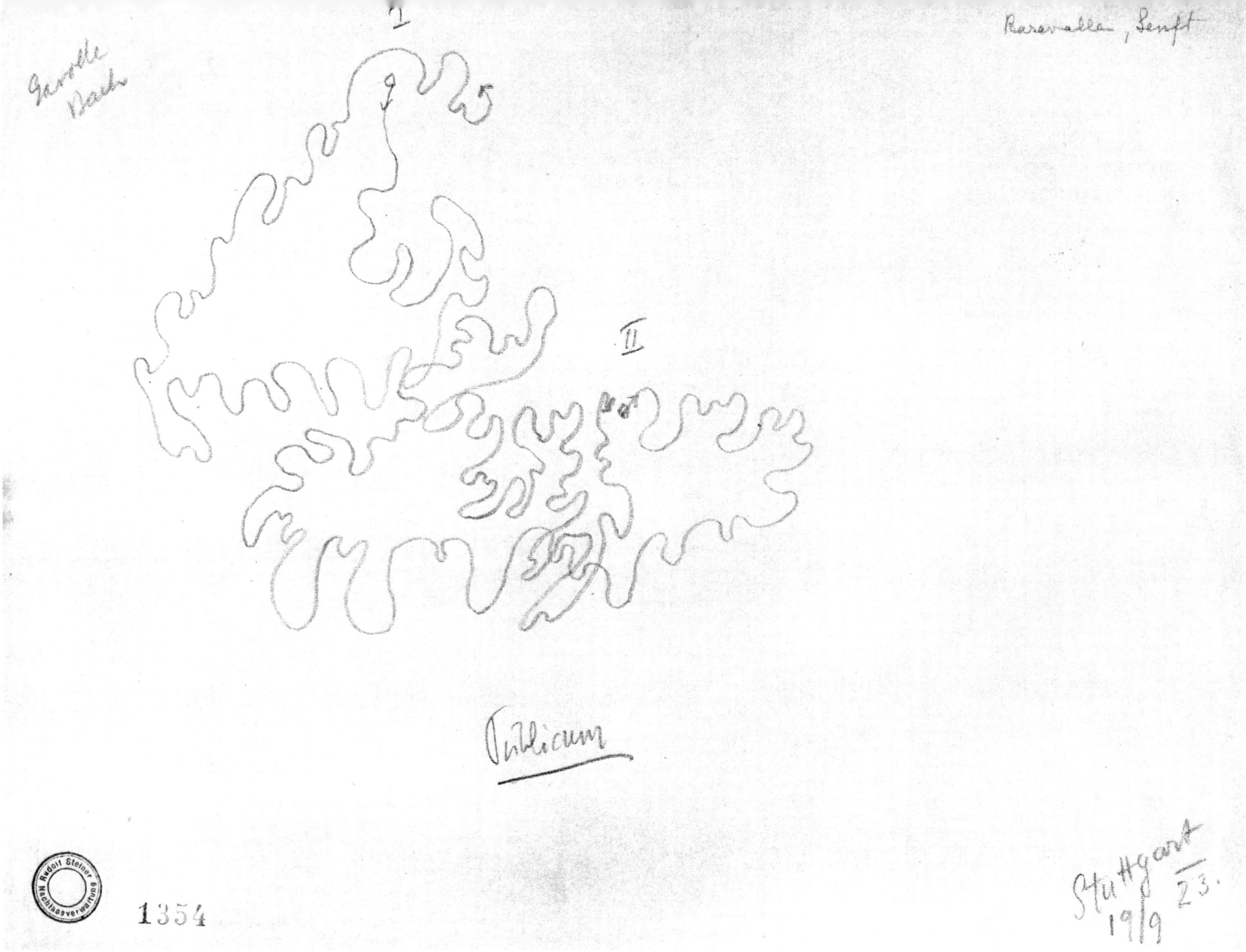

J. S. Bach – Gavotte I, arranged for violin and piano

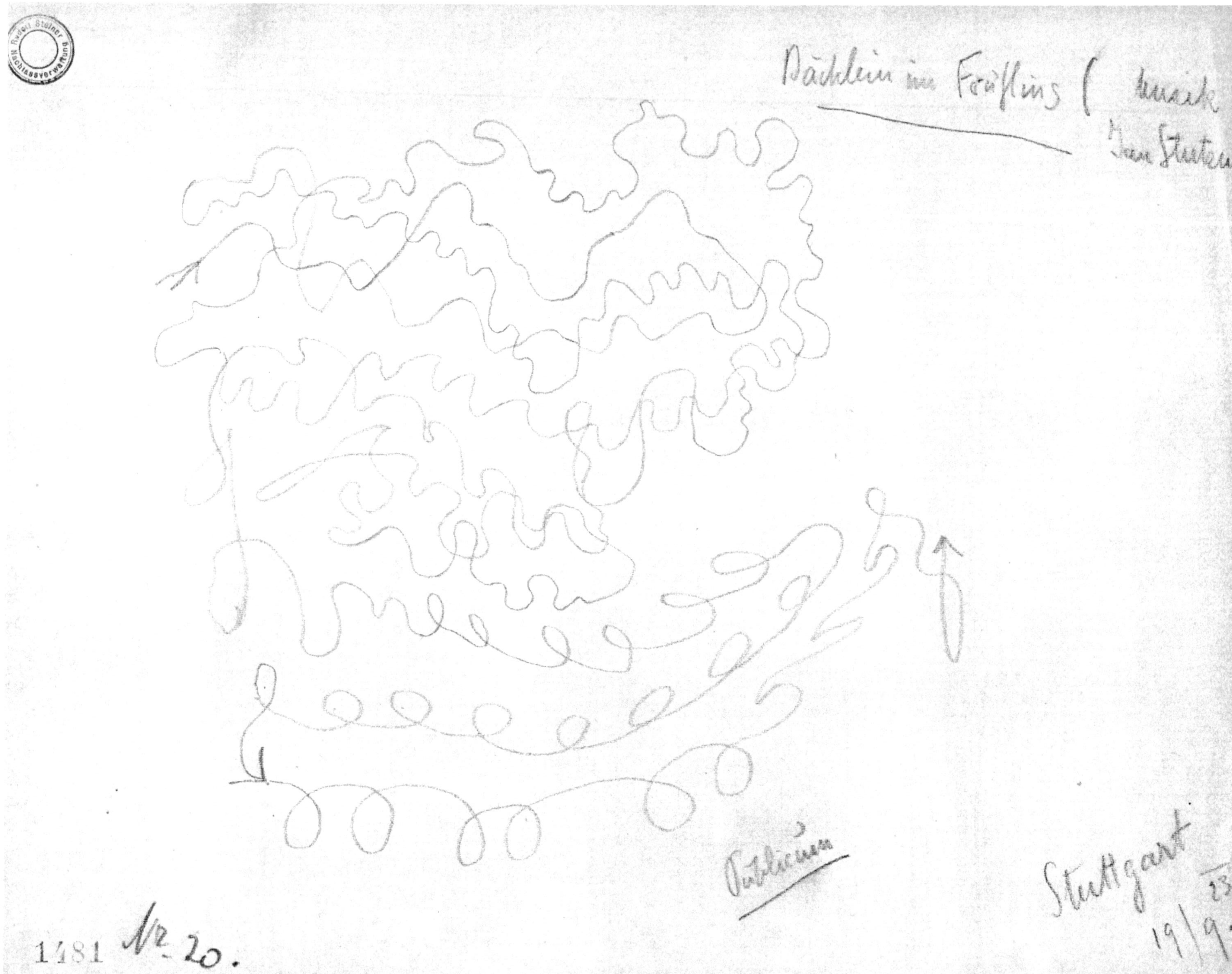

J. Stuten – “März, Bächlein im Frühling” [March, Little brook in spring]

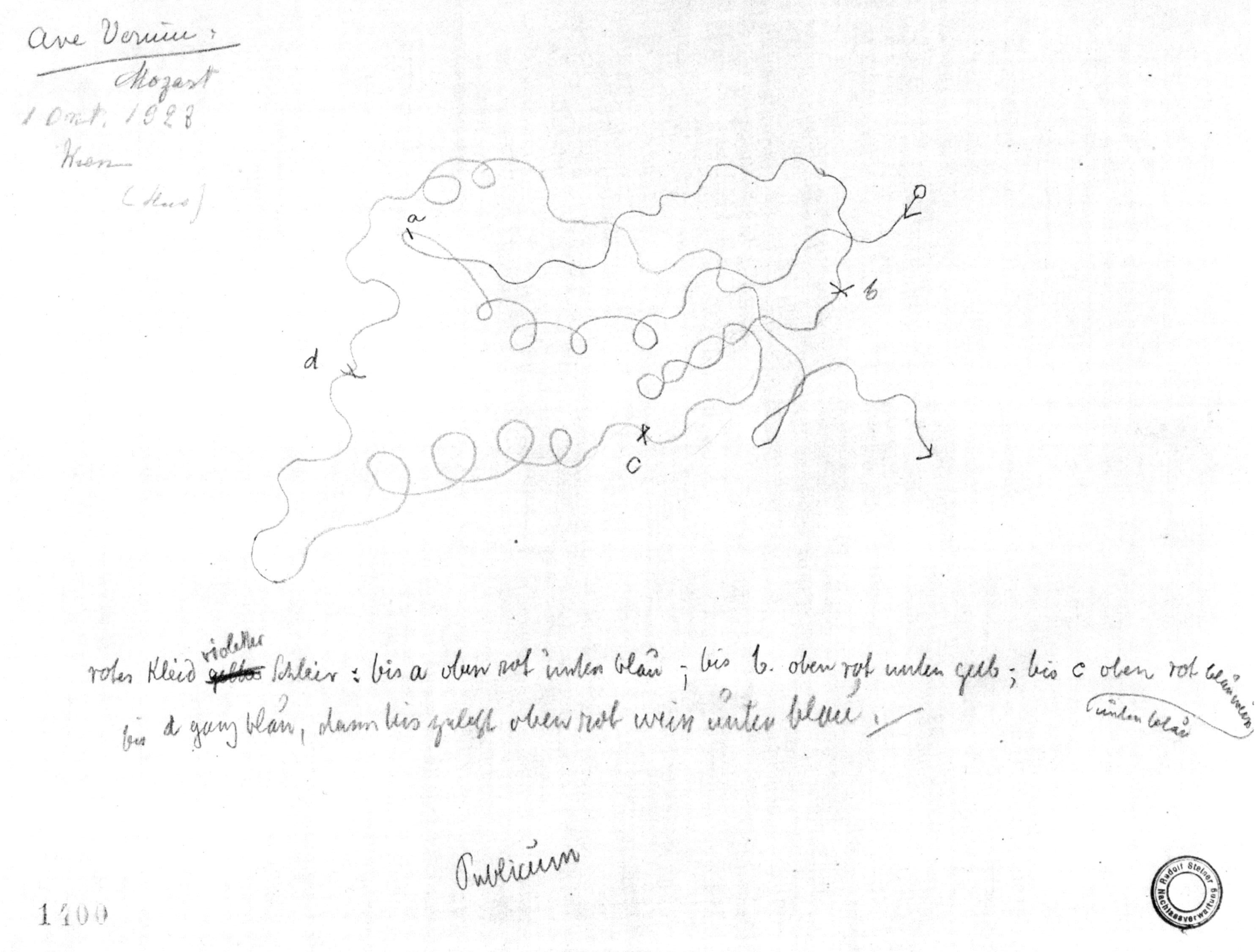

W. A. Mozart – Ave verum, arranged for violin and piano

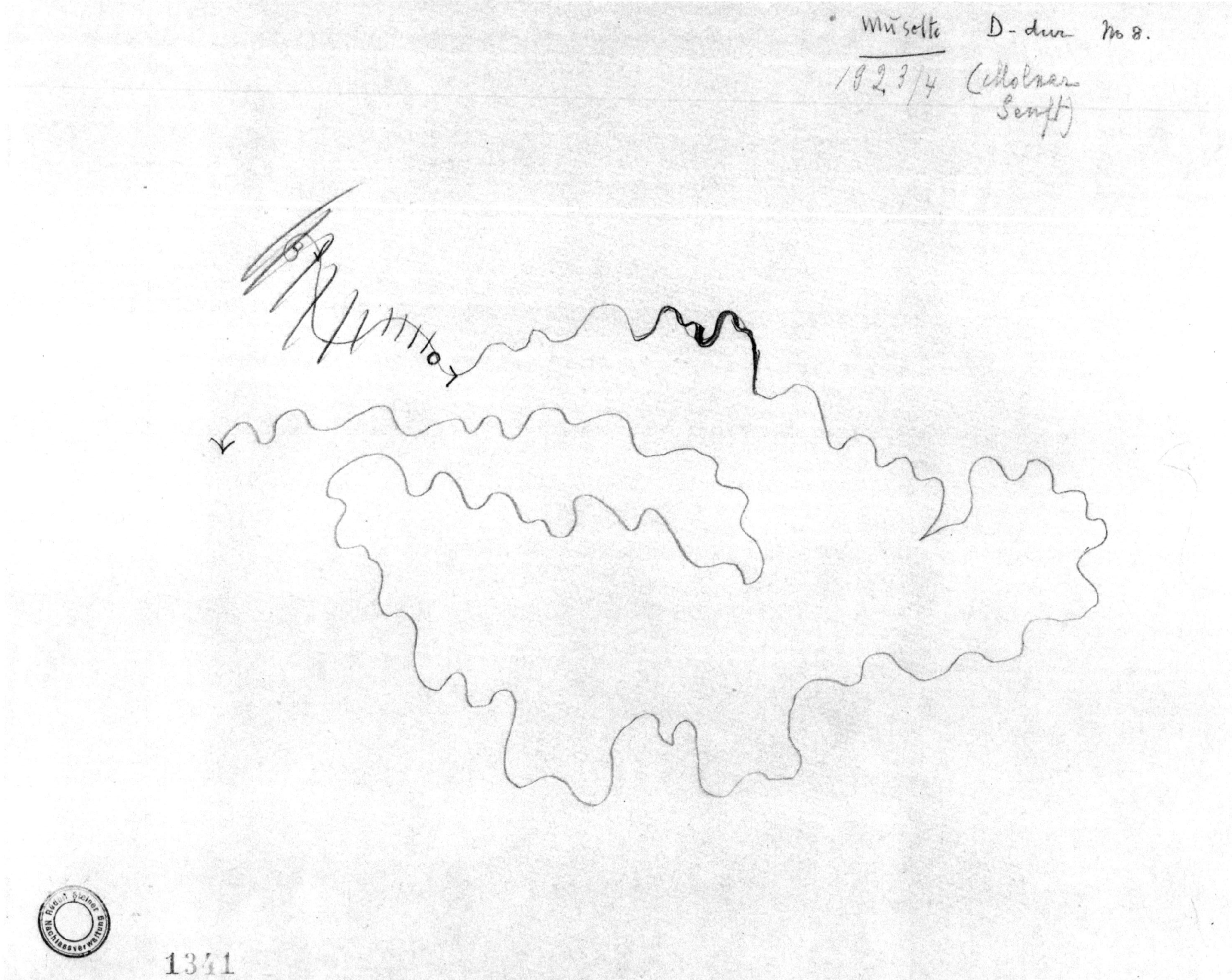

Notebook for Anna Magdalena Bach – Musette, D major

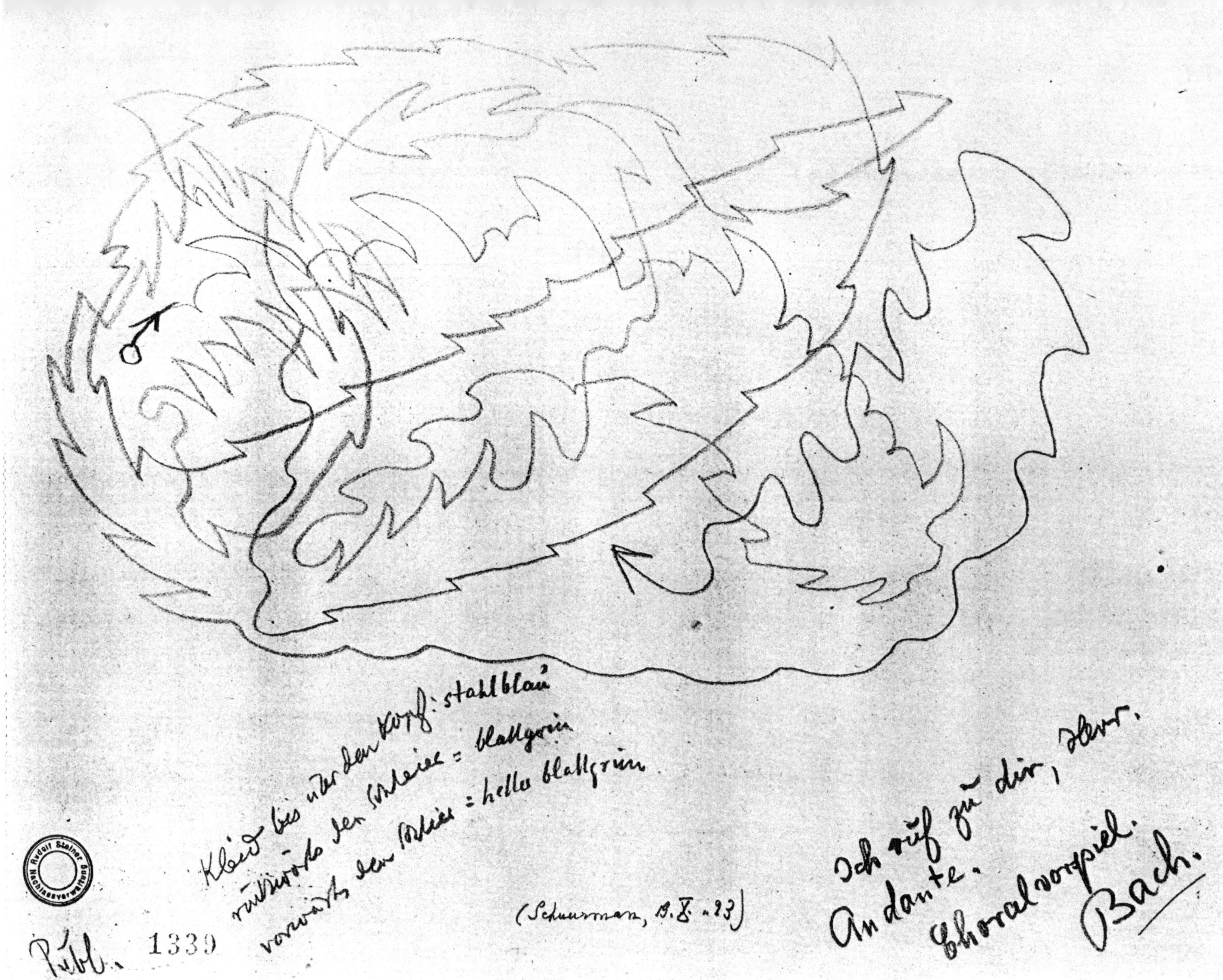

J. S. Bach – “Ich ruf’ zu dir, Herr Jesu Christ” [I call to you, Lord Jesus Christ], Choral introduction

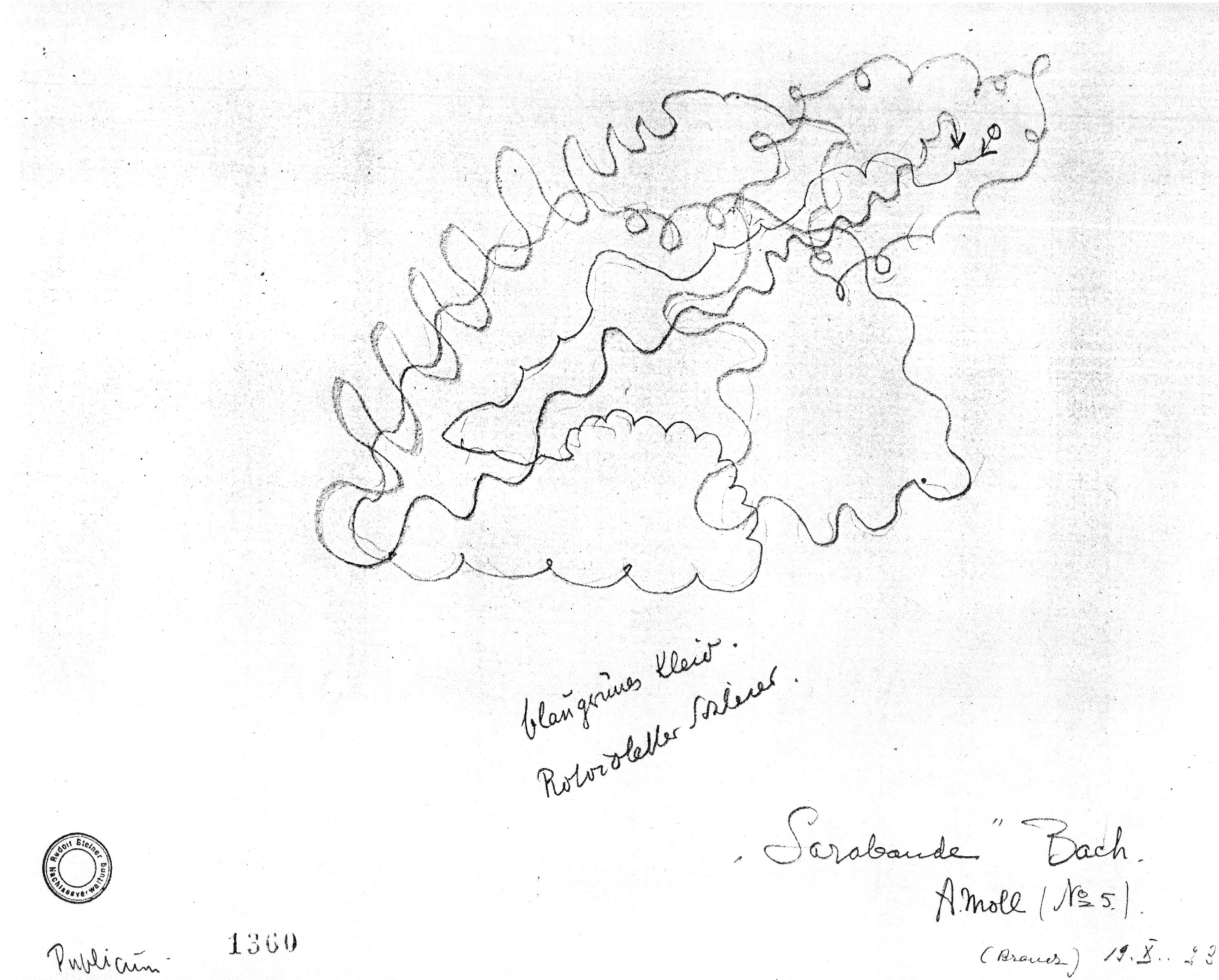

J. S. Bach – Saraband from the English Suite No. 2, A minor

F. Chopin – Étude No. 3, Lento ma non troppo, E major, Op. 10/3

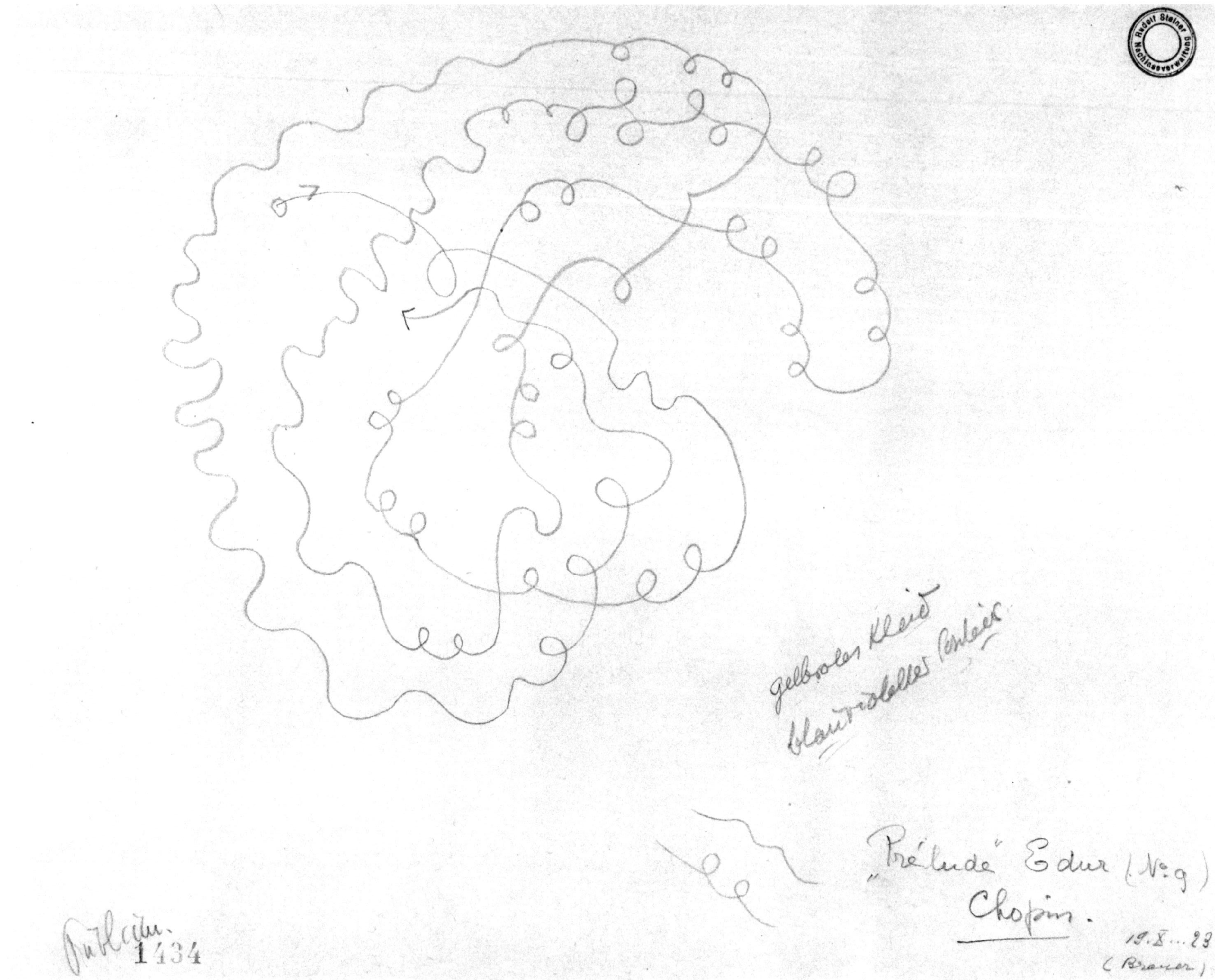

F. Chopin – Prelude No. 9, Largo, E major, Op. 28/9

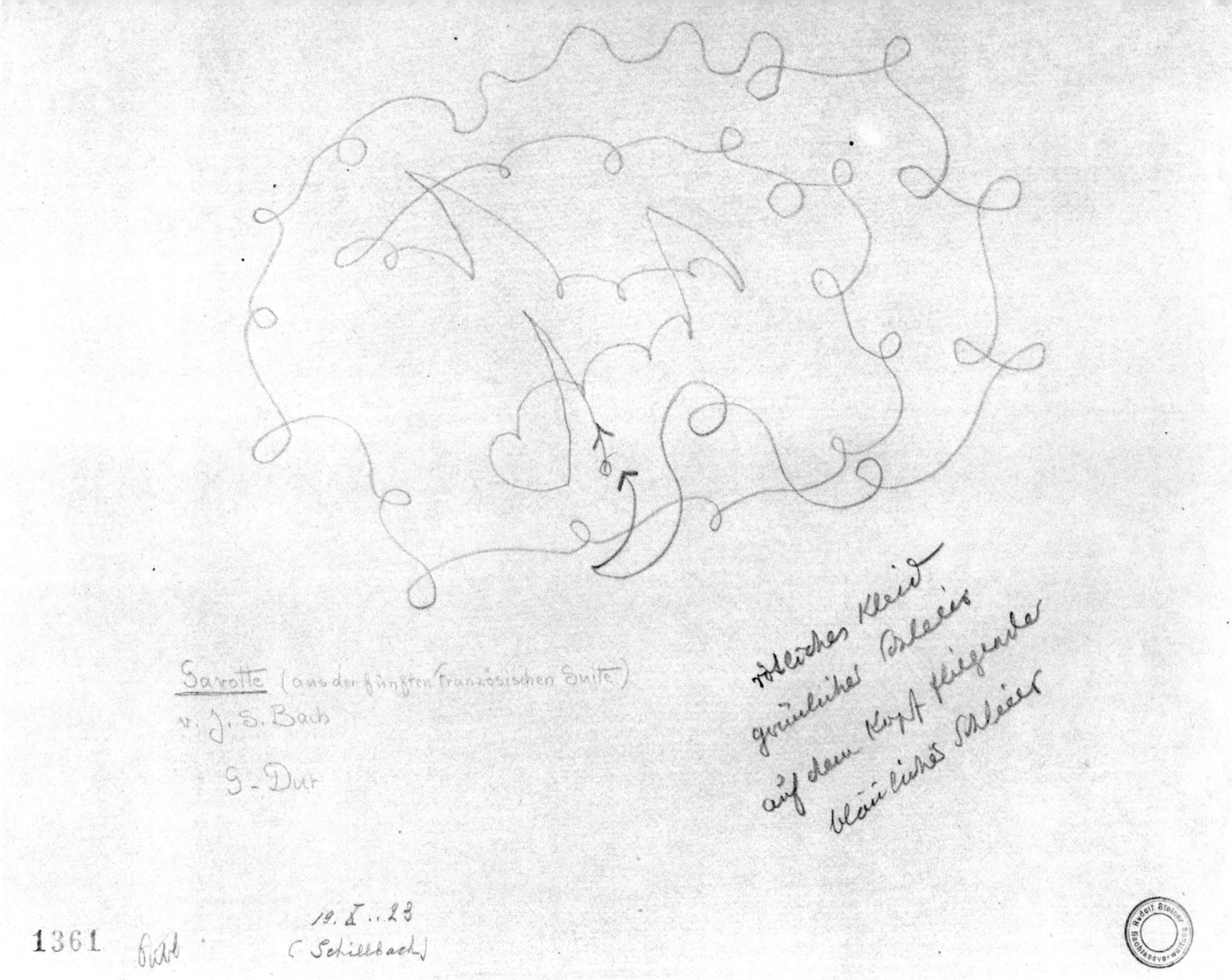

J. S. Bach – Gavotte, G major, from the French Suite No. 5, G major

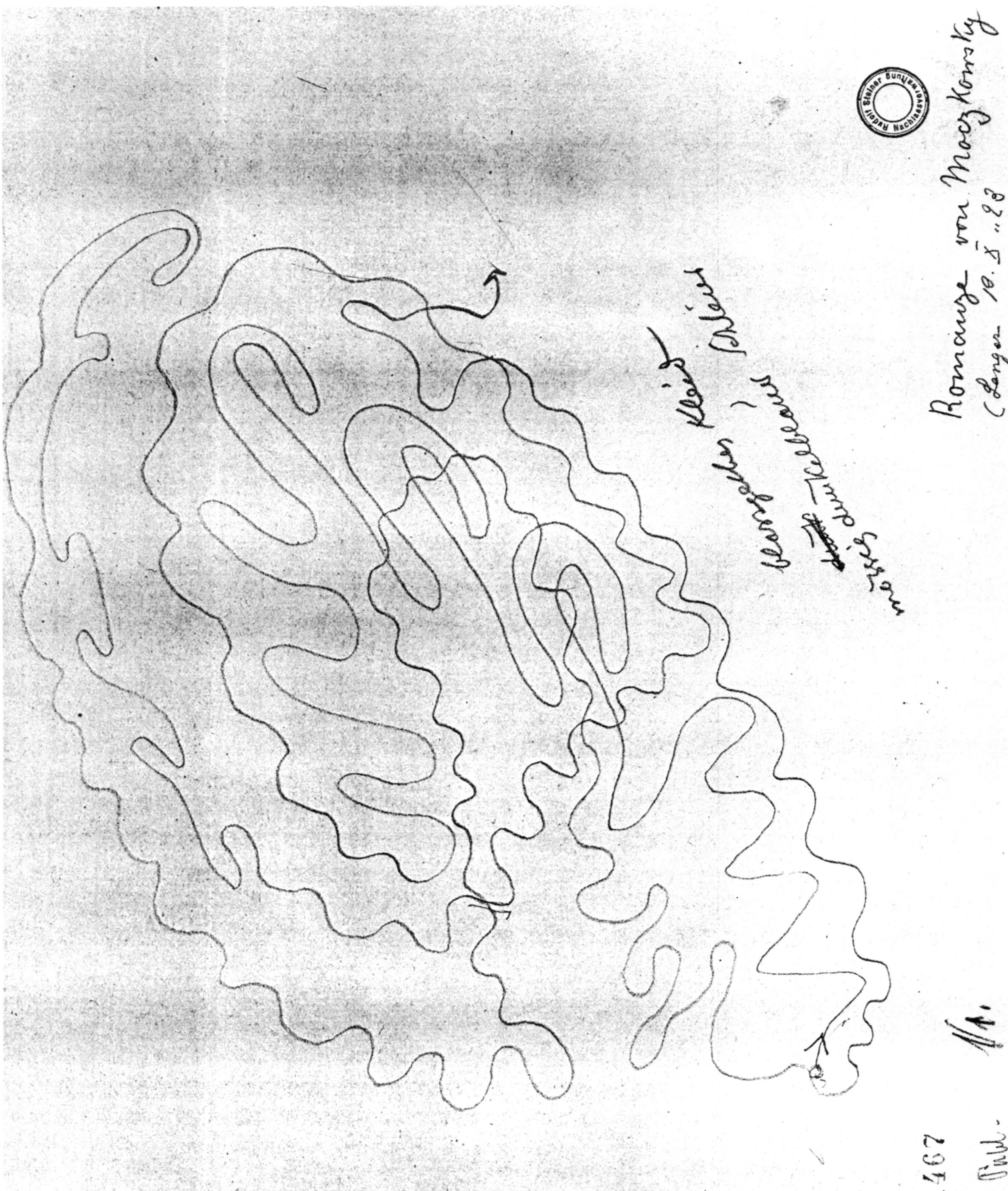

M. Moczkowsky – Romance, Allegretto, Op. 42/1

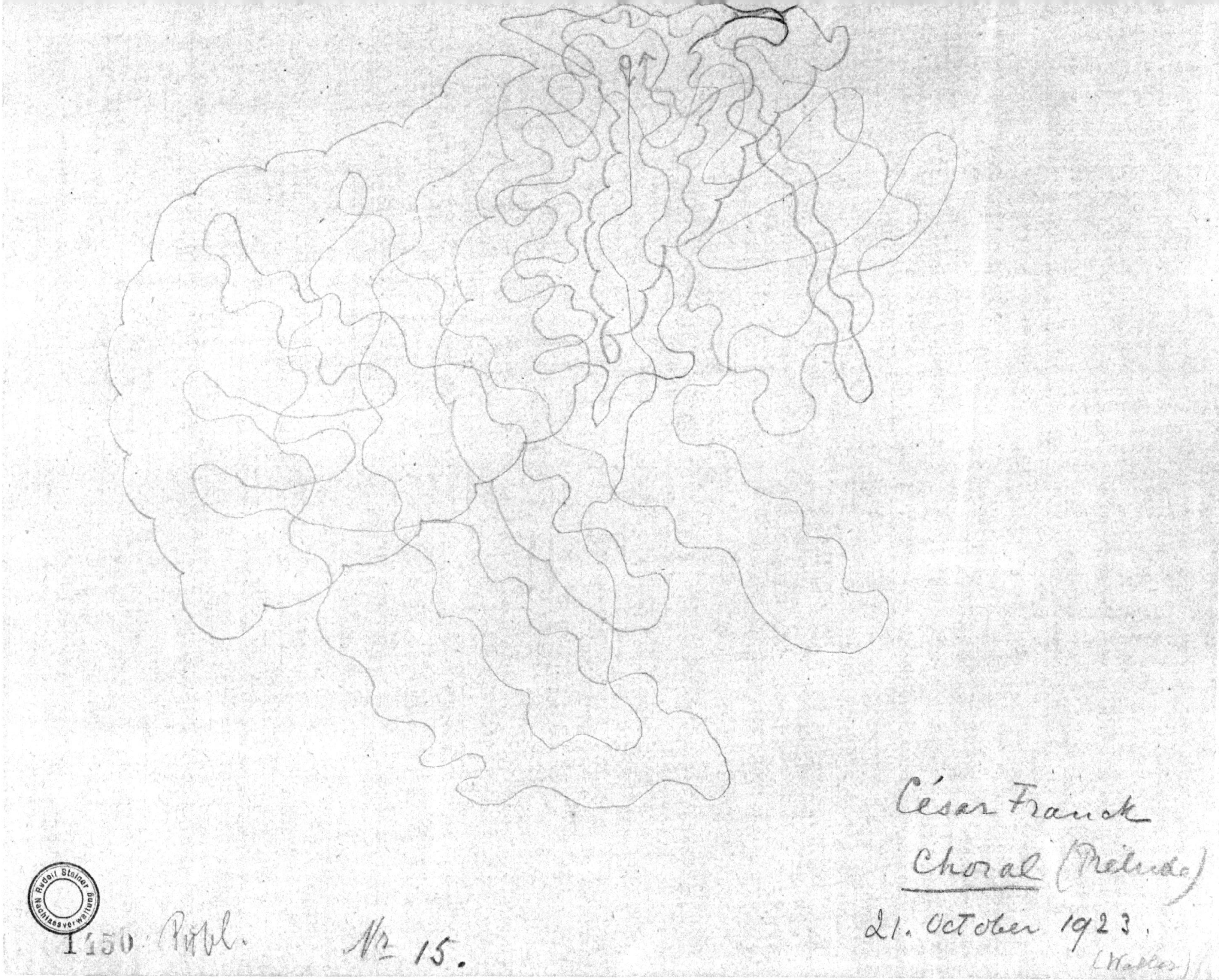

C. Franck – Choral, Poco più lento, E-flat major

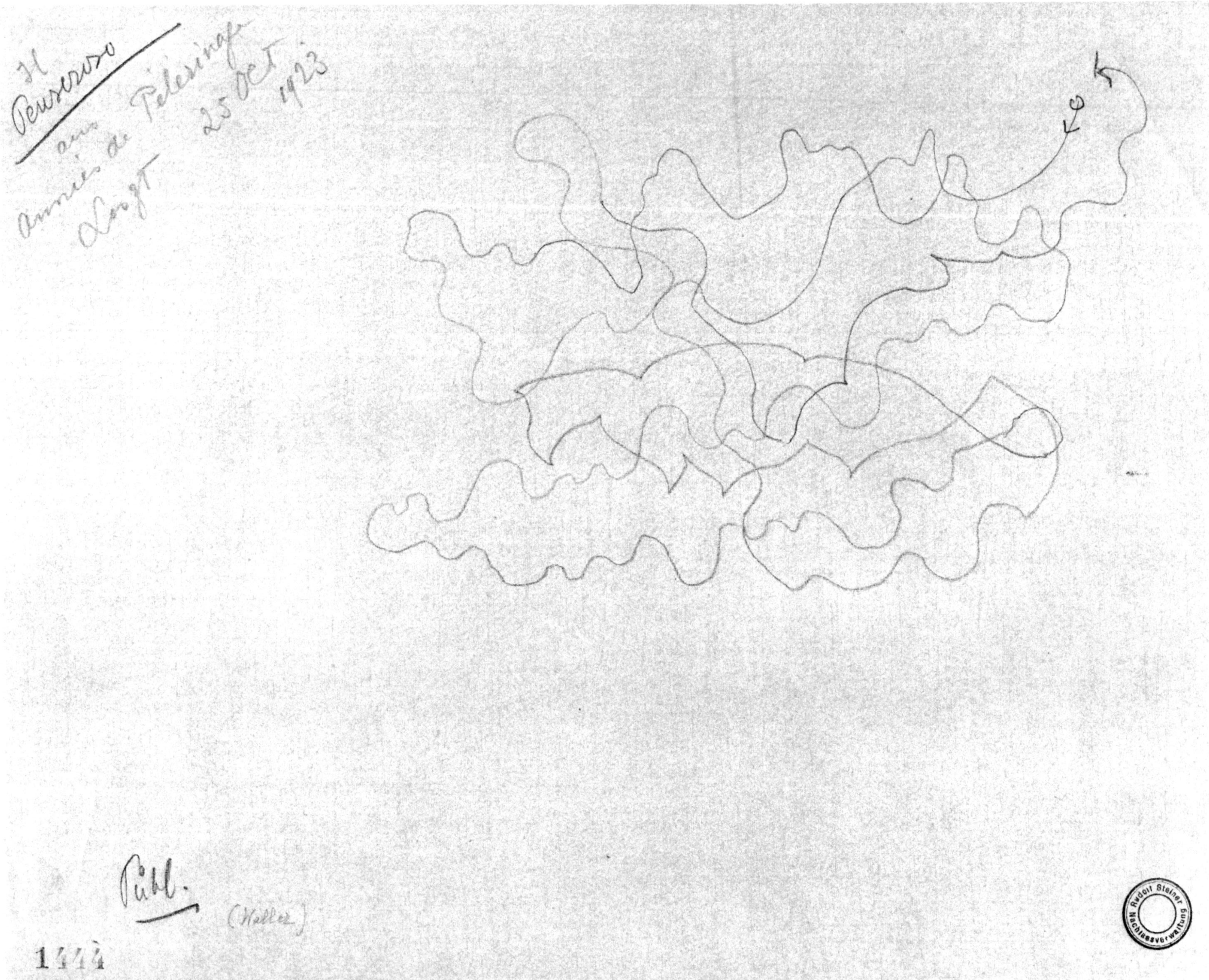

F. Liszt– "Il Penseroso," Lento, No. 2 from *Années de Pélerinage*

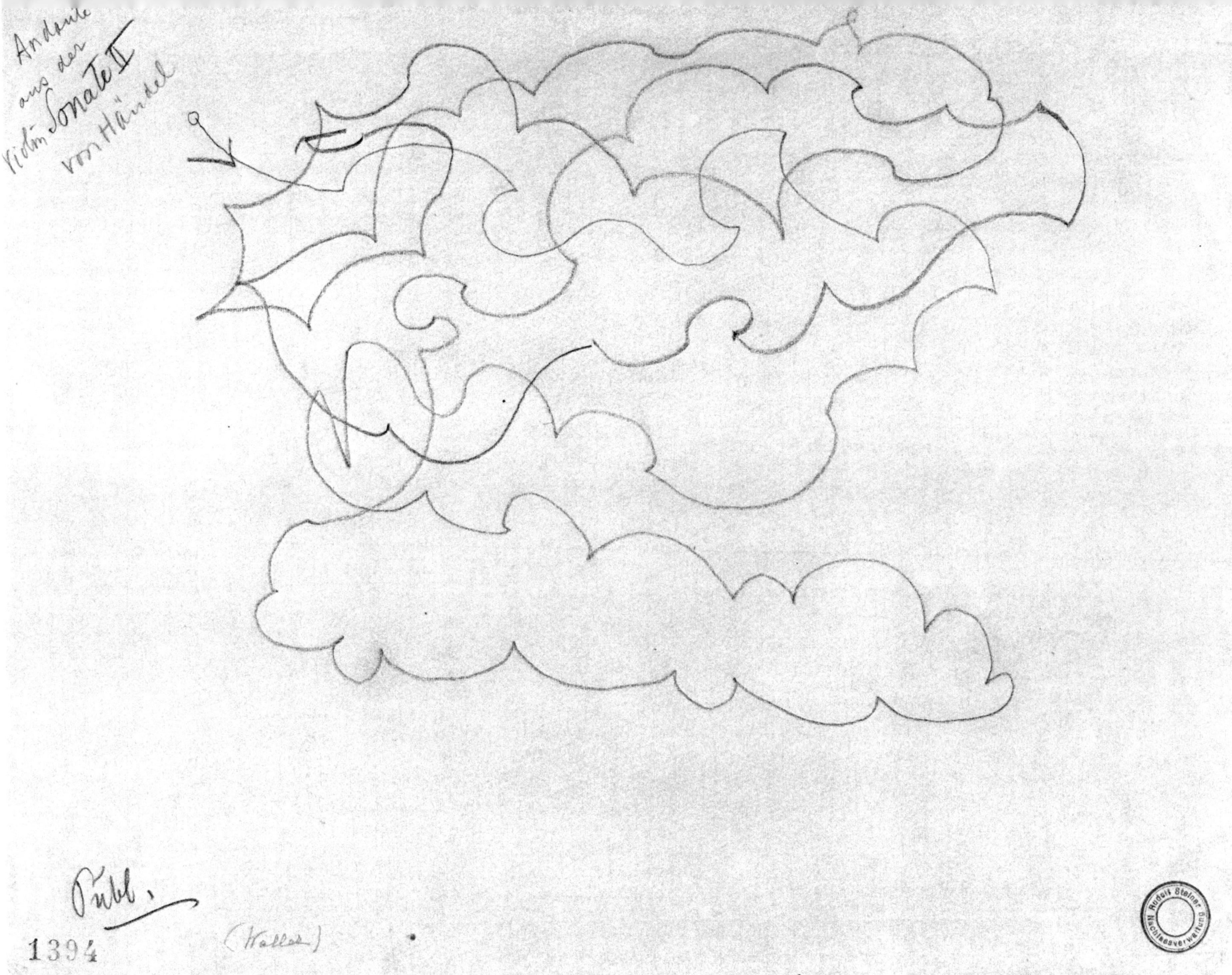

G. F. Händel – Andante, first movement from the Sonata No. 2, G minor

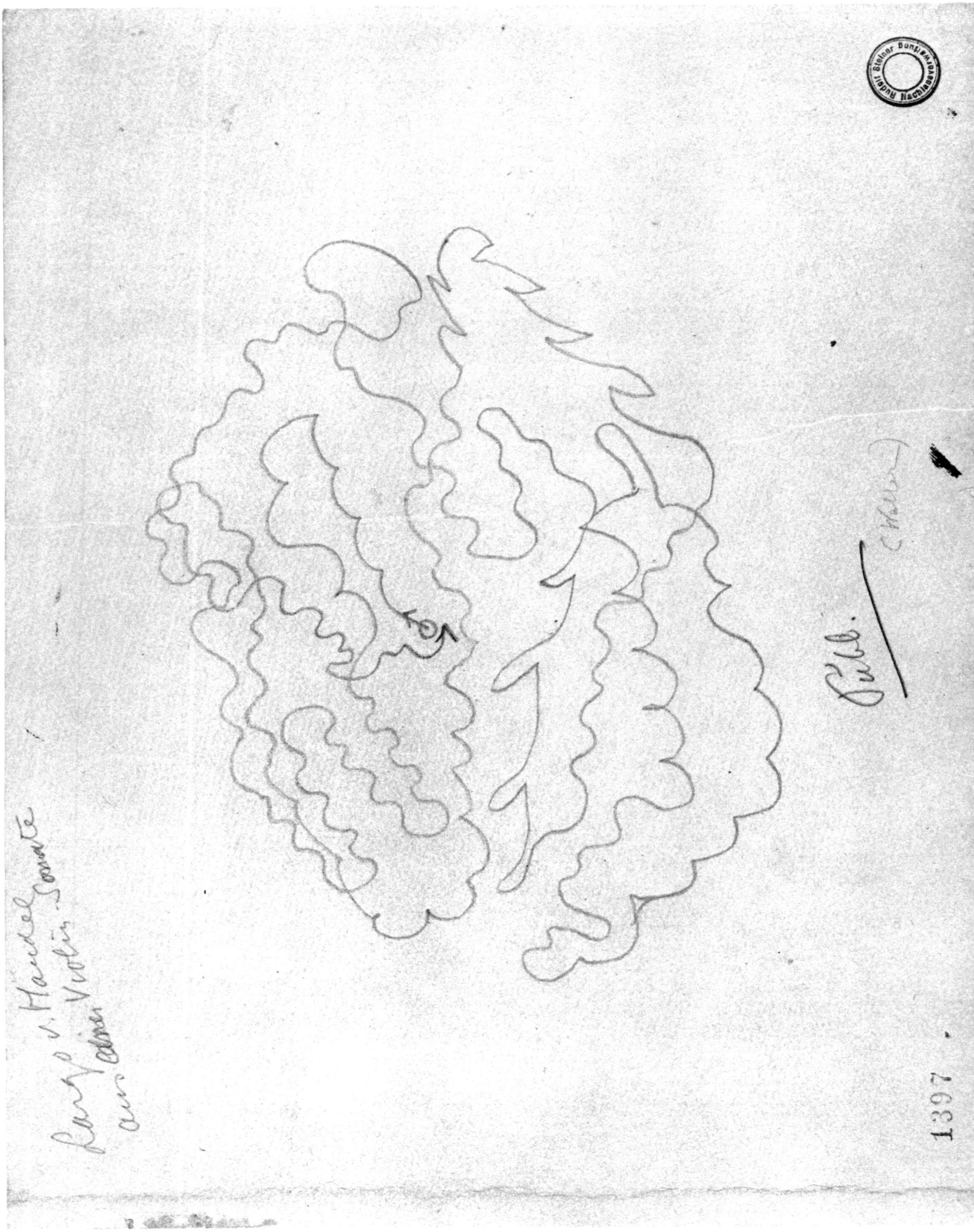

G. F. Händel – Largo, third movement, presumably from the Sonata F Major

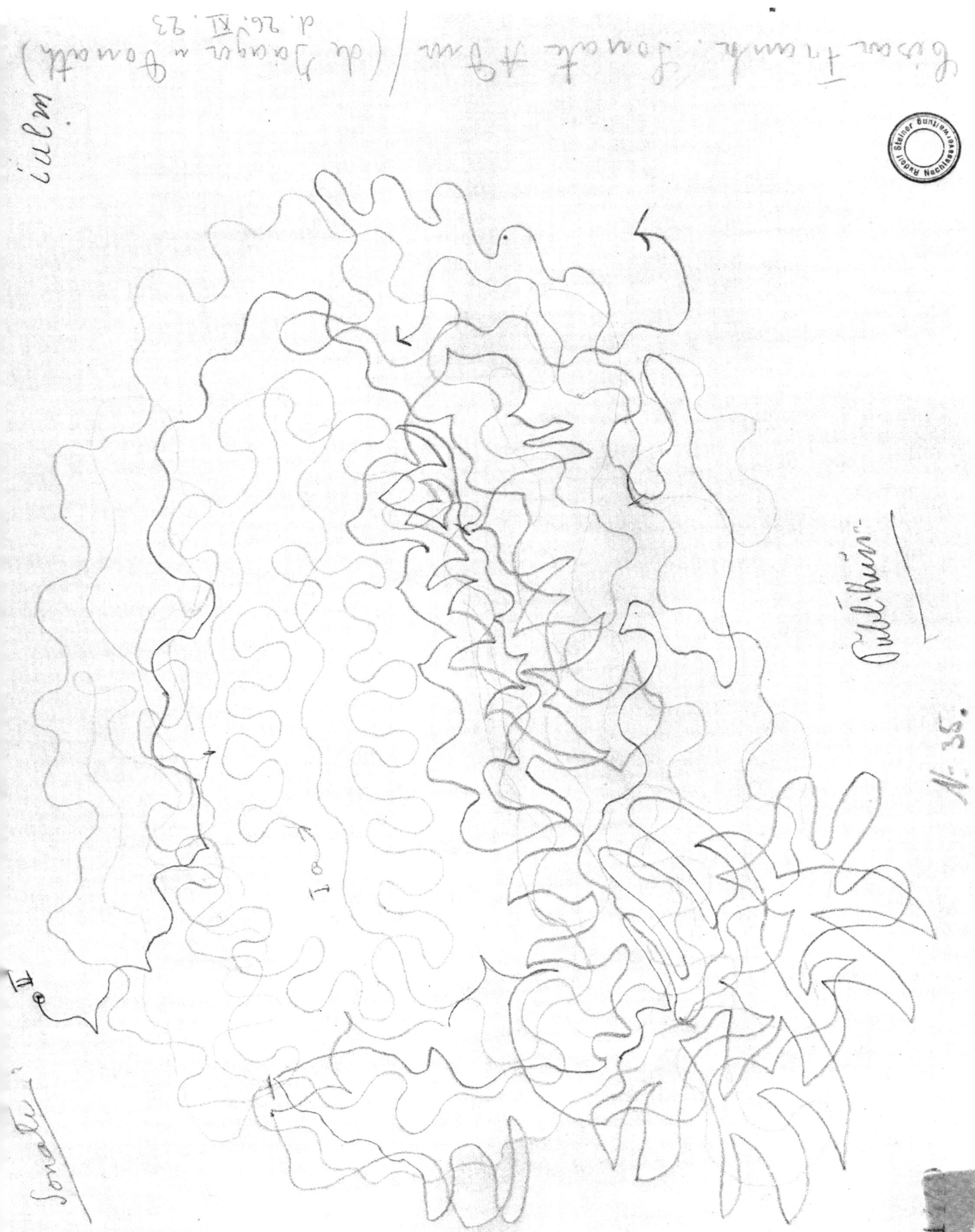

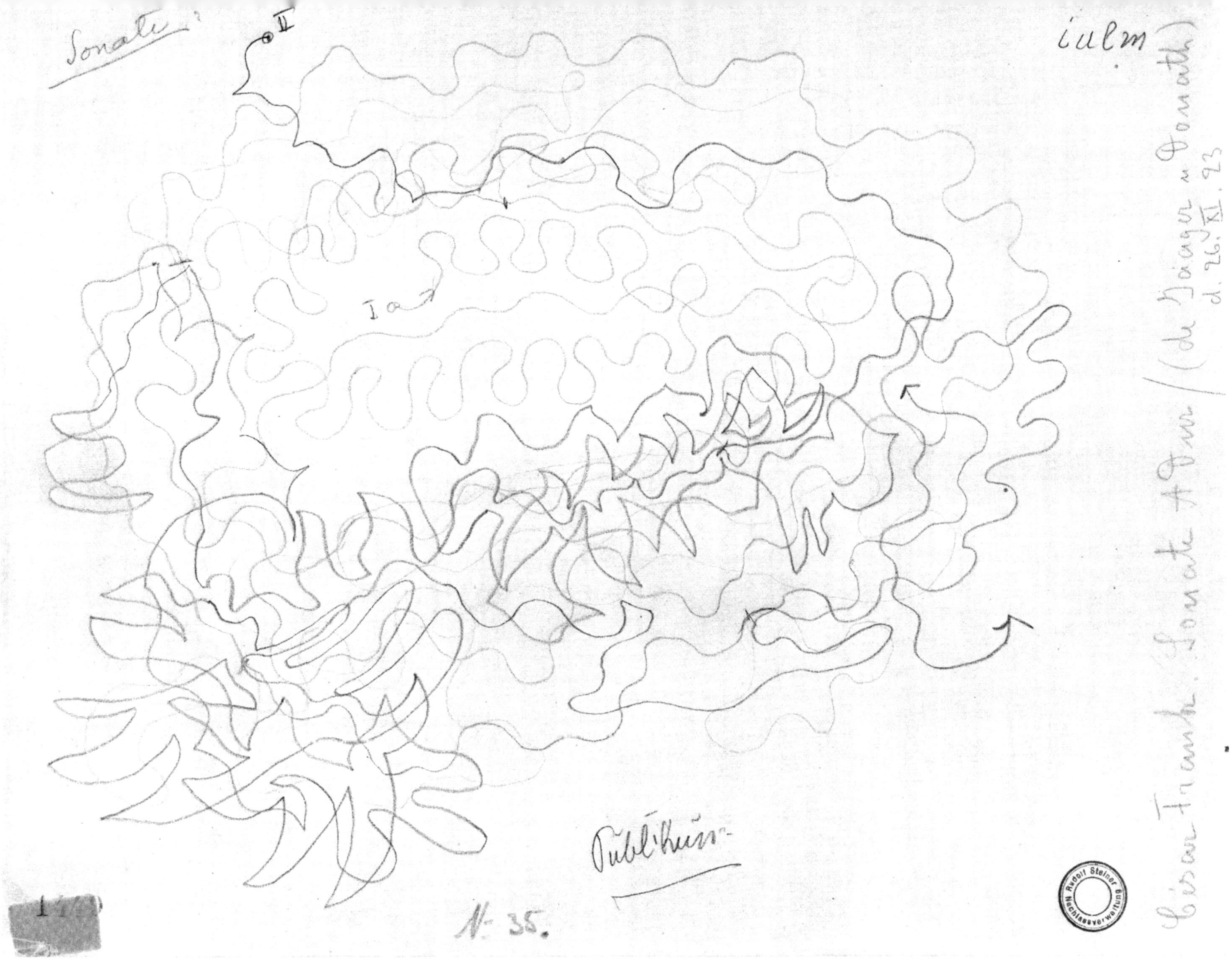

C. Frank – Allegretto ben moderato, first movement from the Sonata A major

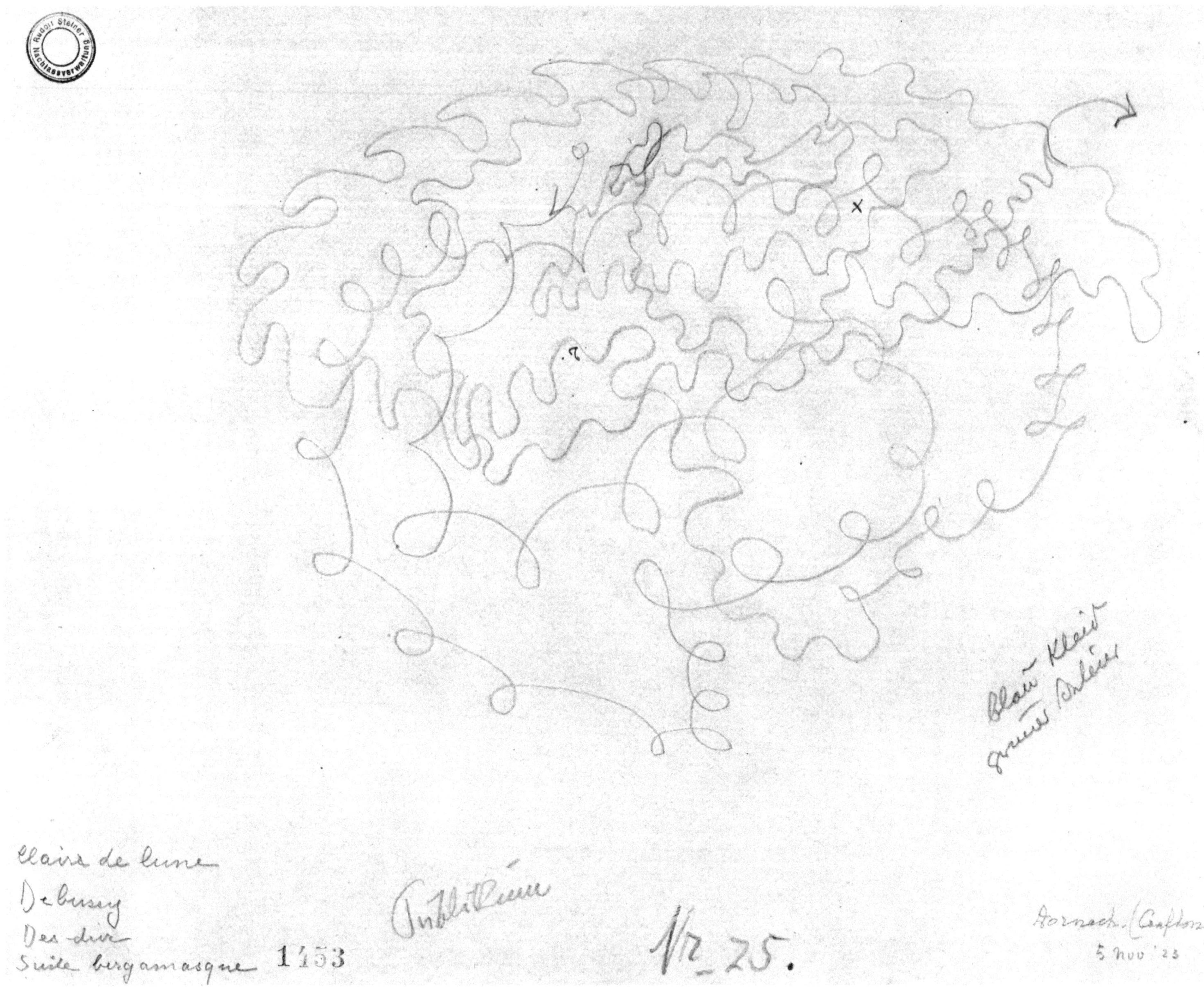

C. Debussy – "Claire de lune," Andante trés expressif, D-flat major

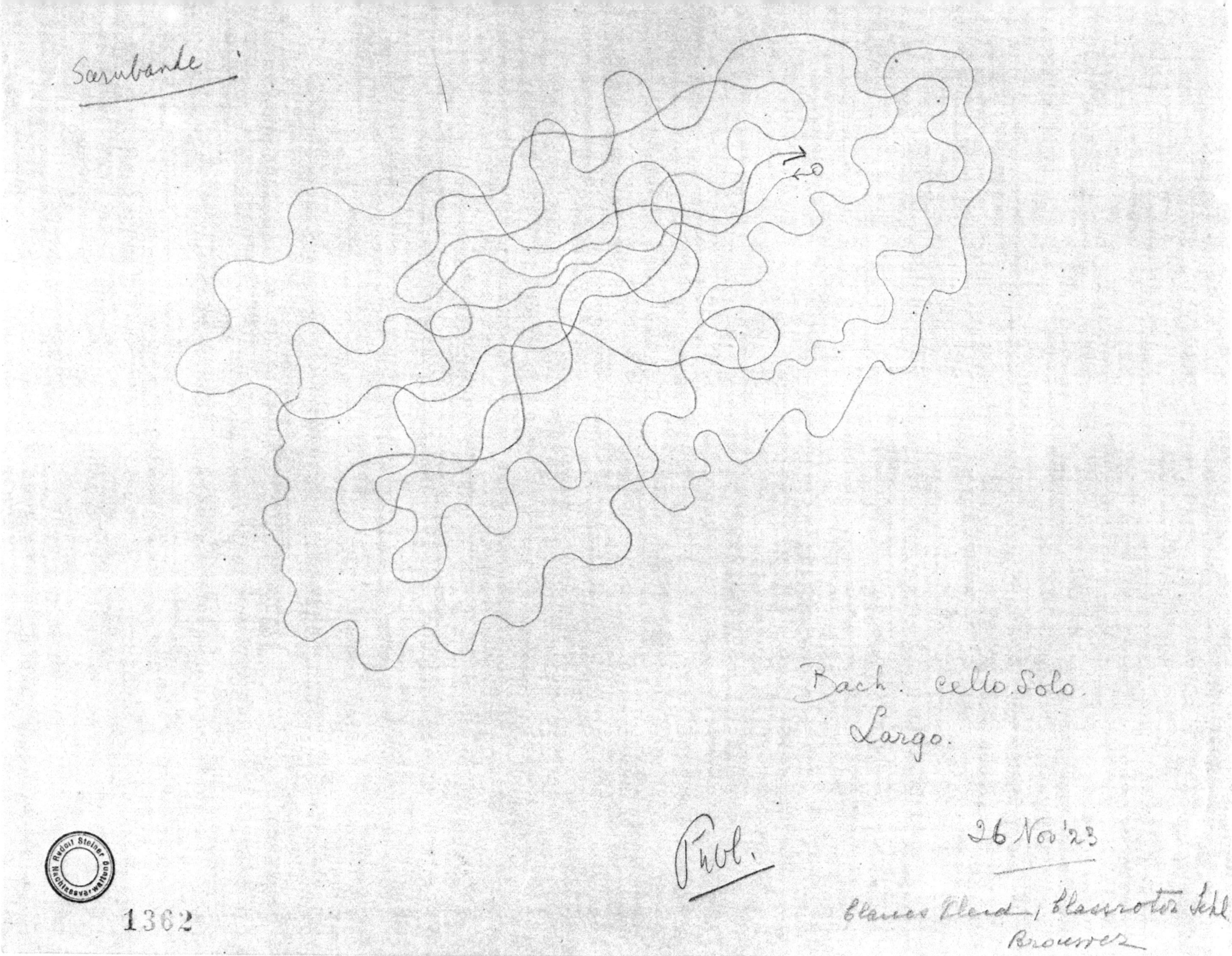

J. S. Bach – Saraband from Suite No. 2 for violoncello solo, D minor

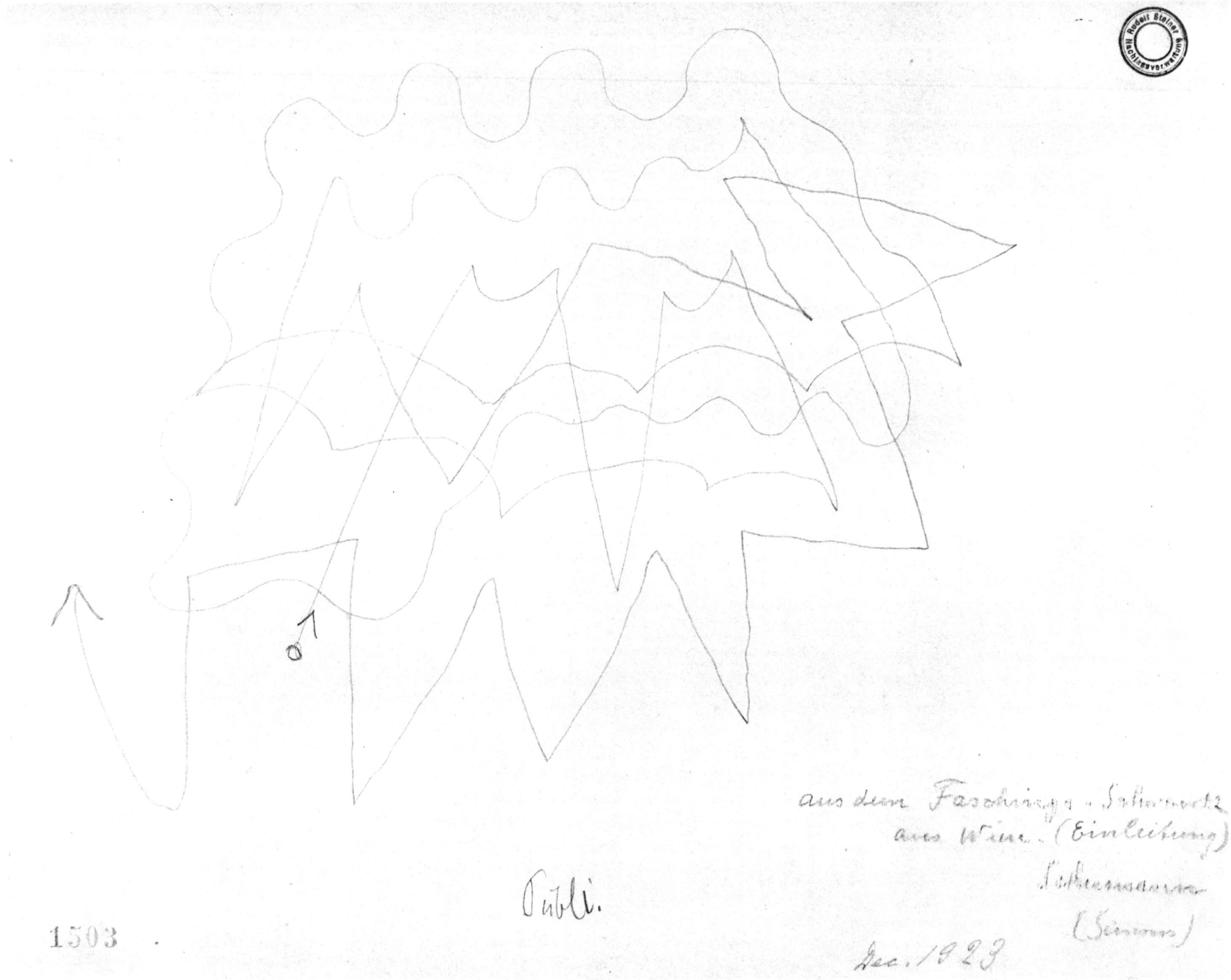

R. Schumann – Allegro (Introduction) from *Faschingschwank aus Wien* [Carnival prank from Vienna], Very lively, B major, Op. 26/1

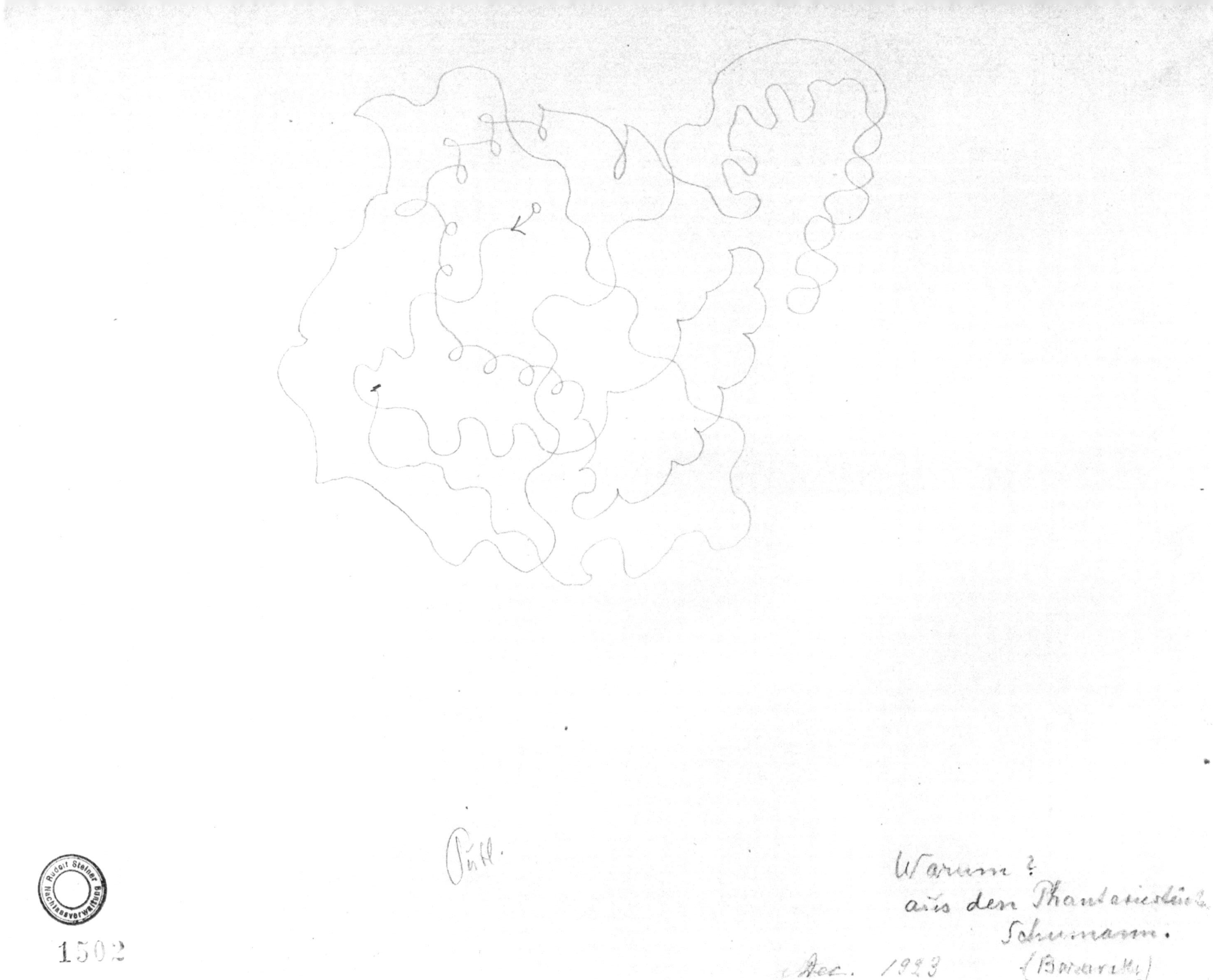

R. Schumann – “Warum?” [Why?] from *Phantasiestücke* [Fantasy pieces], D-flat major, No. 3, Op. 12/3, (Slow and delicate)

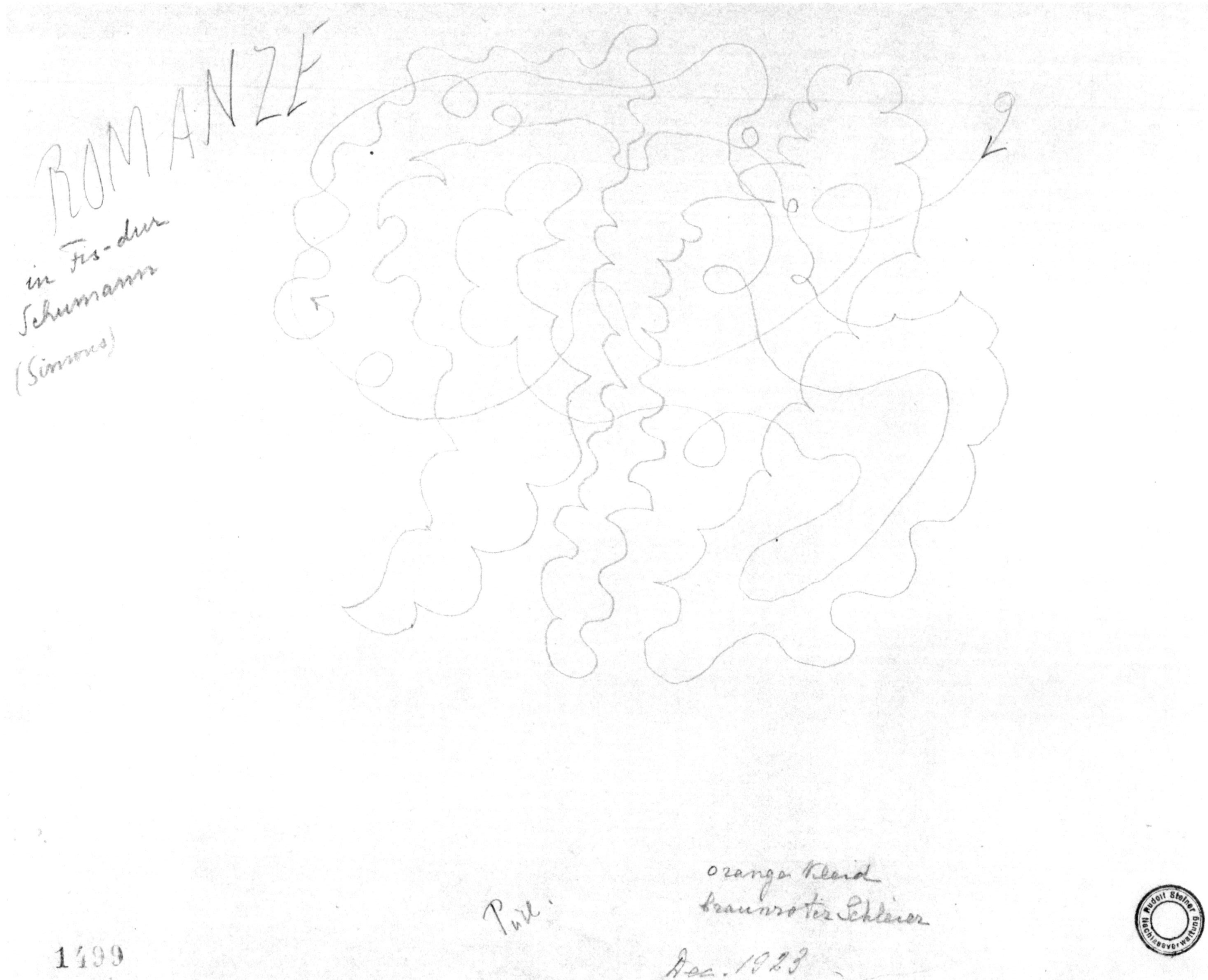

R. Schumann – Romanze [Romance] No. 2, (Simple), F-sharp major, Op. 28/2

F. Kreisler – Prelude in the style of Gaetano Pugnani (1731–1798) from *Klassische Manuskripte für Violine und Klavier* [Classical manuscripts for violin and piano], No. 5

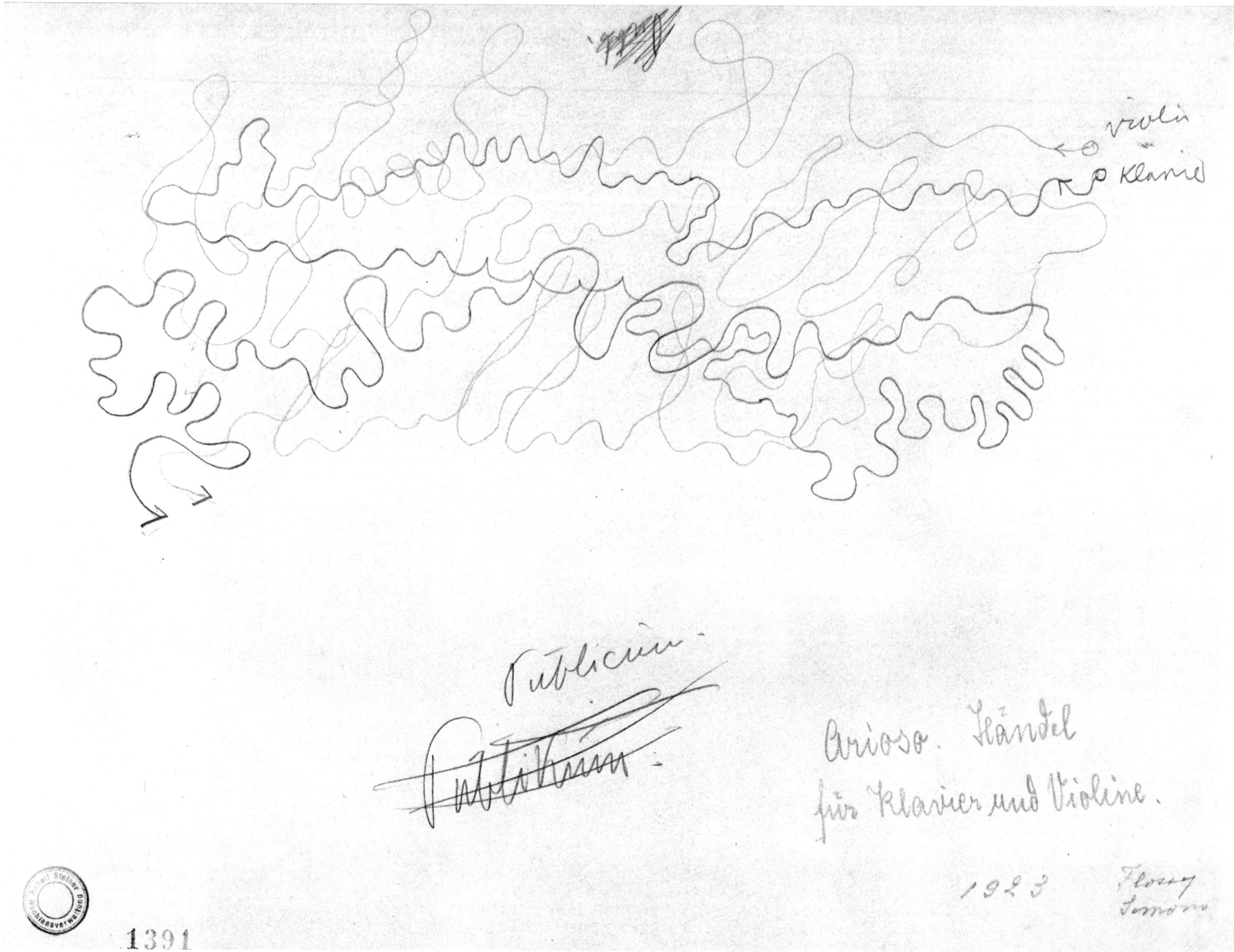

F. G. Händel – Arioso, D major, for violin and piano

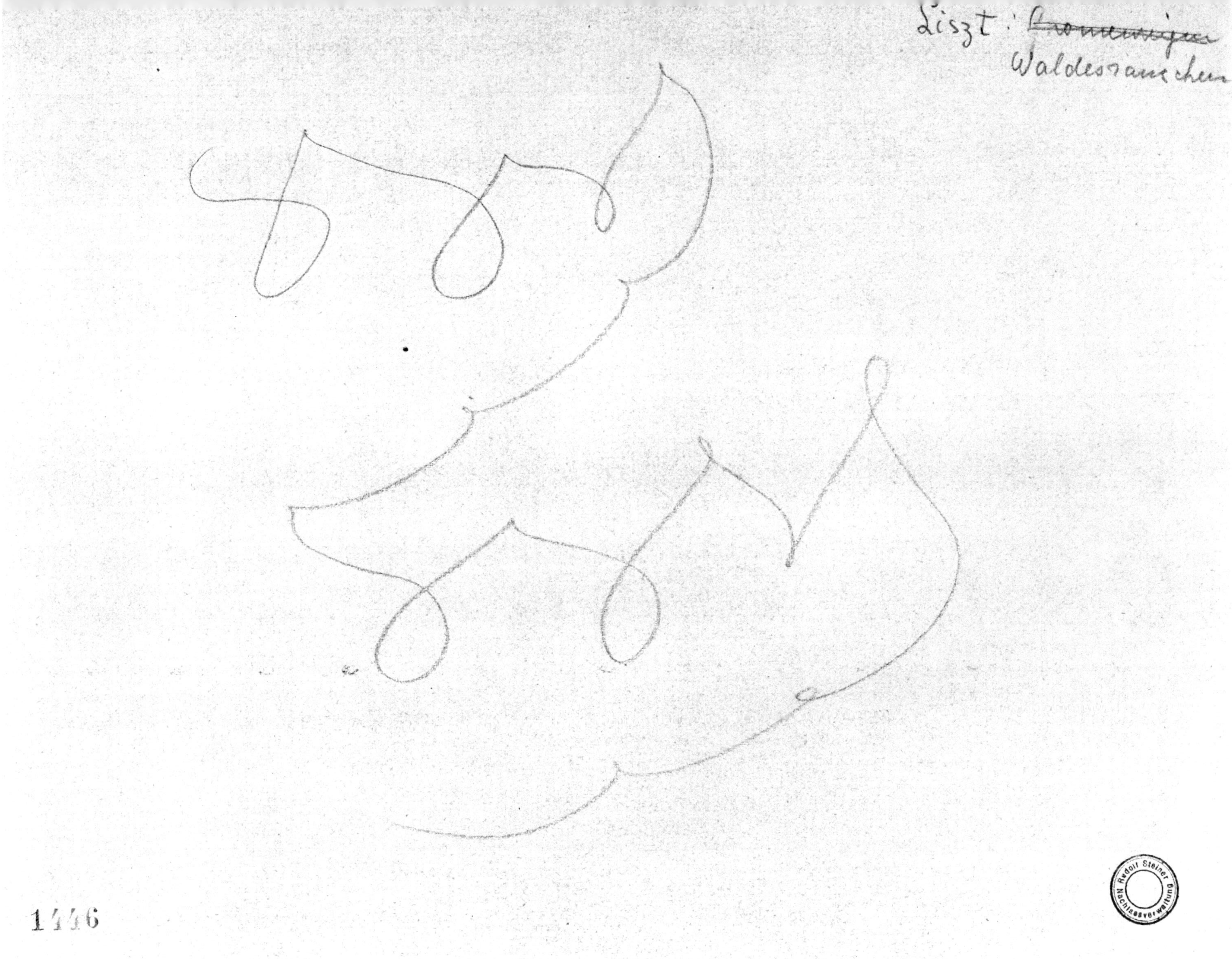

F. Liszt – "Waldesrauschen," [Rustling in the woods], Vivace, Konzertetüde No. 1 [Concert studies]

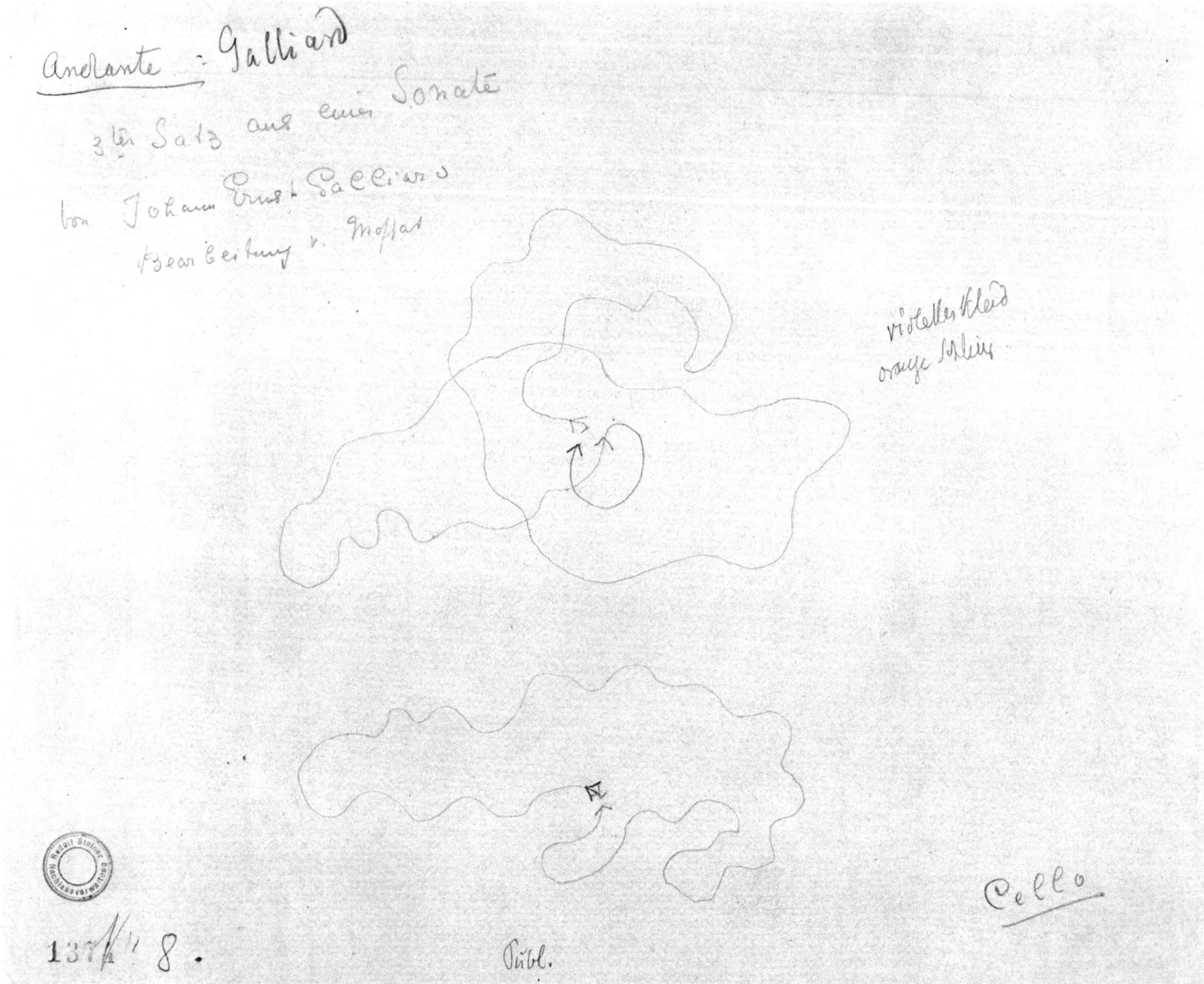

J. E. Galliard – Andante teneramente, F minor, third movement from Sonata No. 3

J. E. Galliard – Allegro spiritoso, fourth movement from Sonata No. 3 for bassoon (violoncello) and basso continuo (piano) (page 1, preliminary)

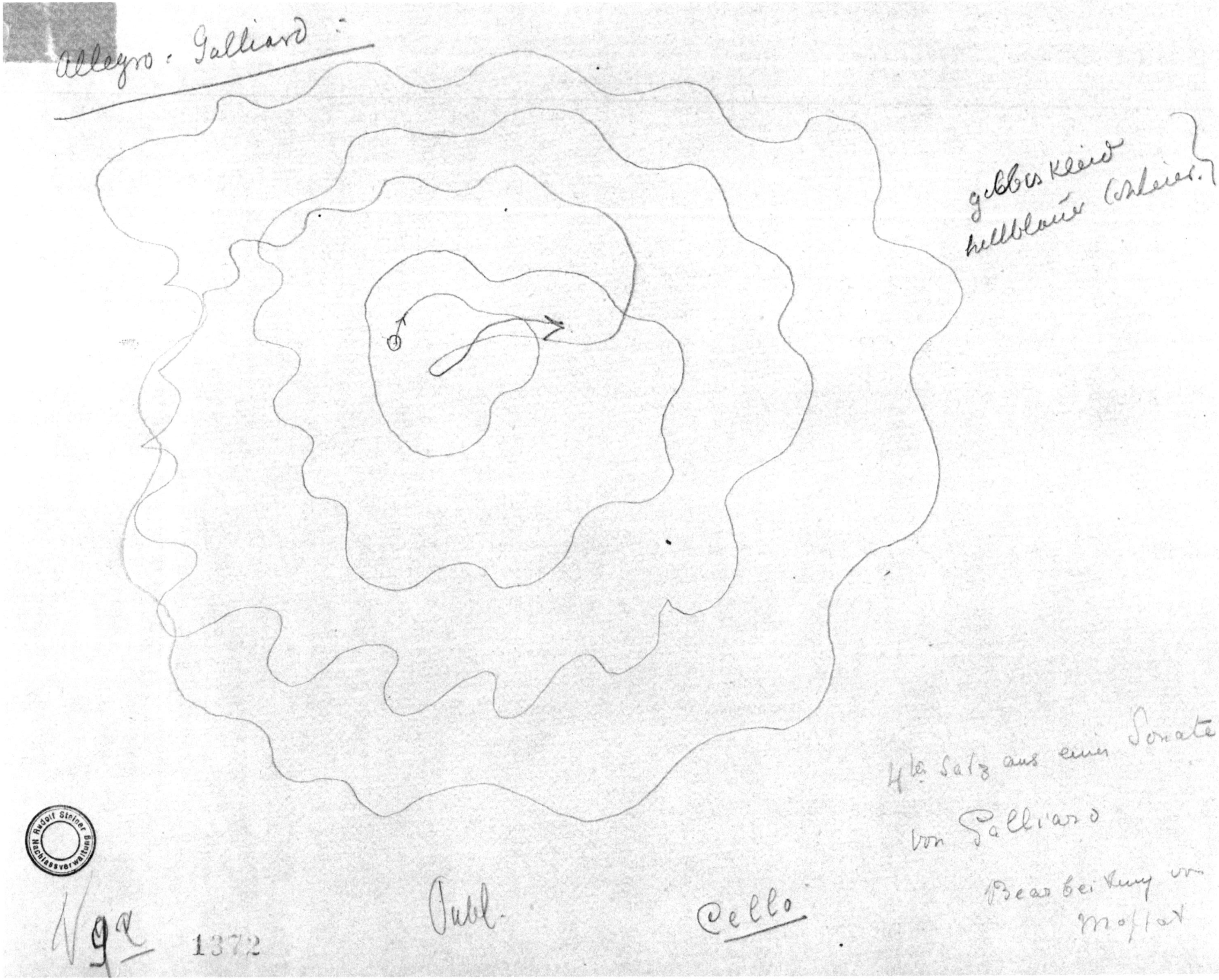

J. E. Galliard – Allegro spiritoso, fourth movement from Sonata No. 3 for bassoon (violoncello) and basso continuo (piano) (page 2, preliminary)

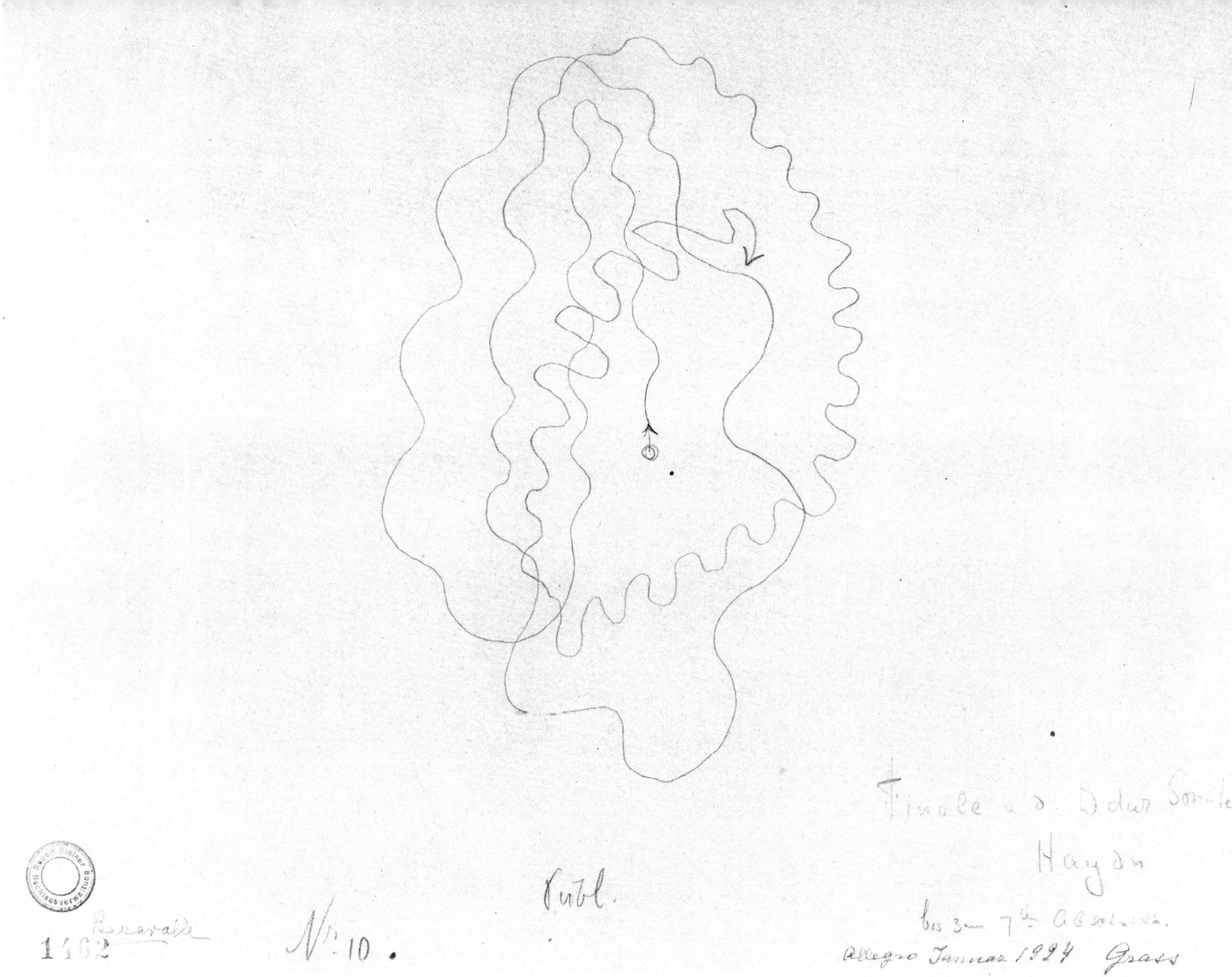

J. Haydn – Finale (Allegro), from the Sonata for Piano, D major

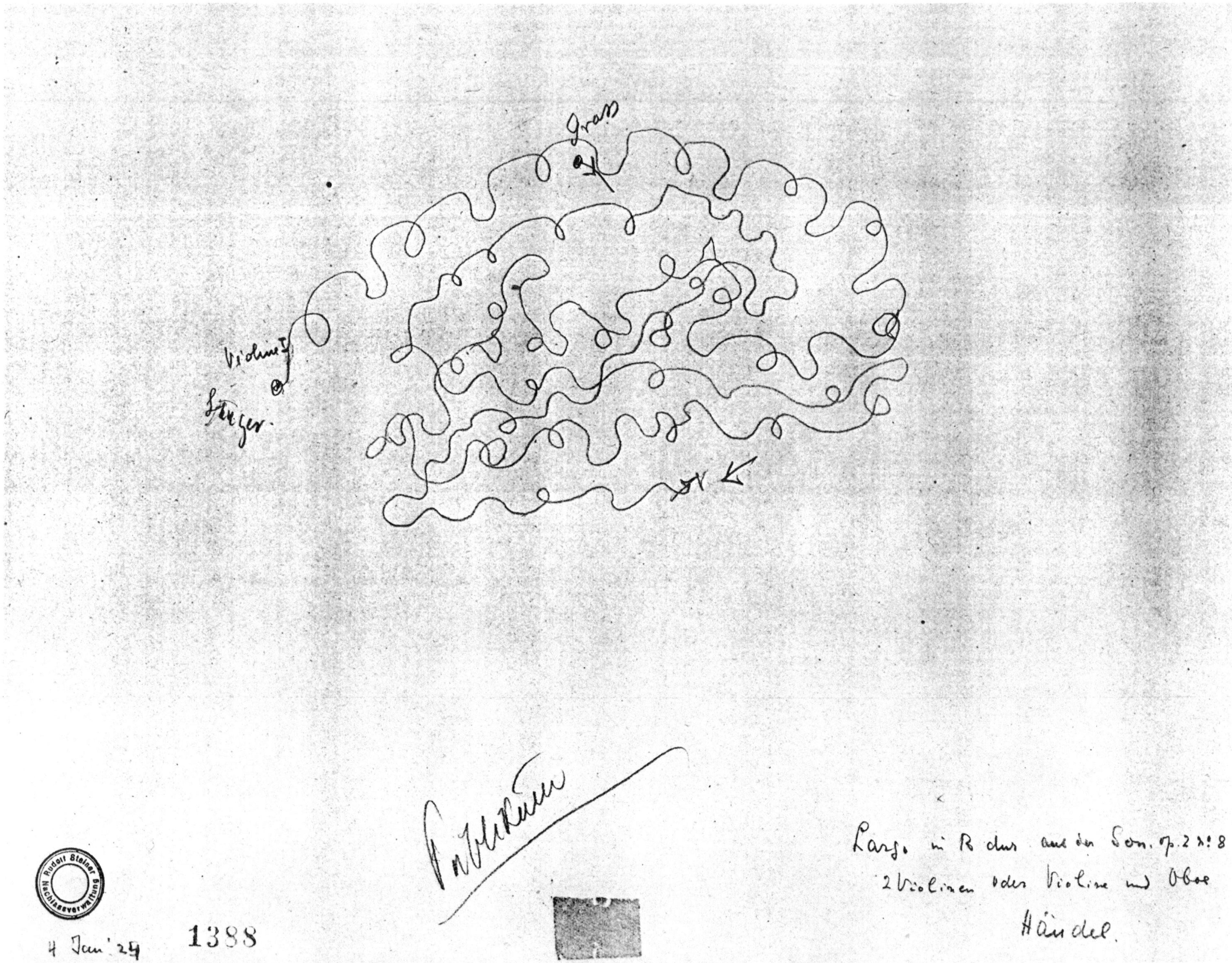

G. F. Händel – Largo, third movement from the Sonata (for violin and oboe), G minor (page 1)

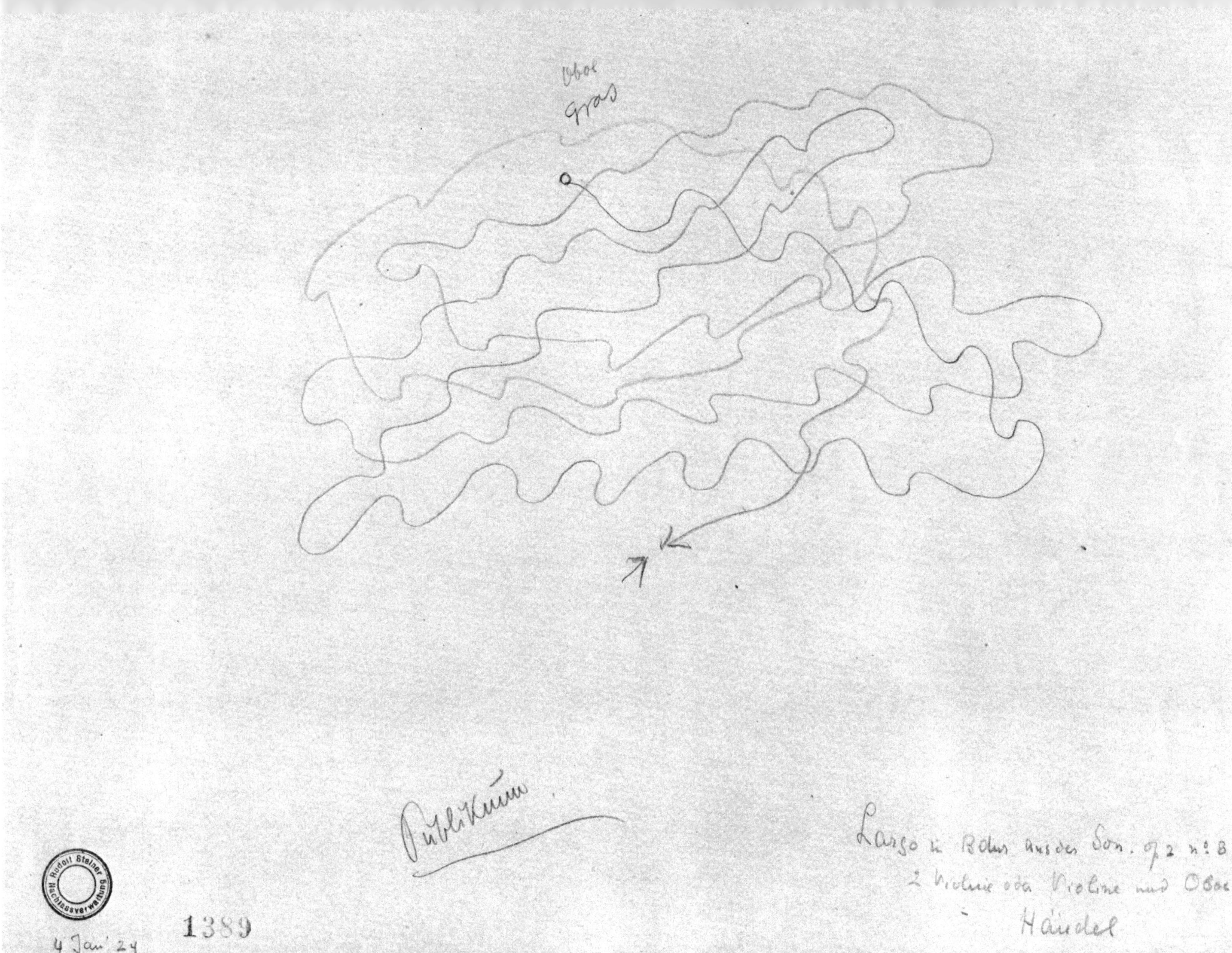

G. F. Händel – Largo, third movement from the Sonata (for violin and oboe), G minor (page 2)

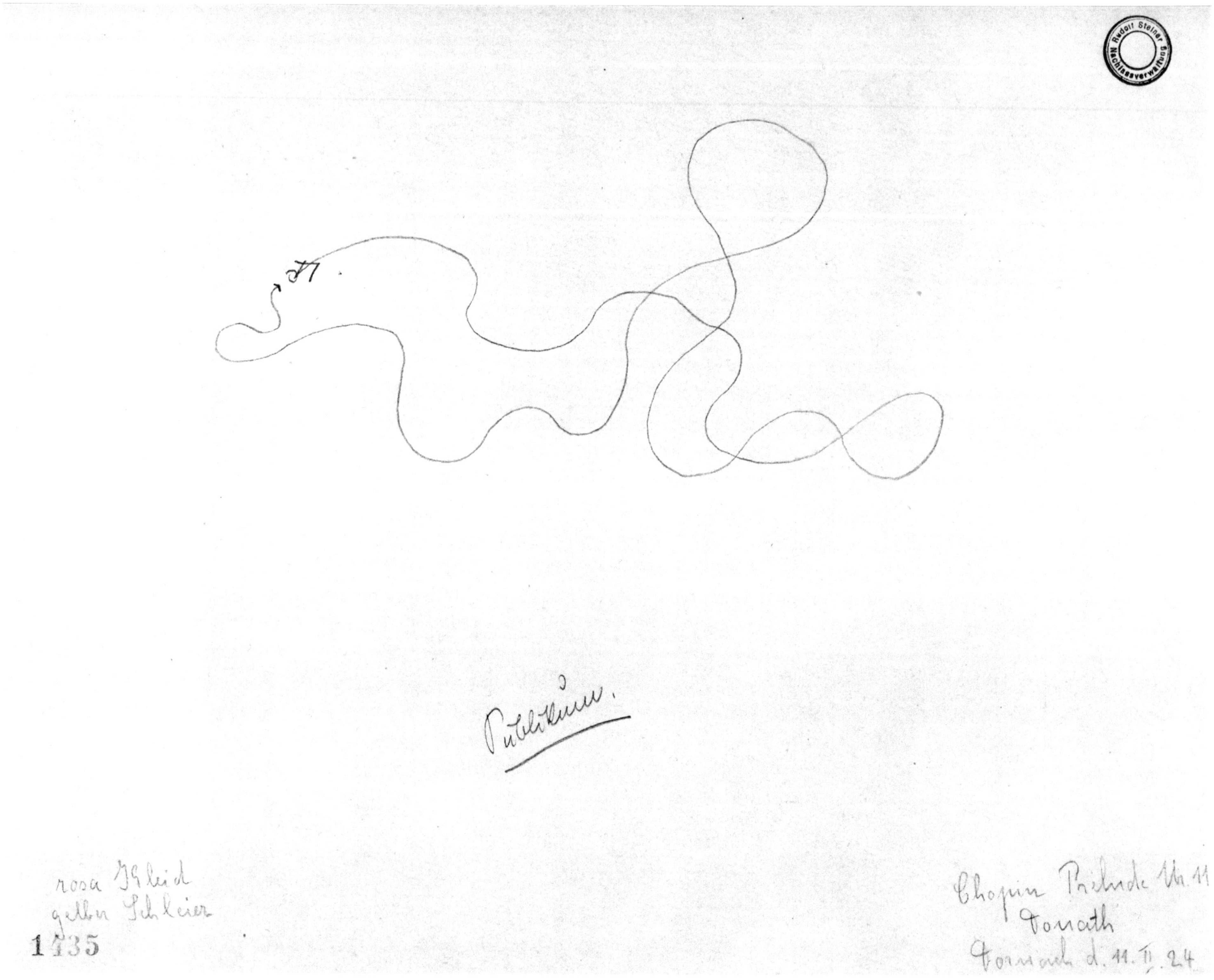

F. Chopin – Prelude No. 11, Vivace, B major, Op. 28/11

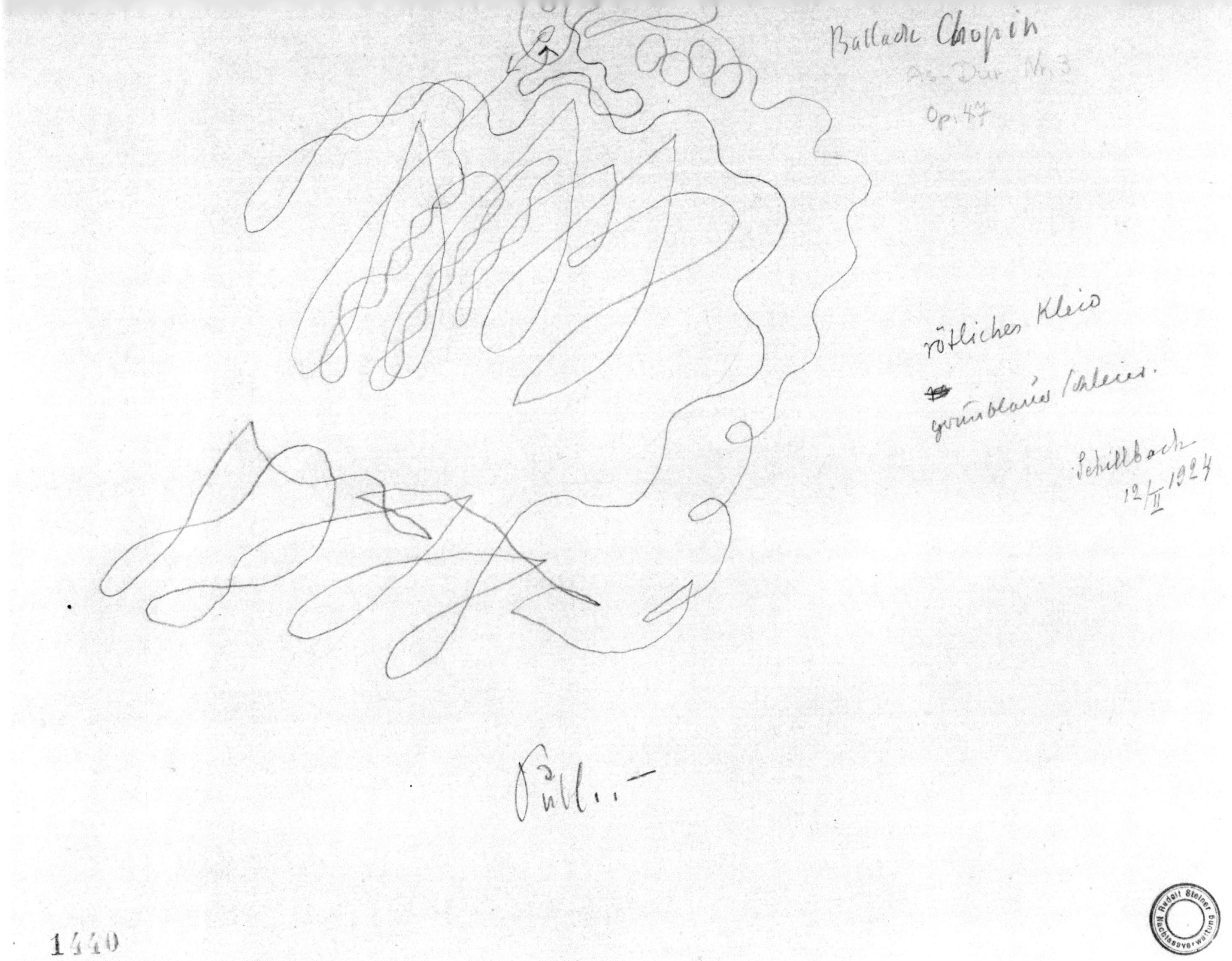

F. Chopin – Ballade No. 3, Allegretto, A-flat major, Op. 47

J. Stuten – "Schmetterlinge," [Butterflies] (light)

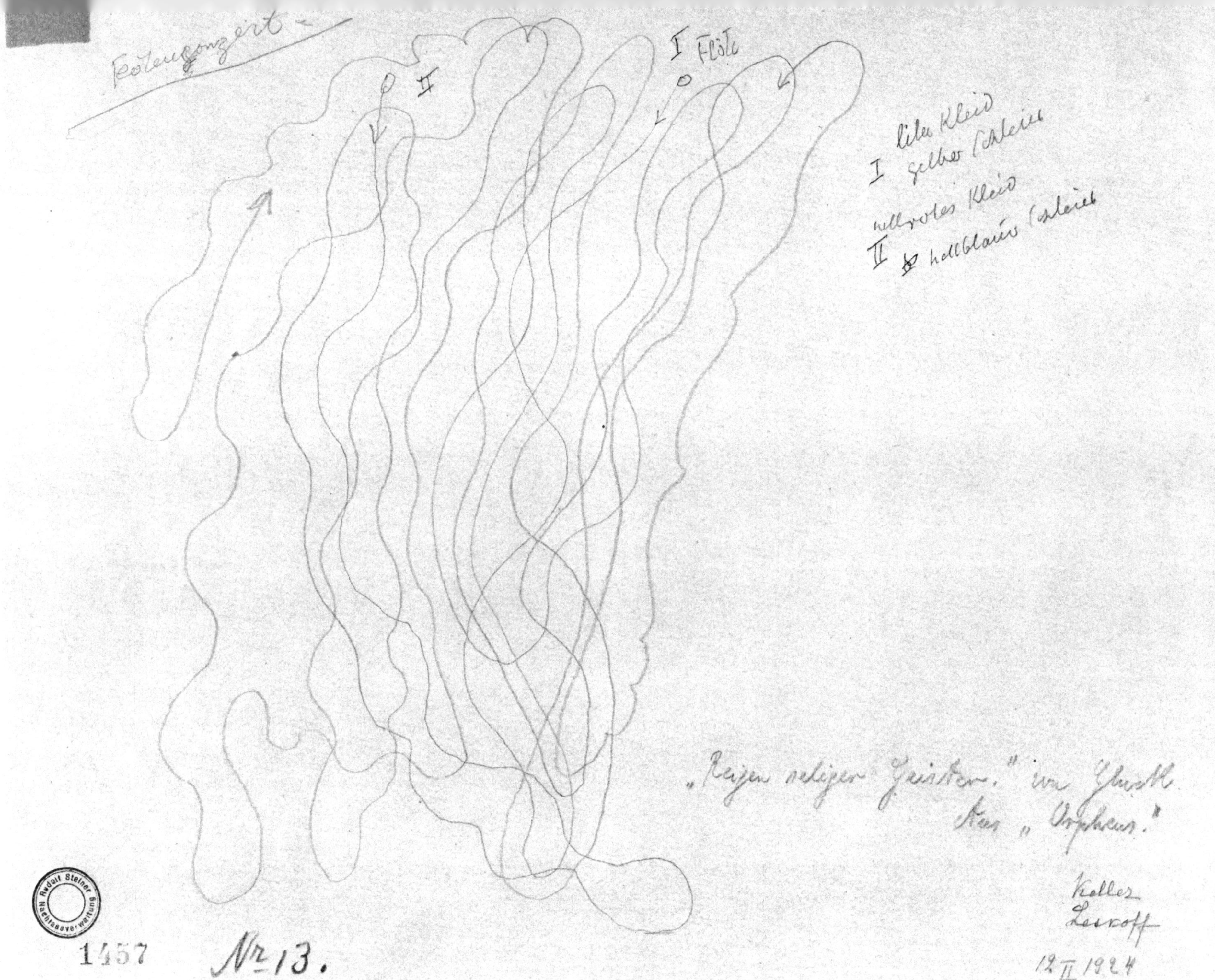

C. W. Gluck – "Reigen seliger Geister," [Dance of the blessed spirits], Andante, from the opera *Orpheus und Eurydike*

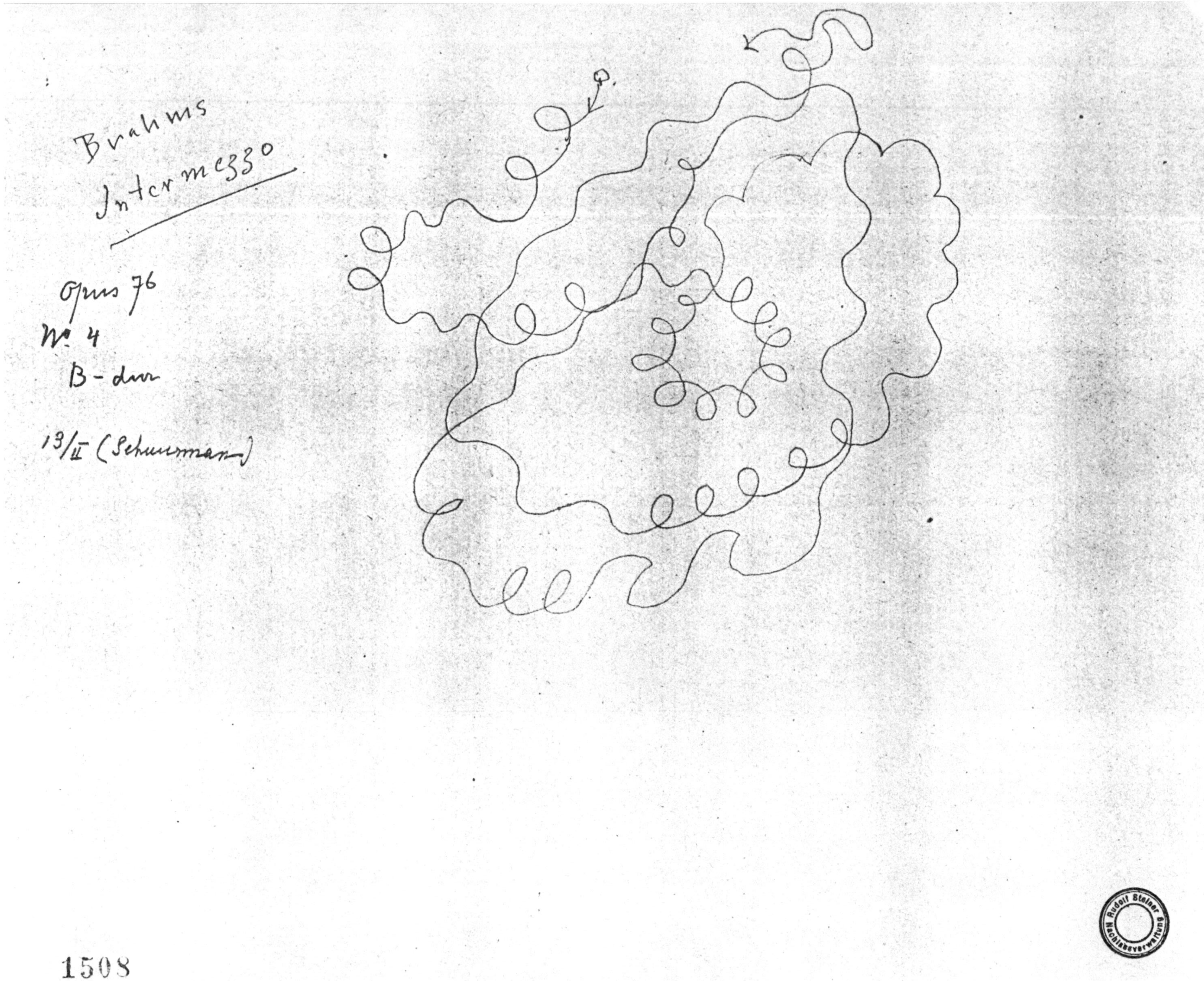

J. Brahms – Intermezzo, Allegretto grandioso, B major, from *Acht Klavierstücke* [Eight piano pieces], Op. 76/4

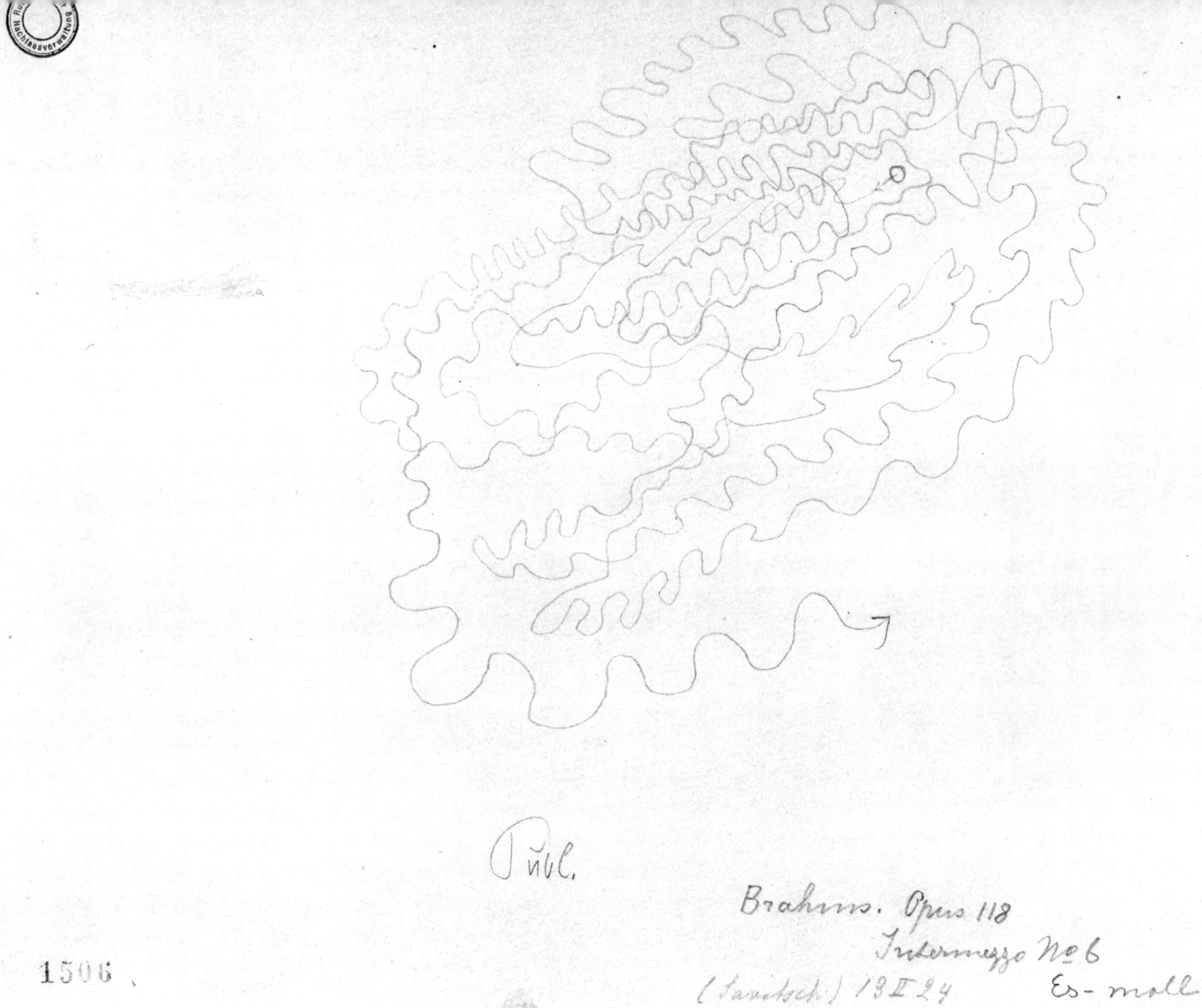

J. Brahms – Intermezzo, Andante, largo e mesto, E-flat minor, No. 6 from *Sechs Klavierstücke* [Six piano pieces], Op. 118/6

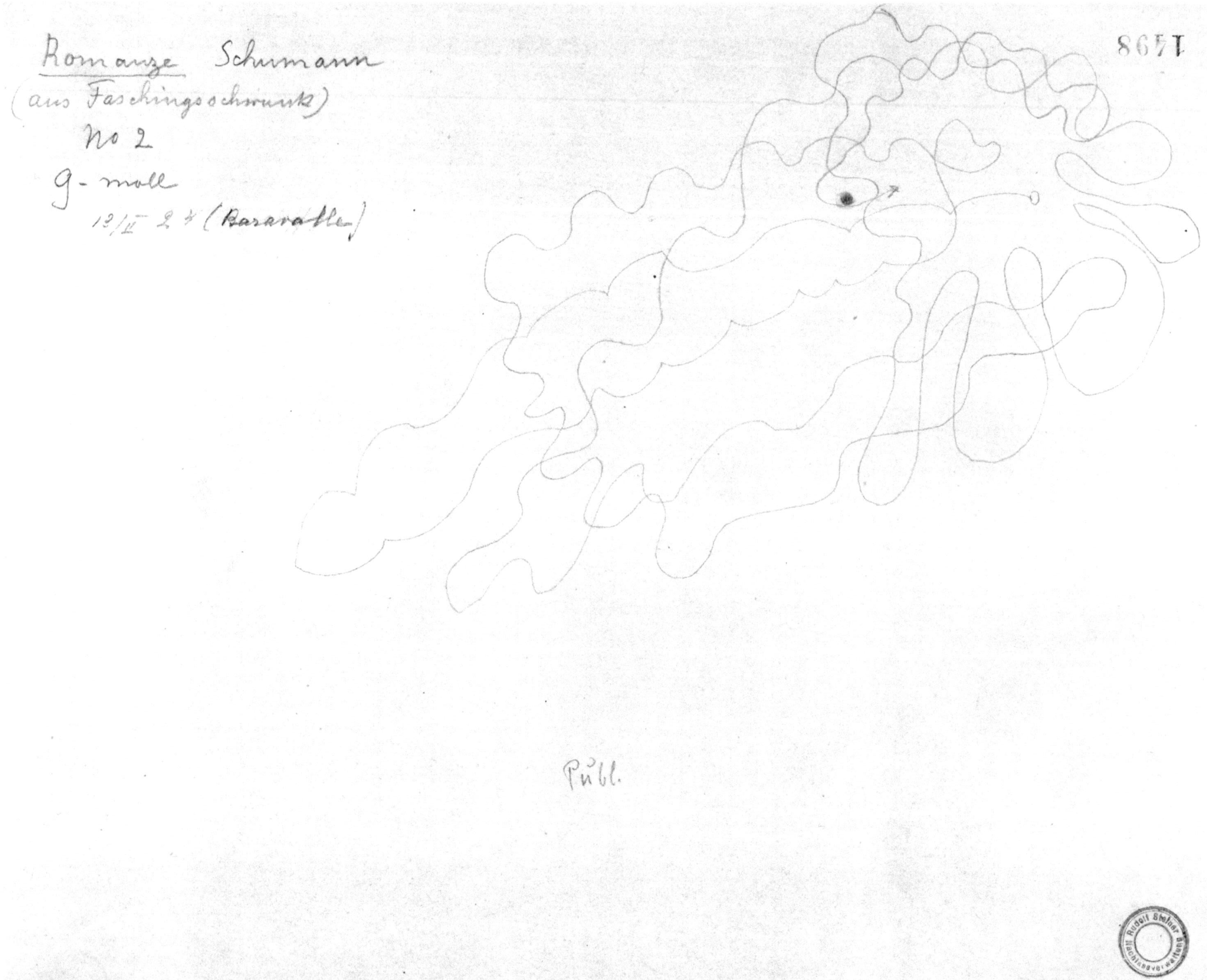

R. Schumann – Romanze, G minor, from *Faschingschwank aus Wien*, [Carnival prank from Vienna], Op. 26/2

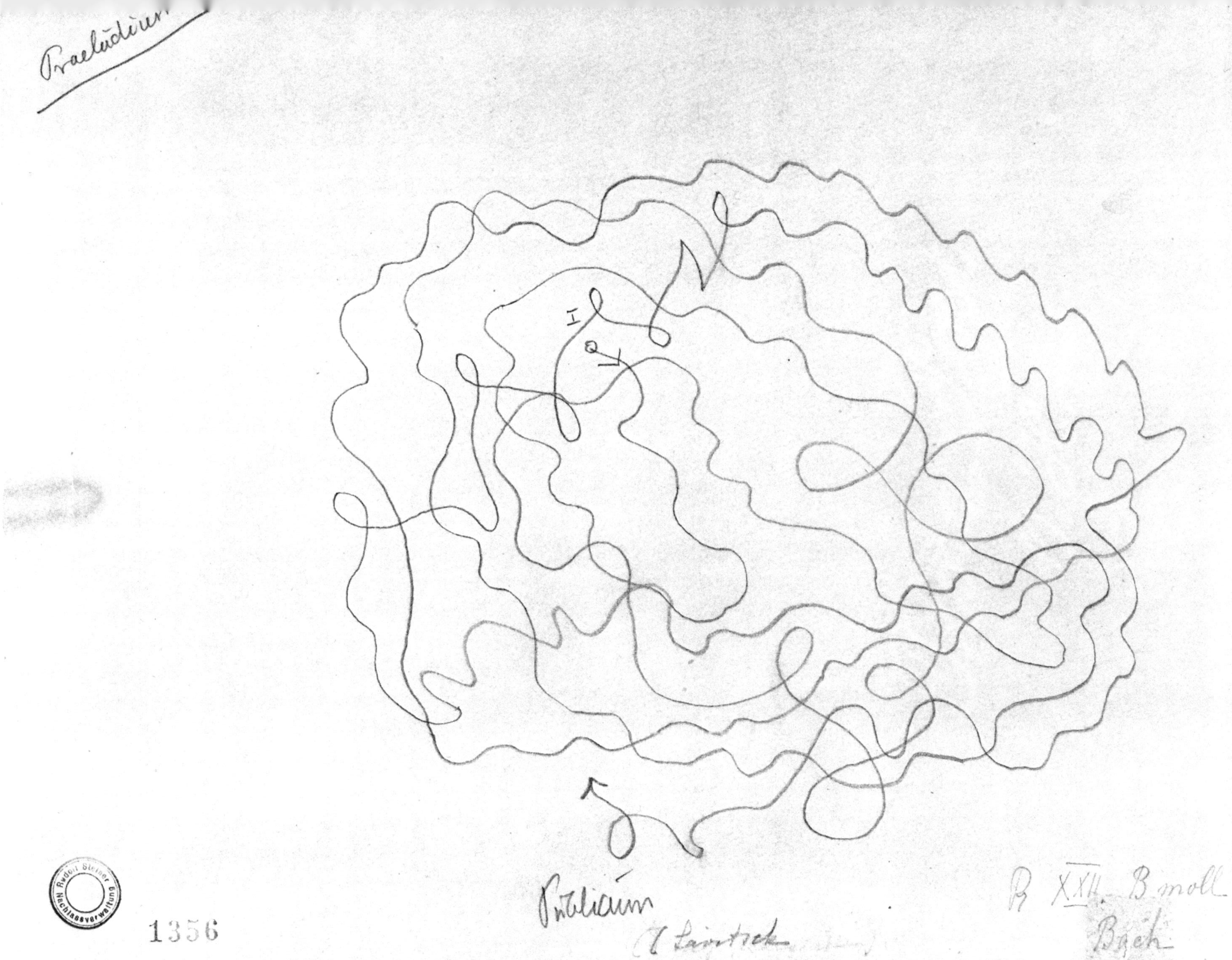

J. S. Bach – Prelude No. 22, B minor, from the *Well-Tempered Clavier II*

G. Tartini – Larghetto affettuoso, first movement from the *Teufelstriller-Sonata* [Devil's trill sonata], G minor

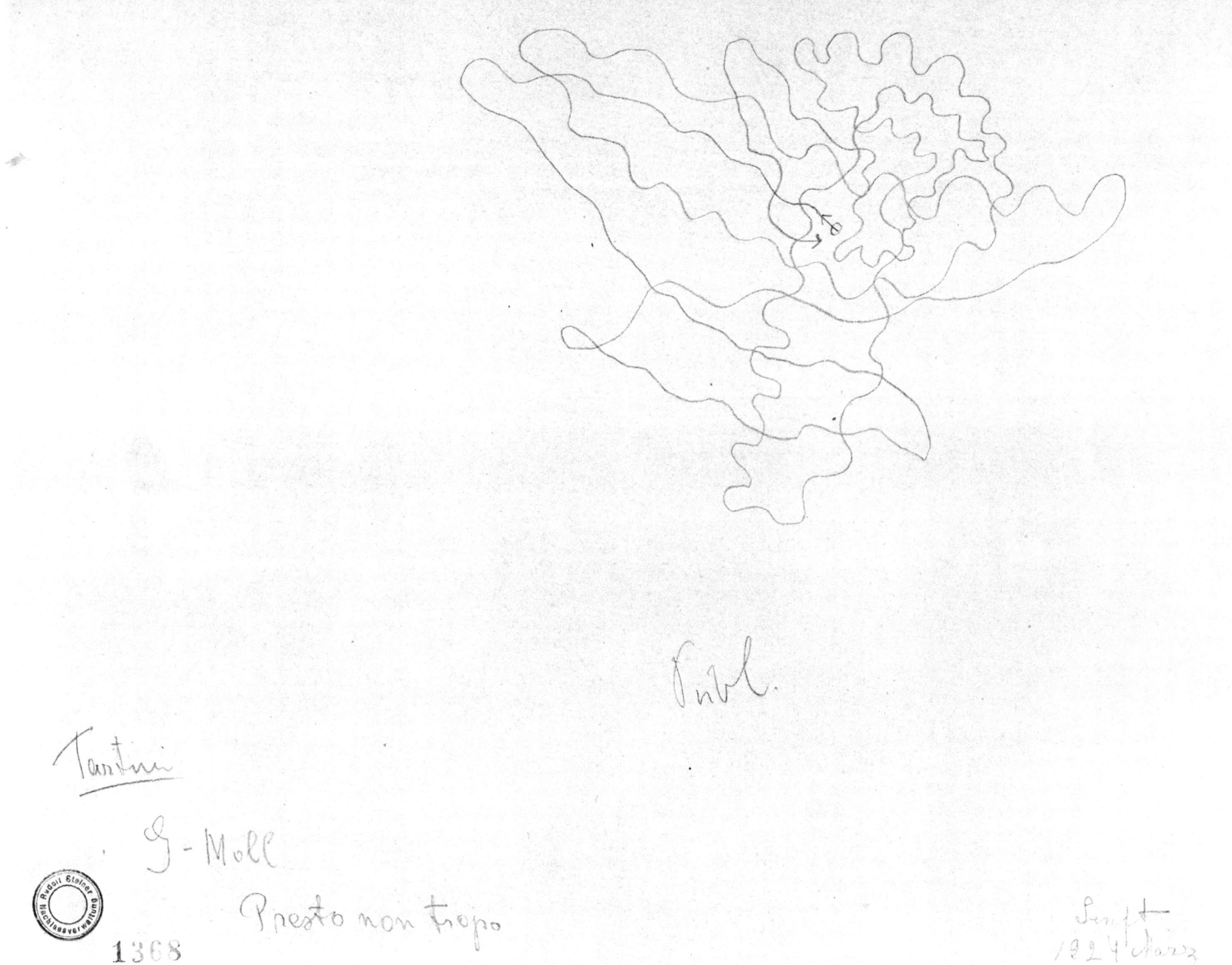

G. Tartini – Presto non troppo (con fuoco), second movement from Sonata (Didonc abbadonata), G minor

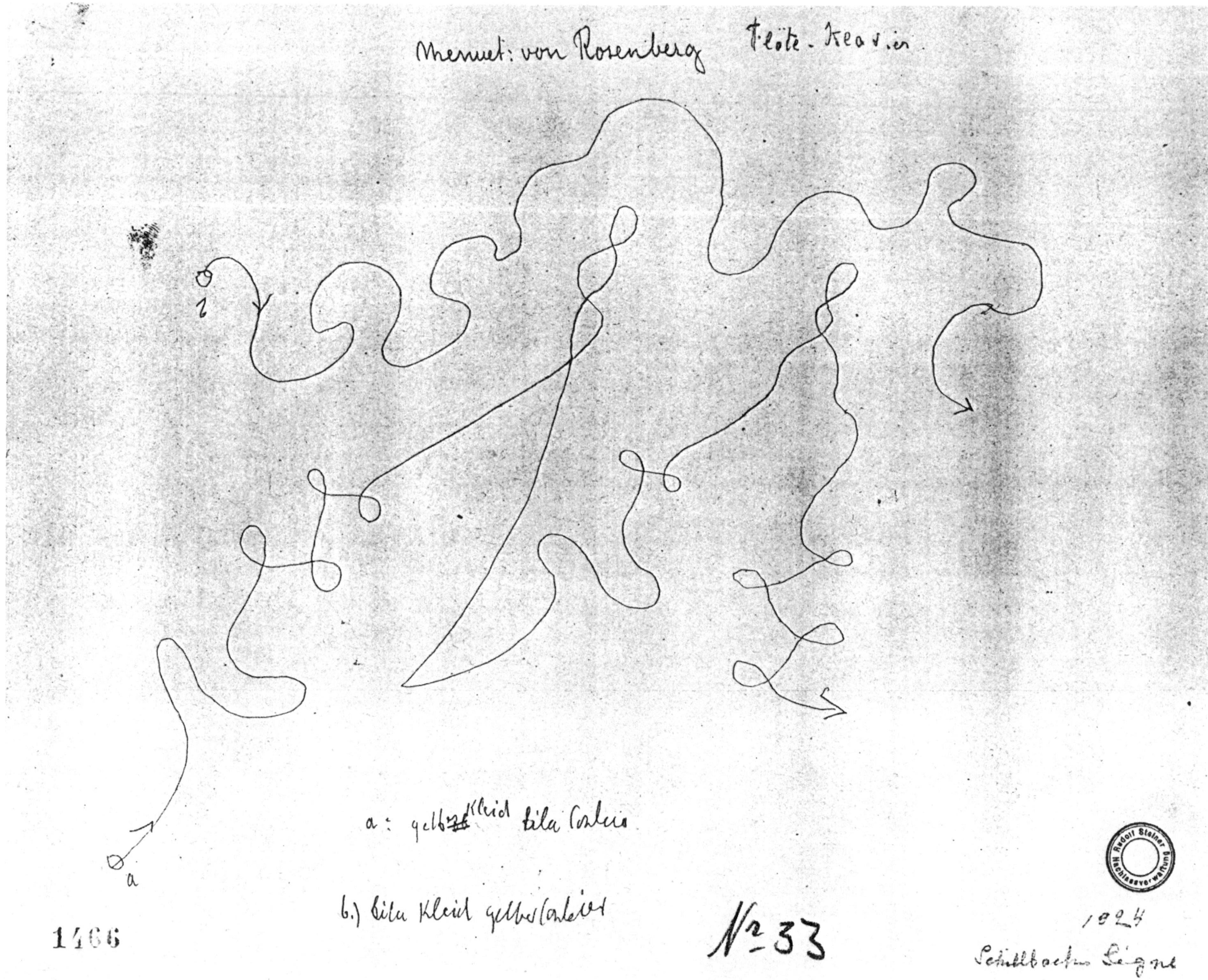

W. Rosenberg – Minuet based on the song: "Ehrlichkeit währt am längsten" [Honesty lasts the longest], for flute and piano

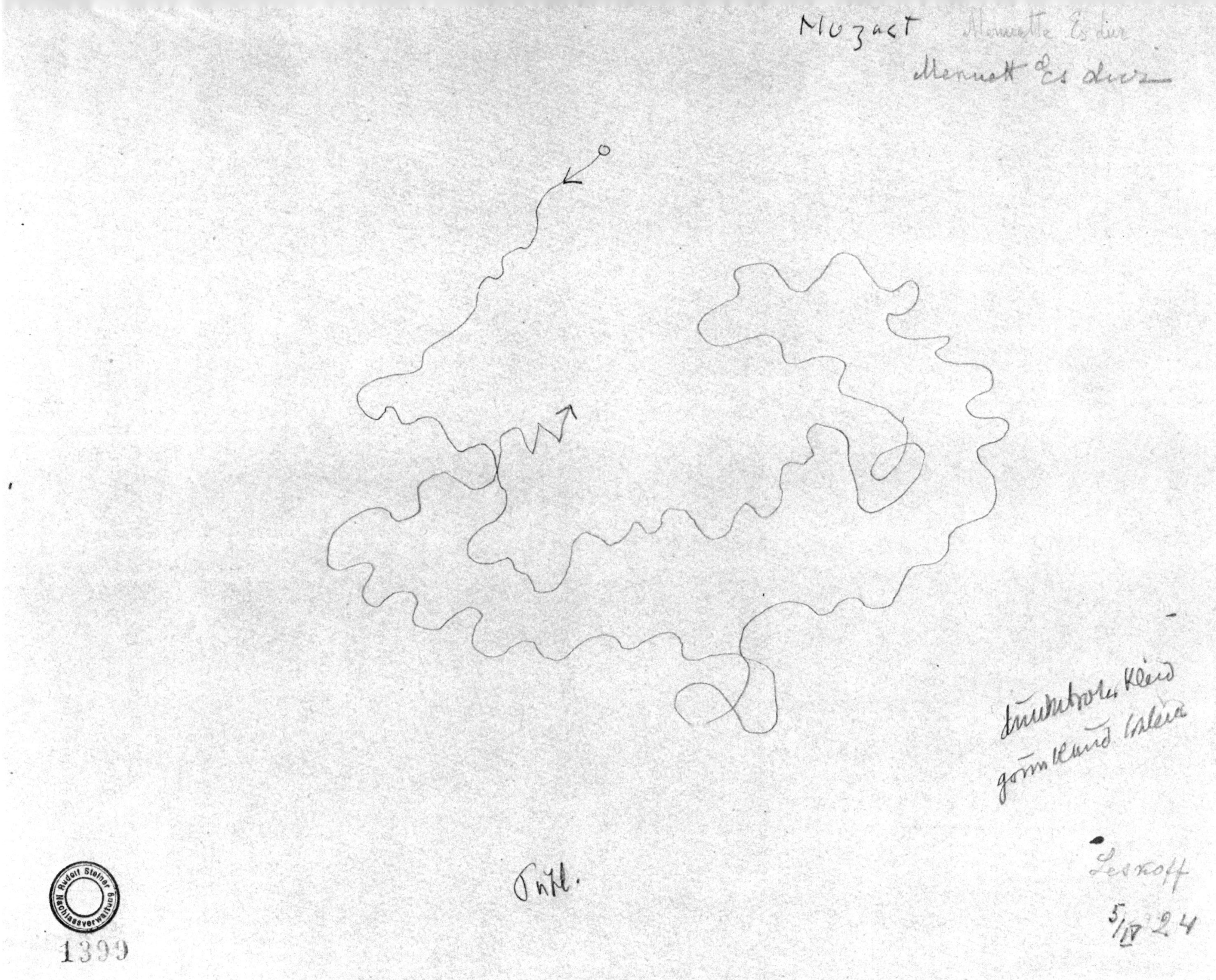

F. Bendel – "Mozart," Menuet favori, un poco maestoso, E-flat major, Op. 14/2

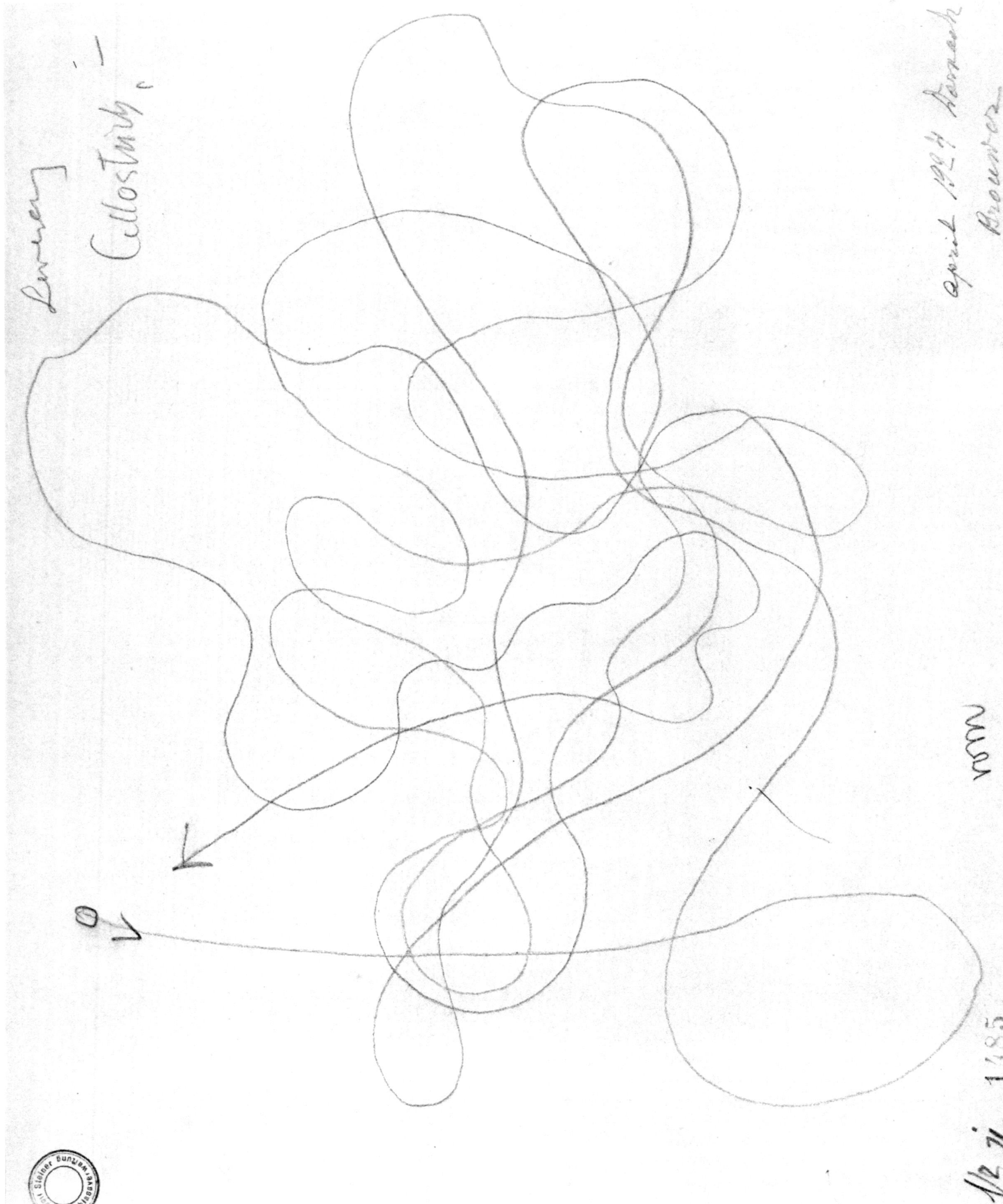

W. Lewerenz – Andante, for violoncello and piano

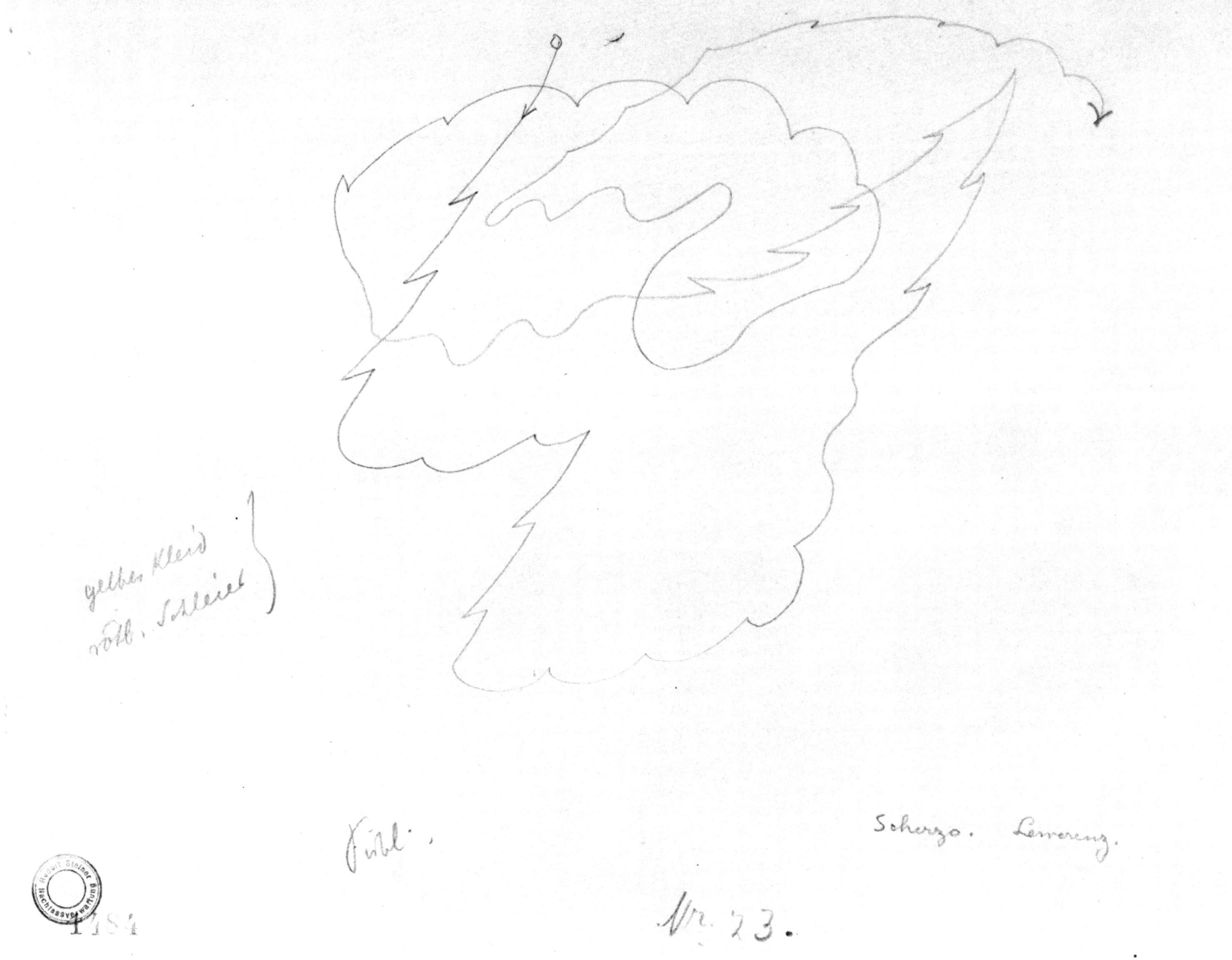

W. Lewerenz – Scherzo, for violoncello and piano

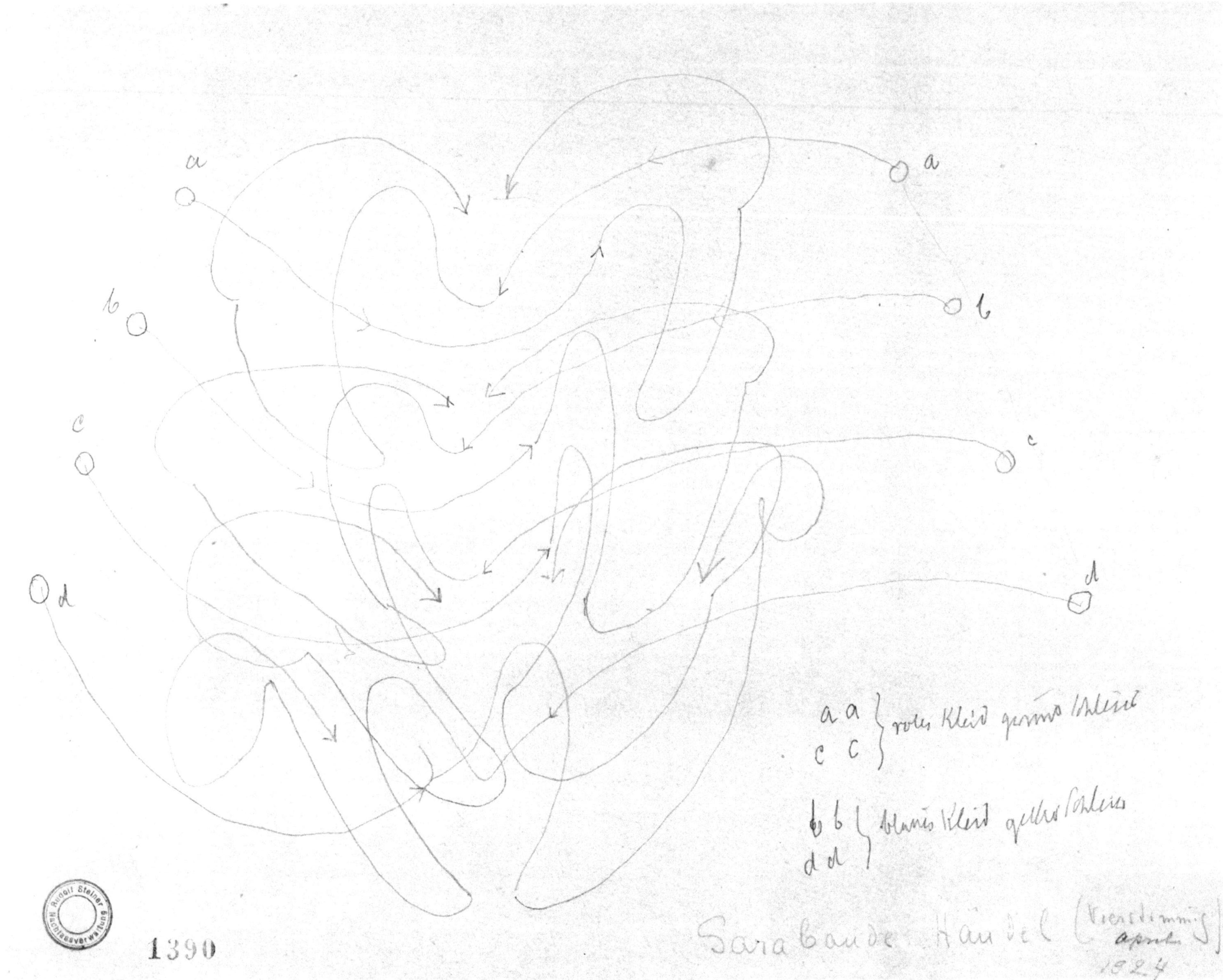

G. F. Händel – Saraband from Suite No. 11 in D minor

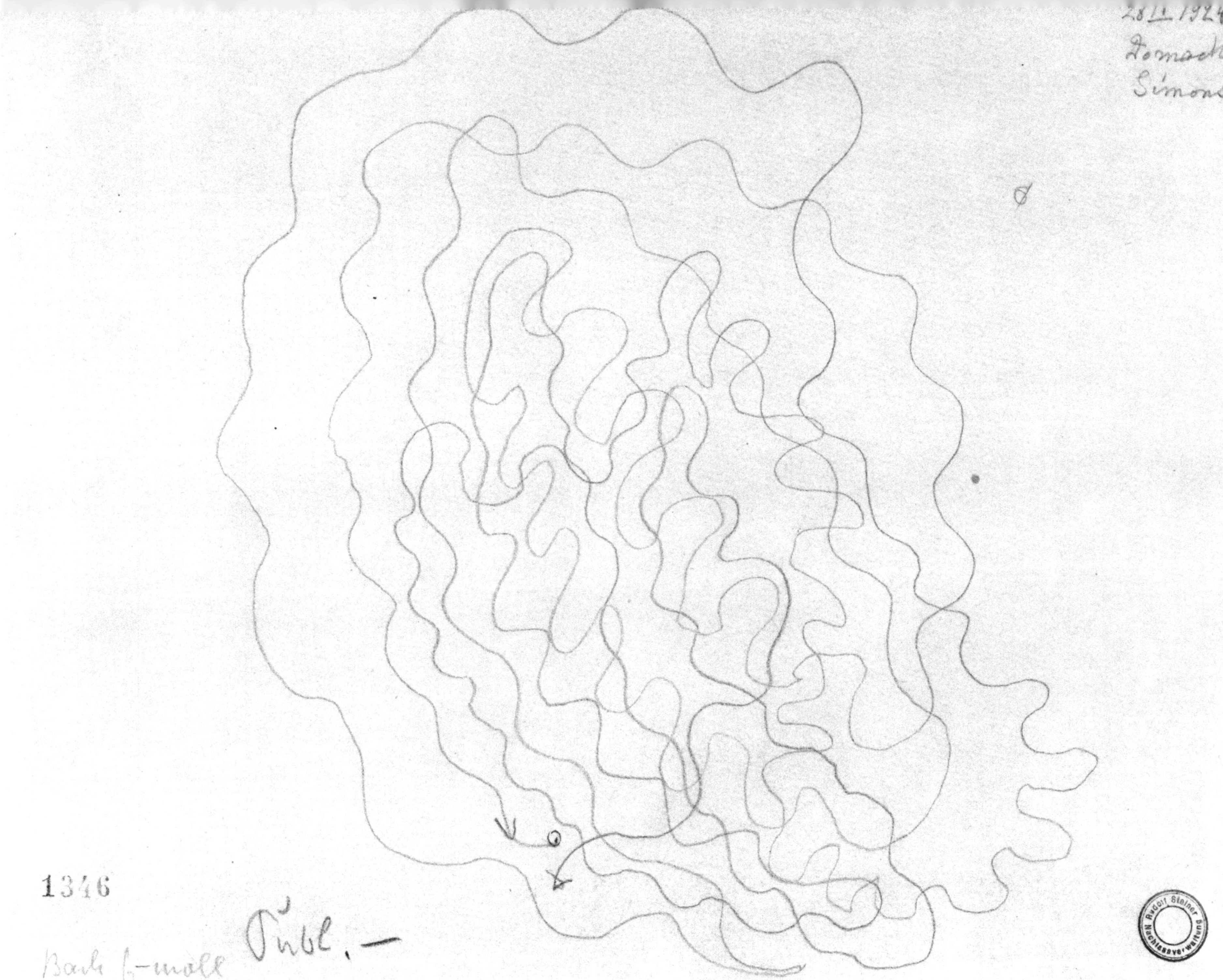

J. S. Bach – Prelude No.12, F minor, from the *Well-Tempered Clavier I*

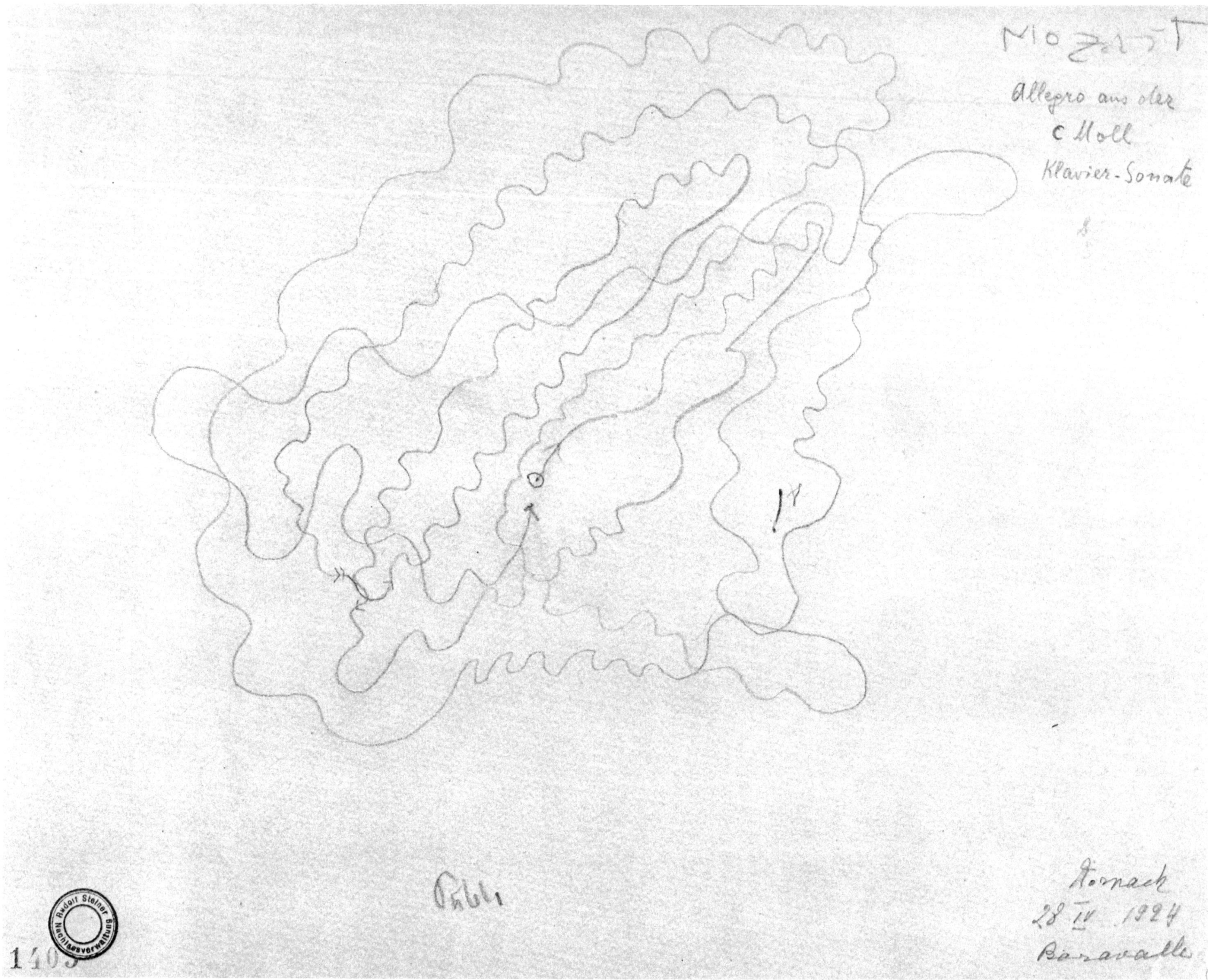

W. A. Mozart – Molto Allegro, first movement from Sonata No. 14, C minor

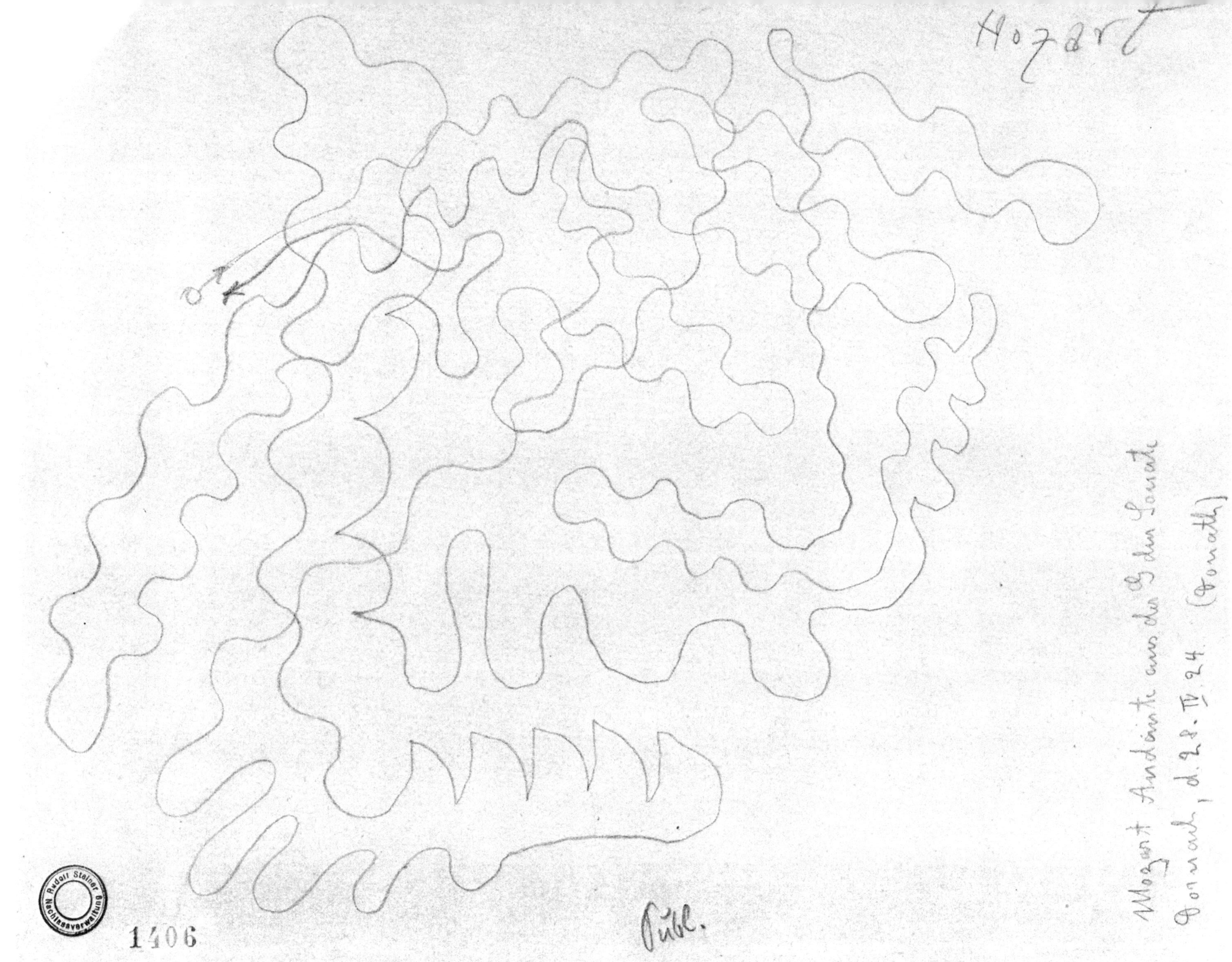

W. A. Mozart – Andante, second movement from Sonata No. 5, G major

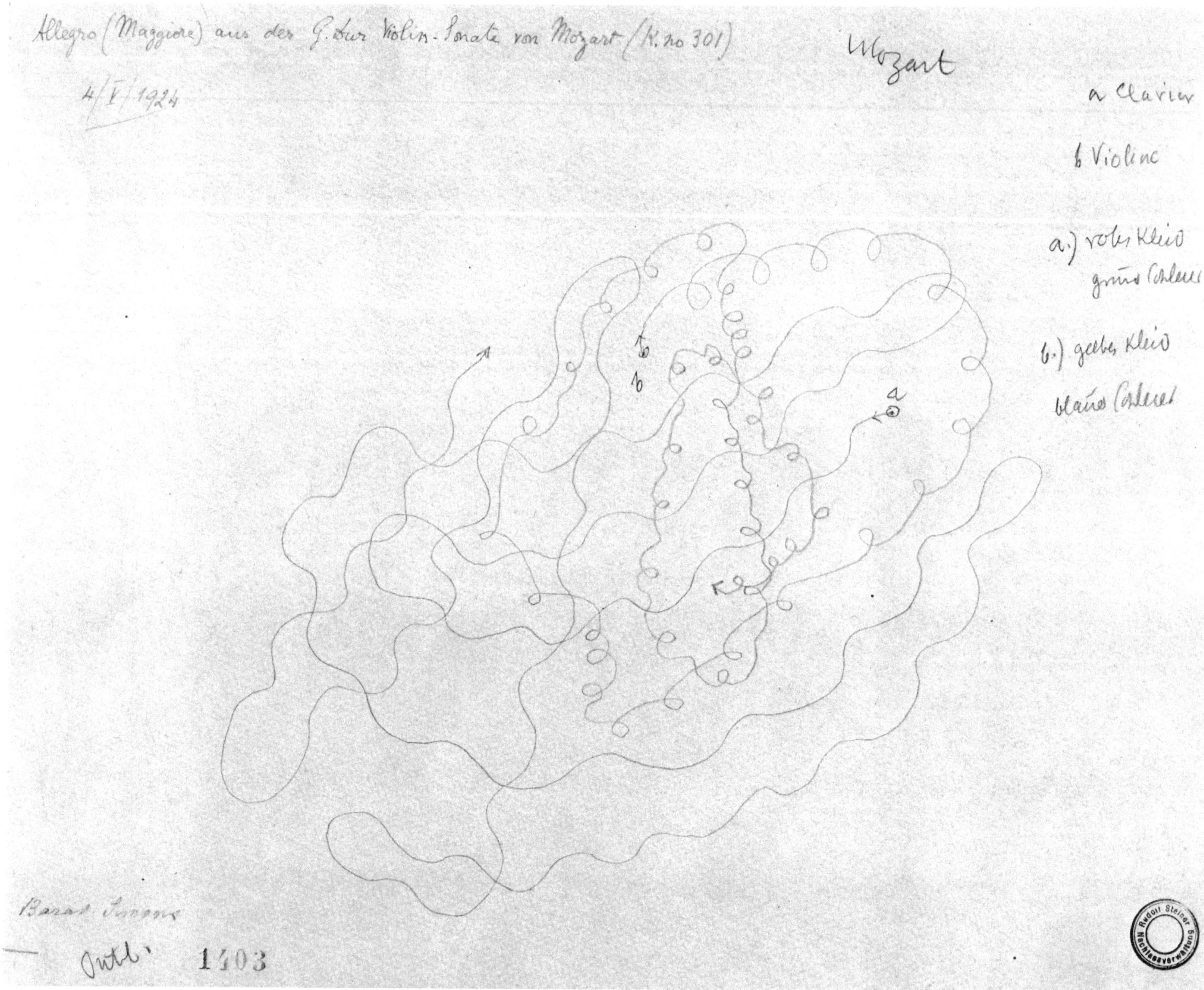

W. A. Mozart – Allegro maggiore, third movement from Violin Sonata, G major

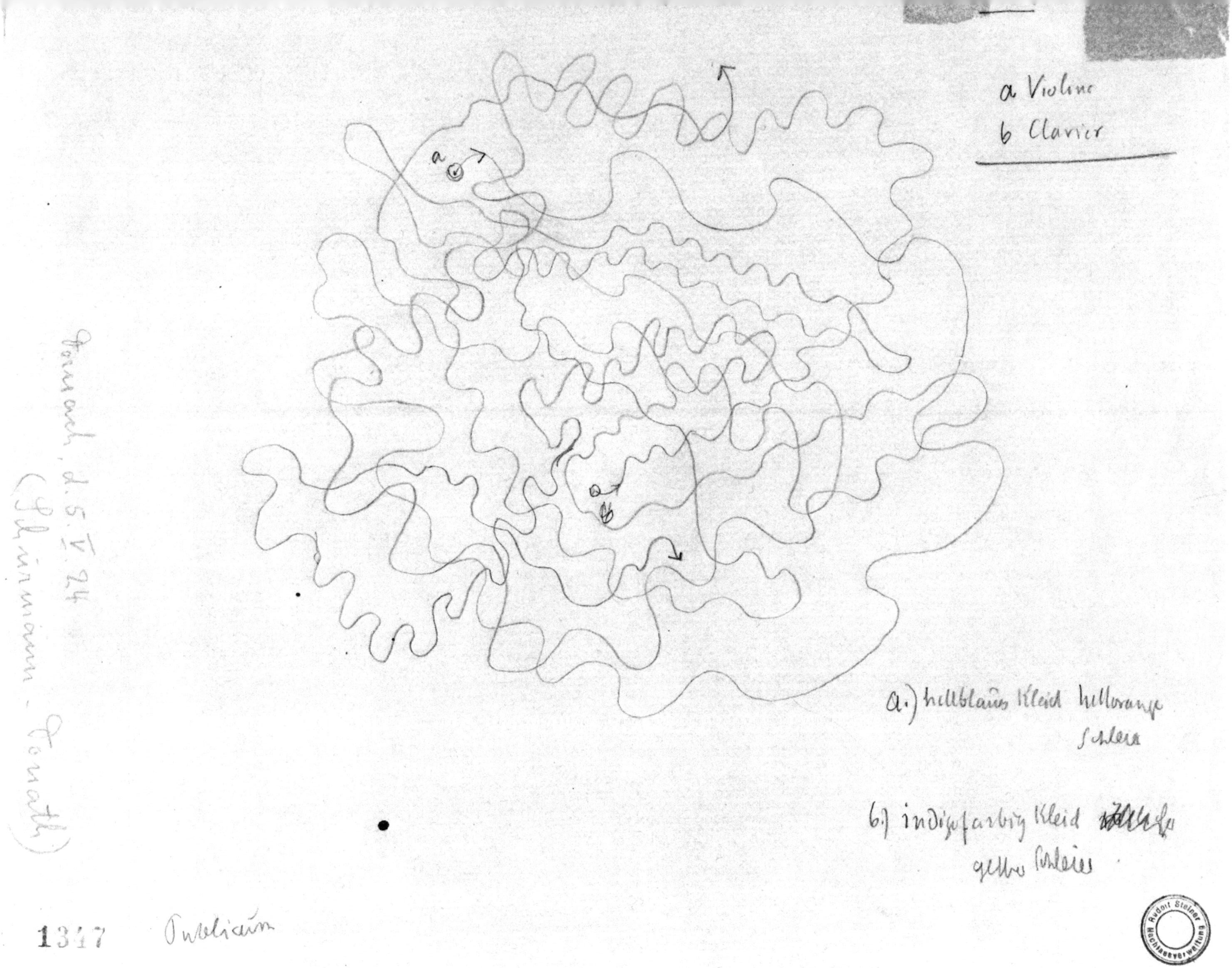

J. S. Bach – Grave, from Suite No. 3 for Orchestra, D major, arranged for violin and piano

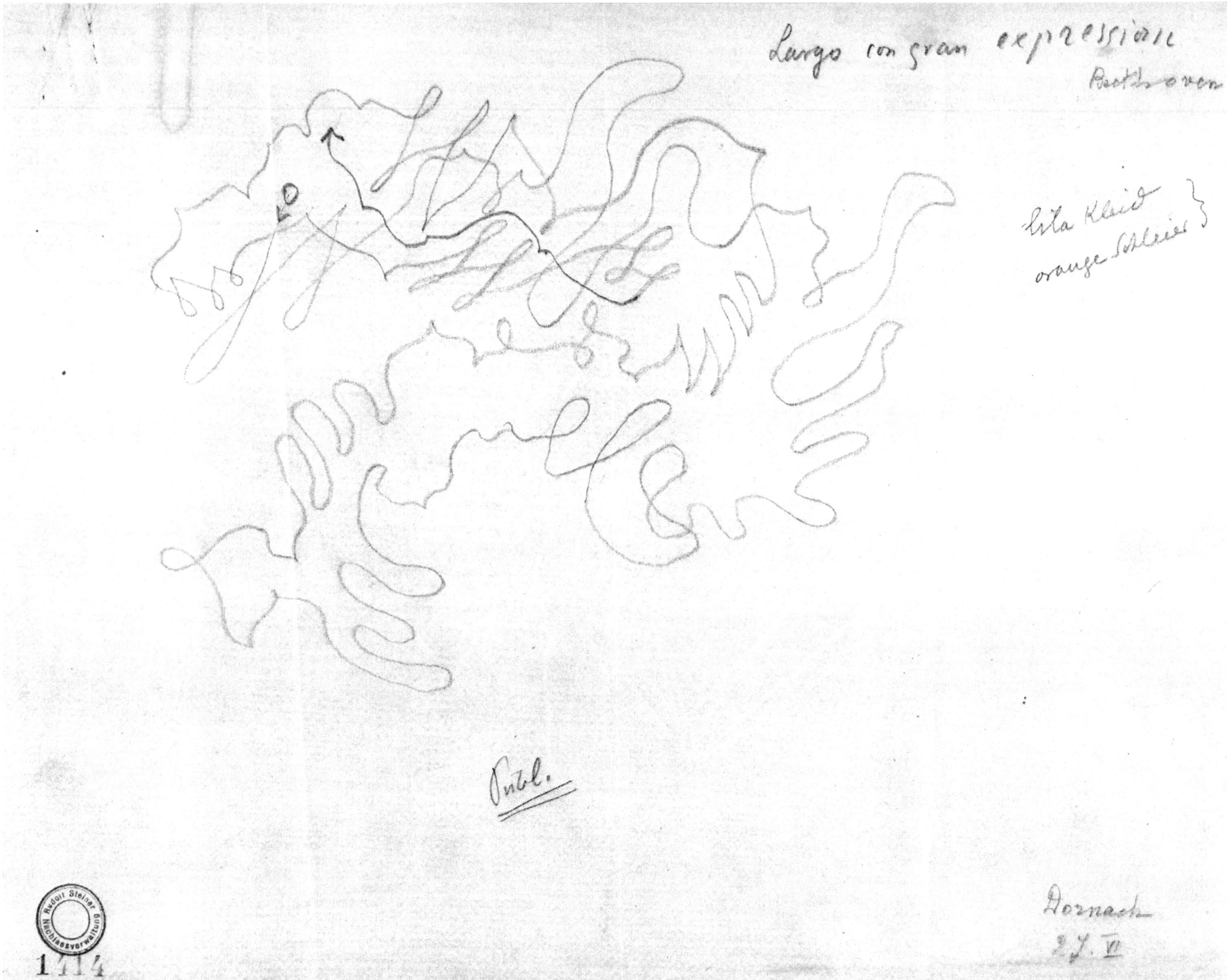

L. van Beethoven – Largo con gran espressione, C major, second movement from Sonata No.4, E-flat major (page 1)

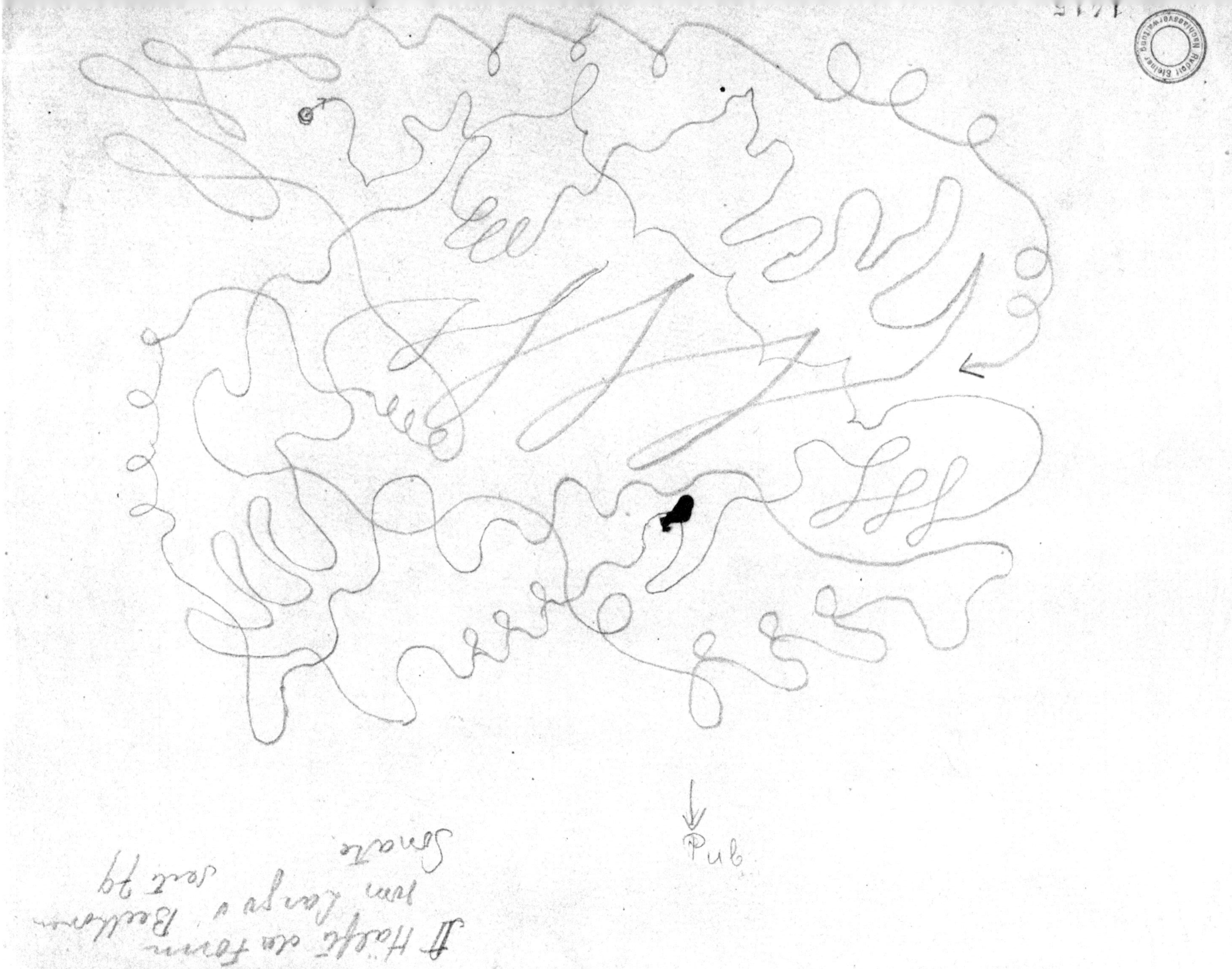

L. van Beethoven – Largo con gran espressione, C major, second movement from Sonata No.4, E-flat major (page 2)

L. van Beethoven–Adagio con espressione, A-flat major, second movement from Sonata No. 13, E-flat major, Op. 27/1

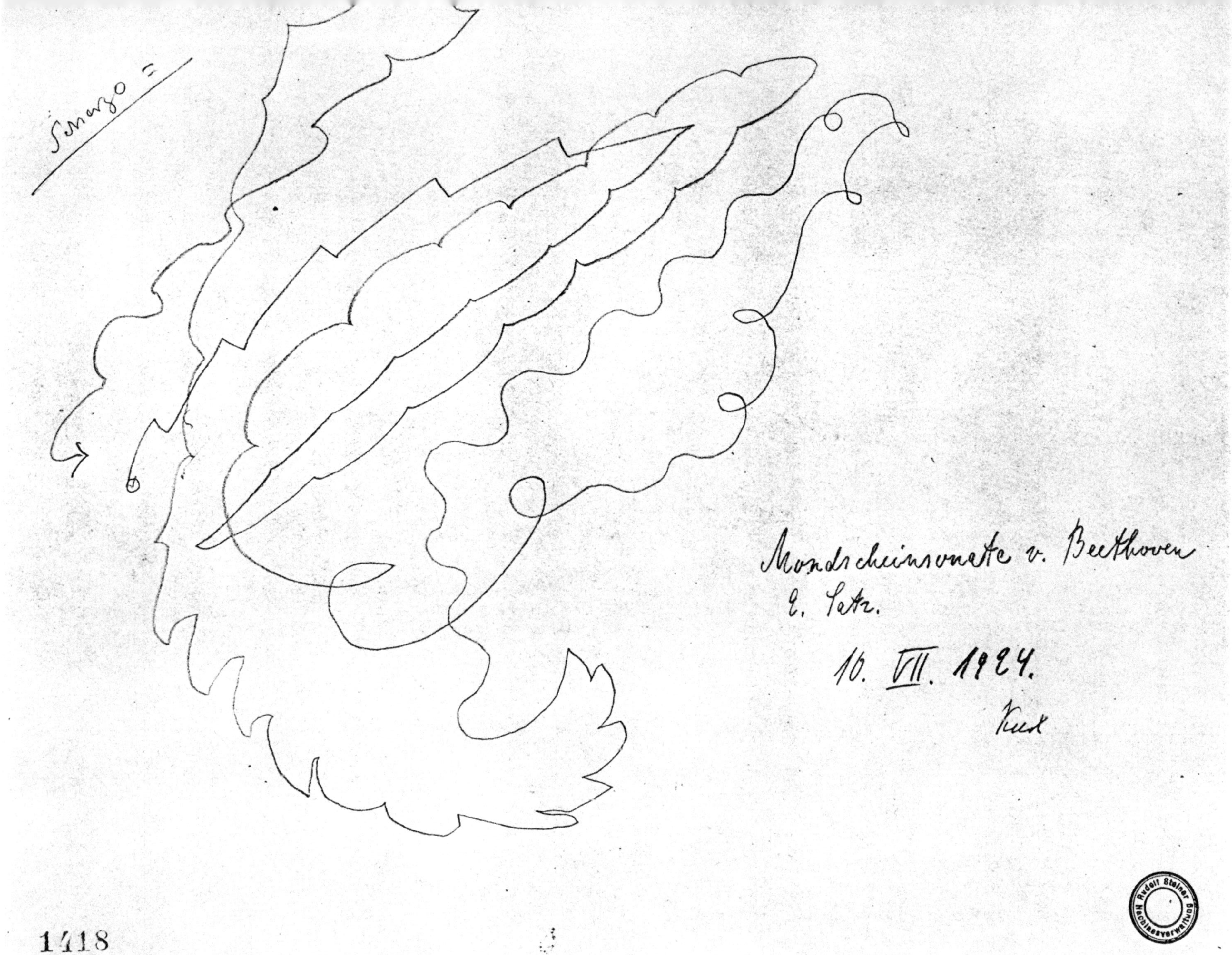

L. van Beethoven – Allegretto, D-flat major, second movement from Sonata No. 14 (*Mondschein*) [Moonshine], C-sharp minor, Op. 27/2

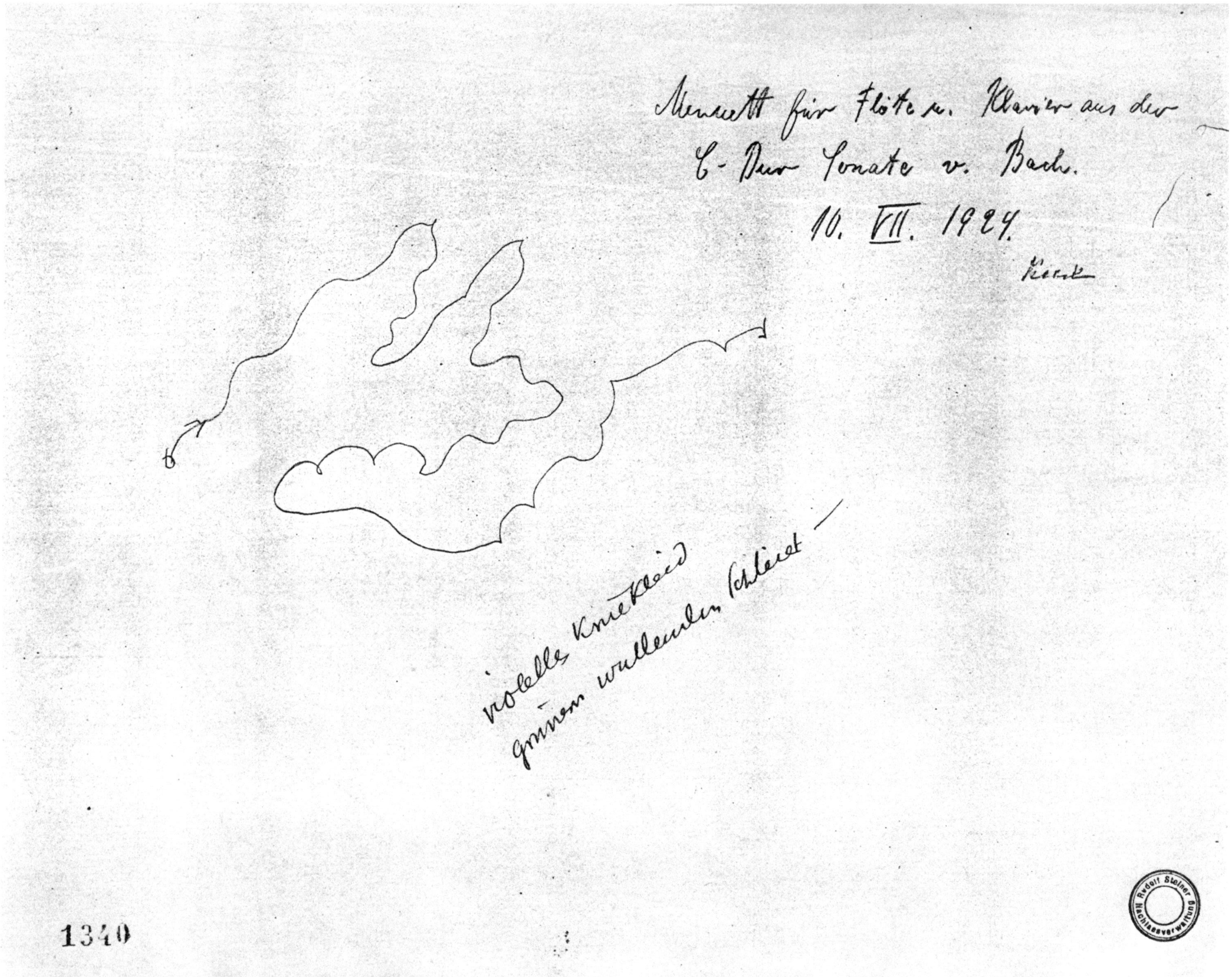

J. S. Bach –Minuet I, fourth movement from Sonata No. 4 for flute and piano, C major (page 1)

J. S. Bach – Costume sketch for Minuet I, fourth movement from Sonata No. 4 for flute and piano, C major (page 2)

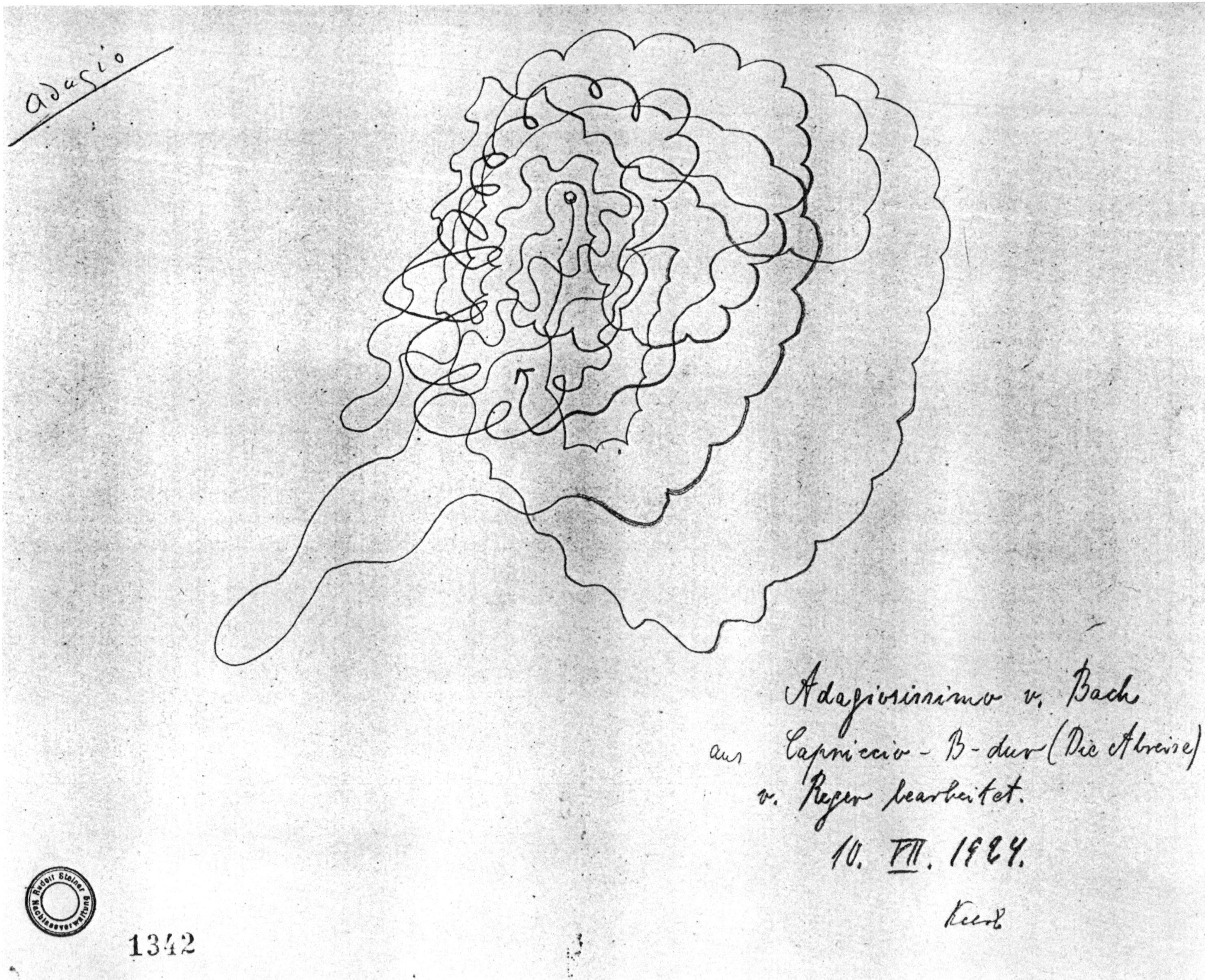

J. S. Bach – Adagiosissimo, F minor, from *Caprice*: "Über die Abreise seines geliebten Bruders," [About the departure of his beloved brother] for piano, B major

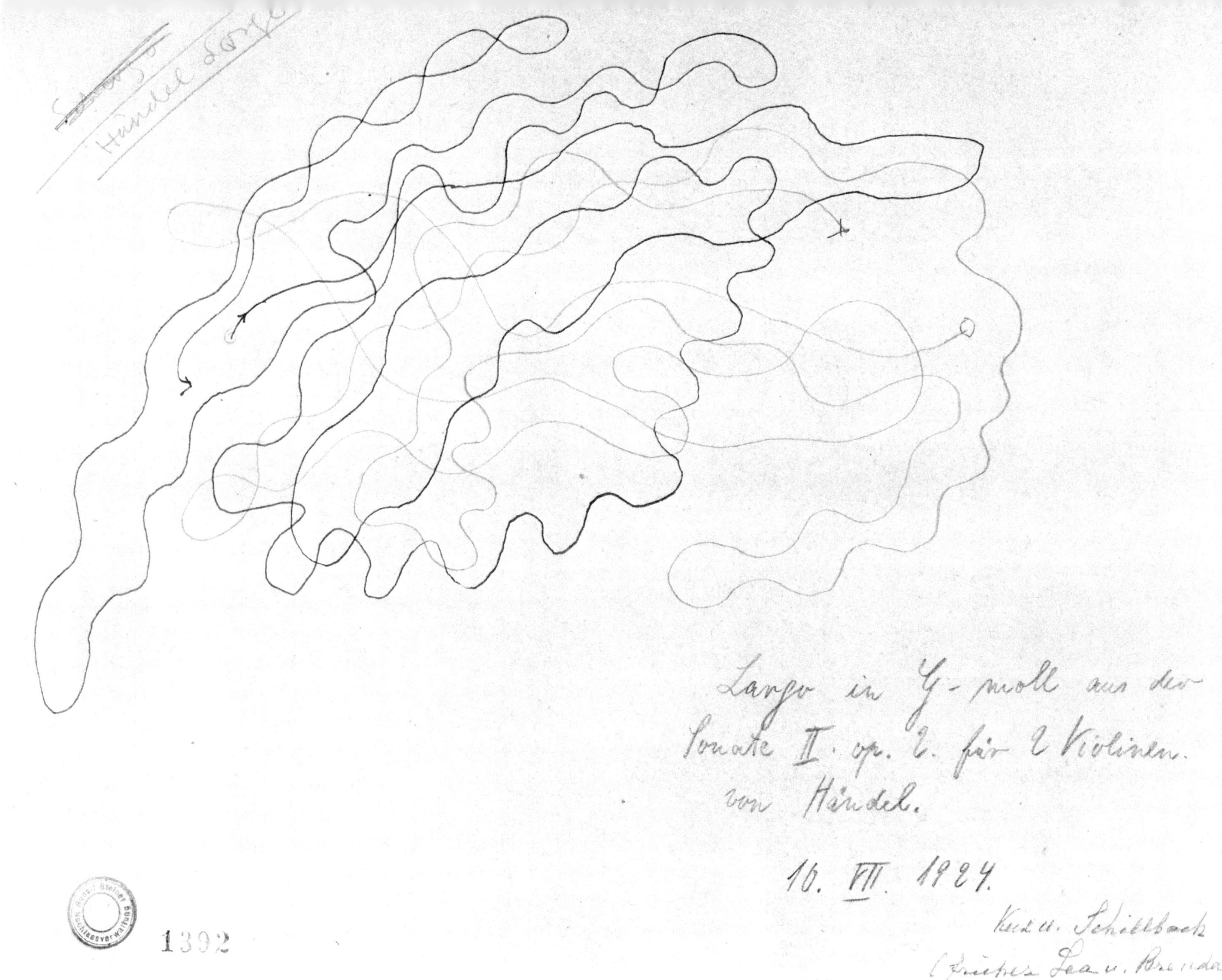

G. F. Händel – Largo, third movement from the Sonata G minor

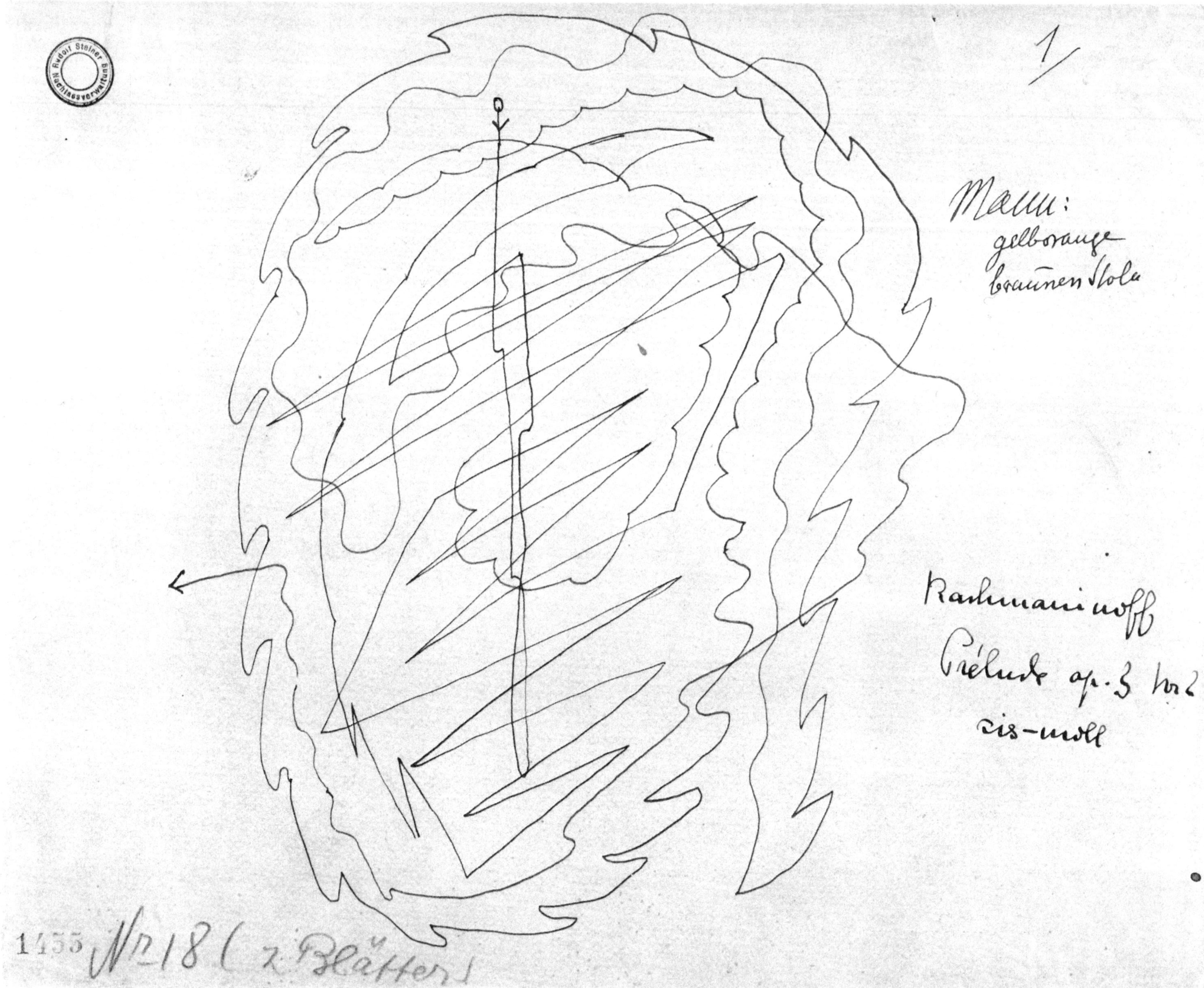

S. Rachmaninoff – Prelude, Lento, C-sharp minor, Op. 3/2 (page 1)

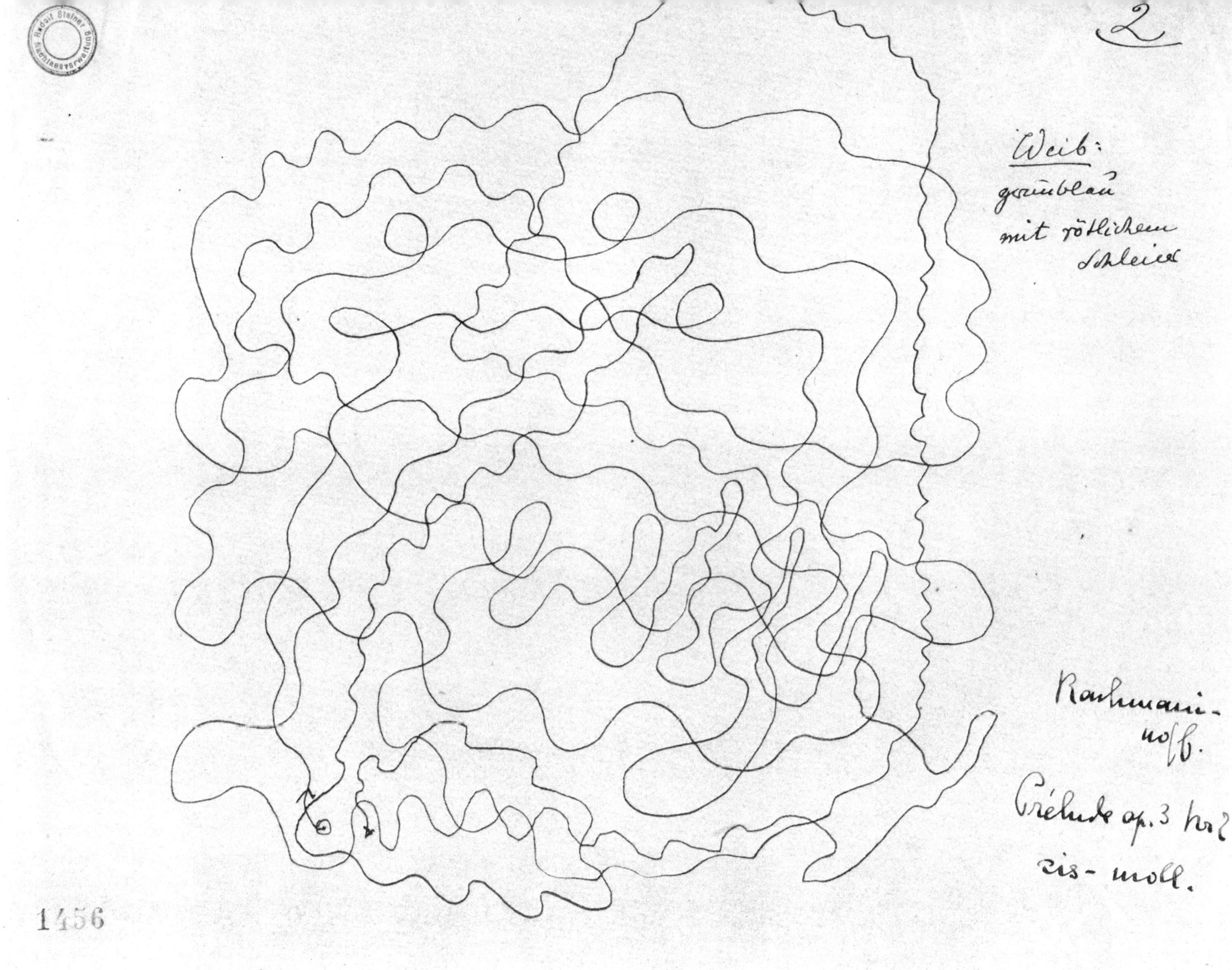

S. Rachmaninoff – Prelude, Lento, C-sharp minor, Op. 3/2 (page 2)

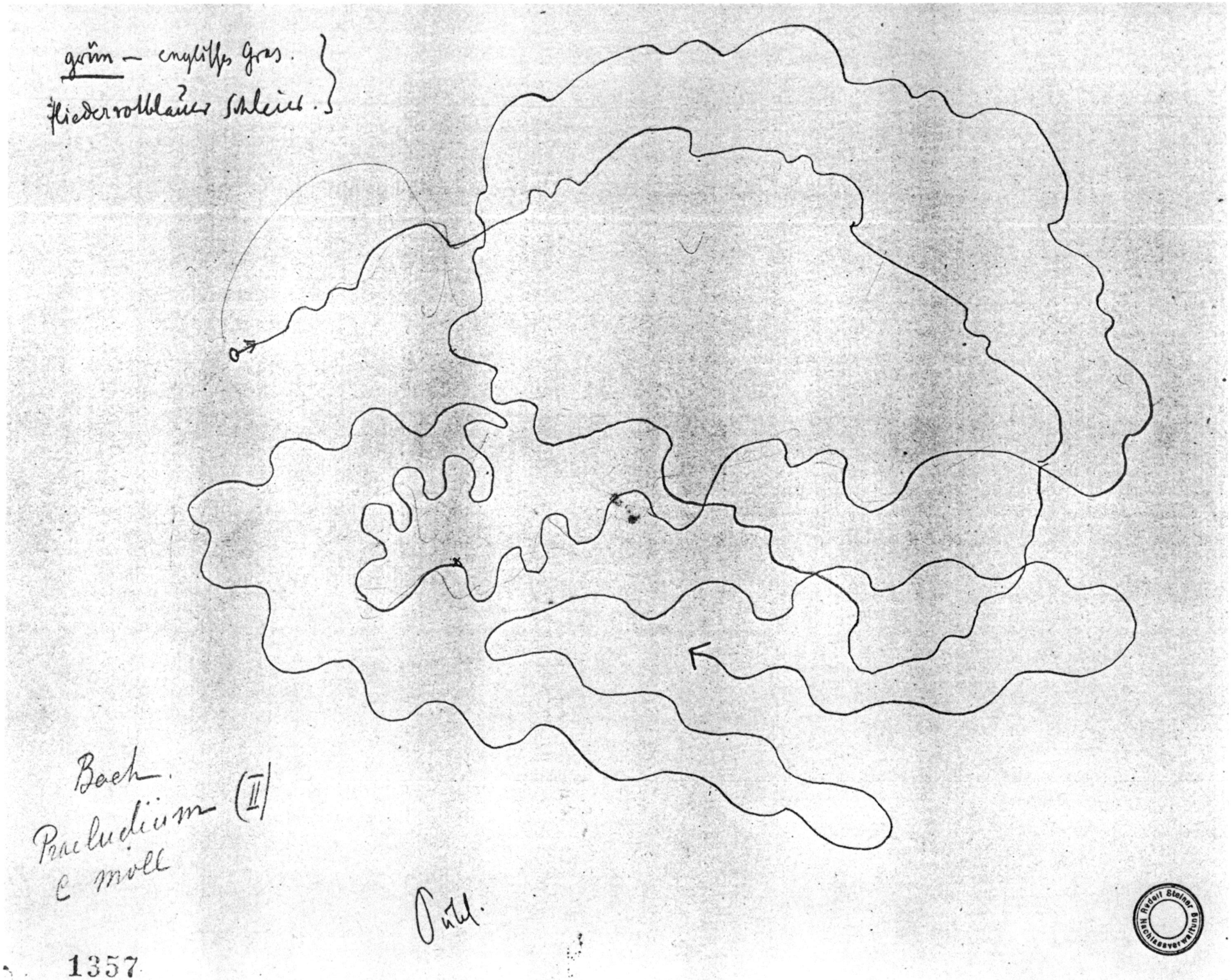

J. S. Bach – Prelude No. 2, C minor, from the *Well-Tempered Clavier I*

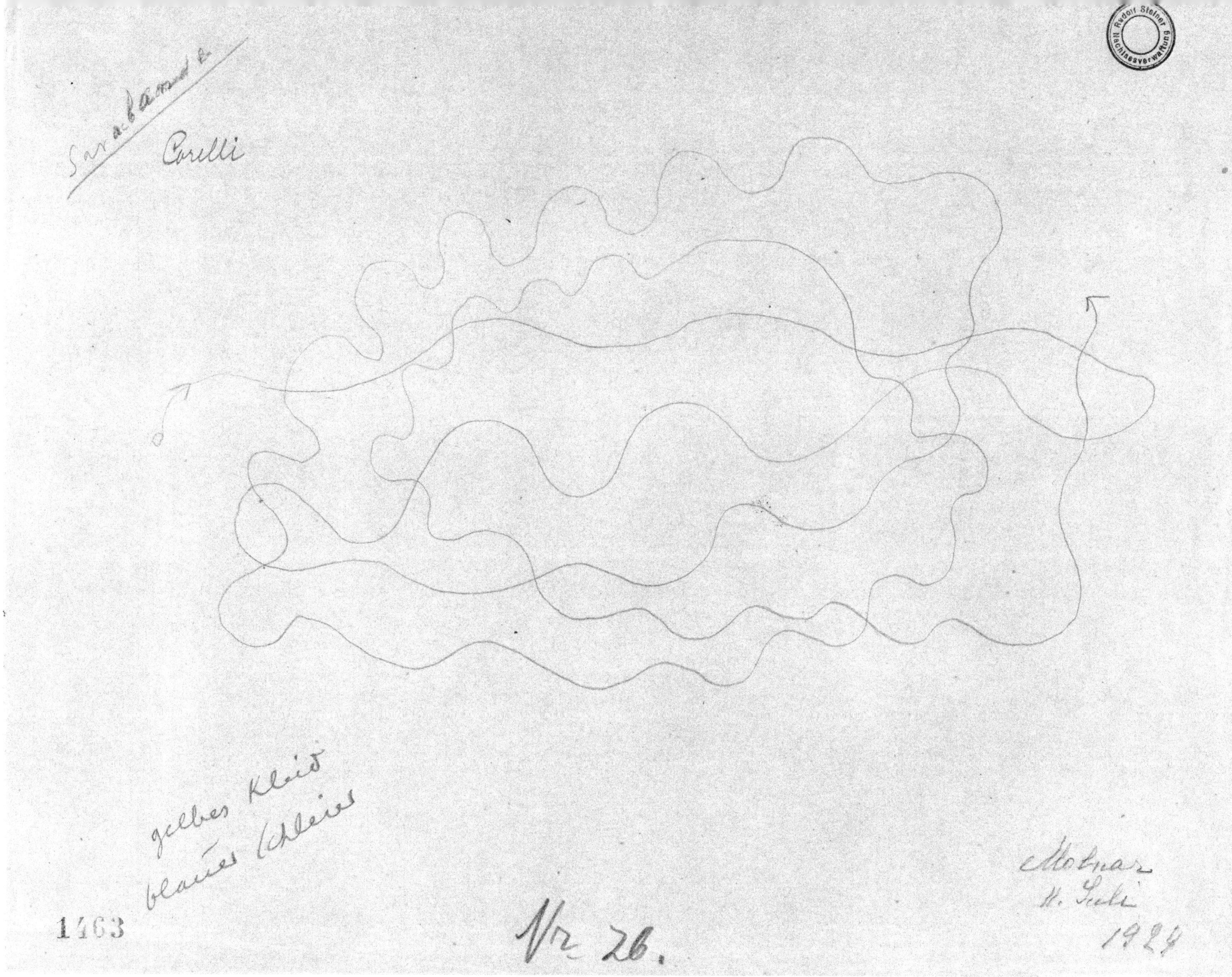

A. Corelli – Saraband, from Sonata No. 8, E minor, for violin and piano

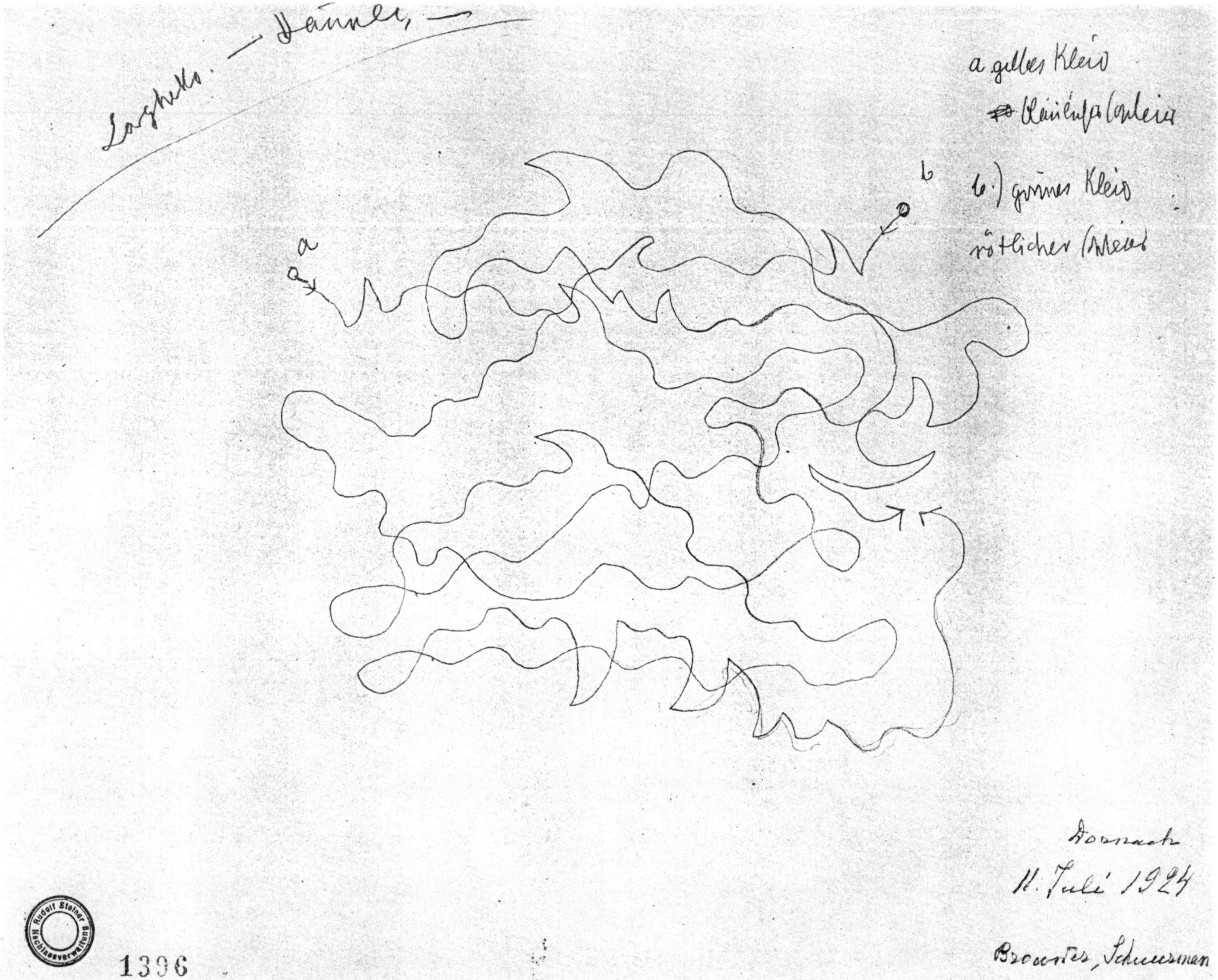

G. F. Händel – Larghetto (Andante), first movement from the Sonata A major

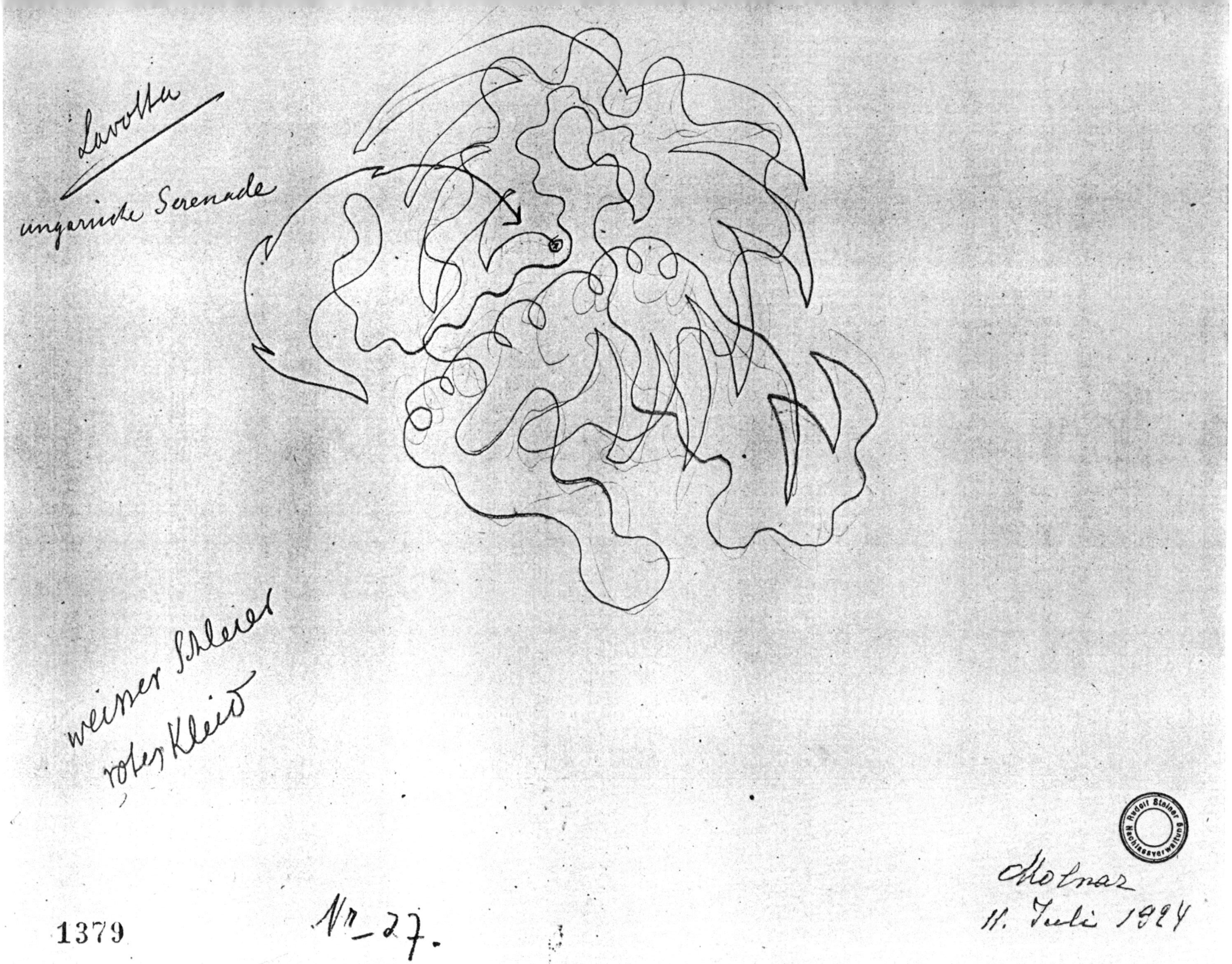

J. Kossowits – "Lavottas erste Liebe," [Lavotta's first love], *Ungarische Serenade* [Hungarian serenade], arranged for violin and piano by Armand Zsadányi

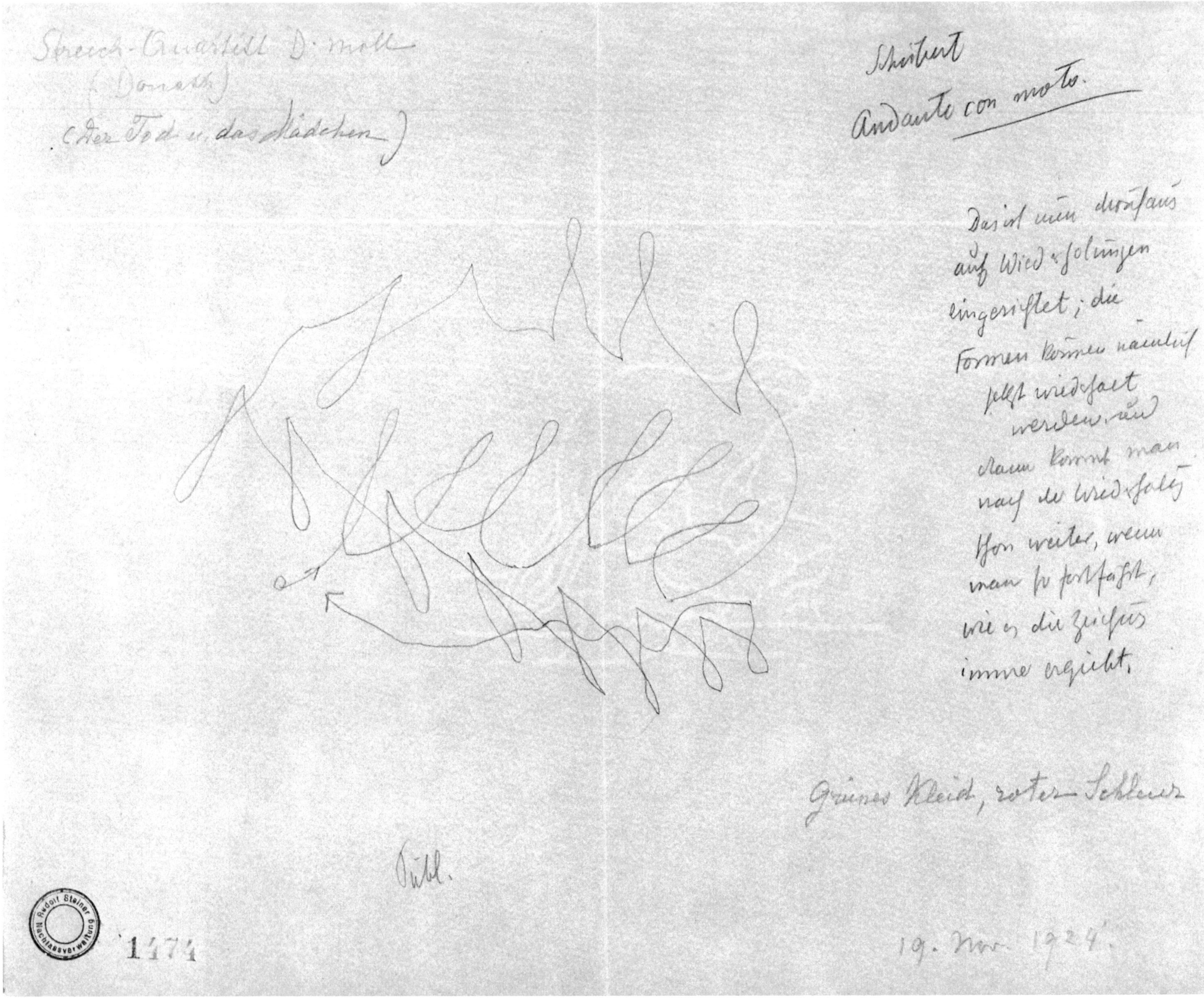

F. Schubert – Andante con moto, second movement from the String Quartet in D minor, *Der Tod und das Mädchen* [Death and the girl]

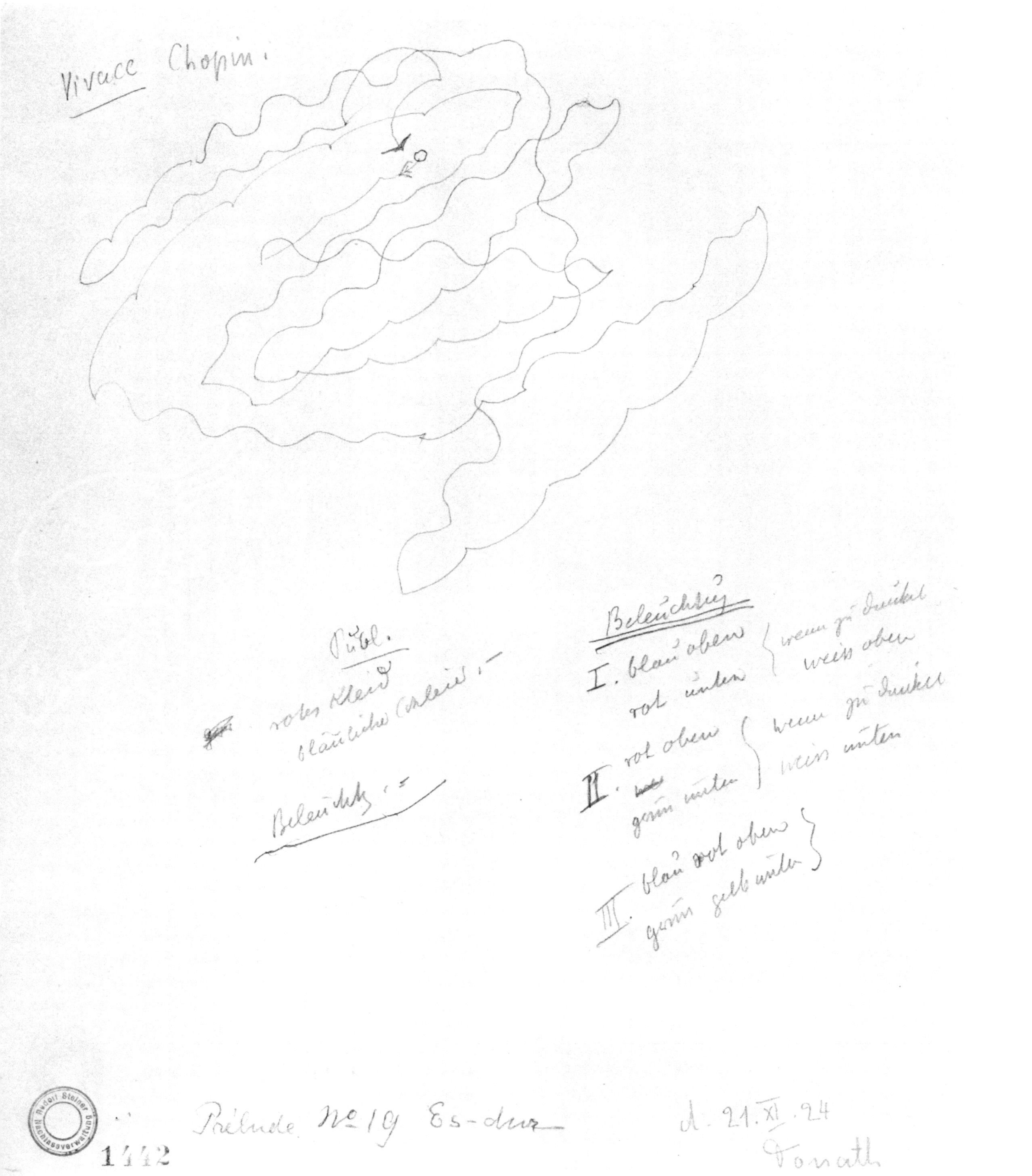

F. Chopin – Prelude No. 19, Vivace, E-flat major, Op. 28/19

R. Dittrich – "Gombei ga tane maku" (merry, moody folk song)

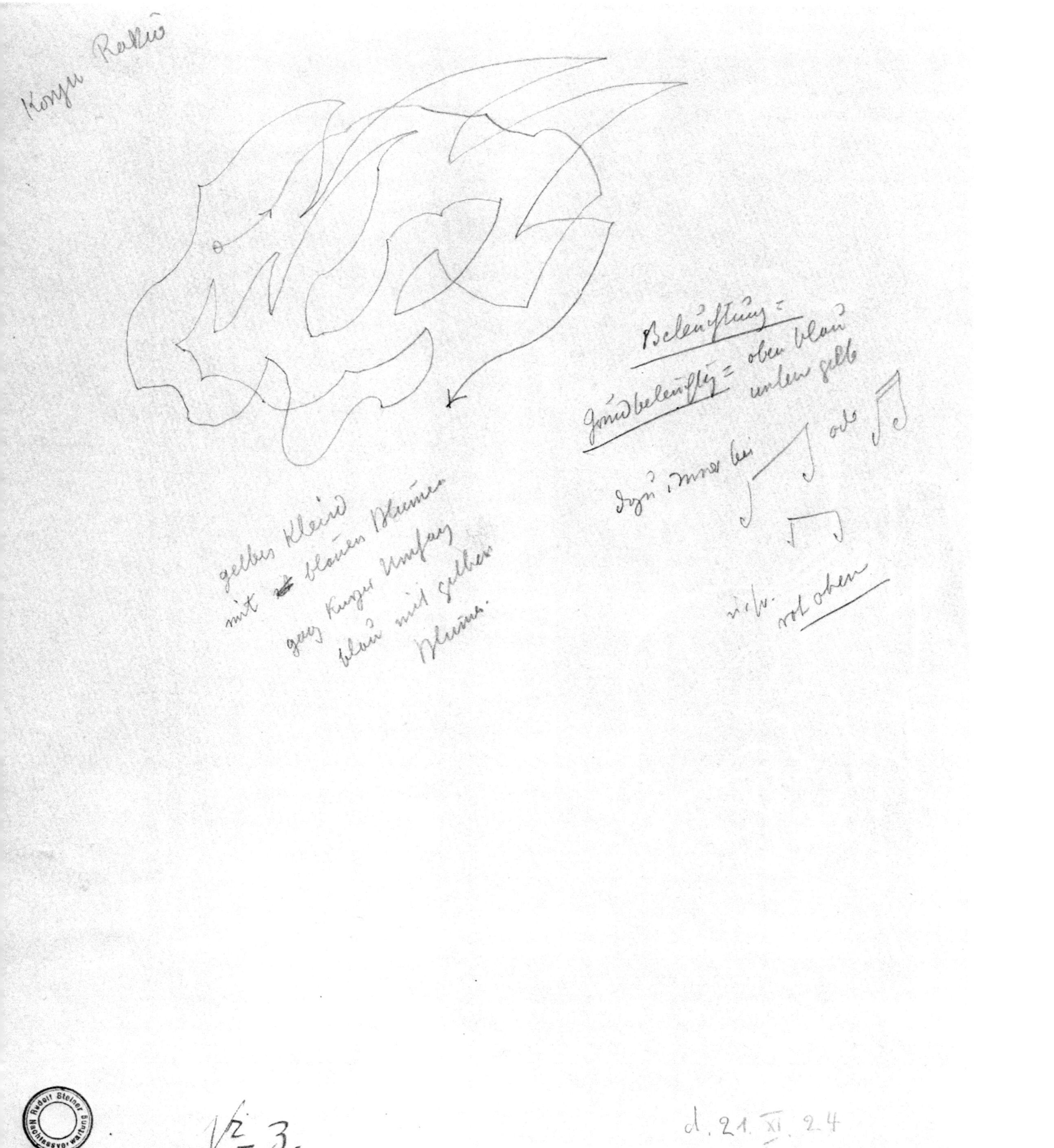

R. Dittrich –"Konju Raku" (Schlangentanz) [Snake dance]

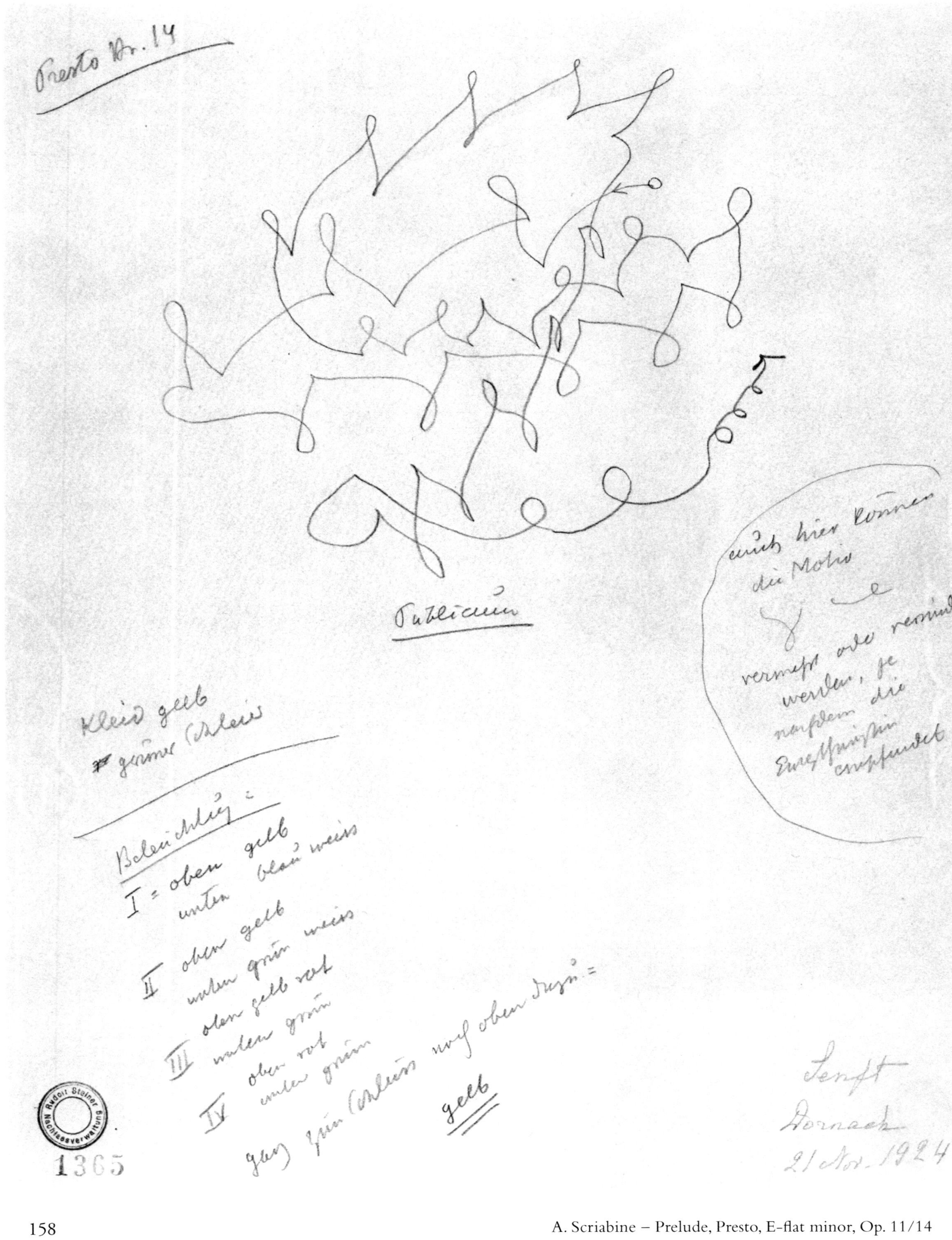

A. Scriabine – Prelude, Presto, E-flat minor, Op. 11/14

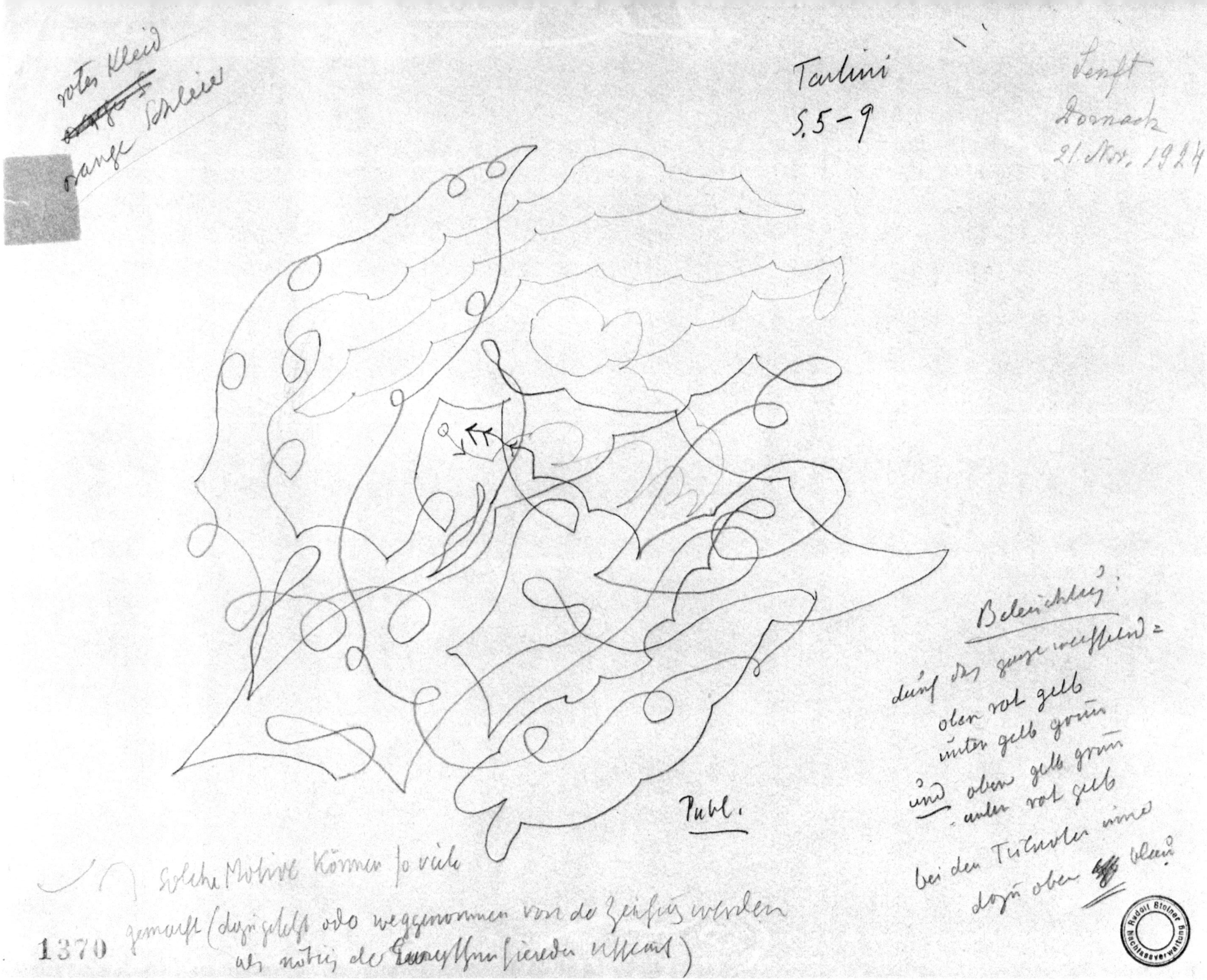

G. Tartini – Allegro, second movement from the *Teufelstriller-Sonata* [Devil's trill sonata], G minor, (known as First Allegro)

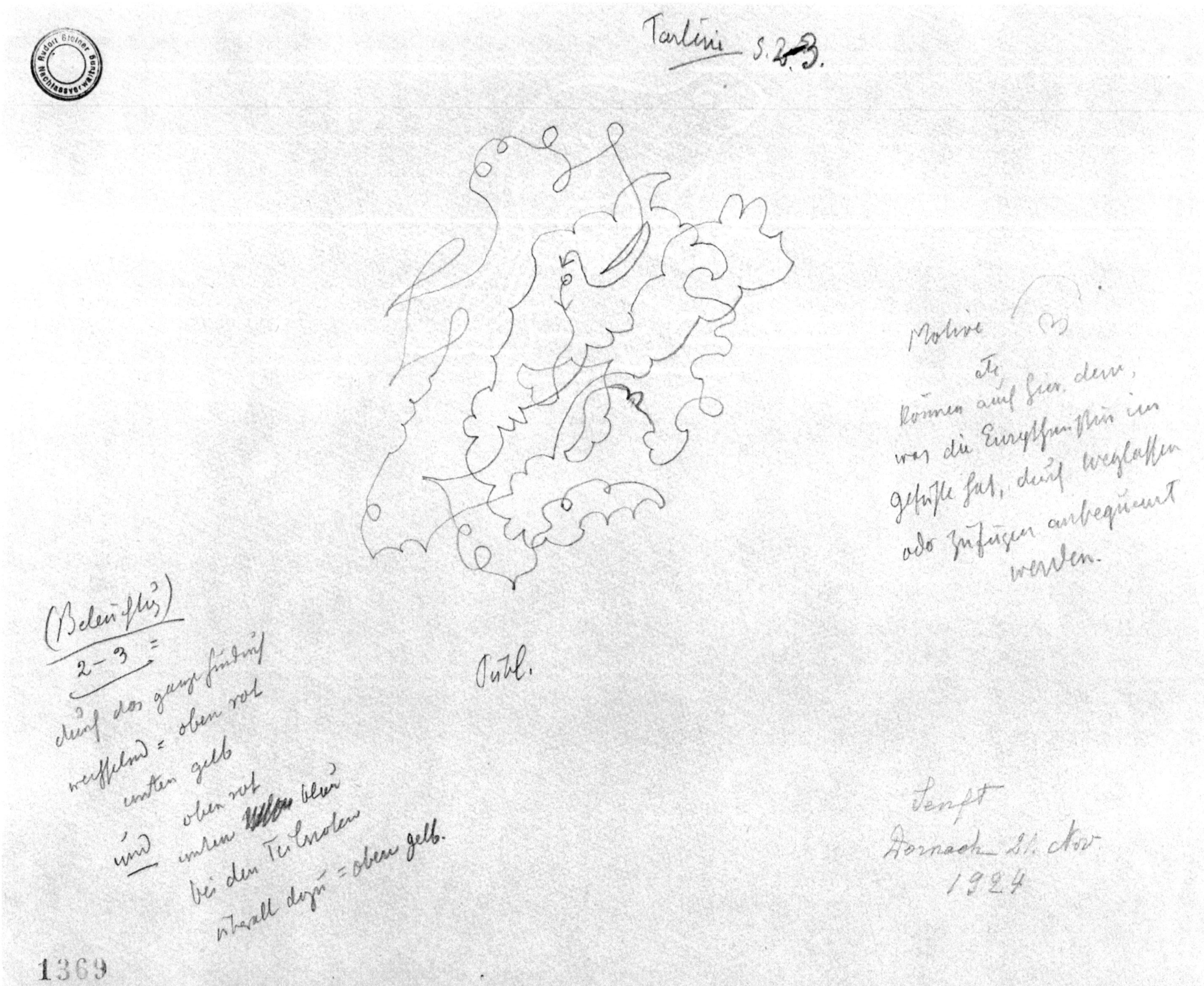

G. Tartini – Allegro commodo, fourth movement from the Sonata (Didonc abbadonata) G minor

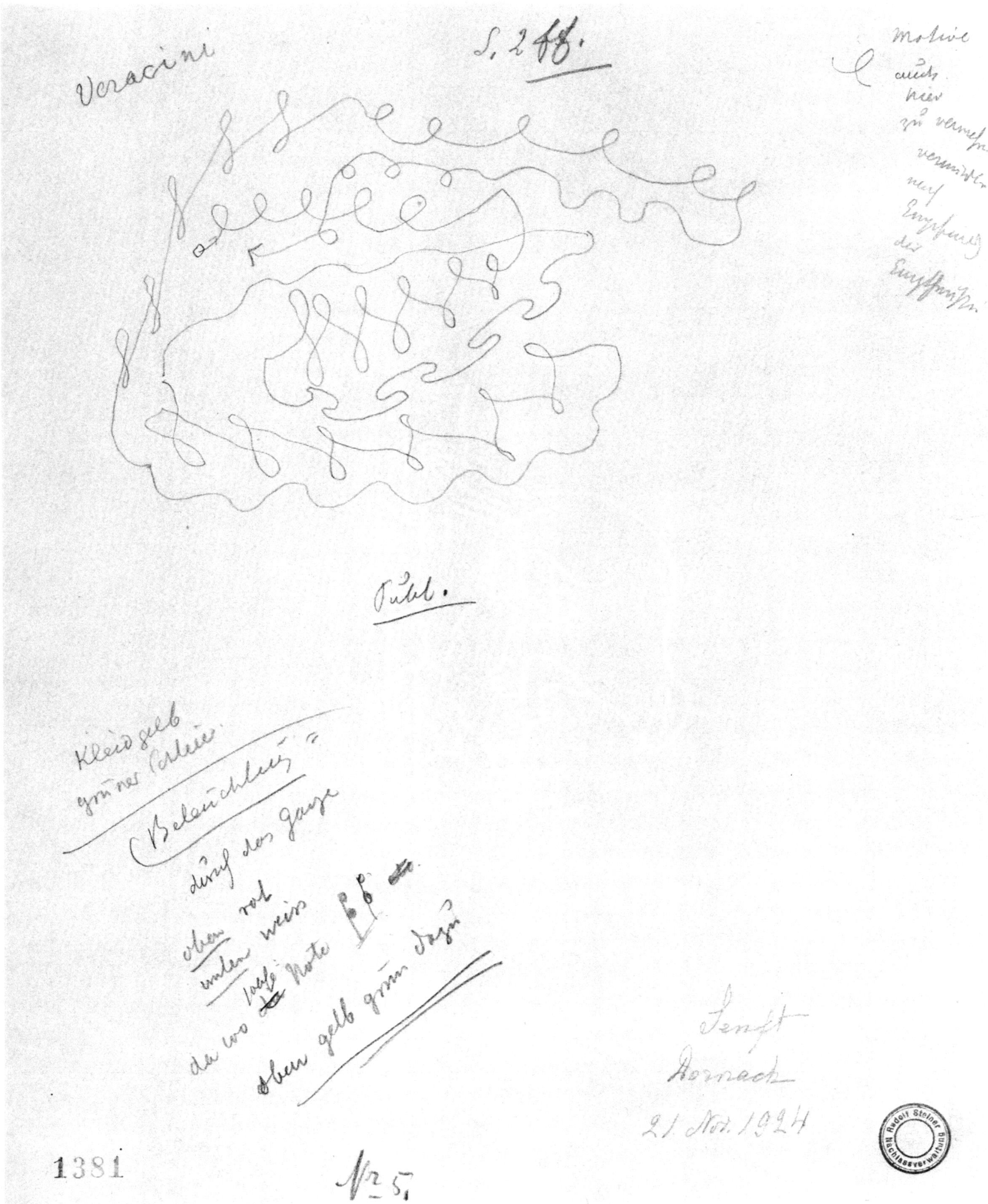

F. M. Veracini – Allegro, fifth movement from Sonata No. 7, A major, for violin and piano

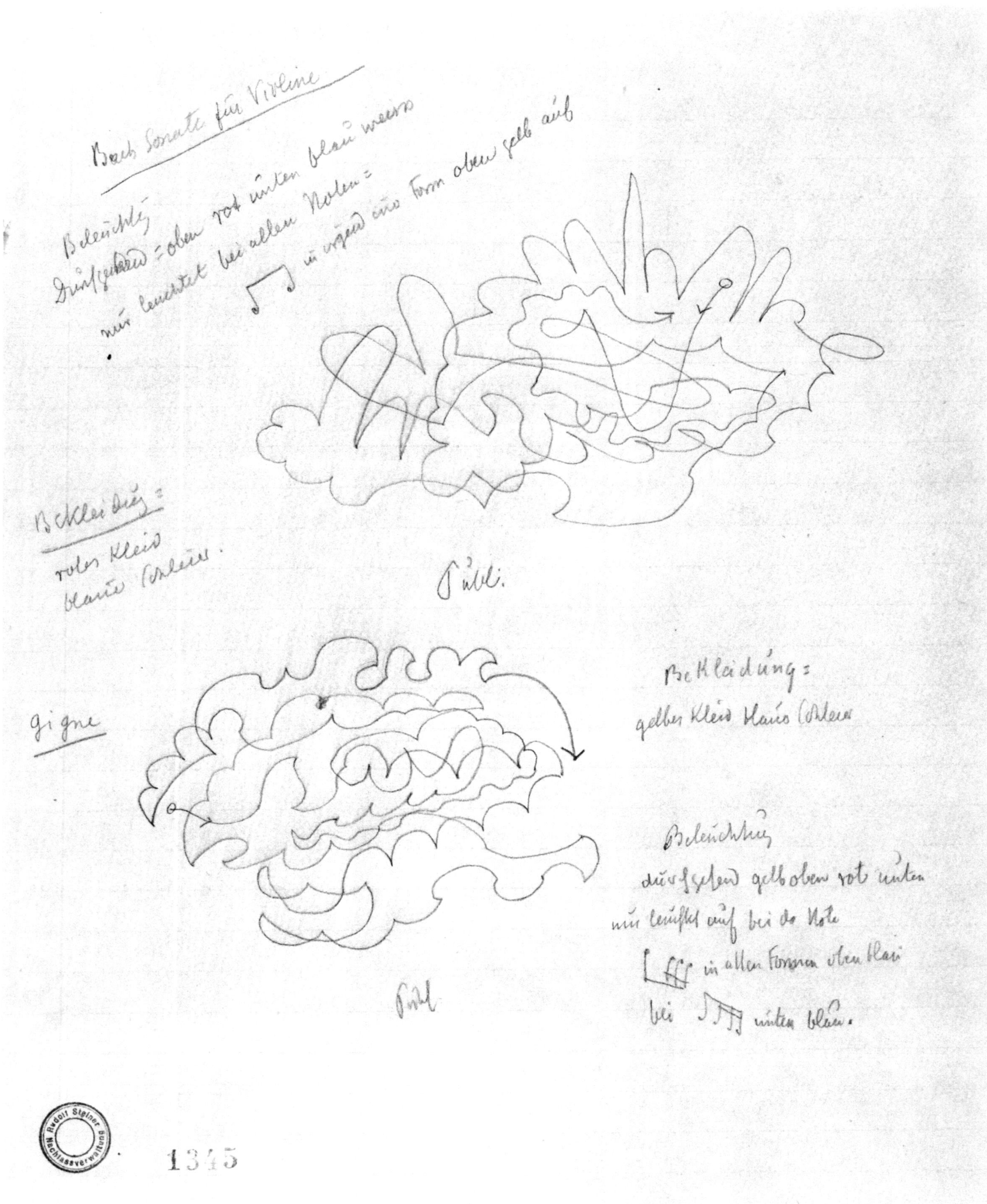

above: J. S. Bach – Adagio, first movement from Sonata No. 1, for violin solo, G minor
below: Gigue, from Suite No. 5 for violoncello solo, C minor

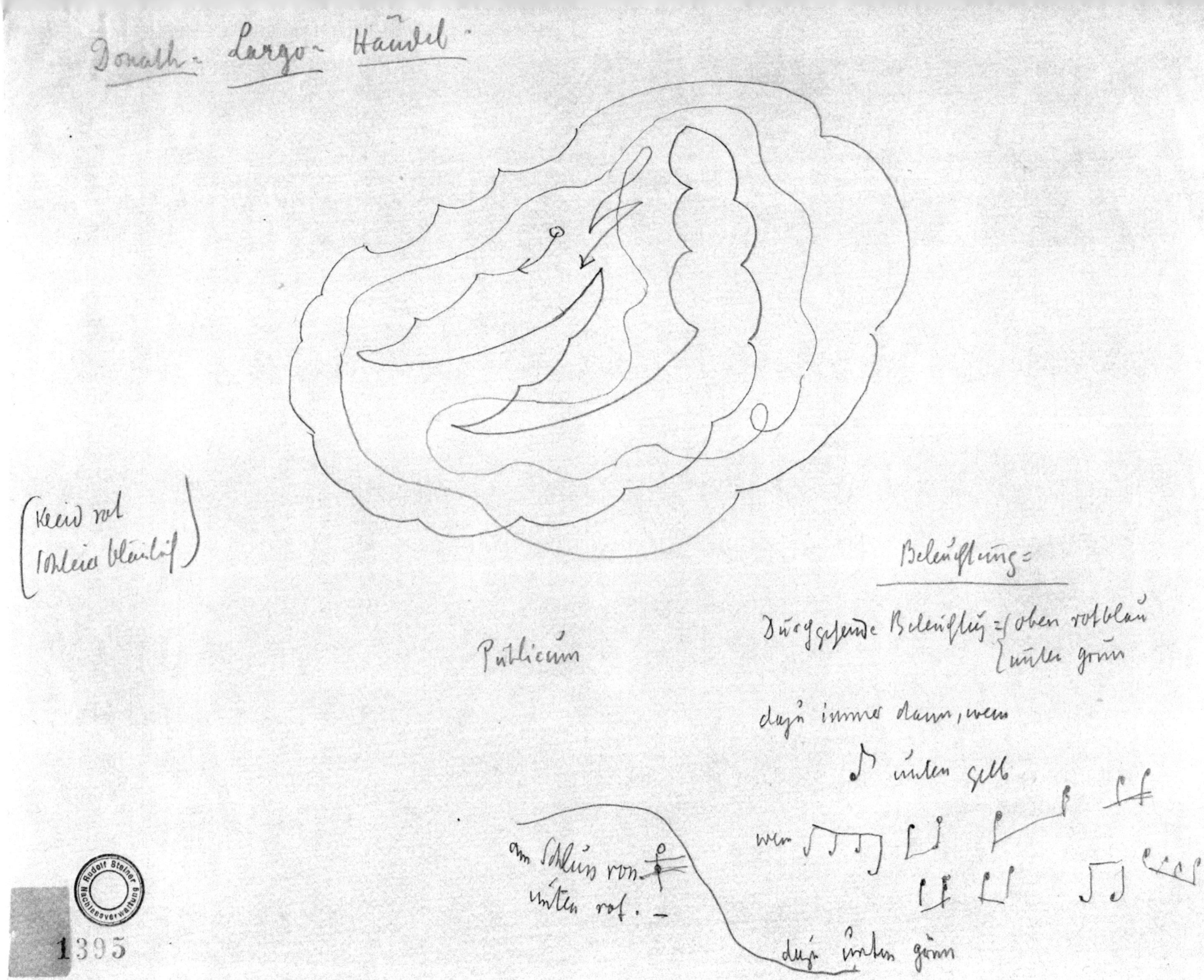

G. F. Händel – Largo, second movement from the Concerto grosso No. 2, B major

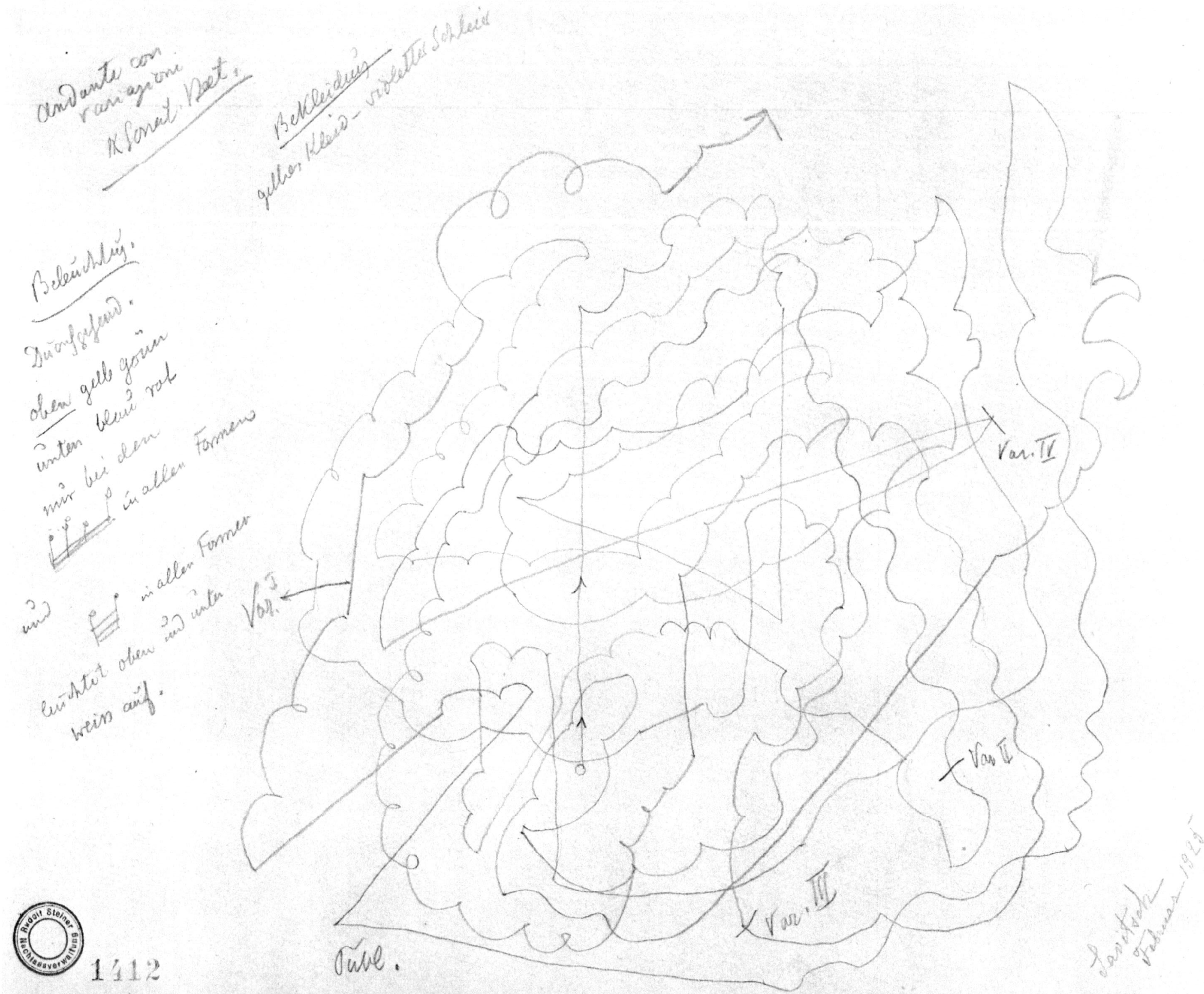

L. van Beethoven – Andante con Variazioni, F major, second movement from Sonata No. 9 (*Kreutzer*), A major, Op. 47

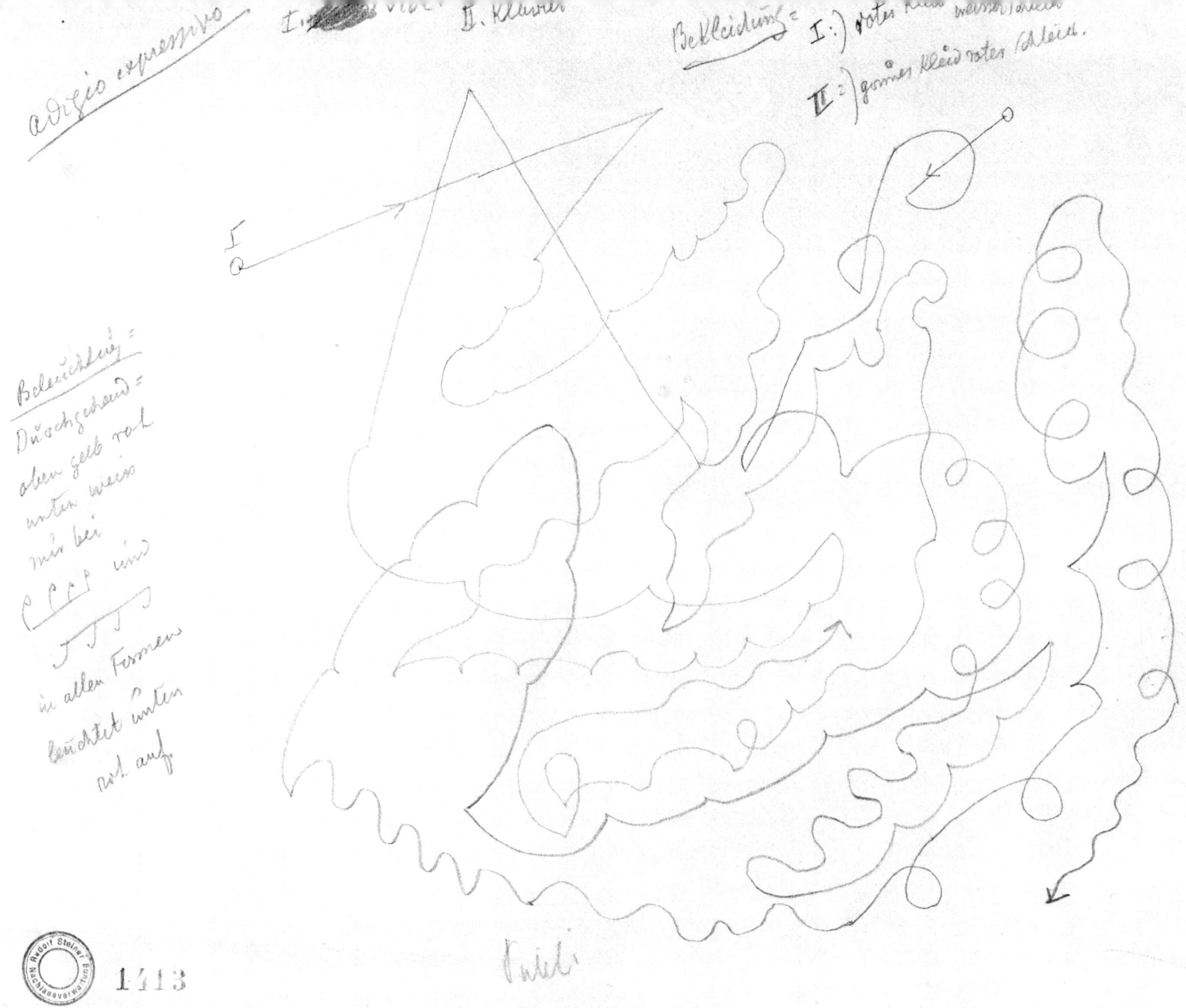

L. van Beethoven – Adagio espressivo, E-flat major, second movement from Sonata No. 10, G major, Op. 96

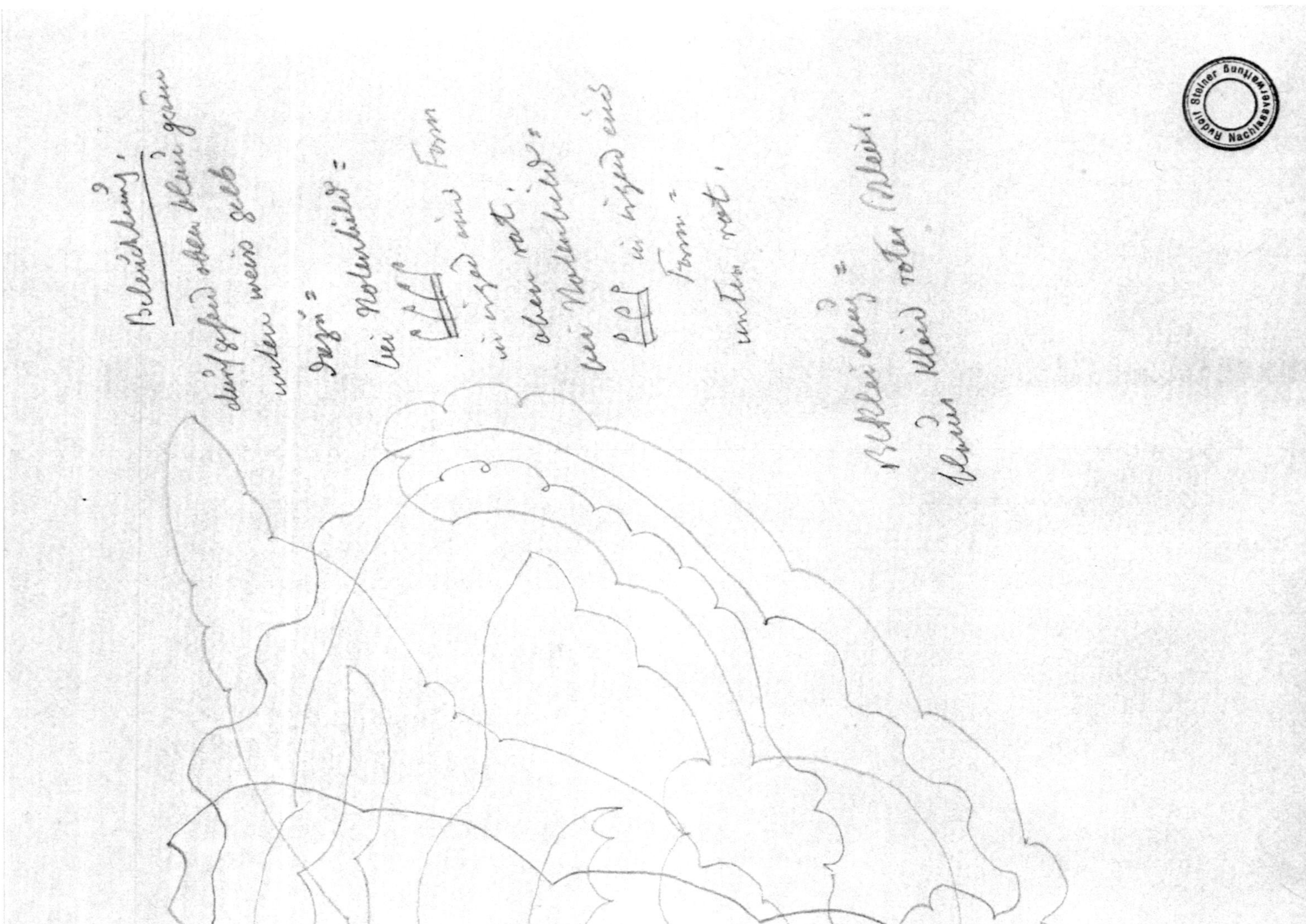

L. van Beethoven – Adagio cantabile, A-flat major, second movement from Sonata No. 7, C minor, Op. 30/2

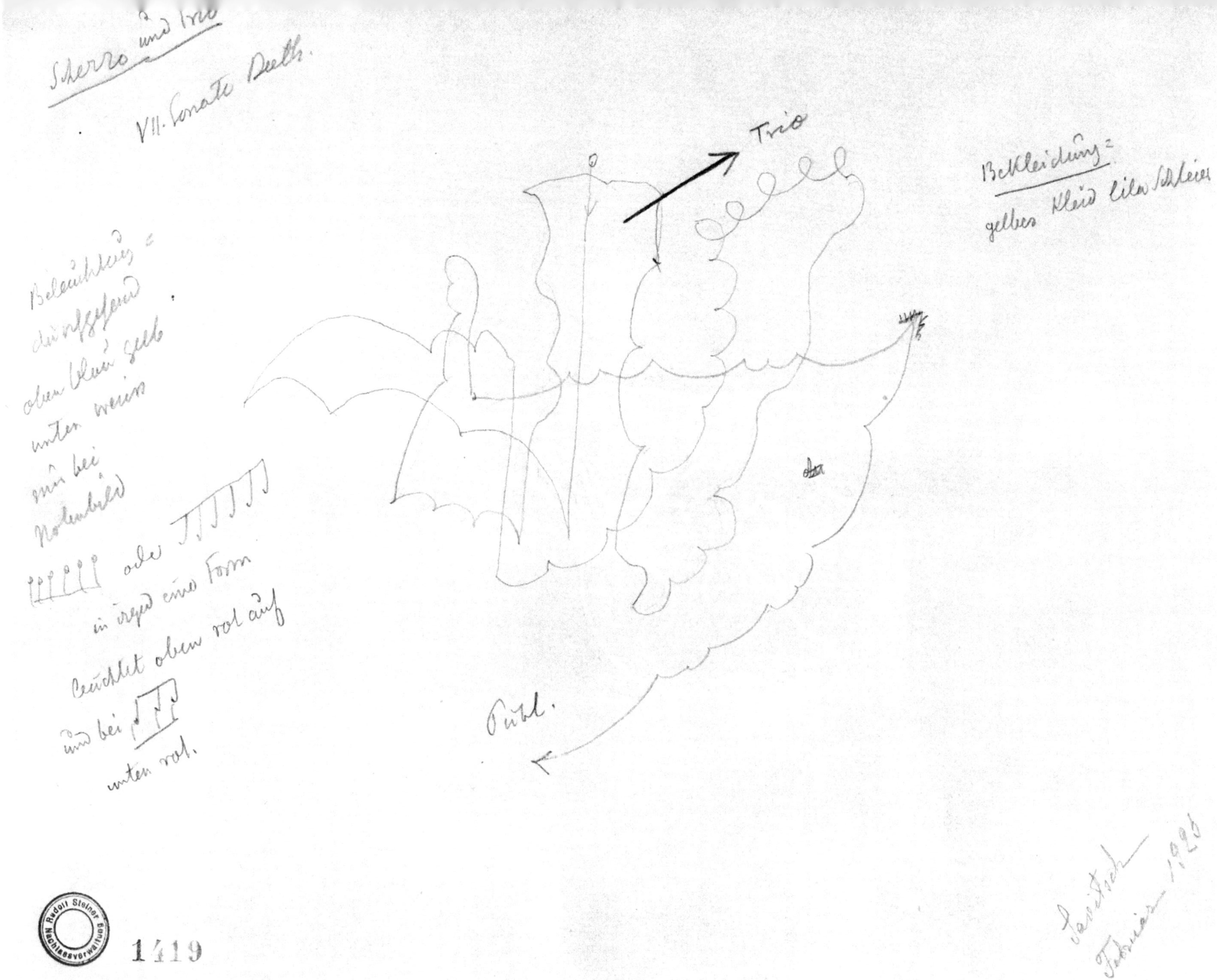

L. van Beethoven – Scherzo, Allegro, C major, third movement from Sonata No. 7, C minor, Op. 30/2

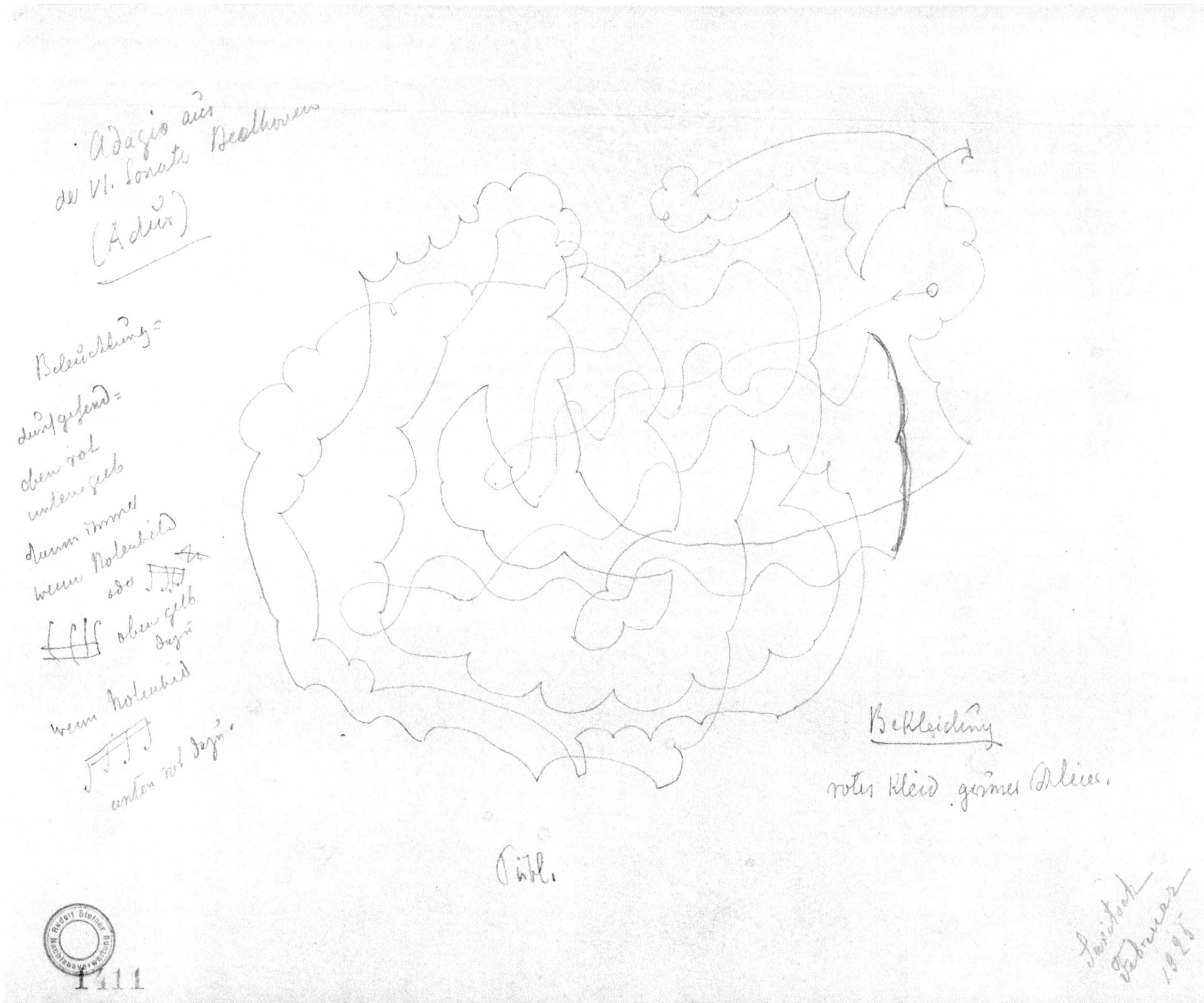

L. van Beethoven – Adagio, molto espressivo, D major, second movement from Sonata No. 6, A major, Op. 30/1

APPENDIX

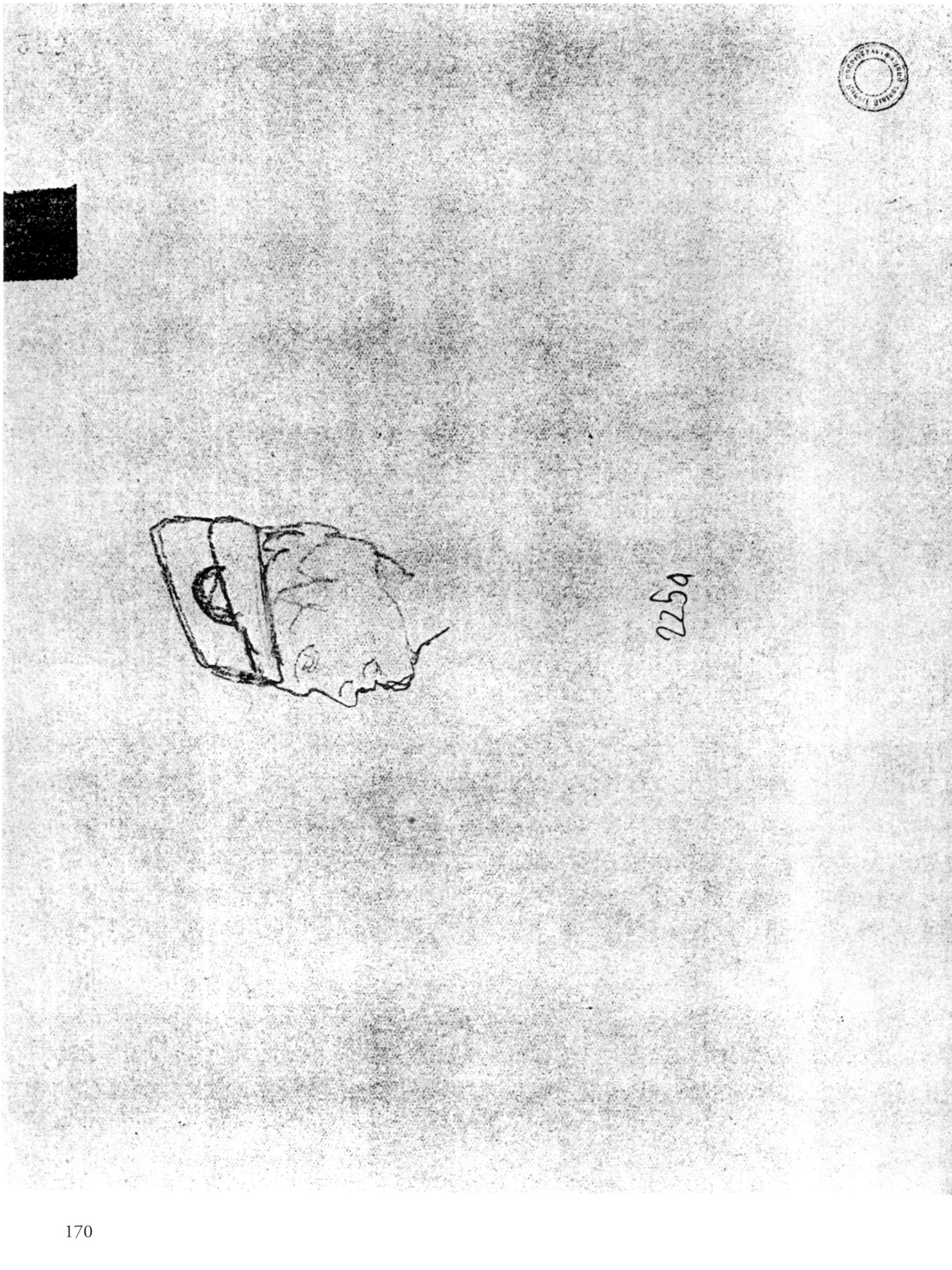

Jan Stuten – Hat for "Nach wächter" [Nightwatchmen] from page 2

Beleuchtungen:

1.) Händel Sonate

I = grüngelb oben
rotblau weiss unten

II = oben rot dazu

III = grün oben
rot unten

IV = rotblau oben
grüngelb unten weiss unten

Kleid grün
Schleier rotblau

2.) Andante con moto = Donath

durchweg { oben rot
unten grün weiss

dazu bei ♩♩ auf allen Linien = oben grün

grünes Kleid rote Schleier

3.) Suite V = Praeludium

I oben rot gelb
unten blau

II oben gelb
unten blau rot

III oben blau
unten grün weiss

IV wie I

Kleid gelb
Umhang = bläulich

4.) Allegretto con moto Bach

Kleid blau
Umhang gelb

I { langsam wechselnd [etwa 3 mal wechseln] = { oben rot
unten grün

oben grün
unten rot

II wechseln ebenso lassen { oben blau
unten gelb

oben gelb
unten blau

III wie I nur dass durch das ganze III nur oben gelb bleibt

IV oben weiss
unten gelb

1. G. F. Händel – Andante from Sonata No. 2 for cello and piano, D minor (no form exists)
2. F. Schubert – Andante con moto from the string quartet in D minor
3. J. S. Bach – Suite No. 5, Prelude (no form exists)
4. J. S. Bach – Gigue, allegretto con moto, from Partita in B major (no form exists)

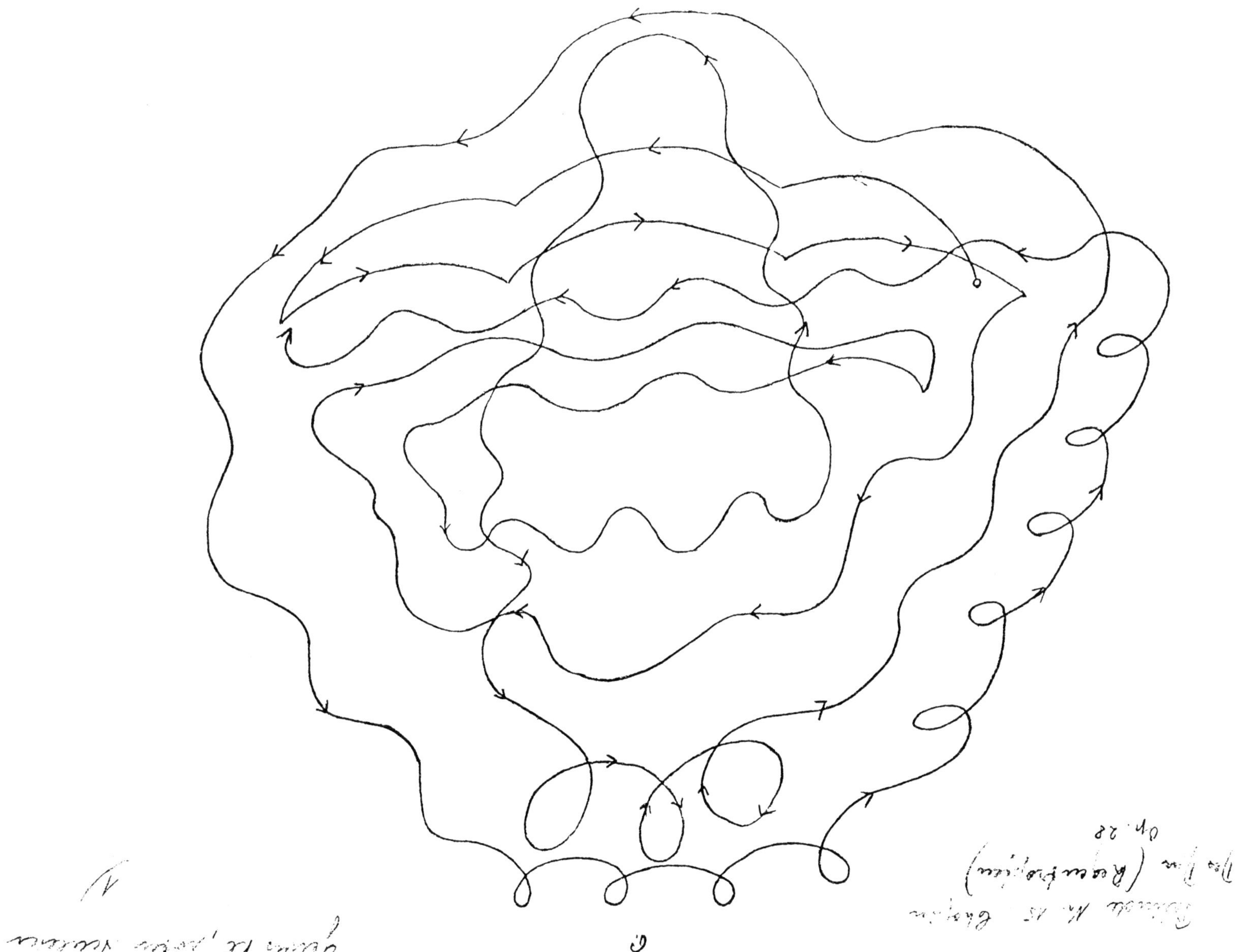

F. Chopin – Prelude, D major, Op. 28/15 (extract on 4 pages, according to Elly Wilke. Drawn by Eva Froböse) (page 1)

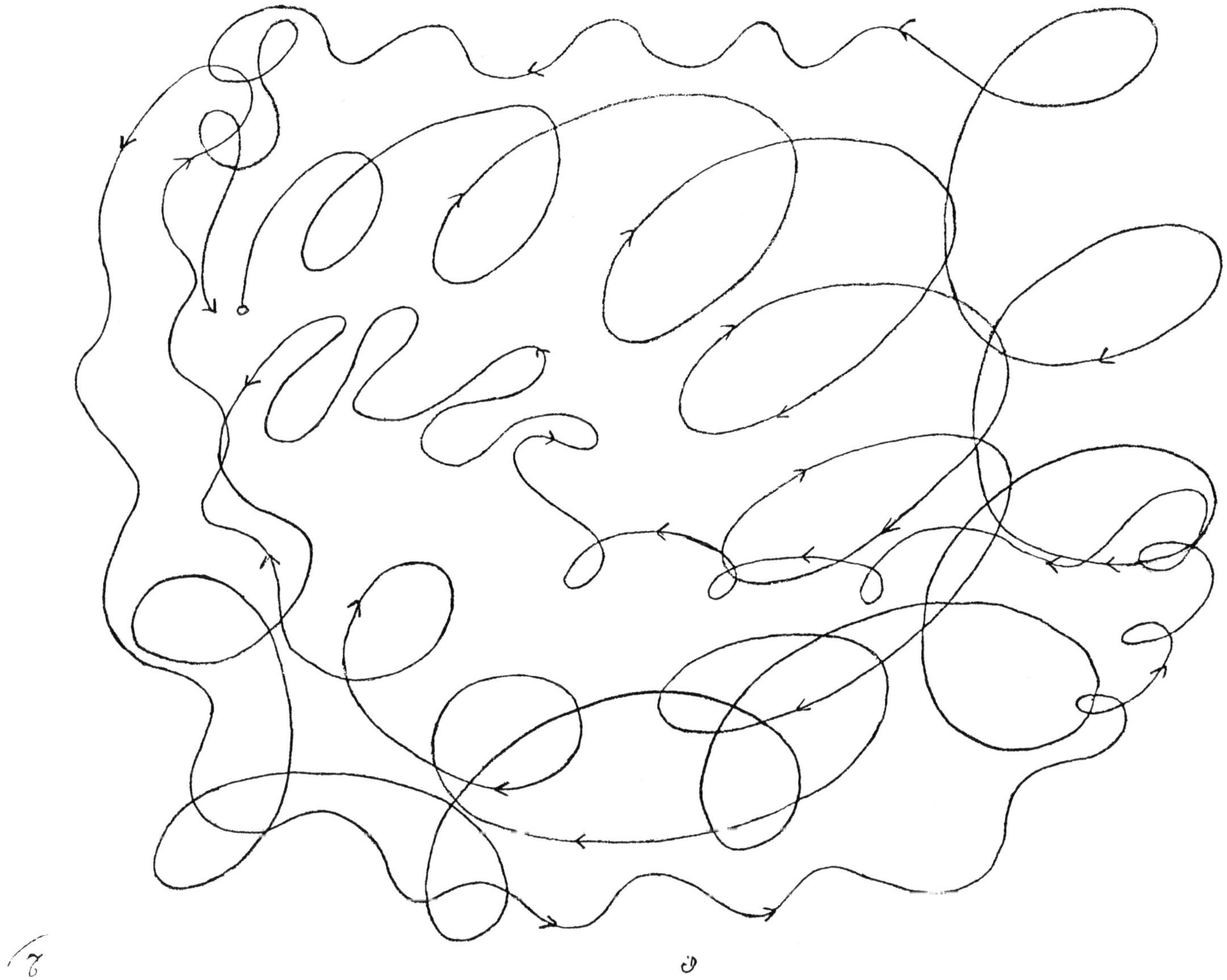

F. Chopin - Prelude, D major, Op. 28/15 (page 2, continuation from page 1)

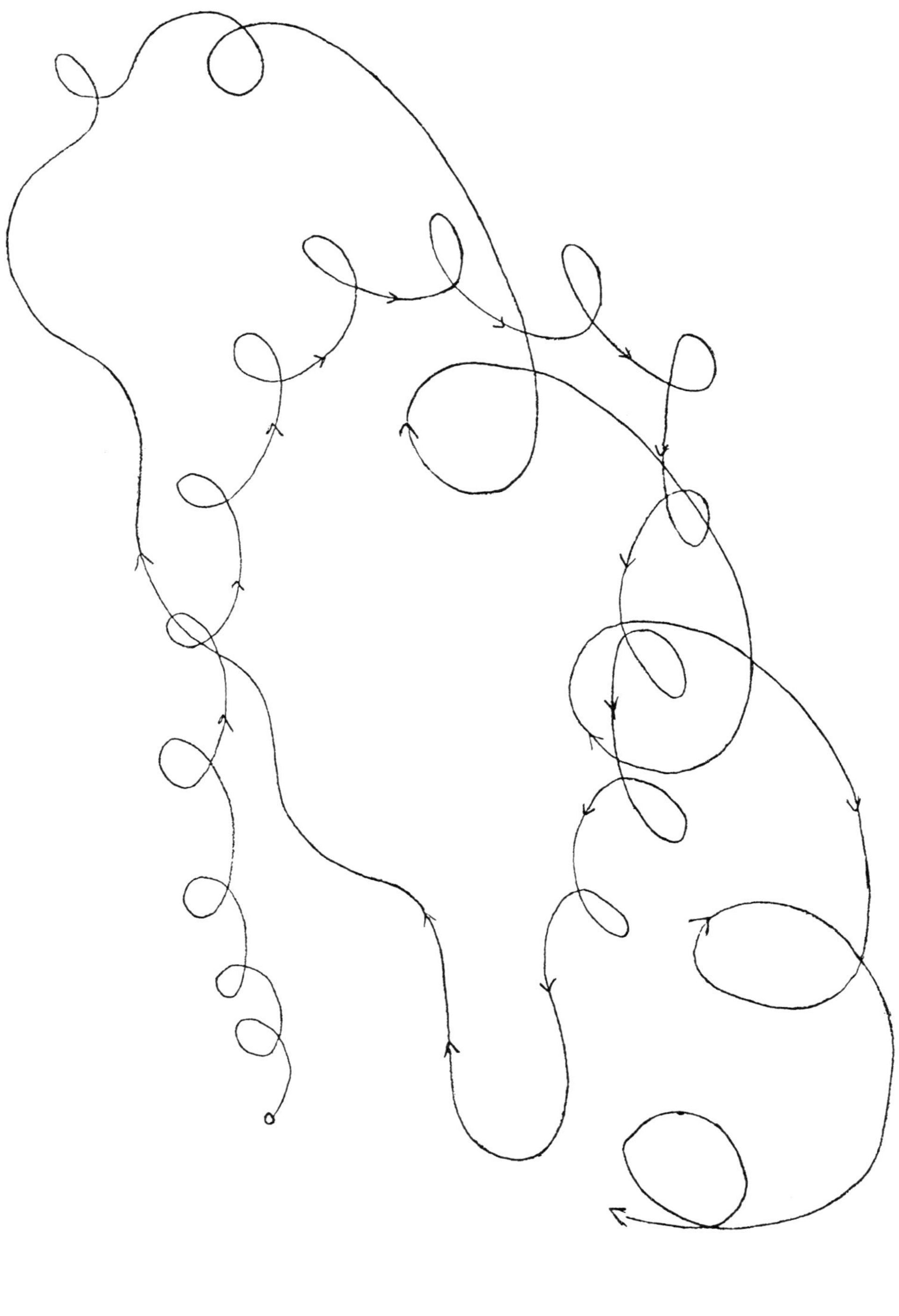

F. Chopin – Prelude, D major, Op. 28/15 (page 3, continuation from page 2)

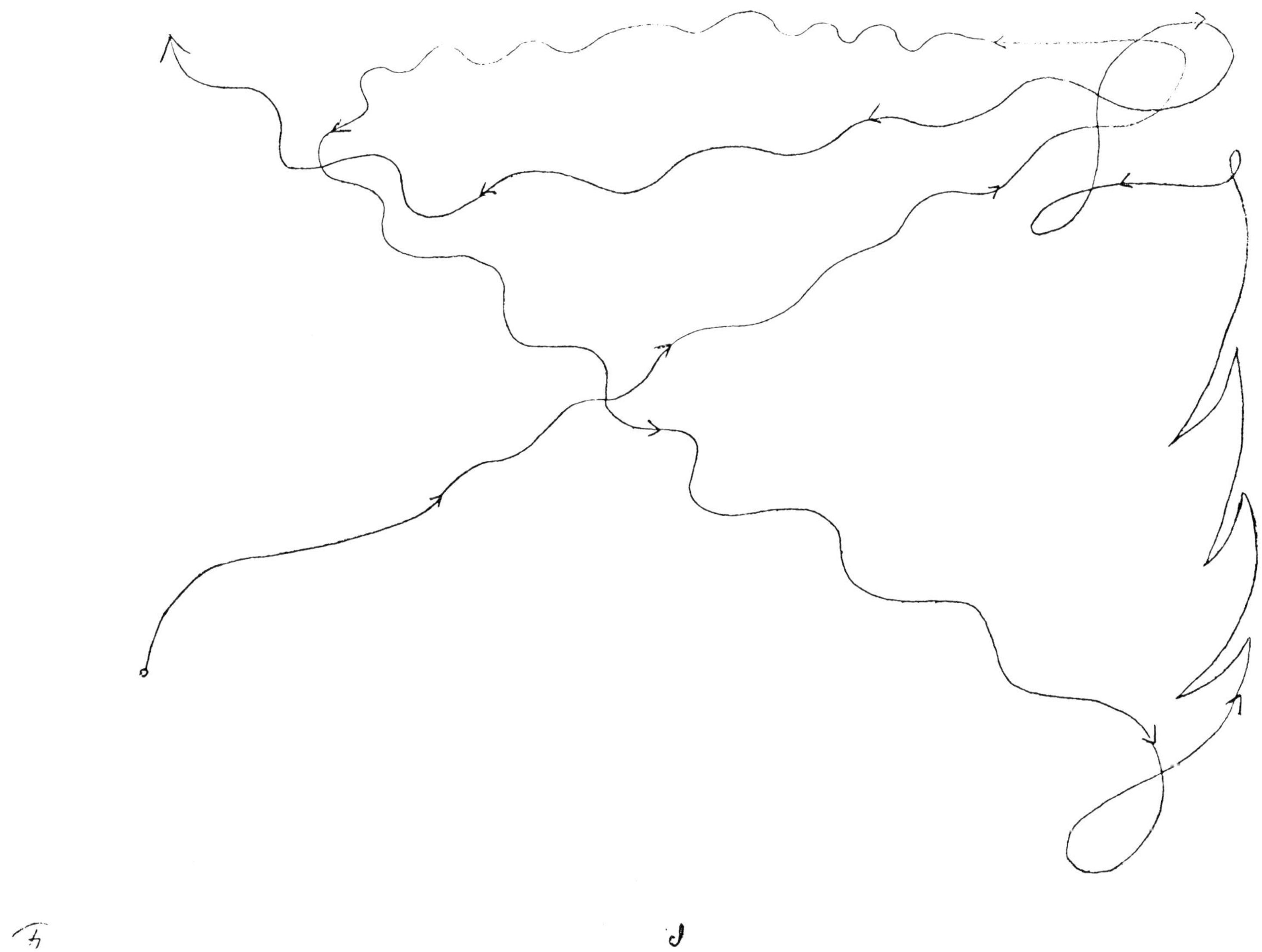

F. Chopin – Prelude, D major, Op. 28/15 (page 4, continuation from page 3)

ADDITIONAL INSTRUCTIONS AND DETAILS

Page XXIX, Chronology

In 1923, through Hedwig Köhler, the first attempt was made within the eurythmy school to eurythmically form an orchestral work (Eighth Symphony by Bruckner). In connection with this effort, Rudolf Steiner gave the principle for working with fashioning the orchestral symphonies.

First, as the focus, the percussion instruments should stand on a platform as the will impulse. The wind instruments should radiate outward to the periphery as thought forces. The string instruments should move around in the surroundings as expression of the feeling. Hedwig Köhler attempted to take up the character of the instruments in the expression of the arms. Rudolf Steiner rejected this, because tone eurythmy is visible singing, and the arms exclusively serve the singing element. On the contrary, the character of the instruments should come to expression in the spatial forms.

In the arranging of the spatial forms for the instruments one should let oneself be inspired by the outer shape of the musical instruments, which originated out of imaginations.

(The indication for a specific hand gesture in connection with a flute part was given for a very specific piece [Minuet by Wilhelm Rosenberg in April 1924 that was performed at Easter 1924. See page 130.])

After this principle for the orchestral arrangement was rehearsed and shown to Rudolf Steiner, he transformed it for the stage presentation. The full circle appeared then as a half circle with the kettle drum in the background. (From Elena Zuccoli's *From the Tone Eurythmy Work at the First Eurythmy School in Stuttgart 1922-1924*, Walter Keller Press, Dornach 1981.)

Elena Zuccoli (born 1901) was a student of the Stuttgart Eurythmeum at that time. She was in the group that showed Rudolf Steiner the symphony movement brought by Hedwig Köhler. After this presentation Rudolf Steiner drew the basic form for the eurythmical arrangements of orchestral works. The original is not available.

Basic form for the eurythmic arrangement of symphonic orchestral works

Instrumental-spatial Forms
The basic form for the string instruments is the lemniscate.

From Elena Zuccoli's *From the Tone Eurythmy Work at the First Eurythmy School in Stuttgart 1922-1924*, Walter Keller Press, Dornach 1981.

"The instruments are all gotten from the spiritual world."

"... Now, what actually is the nature of the musical development of the human being? It proceeds from the experiencing of the spiritual; from making the spiritual present in tone, in the musical tone pattern. The spiritual disappears, but human beings retain the tone pattern and organization. Later they connect it with the word as the remainder of the spiritual, and that which they had earlier as imagination, the instruments, they develop in the physical, making their instruments out of physical matter. The instruments are all gotten out of the spiritual world, inasmuch as they create the musical pitch. When they were no longer able to see the spiritual, human beings simply filled the empty places by making musical instruments. They put physical instruments into the empty places.

You see from this that it is right: one can see in music, more than anywhere else, how the transition into the materialistic age is taking place. There, where musical instruments are heard, spiritual entities actually once stood. They are gone; they have disappeared from the old clairvoyance. When human beings wish to have the music objectively, they need something that is not in the outer nature. Outer nature does not give us a correlate for the musical element. Thus human beings need their musical instruments.

Certainly, the musical instruments give a fundamentally clear impression that music is experienced by the whole human being. The wind instruments are proof of this. The string instruments give lively witness to what is experienced in the chest and comes to expression especially in the arms. Proof that music lives a full life in the third member of the human being, in the limbs, can be found in the percussion instruments or in the transition from string instruments to percussion instruments. However, all that is connected with the wind instruments has a much more intimate relationship to melody than what is connected with the string instruments. The string instruments have a much more intimate relationship to harmony. And percussion is much more connected to inner rhythm. Percussion is related to the rhythmic; the whole human being is within it. And the orchestra is a human being. It is just that a piano must not be in the orchestra.

Why no piano in the orchestra? Well, the other musical instruments are brought down out of the spiritual world. But, it is only in the physical world that the human being has made the piano, where the notes are put together in a purely abstract way. Any piccolo, any violin, all of that is something that came down already as musical from out of the spiritual world. A piano is like a philistine: philistines no longer have the higher human within themselves. The piano is a philistine instrument. It is fortunate that the piano exists. Otherwise the philistines would have absolutely no music. However, the piano arose out of a materialistic experience of the musical element. Thus, the piano is the instrument that one can use the easiest to awaken music within matter. Yet, it is actually pure matter that is enlisted so that the piano can become the expression of the musical element. And so we must say: the piano is naturally a very beneficial instrument—isn't it? Otherwise, we would have to resort to help from the spiritual right from the beginning with music lessons in our materialistic age—but the piano is the instrument that actually must be overcome musically. Human beings must free themselves of the piano impression if they want to experience the actual musical element.

And there one must indeed say: it is always a major experience when the music of a musician like Bruckner, who actually lived completely within the musical element, is played on the piano. The piano disappears from the room. With Bruckner, the piano disappears!

It is actually so with Bruckner. This is proof that something lived in him—even though in a very instinctive way—of the actual spiritual that underlies all music.

(Rudolf Steiner, from the lecture on March 8, 1923, in Stuttgart, in *Das Wesen des Musikalischen und das Tonerlebnis im Menschen* [Published in English as *The Inner Nature of Music and the Experience of Tone*, CW 283.].)

Page 2, Funeral March by Mendelssohn-Bartholdy

Measures 1	– 4	Beginning of the form (the three loops)
Measures 5	– 8	The waves
Measures 9	– 12	The simple lines
Measures 13	– 16	(Major) Repetition of the waves
Measures 17	– 20	Repetition of the simple lines

Measures 21 – 24 ½	Loops
Measures 24 ½ – 26 ½	Turn in the front waves to the end of the form
Measures 26 ½ – 28 ½	Form back (front waves)
Measure 29	Jump to the beginning of the form
Measures 29 – 32	Beginning (the three loops)
Measures 33 – 36	The first waves
Measures 37 – 39	The simple lines
Measures 40 – 44	Loops
Measures 45 – 48	Jump to the beginning of the form; then the three first loops.

Page 12, Minuet in G major for Violin and Piano by L. van Beethoven

An indication for the piano part (II = green) in the minuet-part is known by the eurythmists: foot position is "sympathy." The use of this foot position in that part came about from the form for the eurythmist in question as she practiced, namely, at that place where the peaks or points must be emphasized. Rudolf Steiner found this idea to be quite good, and so, this instruction was kept.

This "sympathy" comes after every motif in the Minuet at the second quarter of the measure. It is, however, not to be used for all minuets. (According to a report by F. Leinhas-von Sonklar.)

This form is drawn with all the repetitions, in the classical style of the Minuet.

Page 14, "Sœur Monique," Rondo for Piano, F major by Couperin

First theme to the double bar = Beginning of the form to the first spiral.
First couplet to the double bar = The form further to the second spiral.
Theme to the double bar = Repetition of the form from the beginning to the first spiral. Jump to the second spiral.
Second couplet = The form further to the third spiral to the double bar = fourth spiral (bow).
The beginning theme to the double bar = The beginning theme.
Third couplet = (Measure 58 ½) = The form with the bow to the end. Then from measure 58 ½ the form backwards to the loop.
Measures 66 – 74 omitted.
Then again the beginning form to the first spiral.
With the jumps to the theme = The beginning form is to be laid out in the space in correspondence with the whole form. (According to the report of an eurythmist who worked with this form with Lea van der Pals in the Eurythmy School.)

Page 24, Prelude, D-flat major, Op. 28/15, (Regentropfen Prelude) [Raindrop prelude] by F. Chopin

"August 23, 1922: … recently I showed the Chopin piece (Prelude in D-flat major) to several women. Now, I tried to see if one could really create the tones/notes in various places without a pose [or special position]. I made an interesting discovery. One place, which doubtlessly was written totally in minor and so should be executed so that it is contracted and downward, had such a delicate tone for me that I decided not to do the whole thing down in the will sphere but rather, though still contracted, up in the spiritual sphere. In the evening I learned that Rudolf Steiner said that one may do such a thing when such parts sound softly. The louder they are, the lower one must do them.

"September 8, 1922, Dornach: ... I performed my Chopin Prelude. Yesterday Rudolf Steiner watched it in the Goetheanum building along with all of the other eurythmists, and he gave me a form! And the form is so magnificent, multifaceted and complicated that everyone, even Marie Steiner, laughed out loud. One said that a person could go crazy with this form. However, Doctor Steiner said quietly and peacefully, "Oh no, one cannot." When I asked him something further about it, he bowed kind-heartedly to me from his chair and said very warmly, "What do you think?" Mrs. Selling (pianist) helped me with it for hours in a very touching manner.

Everyone, even Marie Steiner, pities me! How I will ever get my mind around such a form! Yet nothing is more natural to me. But it is an enormous work!

"February 10, 1923, Dornach: ... It was dress rehearsal and Doctor Steiner sat below in the audience, and I performed my Chopin piece once again. I was in immeasurable despair! ... And this evening after the rehearsal, Marie Steiner came to me and asked if I wouldn't like to go to Doctor Steiner in the morning and show him the "Vöglein" [Little bird] by Grieg and ask for a form for it (See page 51.).

"February 13, 1923: ...The yellow dress with the red veil and the wonderful lighting, through which the red veil sometimes stands out eerily dazzling against the yellow; and sometimes in blue light both together [veil and dress] bore a color in which I swam around with the tones as if in a flowing light. Rudolf Steiner wrote the lighting in my own copy of the music. Sometimes yellow lights up above or below, but at the very end all light above goes out and I disappear with the last tone, while only below a little red still shines. That is what is most wonderful!"

(Elly Wilke)

Pages 25 and 26, Nocturne, E-flat major, Op. 9/2 by F. Chopin

"September 17, 1923: ... Today [Dr. Steiner] gave Miss Donath a form for a Chopin Nocturne [E-flat major]. I sat beside him and stood beside him, along with others, and followed closely as he drew the form. And when he stood up, he turned to me and said: "Now, did you understand it?" I said: "I watched very closely and am disappointed! For always when I expect corners to appear, there come curved lines and visa versa!" Then he said: "Then perhaps you have not watched closely enough." I answered: "Yes, I thought about the form you gave me for the Chopin-Prelude, and here in the music is a very pointed part and the form is always thus: 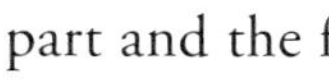." He said: "Well, just try it. You will figure it out." And he said that twice, smiling. Then he left. That was at 8 o'clock. At 8:45 he came back to pick up Marie Steiner, and I stood somewhat off to the side among the rows of chairs. He came there to me and said without leading up to it: "What you earlier experienced as having corners or as angular are not angular or corner-like in the music!" Then he looked at me with eyes wide and drew with his umbrella on an open seat

thusly: I looked him in the eyes for a long time and then put my hand on my forehead and said suddenly after being silent for a while: "Ah, yes!" But those are points; I sensed it then. And he said: "Think about it. You will figure it out." 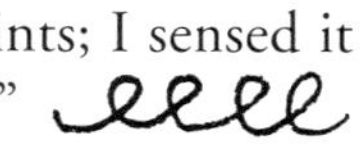

(Elly Wilke)

Page 51, "Vöglein" [Little bird] by E. Grieg
February 12, 1923: …I did the Chopin again. And in the evening Doctor Steiner gave me a really delightful form for my "Vöglein" and thought that I should not obscure the intervals when doing the small tones that I had newly brought out. Then I said immediately: "No, Doctor, I am keeping that in mind, but the notes are still so new that I must practice them first." And he said: "Yes, yes, you will figure it out alright!"
(Elly Wilke [1897-1961], Excerpts of letters from 1922-1923 in *Beiträge zur Rudolf Steiner Gesamtausgabe* [Essays on Rudolf Steiner's collected works], No. 75/76. Dornach 1982.)

Page 61, Aria, Largo by D. Gabrielli
According to a report by Margarete Eckinger (b. 1908) who had to do this part eurythmically.

Page 84, Prelude, F major, Op. 49/2 by Scriabine
Rudolf Steiner had drawn a form for a Prelude (Op. 49, no. 2, Bruscamente) by Scriabine. It had a very violent, hard, and strife-torn character. The woman who had asked him for the form could not cope with it. The piece was too raw for her. Now I took over the task and attempted to portray the character, which indeed went strongly into the unmusical. Marie Steiner looked at the piece, which was certainly considerably daring for the stage of development at which eurythmy was at that time, and let it be performed for Rudolf Steiner. Surprisingly, he was quite satisfied with it and gave the indications for lighting and costuming for the performance. I had the impression that it pleased him to see that I also tried to do modern compositions in tone eurythmy.
(Ralph Kux, [1903-1965], *Erinnerungen an Rudolf Steiner* [Remembrances of Rudolf Steiner], private printing, Lichtendorf, O.J.)

Pages 92 & 113, "März" (Bächlein im Frühling) [March (Little brook in spring)] by Jan Stuten and "Waldesrauschen" [Rustling in the woods] by F. Liszt
Let us look at the compositions for which Rudolf Steiner created forms. He took every suggestion as an opportunity to further tone eurythmy.

Thus he also gave, for instance, forms for "Waldesrauschen" by Franz Liszt and "Bächlein im März" by Jan Stuten. And what did Rudolf Steiner say about these two compositions, which were performed many times in eurythmy programs since the end of 1923, in the fourth lecture of the tone eurythmy course?

"... you will be able to see from all this that nature—the naturalistic—does not form the basis of music, for music must be a creation out of human beings themselves. And if we examine the inner nature of music and speech, we shall realize why it is that music is so far removed from anything naturalistic. Music is a creation out of the human being, and the imitation of nature is a false musical path.

As I said before, I do not mean to cast aspersion on the imitation of rustling forests, soughing [moaning] winds, splashing fountains, or a brook in March. It is far from my intention to criticize these things in any way; but there does lie behind them the urge to pass out of the realm of true music, to enrich music by the introduction of something unmusical. In certain circumstances the result may be very agreeable, for it is possible to enlarge the sphere of every art in every direction; but because eurythmy demands that music be made still more musical than it is in its own nature, terrible difficulties will arise if one attempts to express in eurythmy something that is not truly musical..."

Rudolf Steiner *Eurythmy as Visible Song* (CW 278)

Page 95, Choral Prelude "Ich ruf' zu Dir, Herr Jesu Christ..." [Choral prelude: I call to you, Lord Jesus Christ] by J. S. Bach

"The dress should come right up over the head." Drape a scarf out of the same material in the color of the dress in such a way that it is connected with the dress and leaves only the face free; it receives something then that is strict and nun-like.

Page 120, Prelude, B major, Op. 28/11 by F. Chopin

Once Rudolf Steiner let a form for a Prelude [in B major] by Chopin be done on the stage immediately after drawing it, in order to test its effect. As he saw that the eurythmist could not cope with it, because the form was too long for the short Prelude, he crumpled up the drawing and immediately gave a new, much simpler one. One can see from this that Rudolf Steiner was never pedantic in these matters! He adapted himself to the individuality and ability of the particular person who would be performing the piece.

(Ralph Kux)

Page 140, Largo con gran espressione by L. van Beethoven

[Lighting settings:]	[For measures:]
1. White above, blue below	1-2, 13-14, 18-19
2. In addition green below	3-4, 10, 15-17, 20-21
3. Yellow above, white below	5-9
4. Red above, blue below	11-12, 22-24
(Measure 24-36 to be omitted)	(The End)

[Lighting setting (Set.) from above & the measures for which they are to be used:]

1. Set. 37-40	1. Set. 60	4. Set. 72-76 2/4
2. Set. 41-46	4. Set. 61-62	2. Set. 76 ¾ - 77
1. Set. 47-49	1. Set. 63-64	4. Set. 78-83
2. Set. 50-53	2. Set. 65-67	1. Set. 84-86
3. Set. 54-59	1. Set. 68-71	4. Set. 87-90 Fine

Originally the end was at measure 24 (Sheet 1). Later measures 24-36 were omitted and measures 37-90 Fine were added.

Page 143, Allegretto, D-flat major, second movement from Sonata no. 14 in C-sharp minor (Mondscheinsonate) [Moonshine sonata], Op. 27/2 by L. van Beethoven

... After he had drawn the form for the Beethoven [Allegretto in D-flat major], he gave me the page with a characteristic gesture. He said about it: "This is how you must do it." And made a kind of fourth with his hand, whereby he pressed his fingers together tightly and showed a teasing gesture. His eyes radiated extraordinary cheerfulness in this moment.

(Ralph Kux)

Page 146, Adagiosossimo, F minor from Capriccio [Caprice], "Über die Abreise seines geliebten Bruders" [About the departure of his beloved brother] by J. S. Bach (arranged by M. Reger)

At Whitsun Marie Steiner was on tour with the eurythmy group, and those artists who remained behind in Dornach had to give a performance. This time Rudolf Steiner attended the dress rehearsal by himself. I performed an adagio by Bach-Reger. When I came down off the stage, he said, sitting on his chair and smiling: "Now we also want to give Mr. Kux a eurythmy dress for this." In a somewhat teasing manner, he continued: "Or do you not want a dress?" Naturally, I was enthusiastic about the prospect. He suggested a red eurythmy dress and pointed with a pencil to the edge of my knee pants, indicating that the dress should come to just above the knee. He wanted the blue stole intended for this piece to be somewhat shorter in the back than in the front. The stockings should be in the same color as the stole. At the end he dictated easily, and without stopping, the sequence of the program.

Page 147, Largo, third movement from the Sonata in G minor, HWV 387 by G. F. Händel

Once a woman and I performed a Largo in G minor for two violins by Händel, and Rudolf Steiner said of it: "That is incredibly boring!" He could not calm down over it for a long time. Finally, he said to the two violinists: "Either play it much more slowly or play it faster." It was played faster, as that was more appropriate for the eurythmy. And also here it showed that through a small intervention the piece then had character. Later it actually became a good, successful piece.

(Ralph Kux)

Page 148, Prelude, C-sharp minor, Op. 3/2 by S. Rachmaninoff
He drew a form for me for a further piece that I performed with a woman. It was the Prelude in C-sharp minor by Rachmaninoff. He watched the piece first. Then he had it played for him twice while he drew, and had the eurythmists doing it on the stage at the same time. Through this he showed that he was greatly receptive to one's efforts, taking up what one had worked out with a piece. If he sat in front of the stage and watched, which he always did when possible, one felt him to be like an embodied conscience. If time allowed, he still gave new eurythmy forms right before the dress rehearsal. He drew the forms for the speech eurythmy mostly at home or in his studio, while he usually drew the tone eurythmy forms in the immediate presence of the artist who was to perform the piece. Filled with peace and concentration, he sat in his chair with a blank sheet of paper on his lap. He took the pencil lightly into his hand and let it glide just as lightly across the paper. While the musicians played, he drew the musical piece in mysterious movement-forms on the paper. His expressive hand and the pencil themselves became, as it were, musical rhythm. He sat there totally still and turned inward. Then he took the sheet of paper, observed it with a loving look, and, admiring the forming by the life-world, he showed it to the artists with joy. Everyone gathered around and observed in amazement and joy the new creation that just came into being. A new piece of the world was born, and so one looked reverently into the mysterious working of the musical world that revealed itself in these forms. When it was a matter of a piece that would be performed by several people, he would have the music played several times for him, and each time, he would draw a further form for it. If it was a simple, uncomplicated piece, he drew the form from the music sheet, from the image of the notes, without having it played for him. Thus I experienced it, for example, with a Minuet by Bach for flute and piano. I could stand beside him and see with wonder how he drew a specific form for each and every motif.

(Ralph Kux)

Lighting
Before the dress rehearsal it was customary that the lighting technician come to him and give him the program of poems and musical pieces for the performance. He immediately wrote the lighting instructions into it without hearing the pieces recited or played. The most interesting and most characteristic lighting creations came about in this way. Yes, it was a festival every time for the artists when they did a piece the first time so open to the essential quality of the lighting. I can hardly remember an instance when Rudolf Steiner changed the lighting after he had seen it on the stage. He had the piece that was on the paper before his spiritual eye, and he gave his intentions accordingly. The lighting that he created holds yet many mysteries and is a model or example for a future art of stage lighting.

(Ralph Kux)

Costumes for Women and Men

He gave veils this time for the selections by Bach and Händel. Later he called the veil a shawl or wrap ("Umhang"). In this matter much was tried, but unfortunately, he did not intervene with it again—except for a drawing for the flute Minuet (page 144) by Bach, in which the veil is shown flying strongly over the arm—and thus we were left to our own seeking. We did indeed ask him once whether one could use a harder gauze veil, but he said no to that. One should use a flexible material.

Afterwards he indicated mostly veils, and only rarely stoles, for my pieces. I performed pieces that had earlier been done by women, just as also women performed my pieces. On these occasions I noticed that Rudolf Steiner gave different colors for the costumes every time. Accordingly, it appears to be of importance in selecting the colors whether it is a man or a woman who will perform the piece. A man can wear some colors only with the greatest of caution.

(Ralph Kux)

THE FIRST BEGINNINGS OF TONE EURYTHMY

Hendrika Hollenbach

It was 1919. In Dornach the work on the first Goetheanum, in which I played a modest role, was more or less finished. However, I had heard that Rudolf Steiner had said that it would be good if children were brought together to sing, and because I had experience in this area, the plan ripened in me to form a small children's choir. It seemed to me that the movements for the basic tones of our tone system were the only thing already given in this area that would be appropriate to make beginning theory and simple exercises interesting for the children. Thus I discussed the plan with Marie Steiner. She agreed with it and announced to the members the date and place for the first meeting of the choir. Eight or ten children came, and thus began a work with music, which, little did I forsee at the time, would become the seed for tone eurythmy's development into an independent art in addition to speech eurythmy.

In 1915 Rudolf Steiner gave a lot of new material to the eurythmy teachers present in Dornach at that time. He also gave movements for the colors and for the musical notes. Those of us in Dornach learned these movements in the fourth and fifth eurythmy courses. We worked on a small poem in which the hand movements for the colors were used; worked on a small song with the hand movements for the tones; but we did not go much further than that. The tones were done standing, with a little jump for G, A, and B, as Rudolf Steiner indicated. Several compositions came about at that time, in which—according to indications given by Rudolf Steiner—for the last word of every sentence [of lyrics], more tones came which had to be executed with a jump. Thus was composed the music for the sirens in *Faust* by Leopold van der Pals and for a poem from the *Chemical Wedding* by Max Schuurman. For these numbers in the performance, the text at the end of a movement was not done eurythmically, but instead, the tone sequence was done. I began now, besides practicing somewhat longer songs with the children, to also take them through quite short songs in such a way that half of the group sang and the other half did tone eurythmy. For the time being they did only the melodies that moved in seconds. Then we did the opposite: those who had been singing hopped, and those who had been hopping sang. Thus gradually a light, natural flow with the movements came about. Because the hopping while standing in one spot did not take up much room, a music room was large enough for us. The room had been made available to us by Mrs. Eckinger whose two children I gave piano lessons to at that time. As Christmas approached, we began to practice Christmas songs, and at Christmas in 1919 the choir, which had grown in number in the meantime, appeared for the first time in the Schreinerei. Of course, they only sang.

In the next year I could let the more advanced children do longer songs. When we had a song with three stanzas in the major far enough along three children could hop it nicely in a triangle with free-running transitions between the stanzas that went into a little transition that I had written for it, and when a song in the minor key was rehearsed in a somewhat different way, I asked Marie Steiner to have a look at it. We prepared everything on the stage. The small choir stood toward the front of the stage on the platform. When Marie Steiner saw what the children did, she said, much to our amazement and to the joy of the children: "We will include that in the program on Sunday." The performance was heartily received. Everyone was happy to see the children do something, and after the performance Marie Steiner said to me: "Now my ladies must also learn to hop." She sent me six of the eurythmists at that time, and with these six and six of my most talented children, I started them rehearsing a little Bach composition.

For the first time we left the singing out; the children stood in front in a hexagon and did the treble of the piano; and the women did the bass. At the repetition of the first part a somewhat more complicated transition was done, in order to have a change, and the second part began at a different place. When it was performed, it had to be repeated [due to the audience's request], and on the one side there came a request for special instruction in tone eurythmy, and on the other, the eurythmists asked to practice with me on the stage everyday from 10:00–11:00 am. Then the development really started moving, for often, when Dr. Steiner came through the Schreinerei, we had the opportunity to ask questions. Thus we heard that we could also make the movements for the tones while walking. In the major we hopped only for the notes G, A, and B while walking. However, how we were supposed to indicate the small, differently-natured jump for the minor tones was a problem. When I asked Rudolf Steiner about it, he said one had to stop in one's movement, and when I did not immediately understand what he meant, he had me do it: take one step forward and then place both feet side-by-side; then another step forward and then both feet side-by-side, and so on, so that with the sequence F, G, A, B, C a strong hesitation, like a slight catch, takes place in one's movement. Also the problem of the diverted tones was discussed. First we asked how the tones raised by sharps could be done. He told us that in the place where the original tone occurs, the forearm and upper arm should form a right angle. We practiced this in various ways in the major and minor and asked then about the flats. To our amazement, Dr. Steiner did not feel that the enharmonic tones had to be done differently; G-flat, for example, can simply be done as F-sharp. Because we would gladly have a variation in the movement, we asked if through a soft, inward-turned, rounded hand-position the flats could possibly be intimated. Rudolf Steiner agreed with this. "Yes, you can do it that way," he said. Later he said that for a double sharp, in addition to the angle created by the forearm and upper arm, also another angle could be made between the hand and forearm, at the wrist. We also wanted to know if we could move the major and minor tones into a middle zone at shoulder height where, in the major, the descending tones could be made with the forearms directed upwards and the tones in the minor could done with the arms out at a flat angle. Dr. Steiner agreed with this and added that we could also actually do it behind us, if it were possible. The correct angle appeared to be the important thing in all of these movements.

If one grasped this, then one could metamorphose it and, for instance, make the movements for the tones' smaller area by using only the forearm with the angle at the wrist for the sharps and flats. Now, on the one hand, all of these things had to be taught in the courses—that was my task—and, on the other, the appropriate pieces had to be found for the stage. We performed part of the shepherds' music from Bach's Christmas Oratorio, for which I had asked Dr. Steiner for the first time to draw a form. I remember that he made an appointment to come and hear the piece fairly early. The musicians—the piece was for violin, cello, harmonium, and piano—came upstairs freezing, as it was very cold, and when Dr. Steiner did not come right away, they began to think there had been a misunderstanding, that I had probably not understood Dr. Steiner correctly. Then Dr. Steiner came, and I was embarrassed as I noticed that there was no sheet of paper there for drawing. However, he ripped off a big piece of coarse, brown paper with which the stage was covered and began to draw on it. Thus, this very first tone eurythmy form was a very strange document.

In the next year it was necessary to find something to which moving to the minor key could be practiced. I selected the "Trauer Marsch" [Funeral march] by Mendelssohn for this. Because at the same time a young eurythmist told me that she would like to rehearse a solo in tone eurythmy, wanted to rehearse it with me in the glass house, and asked me to ask Dr. Steiner for a form, I went to Dr. Steiner and asked him to listen to two music pieces: the "Funeral March" by Mendelssohn and "Schmetterling" (Butterfly) by Grieg. He agreed and wanted to listen to them toward evening in the [Goetheanum] building. How amazed I was when I looked at the forms! For the "Schmetterling," he drew two different forms that were quite beautiful. He thought the one on top was most appropriate, however. Besides the large form for the "Funeral March," which I intended to have the group rehearse, Rudolf Steiner drew on the bottom of the page the form small three times and overlapped them, in order to show how the piece could be done by three or more people. He explained: "Then you can use as many people as you want." Although he had heard the music only once the night before, it seemed to be very present for him, for he entered into various details in a loving manner when I asked about the organization of it.

In the meantime the children's group had become a proper tone eurythmy class, with which I practiced in the glass house. After several group pieces had been performed, I began to rehearse solos with the most talented children. The solos were almost always performed in the Schreinerei. Now, twenty-eight years after the very first performance, some of those children of that time are today among the best artists of the Goetheanum ensemble. The stage eurythmists gradually dared to work with more complicated musical pieces and forms, and the younger ones who went through the systematically organized courses or through private instruction could be presented to Marie Steiner, in order to gradually begin performing or be sent to other places to teach what they had learned. The number of forms that Rudolf Steiner gave increased greatly. Often he gave indications for individual pieces that were then later handled thoroughly in his tone eurythmy course. It was wonderful for me when Dr. Steiner confirmed something for me that I had long been seeking and which I thought finally to have found: this is, namely, the connection among the tones, tone eurythmy movements, and the planets. So long as I sought the connection on the basis of our planetary system, I could not find it. Suddenly it came to me one day that it is the cosmic evolution that must connect with the tones. Suddenly a new light fell on the tone eurythmy movements. For just as the arms go downward in three steps in the major scale, and F and G are in the middle position and then go upward again, so too our evolution goes through Saturn, Sun, and Moon to the Earth stage which divides into the Mars and Mercury developments. The same arm positions of F and G suddenly stood in a different light. And raising oneself out of the pull of gravity through the little jumps with G-A-B appeared to make sense for the ascending evolution, where through the arms going upward again the octave is attained, as the stage of the spirit human is attained through the Jupiter evolution and the Venus evolution. Originally Rudolf Steiner said that with the octave one would have to jump up to a higher level or step. This was not easy to accomplish. It was enlightening to see these laws of the descent and ascent of the spirit or of the evolution and involution of matter mirrored in the major and minor, and I was deeply content, when I showed Dr. Steiner a piece of paper on which I had drawn the planets and musical notes and the tone eurythmy movements, and he said: "Yes, that is right." Later I also learned to see how, just as in the diatonic scale we have the seven-fold nature of the planets, we have in the twelve-fold nature of the chromatic scale, in an octave, the compressed twelve-fold nature of the circle of fifths, of which Rudolf Steiner told us that it has to do with the twelve-fold nature of the zodiac. If we take in addition what was given to us in the tone eurythmy course in 1924 and much of what was said in the lectures on music, then we see out of what wonderful depths our tone eurythmy has been drawn, and how worlds of feelings can make us happy if we practice them in the right way.

August 8, 1948
Beiträge zur Rudolf Steiner Gesamtausgabe, No. 75/76, Dornach 1982
[Essays on Rudolf Steiner's complete works]

THE EXPERIENCE OF MAJOR AND MINOR

Lecture (Excerpt), February 19, 1924

RUDOLF STEINER

Speech eurythmy has already reached a certain stage of development, and it may perhaps be said that we have achieved something in this domain. Tone eurythmy, on the other hand, has remained up until now in its most elementary stage; and due to a very remarkable fact that has recently come to my notice, I have been led to give this short course of lectures. It has become markedly evident from various quarters that people have frequently found tone eurythmy more pleasing than speech eurythmy and comparatively easy to comprehend in feeling, whereas speech eurythmy has seemed much more alien to them. This sad fact that more significance is attached to something still in its infancy than to something more fully developed is a proof that at the present time the understanding for eurythmy has not made much headway. It is of utmost importance that this understanding should be fostered; and for this reason I should like today to make certain introductory remarks that may enable you to work for eurythmy in the light of such understanding.

If we try to develop tone eurythmy out of eurythmy in a more comprehensive sense, the opportunity will arise to speak about this understanding at least in an introductory way. From the side of the eurythmists themselves much can be done with a view to increasing a right understanding of eurythmy. And here it is most important to bear in mind what is perceived by the onlookers. The onlookers see not only the movement or gesture that is carried out by the eurythmist, but they also see what the eurythmist is feeling and inwardly experiencing. This makes it necessary that every movement or gesture on the part of the eurythmist should be an actual experience, and this more especially when something is to be performed. In speech eurythmy we must experience the structure and formation of the sounds; and in tone eurythmy, the structure and formation of the tones.

So far, with the exception of the forms that have been made for various pieces of music, tone eurythmy has consisted of the simple tones, the scale as such, and nothing further. If in speech eurythmy we had no more than we have today in tone eurythmy, this would amount to what is comprised in the vowels: a, e, i, o, u.

Just think how little we would have achieved artistically if, in speech eurythmy, we had up to now only been able to make use of the vowel sounds! But artistically we have so far had no more than this in tone eurythmy. This is why it is depressing when the judgments—they were characterized earlier—of tone eurythmy come to meet us. And this also is why I believe it to be necessary that we should now at least begin to lay down the real foundations of tone eurythmy.

Rudolf Steiner
Eurythmy as Visible Singing (CW 278)
The Andenda Music Trust
The Robinswood Press
Stourbridge, England

Rudolf Steiner: Eurythmy Forms for Speech and Tone Eurythmy

Complete Collection in Nine Volumes

I *Eurythmieformen zu Dichtungen von Rudolf Steiner* [Eurythmy Forms for Poetry by Rudolf Steiner] Truth-wrought words, fairy tales, scenes from the Mystery Dramas, humoresques, The Dream Song of Olaf Åsteson (a rendering), introductions (130 pages)

II *Eurythmieformen zu den Wochensprüchen des Anthroposophischen Seelenkalenders* [Eurythmy Forms for the Weekly Verses of the Anthroposophical Calendar of the Soul] by Rudolf Steiner (130 pages)

III *Eurythmieformen zu Dichtungen von Johann Wolfgang von Goethe* [Eurythmy Forms for Poetry by Johann Wolfgang von Goethe] Poems, scenes out of Faust, parts I and II (184 pages)

IV *Eurythmieformen zu Dictungen von Christian Morgenstern* [Eurythmy Forms for Poetry by Christian Morgenstern] Poems and humoresques (255 pages)

V *Eurythmieformen zu Dichtungen von Albert Steffen* [Euryyhmy Forms for Poetry by Albert Steffen] *Poems from Wegzehrung* [Nourishment for the Way] and *Pilgerfahrt zum Lebensbaum* [Pilgramage to the Tree of Life] (133 pages)

VI *Eurythmieformen zu Dichtungen von Fercher von Steinwand, Hammerling, Hebbel, Meyer, Nietzsche und anderen* [Eurythmy Forms for Poetry by Fercher von Steinwand, Hammerling, Hebbel, Meyer, Nietzsche and others] Fercher von Steinwand: "Chor der Urtriebe" [Chorus of the Primal Urges], "Chor der Urträume" [Chorus of the Primal Dreams], *Das Verhängnis* [The Disaster] / Giraud / Hartleben, Hoffmann von Fallersleben, Hegel, Lenau, Mörike, Novalis (244 pages)

VII *Eurythmieformen zu englischen Dichtungen* [Eurythmy Forms for English Poetry] William Shakespeare: Sonnets, elf scenes in "A Midsummer Night's Dream," songs from the plays / Macleod, Blake, Burns, Longfellow, de la Mare, Marlowe, Moore, Nashe, Rands, Rossetti, Scott, Watson (154 pages)

VIII *Eurythmieformen zu französischen und russischen Dichtungen* [Eurythmy Forms for French and Russian Poetry] Giraud, de Hérédia, Hugo, Lafontaine, Leconte de Lisle, Musset, d'Orleans, Rameau, de Ronsard, Samain / Soloviev, Puschkin, Lermontow (149 pages)

IX *Eurythmy Forms for Tone Eurythmy*
For compositions by J.S. Bach, Beethoven, Brahms, Bruckner, Chopin, Corelli, Couperin, Debussy, Dvořak, Franck, Gabrielli, Galliard, Gluck, Grieg, Händel, Lewerwnz, Liszt, Mendelssohn-Bartholdy, Moczkowski, Mozart, Pugnani-Kreisler, Rachmaninoff, Reger, Schumann, Schubert, Scriabine, Stuten, Tartini, Telemann, Tschaikowsky, Veracini (191 pages)

* * *

The following supplement to the eurythmy forms is available:

RUDOLF STEINER: BELEUCHTUNGS- UND KOSTÜMANGABEN
[Rudolf Steiner: Instructions for Lighting and Costumes]

For the speech eurythmy, with corresponding texts

I Deutsche Texte [German texts] (Egyptian – Goethe)

II Deutsche Texte [German Texts] (Hamerling – Schröer)

III Deutsche Texte [German Texts] (Steffen –Volksweise / Belyi, Lermontow, Puschkin, Soloviev)

IV Fremdsprachige Texte [Texts in Foreign Languages] (English and French)

Beleuchtungs- und Kostümangaben für die Ton-Eurythmie [Lighting and Costume Indications for Tone Eurythmy]